ECONOMIC
DEVELOPMENT

THE NEW
PALGRAVE

ECONOMIC DEVELOPMENT

EDITED BY

JOHN EATWELL · MURRAY MILGATE · PETER NEWMAN

W·W·NORTON

NEW YORK · LONDON

© The Macmillan Press Limited, 1987, 1989

First published in
The New Palgrave: A Dictionary of Economics
Edited by John Eatwell, Murray Milgate and Peter Newman
in four volumes, 1987

The New Palgrave is a trademark of
The Macmillan Press Limited

Published simultaneously in Canada by
Penguin Books Canada Ltd.
2801 John Street
Markham, Ontario L3R 1B4

ISBN 0-393-02725-2

ISBN 0-393-95850-7   PBK.

W. W. Norton & Company, Inc.
500 Fifth Avenue
New York, NY 10110

W. W. Norton & Company, Ltd.
37 Great Russell Street
London WC1B 3NU

Printed in Great Britain

1   2   3   4   5   6   7   8   9   0

Contents

Contents

General Preface

The books in this series are the offspring of *The New Palgrave: A Dictionary of Economics*. Published in late 1987, the *Dictionary* has rapidly become a standard reference work in economics. However, its four heavy tomes containing over four million words on the whole range of economic thought is not a form convenient to every potential user. For many students and teachers it is simply too bulky, too comprehensive and too expensive for everyday use.

By developing the present series of compact volumes of reprints from the original work, we hope that some of the intellectual wealth of *The New Palgrave* will become accessible to much wider groups of readers. Each of the volumes is devoted to a particular branch of economics, such as econometrics or general equilibrium or money, with a scope corresponding roughly to a university course on that subject. Apart from correction of misprints, etc. the content of each of its reprinted articles is exactly the same as that of the original. In addition, a few brand new entries have been commissioned especially for the series, either to fill an apparent gap or more commonly to include topics that have risen to prominence since the dictionary was originally commissioned.

As *The New Palgrave* is the sole parent of the present series, it may be helpful to explain that it is the modern successor to the excellent *Dictionary of Political Economy* edited by R.H. Inglis Palgrave and published in three volumes in 1894, 1896 and 1899. A second and slightly modified version, edited by Henry Higgs, appeared during the mid-1920s. These two editions each contained almost 4,000 entries, but many of those were simply brief definitions and many of the others were devoted to peripheral topics such as foreign coinage, maritime commerce, and Scottish law. To make room for the spectacular growth in economics over the last 60 years while keeping still to a manageable length, *The New Palgrave* concentrated instead on economic theory, its originators, and its closely cognate disciplines. Its nearly 2,000 entries (commissioned from over 900 scholars) are all self-contained essays, sometimes brief but never mere definitions.

Apart from its biographical entries, *The New Palgrave* is concerned chiefly with theory rather than fact, doctrine rather than data; and it is not at all clear how theory and doctrine, as distinct from facts and figures, *should* be treated in an encyclopaedia. One way is to treat everything from a particular point of view. Broadly speaking, that was the way of Diderot's classic *Encyclopédie raisonée* (1751–1772), as it was also of Léon Say's *Nouveau dictionnaire d'économie politique* (1891–2). Sometimes, as in articles by Quesnay and Turgot in the *Encyclopédie*, this approach has yielded entries of surpassing brilliance. Too often, however, both the range of subjects covered and the quality of the coverage itself are seriously reduced by such a self-limiting perspective. Thus the entry called '*Méthode*' in the first edition of Say's *Dictionnaire* asserted that the use of mathematics in economics 'will only ever be in the hands of a few', and the dictionary backed up that claim by choosing not to have any entry on Cournot.

Another approach is to have each entry take care to reflect within itself varying points of view. This may help the student temporarily, as when preparing for an examination. But in a subject like economics, the Olympian detachment which this approach requires often places a heavy burden on the author, asking for a scrupulous account of doctrines he or she believes to be at best wrong-headed. Even when an especially able author does produce a judicious survey article, it is surely too much to ask that it also convey just as much enthusiasm for those theories thought misguided as for those found congenial. Lacking an enthusiastic exposition, however, the disfavoured theories may then be studied less closely than they deserve.

The New Palgrave did not ask its authors to treat economic theory from any particular point of view, except in one respect to be discussed below. Nor did it call for surveys. Instead, each author was asked to make clear his or her own views of the subject under discussion, and for the rest to be as fair and accurate as possible, without striving to be 'judicious'. A balanced perspective on each topic was always the aim, the ideal. But it was to be sought not *internally*, within each article, but *externally*, between articles, with the reader rather than the writer handed the task of achieving a personal balance between differing views.

For a controversial topic, a set of several more or less synonymous headwords, matched by a broad diversity of contributors, was designed to produce enough variety of opinion to help form the reader's own synthesis; indeed, such diversity will be found in most of the individual volumes in this series.

This approach was not without its problems. Thus, the prevalence of uncertainty in the process of commissioning entries sometimes produced a less diverse outcome than we had planned. 'I can call spirits from the vasty deep,' said Owen Glendower. 'Why, so can I,' replied Hotspur, 'or so can any man;/ But will they come when you do call for them?' In our experience, not quite as often as we would have liked.

The one point of view we did urge upon every one of *Palgrave*'s authors was to write from an historical perspective. For each subject its contributor was asked to discuss not only present problems but also past growth and future prospects. This request was made in the belief that knowledge of the historical development of any theory enriches our present understanding of it, and so helps to construct better theories for the future. The authors' response to the request was generally so positive that, as the reader of any of these volumes will discover, the resulting contributions amply justified that belief.

Peter Newman
Murray Milgate
John Eatwell

Preface

Economic Development is a subject that did not exist before the Second World War; for example, Seligman's massive *Encyclopaedia of the Social Sciences*, appearing in the 1930s, contained no entry on either 'economic development' or 'development economics'. Of course the same is true of several other important sub-disciplines of economics, such as game theory and financial economics. But while their creation was part of the inevitable speciation that accompanies the natural evolution of economic (or any other) theory, the birth of Economic Development as an academic subject was primarily a response to new and powerful historical forces at work in the outside world.

The European colonial empires were almost completely dismantled between 1945 and 1965, in a process whose speed turned the attention of colonized and colonizers alike to the problem of how fast the newly independent countries could be made to grow. The grim Cold War focused attention on the forced-draft investment policies of the Soviet Union and China, which in turn raised the question whether that was not a faster (and therefore better) path to wealth than that of Western capitalism. Meanwhile, the trauma of the Great Depression of the 1930s had driven both the industrial countries and their raw material suppliers into greater readiness to accept governmental interventions intended to maintain employment and prices, as well as to secure steady growth in output and trade.

The popular subject thus created has always appeared to have a two-fold mission. The first aspect is important and enduring. At any moment in time some nations will be regarded as poor and under-developed, and it will be natural to enquire what must be done to make them wealther. In this sense, Economic Development is a well-established field of applied economics which has existed, in substance if not in name, since at least the time of Adam Smith. Since 'you have the poor with you always', this aspect of its mission is likely to be permanent.

The second aspect is more problematic and, perhaps, temporary. It was the putting into practice of a then widespread belief that, with its 'marginalist' revolution in the last quarter of the nineteenth century, economics had left behind the concern with growth that was central to Classical Political Economy, and that it was high time to return to those earlier concerns. This belief led to some new theory, and to greater attention within standard economics to problems of growth and planning. It also led many students, especially from poor countries, to be given excessive doses of 'development economics', as if that were a substitute for, rather than a complement to, a thorough training in ordinary economic theory.

The many essays in this volume bear witness to the varied and vigorous debates that have taken place in Economic Development, and to the increase in understanding which they have brought. If the subject seems less ambitious now than forty years ago, its foundations are more secure.

The Editors

Development Economics

CLIVE BELL

As we are often reminded nowadays, economic development – in the sense of regular progress and rising prosperity – was a preoccupation of the classical economists. What has come to be called Development Economics, however, is of much more recent origin. Both during and immediately after World War II, the conditions of poverty, illiteracy, disease and mortality in backward agrarian countries aroused keen interest and concern in the West, inspired by humanitarian considerations and, no doubt, those ensuing from the Cold War. The search for ways whereby their people could escape such misery and enjoy rising prosperity engendered a body of diverse doctrines and strong controversy, which has by no means fully subsided.

Then, as now, the comparatively affluent living standards in industrialized societies provided a clear example of what was, in principle, possible. Of course, to reduce thus the problem of economic development to that of building an industrial society is to do it a good deal of violence. For those who place the realization of individual potential at the centre of things, dignity, liberty and satisfaction at the workplace count for quite as much as material affluence; see, for example, Seers (1969). And some writers in a more classical tradition emphasized the importance of expanding the range of choices open to individuals. Yet without claiming any causal connection, there appear to be quite strong associations between the share of industry in national income and at least some of the attributes of a decent life for the mass of the population, a set of regularities explored in considerable detail by Kuznets (1966) and Chenery and Syrquin (1975). There is also the point that industrialism is what most countries in the Third World aspire to. Together, these must do as a defence for the drastic reduction of the problem I have chosen in order to make the scope of this essay manageable.

Two themes are pursued. First, poor countries are starting out in a world in which there are already rich countries. As most of the latter are industrial economies and the former are still heavily agricultural, they will be referred to

1

henceforth as pioneers and latecomers, respectively. In this context, pioneers are inventing new products and processes, even – where legal obstacles are not insuperable – new institutions, such as the joint stock company and the multinational corporation, or, in centrally planned economies, Gosplan. This ferment in capitalist pioneers is the object of Schumpeter's (1926) celebrated work on economic development. Although modern development economics is concerned with the progress of latecomers, an important strand in much thinking on development is that the options and prospects facing latecomers are necessarily influenced by what is going on in pioneers. The very fact that pioneers and latecomers trade in goods, labour, capital and ideas itself suggests that latecomers are affected, though whether they gain or lose thereby is still controversial.

Secondly, much doctrine – and controversy – has been concerned with certain problems of economic coordination that arise in the course of industrialization. In this field, there has been no shortage of challenges to the proposition that economic coordination is best effected by the market mechanism, nor any lack of vigorous defence. It seems fair to say, however, that this is a field in which étatisme is a well-rooted doctrine, which finds ample reflection in the active role played by the state in many latecomers.

Finally, while the classical influence is still strong, development economics has come to absorb a good deal from other fields that are noticeably more 'modern'. Indeed, it might be argued that development economics has been absorbed back into the mainstream, and now enjoys no separate existence. That, too, will be assessed.

1. PIONEERS AND LATECOMERS: CATCHING UP. A summary record of the technological progress of pioneers can be thought of as a metaphorical 'book of blueprints'. Free access to this book is valuable to latecomers, inasmuch as they are then spared the expense of recreating what is already known. This seems to imply that latecomers have a potential advantage over pioneers, an advantage of backwardness, as Gerschenkron (1952) would call it.

While the above proposition looks virtually unassailable, some questions arise. First, is access to the book free? True, knowledge has some of the characteristics of a public good; so that the prices of goods produced by well established and widely diffused methods are unlikely to contain a significant element of rent corresponding to such knowledge. Where newer goods and processes are concerned, however, patent laws and the fact that key elements of know-how are often embodied in factors specific to the firm usually ensure some return to the knowledge possessed. In these cases, therefore, the question is whether the latecomer would be better off developing an alternative technique from whatever knowledge is freely available. Much proprietary knowledge is embodied in specific capital goods, which, with some exotic exceptions, are rarely produced by monopolies. Thus, unless the firm owning the knowledge and/or the producer(s) of the capital goods are able to pursue strategies that leave latecomers at their reservation levels, which may not always be possible, latecomers ought to enjoy a modest surplus over going it alone.

Secondly, many techniques in the 'book of blueprints' that have been discarded by pioneers are no longer available. The firms that produced the capital goods may have gone out of business or lost the intangible knowhow to make the process work; so that if the technique is to be revived, skills and resources will be needed. In many instances, current practice in pioneers will be the only techniques on offer, though it should be noted that this menu still contains many marginal methods, to pioneers at least. For this reason alone, there will be a tendency for latecomers to adopt 'advanced' techniques of production, relative to the pioneers at a comparable stage of their development.

Thirdly, is it socially desirable for latecomers to adopt 'advanced' techniques? To the extent that there is a real choice, advanced techniques may not reflect real scarcities in the economy: loosely speaking, they may be too 'capital-intensive'. In that case, the remedy is to change the incentives favouring advanced techniques through policy reforms, or to licence investments based on their profitability at shadow prices which reflect social scarcities (see Section 5).

If, however, the spectrum of techniques itself is unsatisfactory, rather different considerations arise. If the output(s) in question can be imported, foreign trade provides an alternative to producing them at home. Yet the point at issue is the absence of so-called 'appropriate' techniques for production at home. Now there is always the option of devoting resources to the development of new, 'appropriate' techniques. If such inventive activity is lacking or very limited, it is important to establish why this activity is unattractive relative to, say, producing textiles. It is sometimes argued that latecomers lack the engineers and technicians to undertake such work; but pioneers do not seem to have been greatly handicapped by a lack of card-carrying graduates when they set out. Others argue that the people in question have the wrong sort of training and attitudes, and aspire to emulate inventive activity in pioneers, where many of them were trained. There is some truth in this, inasmuch as men seek prestige as well as profit; but it is not wholly persuasive. It seems more plausible that the limited inventive activity in latecomers directed at 'appropriate' techniques stems largely from its uncertain profitability. Market prices may favour advanced techniques, while the legal system may hold out little prospect that private agents will recover their outlays in royalties or monopoly profits afforded by patent protection. Similarly, it is not clear that the incentives facing public sector agencies, which often employ the majority of a latecomer's technical personnel, are conducive to the development of appropriate techniques.

More generally, if the trappings of modernity are a merit want for governments, entrepreneurs, engineers and final consumers, then 'advanced' is also, for them, 'appropriate'. It can be argued, therefore, that the existence of pioneers is damaging to latecomers, not through the exercise of monopoly power or conspiracy, but through the inevitable demonstration effects on the tastes of latecomers.

In any event, the fact that latecomers face a different spectrum of techniques at the outset leads naturally to the question: will they grow faster than pioneers did at comparable stages, and so eventually catch up? Gerschenkron (1952) argues that this was certainly the case in the 19th century. In the leading sectors, latecomers adopted the latest techniques, and the plants in question were usually larger in scale than representative plants in pioneers. The evidence, such as it is, suggests that some recent latecomers are growing faster still, again drawing heavily on current 'best practice' embodied in large scale plants, albeit not in all industries. While the performance of some other latecomers cautions against any strong claims, this part of Gerschenkron's thesis is given some support by contemporary experience.

Now, if there are constant returns to scale and some measure of choice, it will not usually be efficient for latecomers to adopt the 'best practice' technique – unless, of course, the latter dominates all others in the sense of requiring no more of any input per unit of output and less of at least one input. If, however, there are increasing returns to scale embodied in 'best practice' plant, then slavish imitation of the pioneers' path may be inferior to a leap straight to the most advanced methods. This is a slightly more formal way of stating Gerschenkron's contention that latecomers grow faster because there is greater tension between current practice at the outset in latecomers and unexploited possibilities in the form of current best practice in pioneers. Certainly, it is easier to see how this might be when there are increasing returns.

In the course of adopting and adapting new techniques, increasing returns also appear in the guise of learning-by-doing (Arrow, 1962; Kaldor, 1957). While the process of learning is by no means automatic, firms can expect the efficiency with which they use new techniques to improve following their adoption. Hence, if firms in latecomers organize themselves so as to profit from their accumulated experience as fully as do firms in pioneers and such improvements have a ceiling that is reached in finite time or cumulative output, as seems plausible, then catching up in that particular line of production with the technique in question will be complete.

Thus far, no mention has been made of natural endowments. As a matter of history, industrialization was launched in temperate climates, and most contemporary latecomers are in the tropics and sub-tropics, where pests harmful to man flourish the year round. Advances in medical science and public health, which originated in pioneers and were subsequently put to work in latecomers, have gone a long way towards eliminating this disadvantage, at fairly modest recurrent costs. That leaves the sapping effects of heat and humidity on human effort and efficiency, and poor soils as salient disadvantages of the tropics. Air conditioning deals with the former, just as heating takes care of winter's cold in temperate climes. As for poor soils, these are of no consequence for footloose industries, though a prosperous and productive agriculture may have a beneficial influence on the speed and sacrifice with which an industrial society is built. Besides, the examples of Switzerland, Denmark, Japan and, lately, Singapore and Taiwan indicate that ingenuity and flexibility may count for more than expanses of fertile land and/or an invigorating climate.

2. GROWTH: BALANCED AND UNBALANCED. It has just been argued that the transfer of knowledge and technique from pioneers to latecomers is an inescapable feature

of growth in latecomers. Little was said, however, about the nature of the growth process itself, how it might be launched and sustained, or the forms of economic organization which would make the associated investments in plant and equipment. In particular, the role of the State went virtually unmentioned.

Although the doctrine of 'balanced' growth, as first set out by Rosenstein-Rodan (1943) and subsequently developed and elaborated by Nurkse (1953), certainly appeals to the notion that latecomers can draw on an existing stock of knowledge and techniques, the central problem, as its protagonists saw it, was to get growth started by inducing investment in industry. Now, why did investment have to be induced at all, as opposed to arising naturally and optimally as the result of profit seeking by entrepreneurs? First, it is argued, ruling market prices do not convey all relevant information to private investors. Not only are market structures imperfect, they are also incomplete, insurance markets being conspicuously thin and limited. Secondly, firms perceive their demand schedules to be rather inelastic where an expansion of output is concerned. This assumption of 'elasticity pessimism' was perhaps a natural legacy from the inter-war period. Nurkse, certainly, was pessimistic about the prospects for international trade; but the distinction between tradeable and non-tradeable goods, which is central to Section 5, was not made clearly. In any event, if firms perceive their respective demand schedules to be at all inelastic, they must have significant size, actually or potentially, in their respective markets. Thus, if one firm expands its output, the consequences for other firms are not, in general, completely summarized by market prices.

In Rosenstein-Rodan's example, the workers employed in a new shoe factory spend most of their income not on shoes, but on other wage goods, thereby making it profitable for the industries producing the latter to expand. In turn, an expansion of those industries will lead to a rise in the demand for shoes, but not necessarily such as to validate the initial investment in shoe-making capacity. What matters in establishing equilibrium, therefore, is firms' perceptions of the strategic responses of other firms, not only in competing lines of production, but potentially in all lines. Of course, this is immensely demanding of information for the individual firm, which may confine itself to conjectures about the responses of the firms in the more obvious complementary lines, while entirely ignoring wider ramifications. The more restricted the scope of these conjectures, the more limited is the expansion of output likely to be.

In the case of constant returns to scale – or, more precisely, constant average costs – some output will be produced, provided average cost is less than (perceived) marginal revenue at zero output. If, as seems plausible, initial perceptions are on the conservative side, firms will find demand conditions somewhat more favourable than expected, so that further rounds of expansion may occur. Nevertheless, with Nash conjectures, the resulting equilibrium will still be based on restricted assessments of the ramifications of an individual firm's actions.

The assumption of constant costs does not, however, sit very well with the notion that firms have significant size relative to their respective markets. It seems more fitting to assume that there are increasing returns to scale, at least in the form that the minimum efficient scale of production is large relative to perceived demand, so that average costs may well be falling over the relevant range. In this case, the indivisibility of investment requires the firm to make a substantial and irreversible commitment if any output is to be produced. This it will be reluctant to do, even if it makes extensive and possibly sanguine conjectures about the actions of other firms, unless it has strong assurances that the other firms will make their investments simultaneously. With obvious advantages to hanging back over moving first, it is quite possible that the outcome of this coordination game will be that no investments are made at all. This extreme outcome seems closer to the preoccupations of the balanced growth school than that of limited investment under constant costs, and better to characterize an agrarian economy in which modern industry has not yet been established. Indeed, Rosenstein-Rodan recognizes the importance of increasing returns in drawing upon Young's (1928) example of the tube line. In any event, the resulting failure of economic coordination under the conditions discussed here is greatly intensified in the presence of increasing returns.

Thus far, we have dealt with potentially beneficial effects of an expansion of one firm on the profits of others. But firms also use some of the same inputs, so that simultaneous expansion will raise costs more sharply, unless the inputs in question are in perfectly elastic supply. Thus, there are competitive as well as complementary effects to be considered (Fleming, 1955). The two resources used across the board are, of course, labour and investment.

Where raw, unskilled workers are concerned, no difficulties were anticipated, in view of what was presumed to be a great 'reserve army' of underemployed and unemployed labourers in peasant agriculture and petty trade, which could meet any conceivable (initial) expansion of organized industry. The discipline and rhythms of industrial life, as well as many specific skills, could be acquired on the job through learning-by-doing. Certain special skills, especially those of a technical and managerial nature, might not be so readily created, however, so that they would command a scarcity premium, which would increase with the overall scale of expansion, until additional supplies of such skills were forthcoming. This rise in costs is potentially damaging to the case for simultaneous expansion of all lines of production. In the short run, it could be mitigated by importing foreign technicians. Over the longer run, the training and education of nationals abroad and/or at home would be possible; but the gestation period for workers of this sort is so long that reliance on this option is scarcely feasible if a large programme of industrialization is to start straightaway.

The other resource for which firms clearly compete is capital goods. In a closed economy, the capacity of the machine-building sector will impose a limit on how much investment can be undertaken in other industries even if there is a willingness to save more, a point that is central to the models of Feldman–Domar (1957) and Mahalanobis (1953). If world supplies of such goods are highly elastic, imports remove this bottleneck, so that domestic savings become the limiting factor, provided they can be transformed into foreign exchange through exports.

Most proponents of balanced growth assumed that there was plenty of global capacity to supply the plant and equipment needed at home; but they were less sure that all potential domestic savings could be converted into foreign exchange. Besides, a strong push on many fronts with significant indivisibilities of investment would entail heavy sacrifices in current consumption, even if such conversion were possible at parametric terms of trade. Hence the strong accompanying plea for foreign aid to get the process going without undue pain.

A case for strong government intervention to coordinate individual investments is beginning to emerge from the balanced growth argument. Before addressing it, however, we must also consider the contrary thesis of Hirschman (1958), namely, that the right strategy is to pursue unbalanced growth. In such a strategy, the complementarities discussed above are not simply ignored; rather imbalances between supply and demand are deliberately induced after an examination of where the complementarities lie. The difficulty with Hirschman's thesis is that, unlike the doctrine of balanced growth, it has defied attempts to state it in a formal and rigorous way. This does not, of course, mean that it is wrong; but comparisons with balanced growth are render much more difficult thereby.

There are two features of Hirschman's argument that are particularly relevant here. First, he dismisses all so-called 'obstacles to development' save one, namely, the capacity to make rational economic decisions. If this capacity is adequate, so his argument runs, all the other 'obstacles', should they have an independent existence, will be easily surmountable. Now, the one thing that is needed above all else in pursuing a strategy of balanced growth is the ability to coordinate complementary investments without much help from the price system, so that balanced growth makes intensive demands on the very resource that Hirschman believes to be the scarcest.

How does unbalanced growth economize on this resource? In part, the answer goes, by giving up the attempt at detailed, centralized coordination implied by balanced growth. At first sight, this looks like no strategy at all – if it be granted that the price mechanism is defective – so we move on to the second feature of Hirschman's argument, which is at once poetic and slippery. When growth is unbalanced, capacity in some sectors will outrun others in such a way as to create an imbalance between supply and demand at 'normal' prices. The tension stemming from this excess demand is supposed to induce supplies of whatever is most lacking – savings, entrepreneurship, a decision to build a new road, or whatever. In effect, such tensions focus attention and resources on what should be done, and the stronger the tension, the sharper the focus. This, too, is a form of economic coordination; but if there is anything novel in Hirschman's thesis, it must exert its influence by something other than a change in relative prices under the pressure of excess demand. It is easier to coin descriptive phrases for the process – 'creative tension', for example – than to pin down what is at work and how it operates.

One possible interpretation is that unresolved excess demand induces additional supplies through changes in tastes, endowments or even both. Faced with a particularly lucrative and unusual opportunity a peasant may revise his ideas about how much current consumption and leisure he should sacrifice in order to finance it. Similarly, the need to solve a particularly pressing problem may jolt managers and technicians from their ordinary routines, causing them to summon up hitherto unknown reserves of ingenuity and energy. (The performance of British industry on a three-day work week during the miners' strike of 1974 is perhaps an example.) These changes, it should be emphasized, are not the consequences of changes in relative prices with given tastes and endowments. Rather, they are changes in tastes and endowments triggered by the gap between market and 'shadow' prices when there is unresolved excess demand. Interpreted thus, the theory appears overtly and heavily 'psychological' – and formidably difficult to state precisely, let alone test. Welfare comparisons are also rendered moot, for once a man has eyed a prospect under such conditions, he is no longer the man he was. The idea that individuals are thus transformed by experience is not wholly alien to economics; but many economists would be bemused, rendered giddy even, by this version of it.

As strategic doctrines, balanced and unbalanced growth appear to call for very different roles for the State as an agent in promoting industrialization. Given its assumptions, balanced growth really expresses the desirability of exploiting complementarities through central coordination when the price mechanism cannot do the job efficiently. Inspired perhaps by the Soviet example, the proponents of balanced growth drew the conclusion that an optimal level and pattern of industrial development requires that all investment decisions be made centrally. In the presence of increasing returns and lumpy investments, the problems of isolation and assurance would also arise in a particularly acute form, with a high prior profitability of bankruptcy for the individual firm acting in isolation. Thus, if firms were privately owned, they would have to have a voice in the proceedings. The desire to reduce current sacrifices to manageable proportions through foreign aid and commercial capital also introduced lender's risk and lender's interest. These foreign agencies were therefore to have their seats on Rosenstein-Rodan's Investment Board as well. Thus, what starts out as an argument for the desirability of central coordination begins to look like a manifesto for the Corporate State. Even leaving aside this inherent element of political economy, one is still struck by the staggering demands for detailed information that such a central body would make in its attempts to realize a full optimum.

A government pursuing an unbalanced growth strategy will clearly eschew any scheme of the above kind, but it will not leave matters entirely to the market. To the extent that such things can be assessed, it will promote growth in sectors that generate the right measure of creative tension, and this will need occasional revision as the process unfolds. The promotion could take a number of forms, from taxation to investment by the state itself. Moreover, the decision concerning which sectors to promote is itself a central one, requiring much information, though not as much as balanced growth. Thus, unbalanced growth certainly implies an active role for the state, though its rationale favours intervention in a decentralized form.

In this connection, Hirschman makes an orthodox and telling argument against balanced growth – or rather, the centralized mechanism balanced growth demands. Although the Investment Board might succeed in exploiting complementarity and increasing returns in a given state of knowledge, the very detail and scope of its investment plan would make it resistant to changes. If new information or more efficient techniques of production become available, the Board's tidy scheme of things may be upset by attempts to accommodate them. In an unbalanced growth strategy, however, such disturbances may be positively welcomed, since they offer the opportunity to shake up the system. Moreover, in a decentralised system, agents will have stronger incentives to keep an eye out for new developments. Although the context is rather different, this is tantamount to standing Schumpeter's conclusion about monopoly on its head: by practicising static virtue, the Investment Board falls into dynamic vice.

Finally, it is not clear that a presumption of market failure warrants the conclusion that direct, central coordination of investments is necessary. For if isolation and assurance are the problem, then an alternative way to get firms to commit themselves is to offer subsidies, the schedules of which depend on whether other firms have made commitments. Those moving early would receive larger subsidies until other firms followed. As more firms made commitments, subsidies would fall, since profits (losses) would rise (fall) as complementarities in demand began to make themselves felt. Once all firms had moved, all subsidies would cease and profits would be taxed according to some schedule announced in advance. Indeed, with the information available to the Investment Board, it should be possible to devise a schedule of subsidies that would induce firms to commit themselves in an optimal sequence, the resulting final pattern of investment being identical to that chosen by the Board. In practice, however, such refined calculations seem a rather implausible ideal. Instead, crude calculations would underpin an initial announcement of the schedule of subsidies. If no firms moved, the subsidies to early movers could be increased until some found it worthwhile to make investments, and further revisions would almost certainly be needed as the process unfolded. A lurching sequence of this sort, prodded by occasional revisions to tax policy, looks uncommonly like a form of unbalanced growth, even though its ultimate object is a balanced growth allocation that exploits complementarities in demand and economies of scale. Of course, as new data and techniques become available, revisions to the schedule of subsidies will be in order; but in this decentralized setting, only the schedule will be of inherent interest to the individual firms considering new investments.

3. THE DUAL ECONOMY. As we have seen, the assumption that labour is in highly elastic supply is an important element in balanced growth doctrine; for if wages are bid up significantly by a big push on many fronts, the very profitability of that coordinated effort may be undermined. Yet above all else, elastic supplies of labour bring to mind the classical tradition, and hence Lewis's (1954) celebrated article. Lewis was not, however, so much concerned with the problem of coordinating investment that exercised Rosenstein-Rodan and Nurkse. True to

the classical tradition, what mattered to Lewis is that capital be continuously accumulated and hence that there be a high marginal propensity to save. This would come about, for example, if the proceeds of growth accrued largely to capitalists and capitalists were abstemious – though whether the capitalists were private entrepreneurs or state functionaries was all the same to Lewis. (One should add that Hirschman's thesis makes light of a possible shortage of savings: if the right inducements to invest are present, such shortages will simply vanish.)

Perfectly elastic supplies of labour play a crucial role in Lewis's model. At a constant real wage, capitalists will choose a particular technique of production and, if there are constant returns to scale, earn a constant rate of profit. With classical savings behaviour, the rate of growth of the capitalist sector will be equal to the rate of profit multiplied by capitalists' marginal propensity to save. In the face of a stagnant subsistence sector, therefore, the structure of the economy will become steadily more capitalistic and the overall growth rate will continue to accelerate until the capitalist sector has exhausted all reserves of labour in the subsistence sector. If, at length, the wage should rise, the rate of profit will fall (in both Solovian and neo-Ricardian worlds). Thus, progressive rises in wages induced by the expansion of the capitalist sector will cause growth to peter out.

A notable feature of this process is that the distribution of national income shifts steadily in favour of profits so long as the real wage remains constant. Once the real wage begins to rise, the share of profits may continue to increase for a while if the share of the capitalist sector is still rising rapidly enough; but eventually it seems to have a tendency to fall. In any event, an increasing share of profits is likely to go with a more unequal distribution of incomes. To that extent, the evolution of Lewis's dual economy is consistent with Kuznets's hypothesis (1955) that the distribution of income at first becomes less equal as development proceeds and does not improve until industry accounts for a rather large share of national income.

There has been some dispute as to whether the marginal product of labour in the subsistence sector must be zero for Lewis's argument to go through. As should now be clear, all that matters is that the capitalist sector be able to attract workers at a constant real wage as it expands. Whether this constancy comes about through population growth, changing attitudes towards the participation of women in the labour force, a constant marginal product of labour in the subsistence sector, or some combination thereof is immaterial. Once the real wage begins to rise, however, Lewis's story is at an end.

Lewis's economy is certainly 'dual', in the sense that reproducible capital is used only in the capitalist sector and output per worker is much higher in that sector. Yet nowhere in the above account has it been necessary to appeal to increasing returns. This prompts one to ask whether Lewis's account of the development of the dual economy needs to be modified for successive waves of latecomers. If, at the outset, latecomers adopt more 'advanced' techniques, as embodied in large scale plants, dualism will be sharper than it was in pioneers. A higher rate of profit will yield a higher rate of growth of the capitalist sector, but if the latest techniques are adopted for their own sake, that will scarcely improve profits. Moreover, if such techniques employ fewer workers for each unit of investment, employment in the capitalist sector will be lower in latecomers than in pioneers at a comparable stage of development. Hence, the onset of rising real wages as a result of a depleted reserve army in the subsistence sector will be delayed. Dualism, therefore, will be not only sharper, but also more protracted than was the case historically.

4. GROWTH AND TRADE. Section 1 dealt mainly with the transfer of knowledge, albeit some of it embodied in specific capital goods and skilled workers. The consequences of trade between pioneers and latecomers will now be addressed in greater detail.

In the early literature, the thesis that the net barter terms of trade have a secular tendency to move against latecomers, which are presumably exporters of primary products, was stated by Prebisch (1950) and Singer (1950). This adverse shift stems, so the argument runs, from a combination of low price and income elasticities of demand for such products and an alleged bias towards the saving of raw materials in technical progress in industrialized countries. Thus, economic forces in pioneers produce damaging effects on latecomers. If true, the thesis implies that the later the start, the greater the difficulties of getting started. It was also used to support the argument that industrialization in latecomers should not be shaped by the prevailing structure of world prices for traded goods.

In the orthodox view, the individual latecomer to industrialization is a small country facing parametric prices for traded goods, in a given state of knowledge and with given endowments and tastes. The latecomer has the potential advantage of access to a larger set of techniques through transfers of knowledge, though the modern theory of distortions warns us that the right economic policies are needed to realize this advantage (Bhagwati and Ramaswami, 1963). As for the opportunities presented by trade, these are completely summarized by world prices. The latter may be more or less favourable to today's latecomers than those of a century ago, but the only relevant thing is their structure. There is no room in this account for the explicit operation of the king of 'system' embracing pioneers and latecomers that is central to the dependencia school. If there were such a mechanism, the movements of the barter terms of trade would be, for the orthodox, a sufficient statistic of its inner working.

Accepting this conclusion for the moment, what has actually happened to the barter terms of trade between pioneers and contemporary latecomers over the past century? Despite fierce controversy, the answer is: probably not much (Spraos, 1980). This agnostic conclusion is strengthened if allowance is made for improvements in the quality of manufactures, which are inadequately reflected in individual price series. If a recent and much shorter period is taken – the one favoured by proponents of the Prebisch–Singer thesis is from the peak of the Korean boom to the recession of the early 1980s – and petroleum is excluded, then things do look rather bleak for latecomers. The appeal to such a period is, however, questionable. Thus, theory and the facts appear to combine to confer a distinct advantage on today's latecomers.

It is still interesting to examine the gloomy case. Suppose, therefore, that manufactures become more expensive relative to primary commodities, which are exported. The standard 2×2 model tells us that with given knowledge and endowments, the domestic output of manufactures will increase. If the objective is a larger share for industry, the shift in relative prices is welcome – though there is an attendant loss of real income.

The assumption of just two goods and perfectly malleable and mobile capital may, however, obscure rather than illuminate matters. Industrial capital, in the sense of plant and equipment, is made up of produced goods. In the short run, this stock is specific and fixed. Over the longer run, latecomers cannot augment it by drawing upon a stock of malleable stuff called capital that was previously employed in the sector producing primary commodities for export. The plant and equipment in question is produced only in pioneers: for latecomers, it is a non-competitive import, and must be paid for with primary exports.

To capture this aspect, three goods are needed: primary exportables; standard manufactures, including simple producer goods like cement and fertilizers, plants for which can be bought off the shelf; and sophisticated producer goods, including cement and fertilizer plants. Now, with three goods, the conditions for technology and tastes to be well-behaved do not always suffice to ensure uniqueness of equilibrium; so that the usual caveat applies to what follows. When the relative price of manufactures rises, a shift towards standard manufactures at the expense of primary exportables looks attractive; but the purchasing power of exports over producer goods falls even with unchanged domestic productions, so that an important element in the cost of producing standard manufactures also rises in terms of primary commodities. If (i) the real wage declines and (ii) domestic labour is a good substitute for producer goods, a substantial shift towards standard manufactures may still be profitable. Even though condition (i) may be satisfied, (ii) looks distinctly dubious, so that only a modest shift may be warranted. More generally, if producer goods from pioneers form a large and indispensable component of capital formation in latecomers, adverse movements in the barter terms of trade will certainly slow accumulation in the latter. For domestic savings measured in units of exportables are likely to fall, too. This, therefore, is a fairly orthodox argument that the industrialization of latecomers may be set back by a secular decline in their terms of trade – if such a process is at work.

In a departure from orthodoxy, consider the effects of increasing returns in the form of learning-by-doing. Here, knowledge is not freely transferable, but must be acquired through independent effort and experience. The people who acquire such knowledge become specific factors by virtue of their experience, and so are produced factors. Thus, if latecomers and pioneers face nominally identical prices, pioneers will have lower costs: latecomers will catch up, but they cannot compete. This apparent paradox is resolved if pioneers encounter rising costs as the gains from learning are largely exhausted. Rising real wages in pioneers, for example, will then open the door to competition from latecomers. Industries which are mature in the sense of having little further scope for learning-by-doing will tend to shift from pioneers to latecomers, leading to product-cycle trade.

Some arguments for the (temporary) protection of infant industries also hinge on an appeal to learning-by-doing, but some care is needed. If all the effects thereof are internal to the individual firm, capital markets are perfect and there are no other distortions, there is no case for protection. If learning-by-doing does produce factors and inventive activity in the form of adaptation that are not wholly specific to the firm, then there is a prima facie case for protecting industry in latecomers at the expense of agriculture, given that such externalities are weak or non-existent in agricultural pursuits. It is not, however, an argument for uniform protection, since there are scant grounds for supposing that all industries produce equally strong externalities of this sort.

We must now consider what the existence of international trading opportunities at parametric prices does to the arguments for balanced growth. In the face of perfectly elastic demand schedules, the coordination problem vanishes for firms considering the production of tradeables. Moreover, there will be no reasons for (static) economies of scale to remain unexploited for want of demand. The only reservation here is that the 'natural' wedge between c.i.f. and f.o.b. prices be not so large as to make domestic prices appreciably sensitive to domestic demand and cost conditions. With this proviso, the problem of economic coordination that was the focus of Section 2 disappears.

Does this sound the knell for balanced growth and the Investment Board? Not quite; for there are still the non-tradeables to be considered, some of which – utilities, transportation and communications, for example – have precisely the characteristics of increasing returns and lumpiness in investment which sharpen the argument for some form of central coordination. Thus, there seems to be a sort of reprieve for balanced growth doctrine, the exact form of which is deferred until the next section.

5. PROTECTION AND COST-BENEFIT ANALYSIS. As it turned out, industry in the Third World has grown at a fast clip since 1950, though somewhat more slowly since 1974. Both the pace and pattern of industrial growth have been influenced by a plethora of protective tariffs, subsidies, rebates, quotas and licences, as well as direct investments by activist states. These interventions began to attract the attention of development economists in the sixties, many of whom were exercised by the effects of these interventions on incentives and resource allocation. The patterns of nominal protection revealed, on further investigation, quite higgledy-piggledy structures of effective protection, the only discernible regularity being the taxation of agriculture and the subsidization of industries as a group, and especially those producing consumer goods (Balassa, 1971; Little, Scitovsky and Scott, 1970).

In such a setting, market prices are a poor, if not quite misleading, guide to relative scarcities. To get at the latter, however, something more precise and firmly grounded in theory is needed than the concept of effective protection, particularly in the face of imperfections in factor markets. Rigorous foundations were supplied by the theory of optimal taxation (Diamond and Mirrlees, 1971), which yielded an important and fairly robust result: that, in the small country case, the relative scarcities of tradeable goods are the same as their relative world prices. Thus, the point of departure is the same as that for a calculation of effective protection. Next, suppose that non-tradeables are produced under constant returns to scale with no joint production. Then, if the shadow price of a non-tradeable is equal to its social marginal cost of production, we have

$$p'_N = p'_T A_{TN} + p'_N A_{NN} + \omega l_N \tag{1}$$

where p'_N and p'_T are the vectors of shadow prices of non-tradeables and tradeables, respectively, A_{NN} and A_{TN} are their respective submatrices of input-output coefficients for producing non-tradeables, ω is the shadow wage rate and l_N is the vector of labour input coefficients for non-tradeables. The shadow wage rate, in turn, comprises the value of the worker's marginal product (at shadow prices) in alternative employment (m) plus the social cost of the worker's additional consumption, if any, arising out of his transfer from such alternative employment.

$$\omega = m + \lambda(p_T, p_N) b \cdot \Delta y \tag{2}$$

where b is the vector of the amounts of goods consumed by the worker out of an extra unit of income, Δy is the increase in income arising from a shift from alternative employment and λ is the social value of an extra unit of private income relative to the *numéraire*, which in this case is uncommitted government income. Given p_T, λ, b, Δy and the technology for producing non-tradeables (A_{TN}, A_{NN}, l_N), the shadow prices of non-tradeables and labour follow at once from (1) and (2).

This, in essence, is the scheme advocated by Little and Mirrlees (1969), a work that has been deeply influential since its appearance. Non-tradeables are produced by means of tradeables, non-tradeables and labour; labour, in turn, produces tradeables or non-tradeables in alternative employment and spends any extra income on tradeables and non-tradeables. Thus, non-tradeables and labour can be decomposed ultimately into tradeables valued at world prices, a process of decomposition which corresponds to the matrix inversion needed to solve (1) and (2) for p_N and ω.

What does all this have to do with balanced growth? In the balanced growth schema, all goods are non-tradeables at the margin. Specializing (1) and (2) appropriately, it is immediately clear that, aside from commodity taxes, market prices will then diverge from shadow prices only if there is a distortion in the labour market or savings are deemed socially suboptimal ($\lambda < 1$). In most Less Developed Countries (LDCs), one can safely assume one or the other, if not both, so that trade and other tax distortions aside, market prices are still not 'right'.

When tradeables are introduced at parametric world prices, all shadow prices get anchored to the latter. Yet the derived demands for non-tradeables arising from the extra output and final consumption of non-tradeables are very much at work in (1) and (2). Indeed, they are precisely expressed by the matrix inversion that yields p_N and ω. It should be added that labour is usually assumed to be drawn ultimately from a 'subsistence' sector, where its marginal product is constant (not necessarily zero) but income is lower than in organized employment. Thus, the 'dual' economy makes an appearance, too. Shorn of increasing returns and straitjacketed by international trading opportunities at parametric prices, this is the residue of balance growth doctrine to have surved in the modern approach to assessing the social profitability of projects in distortion-ridden economies.

The focus on projects rather than plans is significant. True, good plans need good projects; but in the balanced growth scheme of things what is a good project cannot be determined independently of all the other projects making up the plan. The salient feature of the system of shadow prices derived above, however, is that it permits investment decisions to be decentralized. When the Ministry of Industry considers a proposal to build a textile factory, it need not worry about road-building proposals before the Ministry of Works. This arrangement is a far cry from Rosenstein-Rodan's Investment Board; but one thing they do have in common is the use of similar information. A glance at (1) and (2) reveals that there is not much difference in procedure between the derivation of shadow prices and the sort of calculations pursued by the 'traditional' sort of planners with input-output models. Dismissal of the latter as outmoded, if not positively harmful, therefore implies distrust of the former, a connection that some critics of 'planning' seem not to have recognized.

Be all that as it may, the widespread adoption of systems of project appraisal based on the use of the world prices carries another implication. For the individual country, world prices are the pivot on which all scarcities turn. True, the shadow prices of non-tradeables and labour will not bear exactly the same relation to the shadow prices of tradeables across all countries; but the latter exercise such a strong influence on the former that world prices will often exert a decisive influence over what is judged to be profitable, especially where industrial projects are concerned. In that case, these systems of shadow prices seem to impose the disciplines of free trade by stealth. Taken individually, each latecomer should benefit if the necessary conditions for the associated shadow prices to reflect real scarcities are satisfied. Taken as a group, however, the allocation of resources thus induced may worsen the terms of trade, which each latecomer has taken as parametric, so that problems of coordination may reappear at another level.

6. CONCLUDING REMARKS. The early writings in development economics are by no means doctrinally monolithic. Some can claim a classical lineage, while others are eclectic. If they share anything in common, it is a distrust of the proposition that matters can be left to the market. Even here there are exceptions, Bauer's being a notable (and sustained) voice of dissent; see, for example, Bauer and Yamey (1957). In fairness to Bauer, it should be said that while he has extolled the unalloyed virtues of individual enterprise and the importance of keeping markets free of intervention, he has never advocated pure laissez faire. On the whole, however, the early writings have a decidedly étatiste flavour.

Thereafter, there has been a steady intrusion of what can be loosely termed 'neoclassical' influences. In pursuing the themes of this essay, these influences have appeared in the shape of the theories of international trade and optimal taxation. Together, they have quite transformed the discussion of how industrialization should be approached. Even institutions do not survive unscathed: the full blooded Ministry of Planning is replaced by the mild-mannered Central Office of Project Evaluation. Where the other theme is concerned – that today's numerous latecomers are setting out in a world in which there are many mature pioneers – it is natural that international economics should have a prominent place in the study of development problems. Indeed, the ubiquitous term 'Trade and Development' suggests that the latter is a sort of dependent companion of the former. What is troubling is that the 'Trade' partner in this pairing is usually unswervingly neoclassical. Thus, the implicit claim that economic relations are mutually beneficial makes 'Development' appear as a corollary to 'Trade'. Perhaps the proposition is correct; but it needs critical scrutiny.

This suggests that development economics is being drawn back into the fold, where it might lose its claim to an independent existence. In that case, students of the subject would require no special preparation: the usual drilling in micro- and macroeconomics, suitably buttressed by field courses in trade, public economics and labour economics, would suffice. No doubt some movement of this sort is occurring. Yet two closing remarks are in order.

First, the traffic in ideas is not wholly in one direction. For example, in struggling to understand the persistent macroeconomic problems that have plagued Latin American economies for several decades, writers in both the 'structuralist' and orthodox traditions have influenced writing on mature economies. Similarly, the diverse contractual arrangements found in the markets for labour, tenancies and credit in agrarian economies have inspired a good deal of work in some branches of microeconomic theory, especially risk-sharing, incentives and the economics of information. (The peasant, who is the leading player in this drama, is no longer a creature of habit and tradition, but rather a relentless maximizer within the scope of the control variables at his disposal.)

Secondly, although it is difficult to sustain all of the structuralist's assumptions of rigidity in the face of the accumulated evidence of the responsiveness of individuals and markets, it does not follow that reservations about the efficacy of the market mechanism can be set aside. LDCs, in which insurance and forward markets are conspicuously thin and incomplete, are very far removed from the Arrow–Debreu ideal; and in the absence of a complete set of markets, market outcomes will not, in general, be (constrained) efficient. Thus, (neoclassical) theory lends no immediate support to the contention that intervention will invariably make matters worse. One cannot, however, rush to the opposite conclusion: that the case for direct interventions and control by the state is, once more, nicely sewn up. Indirect intervention through the market may be superior to direct allocations, and doing nothing may be better than either. Whether to intervene and if so, in what form, will depend on circumstances. This sort of pragmatic tinkering will not appeal to doctrinal purists; but if development economics is to make further progress towards becoming a mature branch of applied economics, these are among the important questions to be posed and answered.

BIBLIOGRAPHY

Arrow, K.J. 1962. The economic implications of learning by doing. *Review of Economic Studies* 28(3), June, 155–73.

Balassa, B. et al. 1971. *The Structure of Protection in Developing Countries.* Baltimore: Johns Hopkins University Press.

Bauer, P.T. and Yamey, B.S. 1957. *The Economics of Underdeveloped Countries.* Chicago: University of Chicago Press.

Bhagwati, J.N. and Ramaswami, V.K. 1963. Domestic distortions, tariffs and the theory of optimum subsidy. *Journal of Political Economy* 71, February, 44–5.

Chenery, H.B. and Syrquin, M. 1975. *Patterns of Development. 1950–1970.* London: Oxford University Press.

Diamond, P. and Mirrlees, J.A. 1971. Optimal taxation and public production I: Production efficiency and II: Tax rules. *American Economic Review* 61, January and June, 8–27 and 261–8.

Domar, E.D. 1957. *Essays in the Theory of Economic Growth.* New York: Oxford University Press.

Fleming, J.M. 1955. External economies and the doctrine of balanced growth. *Economic Journal* 65, June, 241–56.

Gerschenkron, A. 1952. Economic backwardness in historical perspective. In *The Progress of Underdeveloped Countries*, ed. B. Hoselitz, Chicago: Chicago University Press.

Hirschman, A.O. 1958. *The Strategy of Economic Development.* New Haven: Yale University Press.

Kaldor, N. 1957. A model of economic growth. *Economic Journal* 67, December 591–624.

Kuznets, S.S. 1955. Economic growth and income inequality. *American Economic Review* 45, March, 1–28.

Kuznets, S.S. 1966. *Modern Economic Growth: Rate, Structure and Spread.* New Haven: Yale University Press.

Lewis, W.A. 1954. Economic development with unlimited supplies of labour. *Manchester School* 22, May, 139–91.

Little, I.M.D., and Mirrlees, J.A. 1969. *Manual of Industrial Project Analysis in Developing Countries*, Vol. II, *Social Cost-Benefit Analysis.* Paris: OECD.

Little, I.M.D., Scitovsky, T. and Scott, M. 1970. *Industry and Trade in Some Developing Countries.* London: Oxford University Press.

Mahalanobis, P.C. 1953. Some observations on the process of growth of national income. *Sankhya* 12(4), September, 307–12.

Nurkse, R. 1953. *Problems of Capital Formation in Underdeveloped Countries.* Oxford: Blackwell; New York: Oxford University Press.

Prebisch, R. 1950. *The Economic Development of Latin America and Its Principal Problems.* New York: United Nations.

Rosenstein-Rodan, P.N. 1943. Problems of industrialization of Eastern and South-Eastern Europe. *Economic Journal* 53, June-September, 202–11.

Schumpeter, J.A. 1926. *Theorie der Wirtschaftlichen Entwicklung.* 2nd edn, Leipzig: Duncker & Humblot. Trans. as *The Theory of Economic Development*, Cambridge, Mass.: Harvard University Press, 1934.

Seers, D. 1969. The meaning of development. *International Development Review* 11(4), 2–6.

Singer, H.W. 1950. The distribution of gains between investing and borrowing countries. *American Economic Review, Papers and Proceedings* 40, May, 473–85.

Spraos, J. 1980. The statistical debate on the net barter terms of trade between primary commodities and manufactures. *Economic Journal* 90, March, 107–28.

Young, A.A. 1928. Increasing returns and economic progress. *Economic Journal* 38, December, 527–42.

17

Absorptive Capacity

RICHARD S. ECKAUS

The idea that the productivity of new investment is a declining function of the rate of investment – the concept labelled 'absorptive capacity' – has attracted attention in development economics because of its implications as a constraint on growth.

The hypothesis began to emerge most clearly in the 1950s in the form of a limit on the total amount of investment which could be carried out and/or used in any period, as if the marginal productivity of resources devoted to investment would, at some level of total investment undertaken, fall to zero. This was the position taken by Horvath (1958), citing experience in Yugoslavia and Eastern Europe. An Economic Commission for Asia and the Far East (ECAFE) report claimed that 'capacity sets a limit to the amount of efficient investment physically possible', introducing the distinction between 'efficient' and, presumably, 'inefficient' investment (ECAFE, 1960). In the early discussions, the concept was used to represent all the constraints on development which economists could not easily put into the conventional production function, 'the supply of skilled labour, administrative capacity, entrepreneurship and social change' (Marris, 1970).

Rosenstein-Rodan (1961), Adler (1965) and others described the absorptive capacity content as a relationship between the productivity and the rate of investment, rather than as an absolute ceiling on investment's productivity. The sources of the relationship were not discussed in depth nor investigated empirically and it remained a 'black box' whose inner workings were never fully explained. Nonetheless, by the mid-1960s the absorptive capacity idea had become a part of the standard toolbox of development economics and was used readily to explain difficulties experienced in attempts to accelerate economic growth.

Research on growth and planning models led to both a refinement of the concept and new speculation about its sources. Kendrick and Taylor (1969), following a suggestion by Dorfman and Thoreson (1969), modelled the absorptive capacity constraint as a permanent reduction in the productivity of new investment related to the rate of investment, as if an increase in investment were accompanied by the use of progressively inferior engineering design and materials. Eckaus (1972) formulated the constraint by making the productivity of successive tranches of investment in any year decline relative to the original tranche with, however, the decline only being temporary. In subsequent periods after the new capital was completed, its productivity would grow to 'rated' levels. He offered the hypothesis that, as investment increases, less and less well qualified engineers and workers and less suitable equipment are employed in producing the new capital goods and bringing them into production.

The absorptive capacity concepts came to play a critical role in the economy-wide policy models which were formulated as linear programming problems. If the objective function in such models is linear, for example, the simple discounted sum of aggregate consumption over the plan period and, if all the constraints are linear and do not control the timing of consumption, the solutions of the models, will exhibit 'flip-flop' or 'bang-bang' behaviour. Aggregate consumption will be concentrated either at the beginning or at the end of the planning period. This unrealistic and undesirable result can be controlled by constraints on the timing of consumption (Eckaus and Parikh, 1968). An aggregate utility function with declining marginal utility as a nonlinear objective function and/or absorptive capacity constraints, which are essentially nonlinear relations between investment and increments in output, are, however, theoretically more satisfactory means of avoiding 'bang-bang'.

The absorptive capacity concept is related closely to a generalization which emerged quite independently of the development literature from the study of factors constraining the growth of firms in advanced countries (Penrose, 1959). This was embodied in a theoretical growth model by Uzawa (1969). The concept is also a close relation, if not the twin, of an idea which appeared early in the macroeconomic analysis literature only to be lost and then revived once more. In chapter 11 of the *General Theory*, Keynes describes the marginal efficiency of capital, that is, the productivity of new investment, as declining with the rate of new investment because, 'pressure on the facilities for producing that type of capital will cause its supply price to increase' (Keynes, 1936). Under the title of 'adjustment costs', this characterization began to figure prominently in the macroeconomic literature in the late 1960s (Lucas, 1967).

'Adjustment costs' is a phrase which is as appealing as 'absorptive capacity'. The phenomenon is not explained by giving it a name, however. While the fact that economists continue to resort to the idea might be counted as evidence that it reflects a reality, the empirical research on its sources is still limited.

BIBLIOGRAPHY
Adler, J. 1965. *Absorptive Capacity and Its Determinants.* Washington, DC: Brookings Institution.
Dorfman, R. and Thoreson, R. 1969. Optimal patterns of growth and aid with diminishing returns to investment and consumption. *Economic Development Report* No. 142, Development Research Group, Harvard University, Cambridge, Mass.

Eckaus, R.S. 1972. Absorptive capacity as a constraint due to maturation processes. In *Development and Planning: Essays in Honour of Paul Rosenstein-Rodan*, ed. J. Bhagwati and R.S. Eckaus, Cambridge, Mass.: MIT Press.

Eckaus, R.S. and Parikh, K.S. 1968. *Planning for Growth*. Cambridge, Mass.: MIT Press.

Economic Commission for Asia and the Far East (ECAFE). 1960. *Programming Techniques for Economic Development*. Bangkok: United Nations.

Horvath, B. 1958. The optimum rate of investment. *Economic Journal* 68, 747–67.

Kendrick, D.A. and Taylor, L.J. 1969. A dynamic nonlinear planning model for Korea. In *Practical Approaches to Development Planning*, ed. I. Adelman, Baltimore: Johns Hopkins Press.

Keynes, J.M. 1936. *The General Theory of Employment, Interest and Money*. London: Macmillan; New York: Harcourt, Brace.

Lucas, R. 1967. Adjustment costs and the theory of supply. *Journal of Political Economy* 75, August, 321–34.

Marris, R. 1970. Can we measure the need for development assistance? *Economic Journal* 80, 650–68.

Penrose, E. 1959. *The Theory of the Growth of the Firm*. Oxford: Blackwell; New York: Wiley.

Rosenstein-Rodan, P.N. 1961. International aid for underdeveloped countries. *Review of Economics and Statistics* 43(2), 107–38.

Uzawa, H. 1969. Time preference and the Penrose effect in a two-class model of economic growth. *Journal of Political Economy* 77, 628–52.

Agricultural Growth and
Population Change

E. BOSERUP

The macroeconomic theory of the relationship between demographic and agricultural change was developed by Malthus and Ricardo in the early stage of demographic transition in Europe, and interest in classical theory was revived in the middle of this century, when economists became aware of the unfolding demographic transition in other parts of the world. Ricardo (1817) distinguished between two types of agricultural expansion in response to population growth. One is the extensive margin, the expansion into new land which he supposed would yield diminishing returns to labour and capital because the new land was presumed to be more distant or of poorer quality than the land already in use. The other type, the intensive margin, is more intensive cultivation of the existing fields, raising crop yields by such means as better fertilization, weeding, draining, and other land preparation. This also was likely to yield diminishing returns to labour and capital. Therefore Ricardo assumed, with Malthus (1803), that population increase would sooner or later be arrested by a decline in real wages, increase of rents, and decline of per capita food consumption.

This theory takes no account of a third type of agricultural expansion in response to population growth: using the increasing labour force to crop the existing fields more frequently. This was in fact what was happening in England in Ricardo's time, when the European system of short fallow was being replaced by the system of annual cropping. Fallows are neither more distant nor of poorer quality than the cultivated fields, but if fallow periods are shortened or eliminated more labour and capital inputs are needed, both to prevent a decline of crop yields and to substitute for the decline in the amount of fodder for animals, which was previously obtained by the grazing of fallows. Therefore, this type of intensification is also likely to yield diminishing returns to labour and capital, but the additions to total output obtained by increasing the frequency of cropping are much larger than those obtainable by use of more labour and capital simply

21

to raise crop yields. In fact, the Ricardian type of intensification is better viewed as a means not to raise crop yields, but more to prevent a decline of those yields as fallow is shortened or eliminated. When this third type of agricultural expansion by higher frequency of cropping is taken into account, elasticities of food supply in response to population growth are different from those assumed in classical theory.

The failure to take differences in frequency of cropping into account renders the classical theory unsuitable for the analysis of agricultural changes which accompany the demographic transition in developing countries in the second half of this century. Differences in population densities between developing countries are very large, and so are the related differences in frequency of cropping. The relevant classification for analysis of agricultural growth is not between new land and land which is sown and cropped each year, but the frequency at which a given piece of land is sown and cropped. Both in the past and today, we have a continuum of agricultural systems, ranging from the extreme case of land which is never used for crops, to the other extreme of land which is sown as soon as the previous crop is harvested. Increasing populations are provided with food and employment by gradual increase of the frequency of cropping.

In large, sparsely populated areas of Africa and Latin America, the local subsistence systems are pastoralism and long fallow systems of the same types as those used in most of Europe in the first millenium AD and earlier. In areas with extremely low population densities, twenty or more years of forest fallow alternate with one or two years of cropping, while four to six years of bush fallow alternate with several years of cropping in regions where population densities have become too high to permit the use of longer fallow periods. Methods of subsistence agriculture in developing countries with even higher population densities include short fallow systems (i.e. one or two crops followed by one or two years fallowing) or systems of annual cropping. In countries with very high population densities, including many Asian countries, some of the land is sown and cropped two or three times each year without any fallow periods.

If these differences in frequency of cropping are overlooked, or assumed to be adaptations to climatic or other permanent natural differences, the prospects for agricultural expansion in response to the growth of population and labour force look either more favourable, or more unfavourable, than they really are. In sparsely populated areas with long fallow systems, the areas which bear secondary forest or are used for grazing may be assumed incorrectly to be new land in the Ricardian sense, it being overlooked that they have the functions of recreating soil fertility or humidity, preventing erosion or suppressing troublesome weeds before the land is again used for crops. If neither the local cultivators nor their governments are aware of the risks of shortening fallow periods, and are not taking steps to avoid them, such shortening may damage the land, and erosion, infertility or desertification may result. In such cases, the scope for accommodating increasing populations will prove to be less than expected, and later repair of the damage will become costly, if possible at all. On the other hand, if land presently used as fallow in long fallow systems is assumed to be of inferior quality, in accordance with Ricardian theory, the large possibilities for accommodation of increasing populations by shifting from long fallow to shorter or no fallow, will be overlooked or underestimated.

LABOUR SUPPLIES. When population growth accelerated in the developing countries in the middle of this century, economists applied Ricardo's distinction between expansion of cultivation to new land and attempts to raise crop yields by additional inputs of labour and capital. They therefore focused on the most densely populated countries in Asia, in which there was little new land. Since the possibilities for multicropping were not taken into account, it was assumed that the elasticity of food production in response to population growth would be very low in these countries, and that the acceleration of population growth would soon result in food shortages, high food prices, reduction of real wages, and steep increase of Ricardian rent.

Lewis (1954) suggested that in densely populated countries with little, if any uncultivated land, marginal returns to labour were likely to be zero or near to zero, and that a large part of the agricultural labour force was surplus labour, which could be transferred to non-agricultural employment without any diminution of agricultural output, even if there were no change in techniques. So Lewis recommended that rural-to-urban migration should be promoted, as a means of increasing marginal and average productivity in agriculture and of raising the share of the population employed in higher productivity occupations in urban areas. He confined his recommendation to densely populated countries, but many other economists made no distinction between densely and sparsely populated countries, assuming with Ricardo that uncultivated land must be of low quality so that a labour surplus would exist in all developing countries. The labour surplus theory contributed to create the bias in favour of industrial and urban development and the neglect of agriculture which has been a characteristic feature of government policy in many developing countries.

However, the labour surplus theory underestimates the demand for labour in agricultural systems with high frequency of cropping, based on labour intensive methods and use of primitive equipment. If population density in an area increases, fallow eliminated and multicropping introduced, then more and more labour-intensive methods must be used to preserve soil fertility, reduce weed growth and parasites, water the plants, grow fodder crops for animals, and protect the land. Some of the additional labour inputs are current operations, but others are labour investments. Before intensive cropping systems can be used, it may be necessary to terrace or level the land, build irrigation or drainage facilities, or fence the fields in order to control domestic animals. If these investments are made with human and animal muscle power, the necessary input of human labour is large. Even draught animals cannot reduce the work burden much, if fallows and other grazing land have been reduced so much that the cultivator must produce their fodder.

Part of the investments which are needed in order to increase the frequency of cropping are made by the cultivator with the same tools, animals and equipment that are used for current operations. Estimates of investments and savings in agricultural communities with increasing population are seriously low if they fail to include such labour investments. Due to the larger number of crops, the additional operations with each crop, and the labour investments, the demand for labour rises steeply when intensive land use is introduced. This contrasts with the assumptions of the labour surplus theory, which expects that the effect of population growth is always to add to the labour surplus.

When the theory of low supply elasticity and labour surplus in agriculture is combined with the theory of demographic transition, the prospects for densely populated countries with the majority of the population in agriculture look frightening. With the prospect of prolonged rapid growth of population (as forecast by the demographers) and with the poor prospects for expansion of food production and agricultural employment (implied by the labour surplus theory), it seemed obvious that sufficient capital could not be forthcoming for the enormous expansion of non-agricultural employment and output that was needed. So because the possibilities for adapting food production to population were underestimated, many economists suggested that the best, or even the only means to avoid catastrophe was the promotion of rapid fertility decline by family planning. This in turn overlooked the links between the level of economic development and the motivations for restriction of family size.

The motivation for adopting an additional work load in periods of increasing population, and the means to shoulder it, are different as between agricultural subsistence economies and communities of commercial farmers. In the former, the need to produce enough food to feed a larger family may be sufficient motivation for adopting a new agricultural system which, at least for a time, raises labour input more steeply than output. The way to shoulder a larger work load is to increase the labour input of all family members. In some regions most of the agricultural work is done by men, and in other regions, by women; but when the work load becomes heavier, women become more involved in agricultural work in the former regions, and men more involved in the latter; in both, children and old people have more work to do. For all members of agricultural families, average work days become longer and days of leisure fewer. The whole year may become one long busy season in areas with widespread multicropping, labour intensive irrigation, and transplanting from seed beds.

For commercial producers, the motivation for intensification of agriculture emerges when population growth or increasing urban incomes increase the demand for food, and push food prices up until more frequent cropping becomes profitable, in spite of increasing costs of production or need for more capital investment. By this change in sectoral terms of trade, a part of the burden of rural population increase is passed on to the urban population. The increase of agricultural prices is by no means all an increase of Ricardian rent, but is in good part a compensation for increasing costs of production. If the increase of food prices is prevented by government intervention or by imports of cheap food, the intensification will not take place.

Moreover, in regions with commercial agriculture, work seasons become longer when crop-frequency increases in response to population growth. Therefore the decline of real wages per work hour is at least partially compensated for by more employment in the off-seasons, and by more employment opportunities for women and children in the families of agricultural workers. The discussion of low or zero marginal productivity in agriculture suffers from a neglect of the seasonal differences in employment and wages. Many off-season operations are in fact required in order to obtain higher crop-frequency through labour intensive methods alone, and so may well appear to be of very low productivity if viewed in isolation from their real function. Wages for these operations, or indeed off-season wages generally, may be very low; but the seasonal differences in wages are usually larger. Therefore, accumulation of debt in the off-seasons with repayment in the peak seasons is a frequent pattern of expenditure in labouring families.

Low off-season wages are an important incentive for intensification of the cropping pattern in commercial farms, since much of the additional labour with multicropping, irrigation, labour intensive crops and feeding of animals falls in these seasons. But, when the same land is cropped more frequently in response to population growth, the demand for labour in the peak seasons also rises steeply, perhaps more than the supply of labour. In many cases, a large share of the agricultural population combines subsistence production on small plots of owned or rented land with wage labour for commercial producers in the agricultural peak seasons, and this contributes to considerable flexibility in the labour market. If real wages decline, because population increase pushes food prices up, full-time agricultural workers have no other choice than to reduce their leisure and that of their spouse and children, and offer to work for very low wages in the off-season periods. But workers who have some land to cultivate may choose to limit their supply of wage labour, and instead cultivate their own land more intensively with family labour. Since they took wage labour mainly in the peak seasons, their limitation of the supply of wage labour may prevent a decline of, or cause an increase of, real wages in the peak seasons, and thus put a floor below the incomes of the full-time workers.

The flexibility of the rural labour market is enhanced if not only labour but also land is hired in and out. A family that disposes of an increasing labour force may either do some work for other villagers, or rent some land from them, while a family that disposes of a reduced labour force may either hire some labour, or lease some land to others. With such a flexible system, prices for lease of land and wages will rapidly be adjusted to changes in labour supply. But the smooth adaptation of the system to population change will be hampered or prevented if, for political reasons, either hiring of labour or lease of land is made illegal, or changes in agricultural prices are prevented by government action.

TRANSPORT COST AND URBANIZATION. In Ricardian theory, marginal returns to labour and capital decline in response to population growth, partly because agricultural production is intensified, partly because it is expanded to inferior land, and partly because more distant land is taken into cultivation, thus increasing costs of transport. Thus, when population is increasing, producers have a choice between increasing costs of production, or increasing costs of transport between fields and consumers. However, there is a third possibility, which is to move the centre of consumption closer to land which is of similar quality to that which was used before the population became larger. Communities who use long fallow periods often move their habitations after long-term settlement in a forested area, and move to another area where the fertility of forest land has become high after a long period of non-use. Such movement of villages is likely to become more frequent, as population increases.

In other cases it is not the whole village which is moved, but an increasing number of villagers move their habitation to new lands, where they build isolated farmsteads or new hamlets. This may accommodate additional populations until all the space between the villages is filled up with habitations, and the choice in case of further population growth is between more frequent cropping, or use of inferior land, or long distance migration of part of the population.

The combination of shorter fallow periods and filling up of the space between the villages helps to create the conditions for emergence of small urban centres. Costs of transport are inversely related to the volume of transport, and roads, even primitive ones, are only economical, or feasible, with a relatively high volume of traffic. If fallow periods are very long, and distances between villages are large, there will be too few people in an area to handle both the production and transport which are necessary to supply a town with agricultural products. Urbanization and commercial agricultural production are only possible when population densities are relatively high, and fallow periods short. So when population in an area continues to increase a point may be reached when small market towns emerge, served by road and water transport, as happened in large parts of Europe in the beginning of this millenium.

With further growth of population it will again be necessary to choose between further intensification of agriculture at increasing costs, or moving the additional consumers (or some of them) to another location, where they can be supplied by less intensive agriculture, and with shorter distances of transport. So at this stage of development, new small market towns may emerge in between the old towns, or in peripheral areas together with agricultural settlement. In other words, instead of agricultural products moving over longer and longer distances, thus creating Ricardian rent in the neighbourhood of existing consumer centres, new centres of consumption may appear closer to the fields. In most of Europe, such a gradual spread of decentralized urbanization made it possible to delay the shift from short fallow agriculture to annual cropping to the late 18th or the 19th century. Areas with such a network of market towns have better conditions for development of small-scale and middle-sized industrialization than sparsely populated areas with a scattered population of subsistence farmers.

The long-distance migration from Europe to North America in the 19th century can be viewed as a further step in this movement of European agricultural producers and consuming centres to a region with lower population density, less intensive agriculture, and much lower agricultural costs. The urban centres in

America were supplied by extensive systems of short fallow agriculture at a time when production in Western Europe had shifted to much more intensive agriculture with annual cropping and fodder production.

TECHNOLOGY. From ancient times, growth of population and increase of urbanization have provided incentives to technological improvements in agriculture, either by transfer of technology from one region to another, or by inventions in response to urgent demand for increase of output, either of land, or labour, or both. Until the 19th century, technological change in agriculture was a change from primitive technology, that is, human labour with primitive tools, to intermediate technology, that is, human labour aided by better hand tools, animal-drawn equipment, and water power for flow irrigation. In the classical theory of agricultural growth, such changes are means to promote population growth and urbanization, but they are assumed to be fortuitous inventions, and are not viewed as technological changes induced by population growth and increasing urbanization.

In the course of the 19th century, the continuing increase of the demand for agricultural products, and the increasing competition of urban centres of agricultural labour, induced further technological change in European and North American agriculture. The technological innovations of the industrial revolution were used to accomplish a gradual shift from intermediate to high-level technologies, that is, human labour aided by mechanized power and other industrial inputs. The chemical and engineering industries contributed to raise productivity of land, labour and transport of agricultural products, and scientific methods were introduced in agriculture as a means of raising yields of crops and livestock.

The existence of such high-level technologies improves the possibilities for rapid expansion of agricultural production in developing countries as well, but because in North America and Europe these technologies were used to reduce direct labour input in agriculture, those economists who believed in the labour surplus theory feared that they would further increase labour surplus. However, the idea of a general labour surplus in agriculture in developing countries had never been unanimously agreed, and under the influence of empirical studies of intensive agriculture in densely populated regions, Schultz (1964) suggested that labour was likely to be fully occupied even in very small holdings, when primitive technology was used. Therefore output and income in such holdings could only be increased by introduction of industrial and scientific inputs, and human capital investment of the types used in industrialized countries.

Although proponents and the opponents of the labour surplus theory had different views concerning the relationship between the demand for and supply of labour, they agreed in suggesting a low supply elasticity of output in response to labour inputs, because they overlooked, or underestimated, the large effects on output and employment which can be obtained by using high-level technologies

27

to increase the frequency of cropping. The availability of new varieties of quickly maturing seeds, of chemical fertilizers, and of mechanized equipment for pumping water and land improvements, permits the use of multicropping on a much larger scale, and in much drier and colder climates than was possible before these new types of inputs existed. The new high-level technologies have changed the constraints on the size of the world population from the single one of land area to those of energy supply and costs, and of capital investment.

The new inputs permit a much more flexible adaptation of agriculture to changes in population and real wages. Intensive agriculture is no longer linked to low real wages, and it is possible, by changing the compositions of inputs, to vary the rates of increase of employment and real wages for a given rate of increase of total output. By using a mixture of labour intensive and high-level techniques, adapted to the man-land ratio and the level of economic development, first Japan, and later many other densely populated countries, obtained rapid increases in agricultural employment, output per worker, and total output. This 'Green Revolution' is an example of a technological change in agriculture induced by population change. The research which resulted in the development of these methods and inputs was undertaken and financed by national governments and international donors concerned about the effects of rapid population growth on the food situation in developing countries. Therefore, it focused mainly on improvement of agriculture in densely populated countries, where both governments and donors considered the problem to be most serious.

Agricultural producers who use high-level technologies are much more dependent upon the availability of good rural infrastructure than producers who use primitive or intermediate technologies. Transport and trade facilities are needed not only for the commercial surplus but also for the industrial inputs in agriculture; repair shops, electricity supply, technical schools, research stations, veterinary and extension services, are also needed. Therefore short-term supply elasticities differ between those regions which have and those which do not have the infrastructure needed for use of industrial and scientific inputs in agriculture. In the former, a rapid increase of output may be obtained by offering more attractive prices to the producers, while in the latter, increase of prices may have little effect on output, until the local infrastructure has been improved. Improvement of infrastructure may, on the other hand, be sufficient to obtain a change from subsistence production to commercial production, if it results in a major reduction in the difference between the prices paid to the local producers and those obtained in the consuming centres.

In densely populated regions with a network of small market towns, it is more feasible to introduce industrial and scientific inputs in agriculture, than in regions inhabited only by a scattered population of agricultural producers. Because per capita costs of infrastructure are lower in the first mentioned regions, they are more likely to have the necessary infrastructure, and if not, governments may be more willing to supply it. Thus sparsely populated regions are handicapped compared to densely populated ones, when high-level technologies are taken into use.

TENURE. Changes in output may also be prevented if the local tenure system is ill-adapted to the new agricultural system. Land tenure is different in regions with different frequency of cropping. In regions with long fallow agriculture, individual producers have only usufruct rights in the land they use for cultivation, and the land, the pastures, and the forested land are all tribally owned. Before a plot is cleared for cultivation it is usually assigned by the local chief, and when large investments or other large works are needed the producers are organized by the chief as mutual work parties. If population increases and with it the demands for assignment of land, a stage may be reached when either the chief or the village community will demand a payment for such assignments, thereby changing the system of land tenure. Payments to the chief for assignment of land may turn him into a large scale landowner, and this payment may tip the balance and make more frequent cropping of land more economical than use of new plots, or settlement in new hamlets.

When frequency of cropping becomes sufficiently high that major permanent investments in land improvement are necessary, a change to private property in land may provide security of tenure to the cultivator, and make it possible for him to obtain credits. If at this stage no change of tenure is made by legal reform, a system of private property in land is likely to emerge by unlawful action and gradual change of custom; but in such cases the occupants, who have no legal rights to the land, may hesitate (or be unable) to make investments and land many remain unprotected against erosion and other damage.

In more densely populated areas, with more frequent cropping and need for large-scale irrigation and other land improvement, these investments may be organized by big landlords as labour service or by local authorities as wage labour, financed by local or general taxation. In order to change from a particular fallow system to another that is more intensive, it is likely that not only the ownership system in the cultivated plots but also that for uncultivated land must be changed, as must responsibility for infrastructure investment. Because of the links between the fallow system, the tenure system, and the responsibility for infrastructure investment, attempts to intensify the agricultural system by preservation (for political reason) of the old tenure system and rural organization are likely to be unsuccessful, as are attempts to introduce new tenure systems that are unsuitable for the existing (or the desired, future) level of intensity and technology. Therefore, government policy is an important determinant of the agricultural response to population growth.

During fallow periods, the land is used for a variety of purposes: for gathering fuel and other wood, for hunting, for gathering of fertilizer, for grazing and browsing by domestic animals. Therefore, a change of the fallow system may create unintended damge to the environment unless substitutes are introduced for these commodities, or the pattern of consumption is changed. When hunting land becomes short, the right to hunt may be appropriated by the chiefs (or others), forcing the villagers to change their diet. When grazing land becomes short, enclosures may prevent the villagers (or some of them) from using it, or the village community may ration the right to pasture animals in the common grazing land and fallows, in order to prevent overgrazing and erosion, or desertification. These measures will impose a change of diet, and perhaps a change to fodder production in the fields.

NUTRITION. Both production and consumption change from land-using to less land-using products when population increases and agriculture is intensified. There may be a shift from beef and mutton to pork and poultry, from animal to vegetable products, from cereals to rootcrops for human consumption, and from grazing to production of fodder for animals. Under conditions of commercial farming, the changes in consumption and production are induced by increasing differentials between the prices of land-saving and land-using products. If the process of population growth is accompanied by decline of real wages, the changes in consumption patterns for the poorest families may be large. This may result in protein deficiencies and malnutrition with spread of the disease-malnutrition syndrome; this causes high child mortality because disease prevents the child from eating and digesting food, and malnutrition reduces the resistance to disease.

The classical economists had suggested that continuing population growth would result in malnutrition, famine and disease, which would re-establish the balance between population and resources by increasing mortality. But they also envisaged the possibility of an alternative model, in which population growth was prevented by voluntary restraint on fertility. Mathus (1803) talked of moral restraint and Ricardo (1817) of the possibility that the workers would develop a taste for comforts and enjoyment, which would prevent a superabundant population. However, it was not ethical or psychological changes but the economic and social changes resulting from increasing industrialization and urbanization which induced a deceleration of rates of population growth, first in Europe and North America, and later in other parts of the world.

GOVERNMENT POLICIES. The deceleration of rates of population growth in Europe and North America coincided with a decline in the income elasticity of demand for food due to the increase in per capita incomes. As a result the rate of increase in the demand for food slowed down, just as the rate of increase of production accelerated due to the spread of high-level technologies and scientific methods in agriculture. If it had not been for government intervention in support of agriculture these changes would have led to abandonment of production in marginal land, and use of less industrial inputs in the land that was kept in cultivation. But this process of adjustment was prevented by attempts to preserve the existing system of family farming. Large farms could utilize high-level technologies (especially mechanized inputs) better than smaller ones, but governments wanted to prevent the replacement of small or middle sized farms by larger capitalist farms, or company farming. Therefore, both Western Europe and North America gradually developed comprehensive systems of agricultural protection and subsidization of agriculture, agricultural research, and other rural infrastructure. In spite of this support a large proportion of the small farms disappeared and much marginal land went out of cultivation, while the support actually encouraged large farms, and farms in the most favoured regions, to expand their production; they increased their use of fertilizer and other inputs, and invested in expansion of capacity for vegetable and animal production. So supply still continued to outrun demand, and protection against imports and subsidies to exports still continued to increase, while the industrialized countries turned from being net importers to net exporters of more and more agricultural products.

In the discussions about labour surplus and low elasticity of agricultural production in non-industrialized countries, Nurkse (1953) had suggested that an increase in agricultural production could be obtained if the surplus population was employed in rural work projects. In the period until such a programme, in conjunction with industrialization and a deceleration of population growth, could re-establish the balance between demand for and supply of food, he recommended that temporary food imports (preferably as food aid) should be used to prevent food shortage. Because of the increasing costs of financing and disposing of the food surplus, Nurkse's suggestion of food aid was well received by Western governments, and transfer of food, as aid or subsidized exports, reached large dimensions.

Some governments in developing countries did use food aid and commercial imports of the food surpluses of the industrialized countries as stop-gap measures, until their own promotion of rural infrastructure and other support to agriculture would make it possible for production to catch up with the rapidly increasing demand for food. But for many other governments the availability of cheap imports and gifts of food became a welcome help to avoid the use of their own resources to support agriculture and invest in rural infrastructure. Even in those developing countries with a large majority of the population occupied in agriculture, the share of government expenditure devoted to agriculture and related rural infrastructure is small, and within this small amount priority is usually given to development of non-food export crops, which often supply a large share of foreign exchange earnings. Exports of food crops are unattractive because of the surplus disposal of the industrialized countries, which exerts a downward pressure on world market prices. Therefore, both producers and governments in developing countries focus on the types of crops which do not compete with these subsidized exports. In regions in which the necessary infrastructure was available, employment and output of such export crops increased rapidly, not only in countries with abundant land resources but also in many densely populated countries, which shifted in part from food to non-food crops. This general shift from food to non-food crops contributed to a downward pressure on export prices of the latter crops in the world market.

Food imports can have important short-term advantages for the importing country. Rapidly increasing urban areas can be supplied at low prices and without the need to use government resources to obtain expansion of domestic production. Moreover, counterpart funds from food aid can be used to finance general government expenditure, and in countries with high levies on export crops, government revenue increases when production is shifted from food to export crops. However, although there might be short-term advantages of food imports

31

and food aid, the long-term cost of neglecting agricultural and rural development can be very high. The lack of transport facilities and local stocks, and the lack of irrigation in dry and semi-dry areas, may transform years of drought to years of famine. When governments do not invest in rural infrastructure and fail to provide the public services which are necessary for the use of high technology inputs, the latter can be used only by large companies (who can themselves finance the necessary infrastructure) or in a few areas close to large cities.

Without cost reduction by improvement of the transport network and agricultural production, commercial food production may in many areas be unable to compete with imports. Commercial production will decline and subsistence producers will not become commercial producers. Instead, the most enterprising young villagers will emigrate in order to earn money incomes elsewhere. A larger and larger share of the rapidly increasing urban consumption must be imported, and food imports become a drug on which the importers become more and more dependent. The increasing dependency of many developing countries on food imports and food grants is often seen as a confirmation of the classical theory of inelastic food supply, and an argument for continuation of the policy of production subsidies and surplus disposal in America and Western Europe. Food imports are seen as gap fillers, bridging over increasing differences between food consumption and national food production in developing countries; but in many cases the gap is actually created by the food imports, because of their effect on local production and rural development.

FERTILITY. Contrary to the expectations prevalent in the middle of this century, government policy has proved to be a more important determinant of agricultural growth than the man-resource ratio, and the response to rapid population growth has often been better in densely populated countries than in sparsely populated ones with much better natural conditions for agricultural growth. The differences in agricultural growth rates and policies have in turn contributed to create differences in demographic trends, partly by their influence on industrial and urban development and partly by the effects on rural fertility, mortality and migration.

Because of their preoccupation with the man-land ratio, governments in densely populated countries not only devoted more attention and financial resources to agriculture than governments in sparsely populated countries, they also more often devoted attention and financial resources to policies aimed at reducing fertility. Moreover, tenure systems in densely populated countries usually provided less encouragement to large family size than tenure systems in sparsely populated countries.

In many densely populated countries with intensive agricultural systems, much of the rural population consists of small and middle-sized landowners, and such people are more likely to be motivated to a smaller family size than are landless labour and people with insecure tenure. They are less dependent upon help from adult children in emergencies and old age, because they can mortgage, lease, or sell land, or cultivate with hired labour. They may also have an interest in avoiding division of family property among too many heirs. If they live in areas where child labour is of little use in agriculture, they may have considerable economic interest in not having large families, and be responsive to advice and help from family planning services.

In sparsely populated regions with large landholdings, the rural population seldom has access to modern means of fertility control, and motivations for family restrictions are weak. A large share of the rural population tends to be landless or nearly landless workers, and if not, they may be without security in land. So they are much more dependent upon help from adult children in emergencies and old age than are landowners, or tenants with secure tenure. If, moreover, their children work for wages in ranches, farms and plantations, the period until a child contributes more to family income than it costs is too short to provide sufficient economic motivation for family restriction.

People who use long fallow systems in regions with tribal tenure have even more motivation for large family size than landless workers. The size of the area they can dispose of for cultivation is directly related to the size of their family, and most of the work, at least with food production, is done by women and children. So a man can become rich by having several wives and large numbers of children working for him. Moreover, unless he has acquired other property, a man's security in old age depends on his adult children and younger wives, since he cannot mortgage or sell land in which he has only usufruct rights. Because of the differences in motivations for family size provided by individual and tribal tenure systems, the start of the fertility decline in regions with long fallow systems is likely to be linked to the time when population increase induces the replacement of the tribal tenure system by another system of tenure, and a decline is then more likely if it is replaced by small-scale land ownership than if it is replaced by large-scale farming.

In addition to the tenure system, changes in technological levels in agriculture and the availability of economic and social infrastructure may influence the timing of fertility decline in rural areas. The heavy reliance upon female and child labour in those densely populated areas in which agriculture is intensified by means of labour alone, may provide motivation for large families in spite of the shortage of land. Introduction of higher level technologies may then, in such cases, reduce a man's motivation to have a large family because it reduces the need for female and child labour. Use of intermediate and high-level technologies is nearly always reserved for adult men, while women and children do the operations for which primitive technologies are used. So when primitive technologies are replaced by higher levels in more and more agricultural operations, men usually get more work to do and the economic contributions of their wives and children decline, thus reducing their economic interest in large family size. Moreover, in regions with little rural development high rates of child mortality may delay fertility decline, and the large-scale migration of youth from such areas may have a similar effect if parents can count on receiving remittances from emigrant offspring.

However, the relationship between rural development and fertility is complicated. Parents may want a large family for other than economic reasons, and increases in income due to rural development or to better prices for agricultural products make it easier for them to support a large family, thus preventing or delaying fertility decline. Other things being equal, fertility is positively related to income; but in developing societies most increases in income are caused and accompanied by technological, occupational and spatial changes that tend to encourage fertility decline, and the operation of these opposing effects may result in a relatively long time lag between rural modernization and fertility decline.

BIBLIOGRAPHY

Boserup, E. 1965 *The Conditions of Agricultural Growth.* London: Allen & Unwin; Chicago: Aldine Publishing Company, 1966.

Boserup, E. 1981. *Population and Technological Change.* Chicago: Chicago University Press.

Lewis, W.A. 1954. Economic development with unlimited supplies of labour. *Manchester School of Economic and Social Studies* 22(2), May, 139–91.

Malthus, T.R. 1803. *An Essay on Population.* London: J.M. Dent, 1958; New York: Dutton.

Nurkse, R. 1953. *Problems of Capital Formation in Underdeveloped Countries.* Oxford and New York: Oxford University Press.

Ricardo, D. 1817. *The Principles of Political Economy and Taxation.* Ed. P. Sraffa, Cambridge: Cambridge University Press, 1951; New York: Cambridge University Press, 1973.

Schultz, T.W. 1964. *Transforming Traditional Agriculture.* New Haven: Yale University Press.

Schuttjer, W. and Stokes, C. (eds) 1984. *Rural Development and Human Fertility.* New York and London: Macmillan.

Agricultural Supply

JERE R. BEHRMAN

One of the earliest-investigated and most fruitful areas for econometric studies has been the estimation of agricultural supply functions. Studies date back at least to the work of Smith (1928) and Bean (1929) on US agriculture in the 1920s. Early studies adopted a fairly static view. Nerlove's (1958) work on *The Dynamics of Supply*, with adaptive price expectations and adjustment processes for United States agriculture, spawned renewed interest in specification and estimation issues on this topic. The roughly concurrent controversies about market responsiveness in developing-country agriculture (e.g., Schultz, 1964) led to a shift in emphasis towards this concern. In the last quarter century a veritable flood of such studies has appeared. More recently supply studies have incorporated more systematic emphasis on systemic characteristics, risk aversion, the household/ farm model framework and alternative price expectations. This article reviews these basic developments in empirical studies of agricultural supply by starting with the most common framework for such analyses and then considering what questions arise when some of the traditional assumptions are weakened.

PERFECTLY-COMPETITIVE EQUILIBRIUM SUPPLIES WITH NO RISK. Most empirical studies of agricultural supply have assumed perfect competition, equilibrium, no risk and separability between the farm production decisions and the farm household consumption decisions. Under such conditions the supply function for a specific product of an individual producer is the marginal cost function for product prices sufficiently high so that variable costs are covered (and zero otherwise). The market supply function is the sum of all individual supply functions. As such, the supply function depends on all relevant expected product and input prices, all fixed factors, and technology. There are two important elements of dynamics in the supply process: the adjustment of short-run fixed factors over longer time periods and the creation of expectations for product harvest prices at the time that inputs, especially land, are commited.

Early studies basically posited a supply function as dependent on relevant

35

expected prices (P^*):

$$S = f(P^*) \tag{1}$$

where S is a vector of supplies of different agricultural products and P^* is a vector of expected (or, at least after Nerlove's contributions, expected normal) prices.

Expected prices most commonly were represented by one-period lagged prices for products for which actual harvest prices would not be known until harvest time and by actual prices at the time of the input decision for inputs. Frequently, instead of using supplies as the dependent variable, areas devoted to individual crops were used since land is a critical input for which allocation among crops basically is under the control of the farmer.

The seminal contributions of Nerlove (1956, 1958) were: first to generalize the formation of price expectations with adaptive expectations and second, to incorporate a distributed-lag adjustment process to reflect that adjustment is not costless. His basic model for an annual crop, thus, is:

$$A_t^* = a_0 + a_1 P_t^* + a_2 Z_t + u_t \tag{2}$$

$$A_t = A_{t-1} + \gamma(A_t^* - A_{t-1}) \tag{3}$$

$$P_t^* = P_{t-1}^* + \beta(P_{t-1} - P_{t-1}^*) \tag{4}$$

where

    A_t is actual area number cultivation in period t,
    A_t^* is 'desired' or equilibrium area under cultivation in t,
    P_t is actual product price in t,
    P_t^* is 'expected normal' price in t,
    Z_t is other observed, exogenous factors, and
    u_t is a disturbance term.

Relation (2) states that desired area is a function of expected normal prices, other exogenous factors, and a disturbance term; but neither the desired area nor the expected price typically is observed. Relation (3) states that there is a distributed-lag adjustment in actual area towards desired area, with γ the 'coefficient of adjustment'. Relation (4) states that the expected normal price in period t is the expected normal price in the previous period plus an adjustment for the discrepancy in the previous period between the expected normal and the actual prices. Substitution of (3) and (4) into (2) gives an expression in terms of observable variables:

$$A_t = [(1-\beta)+(1-\gamma)]A_{t-1} - (1-\beta)(1-\gamma)A_{t-2} + a_1\gamma\beta P_{t-1} + a_2\gamma Z_t$$
$$- a_2\gamma(1-\beta)Z_{t-1} + a_0 + \gamma u_t - \gamma(1-\beta)u_{t-1}. \tag{5}$$

Literally hundreds of estimates of some variant of this supply relation have been made. Initially they focused on developed-country agriculture. Due to the debate over the market-responsiveness of traditional developing agriculture, emphasis then shifted relatively to developing-country agriculture in studies by Krishna

(1963, 1965), Behrman (1966, 1968b) and a host of others. Askari and Cummings (1976, 1977) noted over 600 such estimates by the mid 1970s. These studies vary substantially regarding the identification of relevant observed exogenous variables, the treatment of serial correlation in the disturbance term, what prices are included, and the role of yields. Despite such variations they point to a pattern of significant and often substantial price responses in agricultural supplies, with some indication of greater responses for higher-income and more-literate farmers, larger farms, own-operated farms, farms with access to irrigation, and crops with lower yield variability. This price responsiveness in developing-country agriculture suggests that measures to suppress particular agricultural prices significantly discourage domestic agricultural supplies of those products. An aggregate supply response study for a cross-section of developing countries by Peterson (1979) also reports substantial discouragement of aggregate agricultural production in these countries by price policies, though Binswanger, Mundlak, Yang and Bowers (1985) suggest that this result is an artifact of the price data used. The price responsiveness in developed countries suggest that price and income-support programmes induce expanded agricultural supplies for the products affected.

One subset of these studies merits particular mention: those that relate to perennials and livestock. Most of these studies have adapted the above model to incorporate long lags due to the long gestation between investment and production, with adjustment lags posited in respect to desired capital stock or desired investment. In a few cases (e.g. French and Matthews, 1971) there are extensive explicit empirical representations of the various critical variables in perennial and livestock production: production, investment, nonbearing new capital, and old capital removal. In many cases, however, the lack of basic data on capital stocks has left bearing stocks to be inferred from outputs or controlled for by differencing outputs for products such as cocoa in which there is a long period once trees have matured during which yields are approximately constant (e.g., Bateman, 1965, 1968; Behrman, 1968a, 1969). Despite the greater complexities of perennials and livestock production and the greater longevity of the related capital stock, there has been little effort to go beyond an essentially static formulation for the demand for the relevant capital stock. Conceptually this problem can be formulated as a dynamic programming model. But, as Nerlove (1979) notes, severe difficulties exist in the empirical implementation of such a strategy because of data inadequacies and because of the uncertainty of future technological devlopments.

Two additional modifications subsequent to the widespread use of the supply relation in (5) are worth noting. First, the more recent formulation of the supply relation is to start with a profit function and to note that the partial derivative with respect to a particular product price gives the supply function for that product and the partial derivative with respect to the price of production input gives the input demand function. This approach has the advantage of focusing on the interrelations in a system of supply and demand relations within a multi-product and multi-input context and in indicating the nature of cross-equation systemic restrictions. The natural distinction between outputs and inputs within this context also sharpens the question about the frequent usage of area as the dependent variable in supply-response relations; such estimates presumably are characterized better as approximations to input demand relations though, as such, they provide information on the underlying parameters of the system that pertain to supply responses. Examples of profit-function-based agricultural supply studies include Lau and Yotopoulos (1971) and Bapna, Binswanger and Quizon (1984). In most applications of this approach, the concerns of Nerlove (1956, 1958) about the empirical dynamics of price expectation formulation and of adjustment have been ignored. Instead, assumptions of immediate adjustment and static product price expectations (i.e., the previous period's prices) prevail. There would seem to be further gains in understanding from the incorporation of such dynamic concerns into these systems estimates, though full incorporation of such dynamics leads to dynamic programming models with the problems mentioned above.

Second, representations of price expectations have changed. There has been growing emphasis throughout economics on 'rational expectations' (Muth, 1961), which are the minimum mean square forecasts based on the information available at the time of the forecast, including that about the structure of the system. There have been some efforts to incorporate rational price expectations into agricultural supply studies, though with reduced-form relations with the same variables as in relation (4) (e.g., Eckstein, 1984). The question remains open whether such rational expectations are preferable representations of expectations actually held by farmers and, if they are, about what information is available for farmers to utilize in their expectation formulation. Nerlove (1979) observes, for example, that the rejection of the proposition that farmers respond to the expectation of some average of prices in all future periods with adaptive expectations also implies the rejection of the notion that farmers are adjusting to a well-defined, longer-run equilibrium because such an equilibrium is well-defined only for stationary price expectations.

NON-SEPARABILITY BETWEEN FARM PRODUCTION AND CONSUMPTION. For the currently developed countries, the separability assumption probably is plausible. Most production is sold on markets, most consumption goods are purchased on markets, there probably are not consumption-labour productivity links and markets are relatively complete (though risk may be a problem, see below).

For the developing countries, in contrast, the separability assumption may be misleading for millions of farm households. One respect in which these assumptions may be misleading is with regard to responses in total production versus the marketed surplus. Many of these households consume large shares of the basic staples that they produce. As a result, price responses in the marketed surplus may differ substantially from those in total production, depending on what is the household own-consumption response. Krishna (1965) and Behrman (1966) presented early models of the price elasticity of the marketed surplus that incorporate the income elasticity of consumption within the household. Such models demonstrate that the price elasticity of the marketed surplus may differ greatly from those of total supply if own-consumption accounts for a substantial share of production and if either own-consumption price or income elasticities is large.

Two other reasons for which integrated household-farm models have been emphasized are incomplete markets (e.g., Lau, Lin and Yotopoulos, 1978; Barnum and Squire, 1979a, 1979b) and productivity-consumption links (e.g., Leibenstein, 1957; Bliss and Stern, 1978a, 1978b; Stiglitz, 1976; Pitt and Rosenzweig, 1986; Behrman and Deolalikar, 1987; Strauss, 1986). Both these phenomena are thought to be common in developing countries. If they are important, agricultural supply should be explored within the context of the household-farm model. This means that prices for consumption goods and services (e.g., for schools, clothing and health-care) and fixed household assets should enter into the determination of agricultural supplies, in addition to prices of agricultural products and inputs and fixed agricultural factors. For the examination of the determinants of some perennials and livestock, for instance, even the prices that determine births, infant and child mortality and migration in principle should be included since such prices simultaneously determine the long-run agricultural capital stocks (with the obvious link through the long-run availability of household labour). While there are a few studies of agricultural supply that have emphasized the conceptual importance of the farm-household model (e.g., Lau, Lin and Yotopoulos, 1978; Barnum and Squire, 1979a, 1979b), in empirical applications the full ramifications of such demand-production simultaneity are yet to be explored.

RISK AND RISK AVERSION. Farmers are subject to production risk and, for farmers who partake in markets, price and input-availability risks. Once it was established that developing-country farmers seem responsive to expected prices, considerable emphasis shifted to the role of risk and risk aversion in determining agricultural supplies. Many studies have attempted to test for the supply response to risk by including ad hoc empirical measures of risk (e.g., variances in prices or in yields as in Behrman, 1968b) and report some evidence of negative responses to risk. Several experiments have been undertaken to attempt to identify the nature and the magnitude of risk aversion among farms. The most satisfactory of these to date is by Binswanger (1980, 1981) in which the payoffs were real and substantial. He concludes that his results are consistent with expected utility maximizing behaviour (and not with security-based forms of behaviour in which farmers are concerned primarily with avoiding disaster) and that most individuals are risk averse, but not very risk averse.

How should supply responses be modelled given the possibility of risk and risk aversion? Newbery and Stiglitz (1981) provide a recent theoretical synthesis of the implications of risk and risk aversion for modelling supply in their discussion of the theory of commodity price stabilization. They demonstrate that risk may have an impact even on a risk-neutral farmer; such a farmer does not just maximize the product of expected prices and expected quantities minus costs if prices and quantities are correlated (as would be the case for a perfectly competitive farmer in an area which accounts for a large share of the market, as with West African cocoa production), but also must incorporate the price-quantity covariance in order to maximize expected profits. They also argue that rigorous specification of supply behaviour under risk aversion is difficult and should proceed from first principles of constrained utility maximization (which is likely to require a farm-household framework as well). Binswanger (1982) further elaborates on the difficulties of econometric estimation under risk preferences. I am unaware of empirical studies to date that are consistent with such a framework.

DISEQUILIBRIUM. The standard framework for empirical agricultural supply analysis assumes equilibrium, or adjustment towards equilibrium in which observed prices convey all the available information. As Schultz (1975) and Nerlove (1979) emphasize, however, for some important questions such as the nature of the historical transformation of developed-country agriculture and the current transformations of developing-country agriculture, disequilibria are likely to be common and visible prices are not likely to convey all of the relevant information available to farmers. For studies of agricultural supply responses in such contexts, a broader perspective is desirable to represent the impacts of differential capabilities of economic entities to deal with disequilibria, public investments, development of markets, technological and demographic changes, and governmental roles. Embedding supply studies within this larger context in order to attain further understanding remains a major challenge.

BIBLIOGRAPHY

Askari, H. and Cummings, J.T. 1976. *Agricultural Supply Response: A Survey of the Econometric Evidence.* New York: Praeger Publishers.

Askari, H. and Cummings, J.T. 1977. Estimating agricultural supply response with the Nerlove model: a survey. *International Economic Review* 18, 257–92.

Bapna, S.L., Binswanger, H. and Quizon, J.B. 1984. Systems of output supply and factor demand equations for semi-arid tropical India. *Indian Journal of Agricultural Economics* 39(2), April-June, 179–202.

Barnum, H.N. and Squire, L. 1979a. An econometric application of the theory of farm-household. *Journal of Development Economics* 61(1), 79–102.

Barnum, H.N. and Squire, L. 1979b. *A Model of an Agriculture Household: Theory and Evidence.* Baltimore: Johns Hopkins for the World Bank, chs 3–6.

Bateman, M. 1965. Aggregate and regional supply functions for Ghanaian cocoa, 1946–62. *Journal of Farm Economics* 47, 384–401.

Bateman, M. 1968. *Cocoa in the Ghanaian Economy: An Econometric Model.* Amsterdam: North-Holland.

Bean, L.H. 1929. The farmers' response to price. *Journal of Farm Economics* 11, 368–85.

Behrman, J.R. 1966. Price elasticity of the marketed surplus of a subsistence crop. *Journal of Farm Economics* 48, 875–93.

Behrman, J.R. 1968a. Monopolistic cocoa pricing. *American Journal of Agricultural Economics* 50, 702–19.

Behrman, J.R. 1968b. *Supply Response in Underdeveloped Agriculture: A Case Study of Four Major Annual Crops in Thailand 1937–1963.* Amsterdam: North-Holland.

Behrman, J.R. 1969. Econometric model simulations of the world rubber market

1950–1980. In *Essays in Industrial Econometrics*, vol. 3, ed. L.R. Klein, Philadelphia: Economic Research Unit, Wharton School of Finance and Commerce, University of Pennsylvania.

Behrman, J.R. and Deolalikar, A.B. 1987. Health and nutrition. In *Handbook on Development Economics*, ed. H.B. Chenery and T.N. Srinivasan, Amsterdam: North-Holland.

Binswanger, H.P. 1980. Attitudes towards risk: experimental measurement evidence in rural India. *American Journal of Agricultural Economics* 62(3), 395–407.

Binswanger, H.P. 1981. Attitudes towards risk: theoretical implications of an experiment in rural India. *Economic Journal* 91, December, 867–90.

Binswanger, H.P. 1982. Empirical estimation and use of risk preferences: discussion. *American Journal of Agricultural Economics* 64(2), May, 391–3.

Binswanger, H., Mundlak, Y., Yang, M.C. and Bowers, A. 1985. Estimation of aggregate supply response. Washington: World Bank, Report No. ARU 48.

Bliss, C. and Stern, N. 1978a. Productivity, wages and nutrition, part I: the theory. *Journal of Development Economics* 5(4), 331–62.

Bliss, C. and Stern, N. 1978b. Productivity, wages and nutrition, part II: some observations. *Journal of Development Economics* 5(4), 363–98.

Eckstein, Z. 1984. A rational expectations model of agricultural supply. *Journal of Political Economy* 92(1), February, 1–19.

French, B.C. and Matthews, J.L. 1971. A supply response model for perennial crops. *American Journal of Agricultural Economics* 53, 478–90.

Jarvis, L. 1974. Cattle as capital goods and ranchers as portfolio managers: an application to the Argentine cattle sector. *Journal of Political Economy* 82, 489–520.

Krishna, R. 1963. Farm supply response in India-Pakistan: a case study of the Punjab region. *Economic Journal* 73, 477–87.

Krishna, R. 1965. The marketable surplus function for a subsistence crop: an analysis with Indian data. *Economic Weekly* 17, February.

Lau, L.J., Lin, W.-L. and Yotopoulos, P. 1978. The linear logarithmic expenditure system: an application to consumption-leisure choice. *Econometrica* 46(4), 843–68.

Lau, L.J. and Yotopoulos, P.A. 1971. A test for relative efficiency and application to Indian agriculture. *American Economic Review* 61, 94–109.

Leibenstein, H. 1957. *Economic Backwardness and Economic Growth*. New York: John Wiley.

Muth, J.F. 1961. Rational expectations and the theory of price movements. *Econometrica* 29, 315–35.

Nerlove, M. 1956. Estimates of supply of selected agricultural commodities. *Journal of Farm Economics* 38, 496–509.

Nerlove, M. 1958. *The Dynamics of Supply: Estimation of Farmers' Response to Price*. Baltimore: Johns Hopkins University Press.

Nerlove, M. 1967. Distributed lags and unobserved components in economic time series. In *Ten Economic Essays in the Tradition of Irving Fisher*, ed. W. Fellner et al., New York: Wiley, 126–69.

Nerlove, M. 1979. The dynamics of supply: retrospect and prospect. *American Journal of Agricultural Economics* 61(5), 867–88.

Newbery, D.M.G. and Stiglitz, J.E. 1981. *The Theory of Commodity Price Stabilization*. Oxford: Clarendon Press.

Nowshirvani, V. 1971. Land allocation under uncertainty in subsistence agriculture. *Oxford Economic Papers* 23, November, 445–55.

Peterson, W.L. 1979. International farm prices and the social cost of cheap food policies. *American Journal of Agricultural Economics* 61, 12–21.

Pitt, M.M. and Rosenzweig, M. 1986. Agricultural prices, food consumption and the health and productivity of farmers. In *Agricultural Household Models: Extensions, Applications and Policy*, ed. I.J. Singh, L. Squire and J. Strauss, Washington: World Bank.

Schultz, T.W. 1964. *Transforming Traditional Agriculture*. New Haven: Yale University Press.

Schultz, T.W. 1975. The value of the ability to deal with disequilibrium. *Journal of Economic Literature* 13, 827–46.

Smith, B.B. 1928. Factors affecting the price of cotton. US Department of Agriculture Technical Bulletin No. 50, Washington, DC.

Stiglitz, J. 1976. The efficiency wage hypothesis, surplus labour, and the distribution of income in LDC's. *Oxford Economic Papers, New Series* 28, 185–207.

Strauss, J. 1986. Does better nutrition raise farm productivity? *Journal of Political Economy* 94(2), April, 297–320.

Agriculture and Economic Development

S.K. RAO

Most people in developing countries derive their livelihood from agriculture. Agricultural growth, and the conditions governing the distribution of its produce, are, therefore, of direct relevance to them. Agriculture is also important in that if it fails to develop at a suitable pace, it could prove to be a critical constraint on the growth of industrial and other sectors. It is the supplier of an essential wage good, viz. food; it also supplies raw materials to industry and, looked at from another angle, could provide the motive for industrial expansion by being a market for industrial goods.

Compared to just about one-fifteenth of the labour force engaged in agriculture in industrial countries, in developing countries the proportion is often in the range of half to four-fifths of the total. The proportion of output originating in agriculture, however, is much less – reflecting the lower output per man engaged in agriculture compared to other sectors. This disparity in productivity is greater in developing countries than in industrial countries.

The low productivity per worker implies that the proportion of output absorbed within agriculture itself, i.e. self consumption, is high, leaving little surplus for use outside agriculture. In a poor developing country, a farm family produces enough food for itself and two other people; in contrast, in an industrial country like Britain, the proportion of labour force needed to provide food for the whole of its population is less than one-twentieth.

The importance of improved productivity in agriculture can also be viewed from another angle. The larger is the proportion of agricultural output not absorbed within agriculture itself, the greater is the market for non-agricultural goods. Agricultural growth, along with growth in exports and public investment, could constitute an important exogenous source of demand for industry.

The preceding argument can be illustrated with the help of Figure 1. In Figure 1, *ON* represents the level of employment in agriculture; and corresponding to

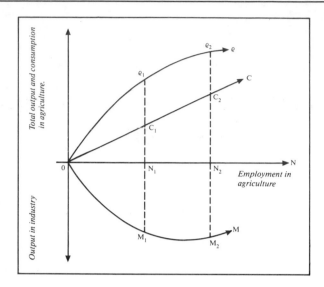

Figure 1

it, there are OQ and OC, which trace the levels of total agricultural output and consumption within the agricultural sector respectively. At ON_1 level of employment, total output is N_1Q_1, consumption is N_1C_1, leaving a surplus of C_1Q_1 for use outside agriculture. The surplus C_1Q_1 sustains a level of employment in the non-agricultural (industrial) sectors, which results in an output level of N_1M_1. The curve OQ has a declining scope reflecting diminishing returns in agriculture. This arises from the finiteness of land and other natural resources, yielding diminishing returns as the scale of other inputs is expanded. Technological progress, however, could result in outward shifts of the curve, so that for any given level of employment, output is higher. It would also result in larger surplus, enabling a larger level of employment to be sustained in the non-agricultural sector.

Productivity-enhancing investment in agriculture, however, depends not only on the state of knowledge, but also on conditions governing the adoption of technology: it depends on the land tenure system which determines how the agricultural produce is divided between owners of land and agricultural labour; on the terms of trade between agriculture and industry, which determine the relative cheapness of industrial inputs vis-à-vis agricultural produce; on the level of demand for agricultural produce; among other things. These issues are discussed below.

LAND REFORM. Land reforms were attempted in several countries not only with a view to improving the distribution of incomes, but also as a means of improving incentives to the farmer. In many countries, historically, land came to be

44

concentrated in large holdings. In some cases, a portion of the landholding was cultivated directly by the landlord, the rest being leased out to tenants either in return for labour services or simply for rent, fixed or as a share of the produce. In some countries, large holdings of plantations developed, often owned and managed by expatriates; in some countries (e.g. the Caribbean, Mauritius, Fiji) labour to work on these plantations was brought over either as slaves or as indentured labour; the labourers were frequently given small plots of land to raise subsistence food and as a means of tying their services to the estate (Byres (ed.), 1983; Bagchi, 1982).

The conventional Marshallian argument for land reform was that in a situation where a tenant is obliged to pay a share of output as rent to the landlord, his incentive to maximize output is lost; instead of applying inputs to a point where the marginal output equals marginal cost, he would apply inputs only to the point where his share of marginal output is equal to the marginal cost. A tenant would also not undertake capital improvements if he did not enjoy security of tenure. It is suggested, therefore, that land reform which confers ownership rights on the tenant or improves the security of tenure would raise productivity. In practice, however, the situation is found to be far more complex than is implied in the above argument. It is found (e.g. South Asia) that land is leased-in and -out by all classes of farmers, big and small, largely because of reasons relating to operational efficiency. Moreover, crop-sharing is adopted to distribute risk, and is sometimes associated with sharing of inputs. Further, in a situation of endemic unemployment and underemployment, a tenant may have no choice but to demonstrate that he is putting in the maximum effort possible, if he is not to be evicted (Bagchi, 1982; Bharadwaj, 1974).

Some scholars have argued that the existing state of land relations in many developing countries may not be conducive to agricultural growth. It is pointed out that where large numbers of households depend on consumption loans to meet their subsistence expenditure from year to year, not only might the landlord find it profitable to use his farm surplus to finance consumption loans at high rates of interest, but he might in fact contrive to create such a situation by fixing his share of produce in such a way that the tenant is perpetually left with no alternative but to depend on consumption loans (Bhaduri, 1983). This view, however, presupposes that the landlord is in a position to fix the share of his produce at his will, which may not be the case. But this points to the class of situations where the savings of a landlord can be absorbed either in productivity-enhancing investments (e.g. irrigation) or unproductive investments (e.g. consumption loans to poor peasantry). In both instances, the landlord obtains a return on his investment, but in one case through increased output while in the other it would be through a change in the distribution of income. It could be argued that in a country such as India, the caste system effectively contrives to prevent a portion of the peasantry from gaining access to markets or resources in a free manner, creating conditions ripe for a strong demand for consumption loans. In such a situation, unless the rate of return on productive investment rises sharply through the availability of new technology (e.g. electrification, high yielding varieties of seeds), a large portion of rural savings might continue to be deployed in unproductive investment. Savings are in effect deployed to improve the share of produce rather than to improve output. In some instances this might even take the form of accumulating land which is not cultivated directly, but nevertheless acquired to prevent the poorer peasantry from breaking out of the vicious circle of poverty.

A redistribution of land is expected to raise output in countries where there is widespread underemployment or unemployment, and labour effort is the main input in agriculture. In those situations, productivity of land is inversely related to size, as the small farmer who relies on family labour for cultivation puts in greater labour effort; the larger, capitalist, farmer who relies on wage labour, restricts labour input to the point where marginal output equals wage (Bharadwaj, 1974). In situations of endemic unemployment in rural areas, land is usually prized as a precious asset and many big farmers accumulate land since it gives them control over rural population, even if they do not put it to immediate use as an income yielding asset. For these reasons, a redistribution of landholdings could raise output. However, land reforms have rarely been successful. In countries where reforms were attempted as a once for all measure, they were widely evaded, and in the subsequent period land transfers were usually reversed through the market. Mexico, Egypt and India are good examples of this phenomenon (Bagchi, 1982).

Interesting exceptions to the above are South Korea and Taiwan, where the American military authorities in the post-World War II period implemented land reforms fairly rigorously in an attempt to ward off the threat of a communist revolution (Ghai et al., 1979). In South Korea, a ceiling of three hectares was imposed and the market in land was virtually abolished. This resulted in increased productivity as well as a reduction in poverty. The success of reform was facilitated by the fact that the industrial, urban population began to absorb a rising proportion of the labour force from about the early 1960s; this reduced the population pressure in the rural area, which usually heightens disequilibriating tendencies.

In general, the economies which inherited a large estate plantation economy, often under expatriate ownership, faced a difficult situation. If they were left as they were, the expatriate owners often did not plough back profit into capital formulation, due to imagined or real political insecurity (e.g. Papua New Guinea, Guyana). In some countries, they were nationalized (e.g. Guyana) or schemes were developed to purchase a proportion of the estates and transfer them to the local communities, sometimes involving a degree of compulsion in the acquisition of land (e.g. Papua New Guinea, Kenya). While in some instances output improved as a result, the results were not uniformly positive. The failure by the erstwhile owners to replant properly had in some cases reduced profitability; in other cases, parcelling out of estates, lack of experience and poor management had reduced productivity (e.g. Papua New Guinea; Sawyerr (ed.), 1984, pp. 50–60).

In socialist countries, land reform occupied a central position in policy. An interesting case is that of China. Following the revolution of 1948, Chinese agriculture was organized on a commune basis. There are various tiers, with the family as the basic unit. The family cultivates a private plot (which absorbs less than a tenth of total cultivated land), husbands small animals such as pigs, collects animal manure for private and collective use, and contributes labour to communal farming. Some 30 to 40 families constitute a production team, which is the basic production unit; it collectively owns the land it cultivates and the tools it uses. It makes the production decisions and distributes income. Superimposed over a production team are a production brigade, consisting of 7–8 production teams, and the people's commune, consisting of 13–15 brigades. The production brigade is responsible for services such as elementary schooling and health, and also organizes small-scale industries. The people's commune is responsible for services and small industries at a higher level, and also undertakes marketing and civil administration.

After deducting a proportion of net output (about a quarter) for collective use – taxes, cash and grain reserves, and a small welfare fund – the rest is distributed by the production team to its members, on the basis of work points accumulated by families at the team, brigade or commune level. But there is also distribution on the basis of an equality principle – on an adult equivalent basis – and to take care of families in persistently difficult circumstances (e.g. old people with no children) or to help maintain floor consumption levels among the poorest teams in the commune; such a distribution could absorb more than two-thirds of the output.

The state's control over the communes is exercised mainly through the supply and marketing system. The state collects produce through taxes, imposes quotas for delivery to the state at fixed prices, and additional deliveries at negotiated prices. It also allocates agricultural inputs and non-agricultural products for consumption. Agricultural plans are prepared at country and higher levels, and for aggregate commodity groups at the state level.

Through the commune system, China was able to improve income distribution. The provision of basic necessities, together with the maintenance of the food security system, has been a notable achievement of China. It was able to achieve this with little dependence on imports, and by absorbing not more than a fifth of the country's total investment resources. Collective labour at commune level was important in building rural infrastructure. China was at the same time able to maintain a rate of growth in total output comparable to that of, say, India (World Bank, 1983; Ghai et al., 1979).

It was clear, however, that for periods the Chinese farm output had suffered markedly as the output distributed on 'the equality principle' predominated and unrealistic physical targets were pursued. Poor management was another problem.

Since 1979, a form of *contractual collectivism* has been introduced in China under which individual or groups of peasant households can enter into a contract with the collective to undertake specialized work or crop production. Under some forms, the households are allocated work points, as before, on fulfilment of the contract; but under *da bao gan* or 'contracting in a big way' the households are allowed to keep the residual after paying the share of the collective's tax and grain sales quotas to the state and any additional sum agreed with the collective. Under the contractual collectivism, land continues to be owned by the collective, but the households can own implements and other working capital – and are sometimes allowed to hire labour. The market has also come to assume a greater role (Blecher, 1985). These changes have led to greater production, with luxury and cash crops expanding rapidly. Some observers see in this trend a resurgence of private property relations, even though, as land is still collectively owned and all households are members of collectives, it is difficult to describe it as such. These changes, while promoting growth, could result in increased rural inequalities, particularly as non-land inputs become important in agriculture. The conflict between working on one's own plot as against working for the collective, a conflict which was always present, could be heightened. The change is also likely to accentuate regional inequalities, as communes in areas endowed with poor natural resources find that the state cannot mediate a transfer of resources from the richer to the poorer communes.

TERMS OF TRADE. The availability of industrial inputs and consumer goods relatively cheaply in terms of agricultural produce enhances agricultural output by promoting productivity-raising investments, as well as by providing incentives to the agricultural sector. On the other hand, as the terms of trade faced by industry worsen, the surplus available within industry worsen, the surplus available within industry for reinvestment decreases; the market available for agricultural goods would also be reduced. For this reason, one could postulate 'equilibrium' terms of trade between agriculture and industry, deviations from which would have growth reducing effects (Thirlwall, 1986).

In market economies, the prices of agricultural products tend to be determined by the balance between supply and demand, whereas prices of industrial goods tend to be determined on the basis of a cost-plus principle. For this reason, improvements in productivity in agriculture are usually passed on through reduced prices to consumers, in contrast to industry where they may be absorbed within the sector itself. Historically, innovation and technological progress in agriculture has been sufficiently strong to outweight the inherent tendency towards diminishing returns in agriculture, resulting in a favourable movement in terms of trade for industry. This had helped industrial growth.

In an attempt to maximize industrial growth, many governments adopted policies which tilted the terms of trade against agriculture. This was sometimes the result of an exchange rate policy which offered greater protection to industry than to agriculture. Where a country's exports consist of agricultural goods, while its inputs are sourced internally, a failure to adjust exchange rates for higher rates of inflation at home could result in an appreciation of exchange rates, tilting the terms of trade against agriculture. In some countries, overvalued exchange rates, pursued in an attempt to secure cheap food supplies for the urban population, seem to have had a negative effect on agricultural growth (e.g. Ghana, Nigeria, Tanzania and Papua New Guinea).

On the other hand, a movement that favours agriculture could depress industrial output by raising primary costs (i.e. costs of agricultural raw materials and money wage costs), and could also result in unacceptable rates of inflation. An end result could be a constraint on growth of aggregate demand in the economy, in an attempt to control inflationary pressures, which could prove to be a depressant of growth (Patnaik et al., 1976). Within rural areas, a favourable movement in terms of trade for agriculture could have the unforeseen consequence of worsening the distribution of income: in economies where land is cultivated by hired labour, money wage rates may fail to keep pace with prices of food; in economies where land is owned collectively (e.g. China), it could worsen the distribution of income between communes which are endowed with naturally rich land and those which are endowed with poor resources. There is some evidence that the favourable movement in terms of trade for agriculture such as that observed in India during the 1960s and 1970s has proved to be a constraint on industrial growth (Mitra, 1977); and in China, where in the late 1970s and early 1980s the terms of trade for agriculture were tilted favourably by supplying inputs at controlled prices and raising prices for output above quota, output seems to have responded favourably, even though the distribution of income between the poor and the rich communes may have worsened.

TECHNOLOGICAL CHANGE. The state played an important role in many developing countries in the provision of inputs for agriculture and in spreading new technology. The scale of this, and the access to it, varied greatly depending on the strength of the farm lobbies and the character of the state. The absorption of these inputs, and their impact on output, also depended upon the land relations that characterized a country. The so-called 'Green Revolution', which consisted of cultivation of high yielding semi-dwarf varieties of wheat and rice, depended upon the availability of irrigation and more intensive application of fertilizer. The yields of these new varieties could be two to three times those of traditional varieties; by the late 1970s, over half the wheat acreage and one-third of paddy fields in developing countries were brought under these varieties. However, the success of the Green Revolution was confined to irrigated regions and somewhat affluent farmers, in countries where land was cultivated privately. It thus tended to increase inequalities across regions as well as classes (e.g. India, Mexico; see Bagchi, 1982). On the other hand, it boosted agricultural growth and enabled industrialization to proceed at a faster pace than might have been possible otherwise. The Green Revolution, by raising the prospect of higher yields, also tended to result in eviction of tenants, as landowners found it more profitable to cultivate land directly than to continue with output sharing arrangements with tenants. In some parts of the world, farmers responded by investing in tube-well irrigation to draw on underground water; where this was not accompanied by careful planning to ensure that adequate replenishment of underground water takes place (through, for example, construction of percolation tanks), it resulted in a gradual sinking of the water table, resulting in increased costs of irrigation all round. Another effect had been a reallocation of land use for the cultivation of high-yield crops, at the expense of others. Where the opportunities for foreign trade were not favourable, this resulted at times in stock accumulations of the favoured grains financed by the state – constituting a source of inflationary pressure.

The Green Revolution in general tended to increase intensity of cropping, and along with it the demand for labour input. In some countries, however, labour-saving mechanization began to displace labour use, partly motivated by the desire to reduce bottlenecks in the availability of labour in peak times, and partly to retain greater control of the labour process by the landowners. While mechanization thus helped in improving labour productivity – and to some extent land productivity – it also tended to result in a worsened distribution of income, even though absolute poverty may have decined. Mechanization facilitates the formation of large holdings and, therefore, can be expected to work in favour of concentration in landholdings.

INTERNATIONAL ENVIRONMENT. Agricultural exports are an important source of income for many developing countries, constituting nearly a quarter of their total export earnings (excluding oil exporting countries); in the case of many low income countries, they comprise virtually their total export earnings. Yet, the international trade environment has not moved propitiously for them in recent years. The terms of trade of agricultural exports deteriorated – by up to a quarter, for example, between 1974 and 1982. This was partly due to a change in the relationship between industrial country growth and the demand for commodities; and, partly, in recent years, due to attempts by developing countries to improve their export earnings simultaneously by substantial devaluations, which may have collectively worsened their terms of trade.

The environment for developing country agricultural exports was made worse by a high degree of protection in industrial countries. In general, farmers in Japan and Europe enjoy higher protection than farmers in those developing countries which depend on agricultural exports (World Bank, 1986). The problem is made worse by the attempts of industrial countries to off-load their farm surpluses at subsidized prices in the world market. By the early 1980s, the budgetary support expenditure in the USA, EEC and Japan had reached $35 billion, amounting to more than half of one per cent of their combined GNP.

While this is an advantage for those developing countries who could trade minerals or manufactures for food or other agricultural commodities, it has a negative impact on those countries which produced agricultural goods for export. Examples were sugar and beef, which were both heavily affected by industrial country protection; in these instances, the World Bank staff estimated that developing countries might have lost $12.5 billion in export revenues in 1983, as a result of industrial country protectionism; for comparison, the aid programmes of all industrial countries totalled $22.5 billion (both figures at 1980 prices; World Bank, 1985).

The policies of industrial countries also create substantial volatility in commodity prices, as the burden of balancing supply and demand is placed on a narrow market outside their own insulated domestic markets. This also increases the costs to the developing countries who depend more on agricultural exports.

An international trade regime which reduces protection for agriculture in industrial countries, and devises a scheme for reducing commodity price fluctuations, such as the Common Fund, will have a beneficial effect on agriculture in developing countries. However, in practice it has proved difficult to devise commodity agreements that can stabilize prices around a long-term trend level.

BIBLIOGRAPHY

Bagchi, A.K. 1982. *The Political Economy of Underdevelopment.* Cambridge and New York: Cambridge University Press.

Bhaduri, A. 1983. *The Economic Structure of Backward Agriculture.* London: Academic Press.

Bharadwaj, K. 1974. *Production Conditions in Indian Agriculture.* Cambridge: Cambride University Press.

Blecher, M. 1985. The struggle and contradictions of productive relations in socialist agrarian 'reform': a framework for analysis and the Chinese case. *Journal of Development Studies* 22(1), October, 104–26.

Byres, T.J. (ed.) 1983. Share cropping and share croppers. Special issue of *Journal of Peasant Studies*, January/April.

Ghai, D., Khan, A.R., Lee, E. and Radwan, S.R. 1979. *Agrarian Systems and Rural Development.* London: Macmillan.

Mitra, A. 1977. *Terms for Trade and Class Relations.* London: Frank Cass.

Patnaik, P., Rao, S.K. and Sanyal, A. 1976. The inflationary process: some theoretical comments. *Economic and Political Weekly* 23, October.

Sawyerr, A. (ed.) 1984. *Economic Development and Trade in Papua New Guinea.* Port Moresby: University of Papua New Guinea Press.

Thirlwall, A.P. 1986. A general model of growth and development on Kaldorian lines. *Oxford Economic Papers* 38(2), July, 199–219.

World Bank. 1983. *China: Socialist Economic Development.* Washington, DC: World Bank.

World Bank. 1985. *World Development Report.* London: Oxford University Press.

World bank. 1986. *World Development Report.* London: Oxford University Press.

Appropriate Technology

ALICE H. AMSDEN

Depending on the decade, different criteria have provided the basis for judging the appropriateness of technology in developing countries. In the 1950s and 1960s, debate centred on whether the choice of technique ought to be guided by the objective of maximizing the growth rate, rather than the level, of output. In the 1970s, the maximand became employment. There was a surge in articles on employment creation through income redistribution and on the merits, more in theory than in practice, of alternative technology life-styles. Soon after, what was considered to be appropriate came once again to mean a competitive market outcome. So defined, the term 'appropriate technology' served no distinct purpose and dropped out of use.

Central to the economic literature in the 1950s and 1960s on how to accelerate development was lengthy discussion of choice of technique. A socialist like Dobb (1963) argued that insofar as the limiting factor consists in the available surplus of foodstuffs and other consumer goods, it will not be the best policy (from the growth standpoint) to invest in low productivity, 'labour-intensive' techniques (as advocated by the twin doctrines of Marginal Productivity and Comparative Cost). Techniques should be chosen that, by achieving a higher level of output per worker, make the surplus product larger. Dobb's point was also made by some adherents of the neoclassical production function who faulted the market model for being too preoccupied with static resource allocation (Sutcliffe, 1974, ch. 5).

Output grew very rapidly in developing countries in this period. Yet outside the socialist bloc, employment growth stagnated. The term 'appropriate technology' was popularized by economists seeking to understand this fact and what could be done about it.

The reasons proffered for slow employment growth amidst rapid rises in output were wide ranging. The majority blamed market distortions. The political clout of urban workers raised wages, subsidization of credit cheapened capital, and overvalued exchange rates invited machinery imports. Another group offered managerial explanations. A choice of technique was not a mere theoretical abstraction, as evidenced by different factor proportions among plants of the same firm ostensibly producing the same product in different countries. But 'engineering man' rather than *homo economicus* did the choosing, and in developing countries chose production processes to raise technical sophistication, reduce labour problems and enhance product quality (Stobaugh and Wells, 1984). A third set of reasons was elaborated by Frances Stewart (1972, 1985). First, she recognized a maximization conflict not merely between output and the growth of output, but also between output and employment. Two techniques of different factor proportions might incur the same total costs, but the technique with a higher ratio of capital to labour might produce higher output. In theory, this technique might generate more employment in the long run, but over time, new technologies would be devised, because innovation occurred in high wage countries. The assumption of a continuous spectrum of techniques to produce a given output, therefore, was belied by history (so lowering wages might succeed only in raising rents rather than employment). At the other extreme, 'technological determinists' were equally wrong in contending the absence of any choice. Yet by varying operating scale and discriminating among products to satisfy consumer wants, the technical menu could be widened.

By this line of reasoning, increasing employment was seen to depend upon choosing appropriate *products* and stimulating small-scale industry. The possibility of specializing through foreign trade in labour-intensive manufactures was underplayed while it was assumed that the consumption bundle of the poor generally involved more labour-intensive production processes than that of the rich. Therefore, employment would rise with a redistribution of income from rich to poor to finance 'informal sector' markets.

The most radical articulation of this view, in the Proudhonian sense, was heard on the fringes of the economics profession. Adherents were sufficiently focused and active to be called a movement, the AT. The Appropriate Technology movement traced its intellectual heritage to Mahatma Gandhi and E.F. Schumacher (1973) and emphasized rural community development. Appropriate technology came to embody self-reliance, a rejection of the technico-economic values of industrialized nations, the use of locally available resources, especially solar energy, and not just a higher ratio of labour to capital (Jequier, 1976). Appropriate technology had to be developed by and for the people who lived by it.

Politically, even the most radical tendencies in the AT movement failed to mobilize mass support. In policy making, not even the moderates made such headway, except possibly in India. Political economy constraints had largely been ignored and demands for income redistribution proved fanciful. The difficulties of devising new technologies and developing local capabilities to assimilate and improve them were underestimated. And at best, all that might be expected was a small surplus and slow growth.

Into this void stepped enthusiasts of export-led growth. Through trade, developing countries could specialize in 'labour-intensive' products without having to redistribute income. With a reduction in market distortions, the choice by profit-maximizing firms of appropriate technology would be automatic. But the conflict between output growth and employment inherent in this reading of appropriate technology was never well understood. Governments in middle income countries with a long-term perspective, appreciative of the high risks of a trade-reliant development strategy amidst rising wages, borrowed heavily abroad. Funds were used to establish new industries with long lead times and high capital requirements in order to stay ahead of competition from even lower wage countries in 'labour-intensive' goods. Debt servicing required access to the markets of advanced countries. Yet as advanced countries climbed up the ladder of comparative advantage, they became less capable of achieving full employment and less willing to relinquish their labour-using industries to imports. Neither the theoretical solution, lower wages, nor the politically popular one, protection, promised relief for indebted nations. Thus, the technologies that seemed appropriate to different groups of countries were out of synchronization. The fast growing, newly industrializing countries and the slower growing advanced economies collided in a widening range of markets for industrial products.

BIBLIOGRAPHY

Dobb, M. 1963. *Economic Growth and Underdeveloped Countries*. London: Lawrence & Wishart; New York: International Publishers.

Jequier, N. 1976. *Appropriate Technology*. Paris: Development Centre of the Organization for Economic Cooperation and Development.

Schumacher, E.F. 1973. *Small is Beautiful*. London: Blond & Briggs.

Stewart, F. 1972. Choice of technique in developing countries. *Journal of Development Studies* 9(1), October, 99–121.

Stewart, F. 1985. Macro policies for appropriate technology: an introductory classification. In *Technology, Institutions and Government Policies*, ed. J. James and S. Watanabe, London: Macmillan.

Stobaugh, R. and Wells, L.T., Jr. (eds) 1984. *Technology Crossing Borders*. Boston: Harvard Business School Press.

Sutcliffe, R.B. 1971. *Industry and Underdevelopment*. London: Addison-Wesley.

Balanced Growth

T. SCITOVSKY

The idea of balanced growth can be traced back to John Stuart Mill's qualified restatement of Say's Law: 'Every increase in production, *if distributed without miscalculation among all kinds of produce in the proportions which private interest would dictate*, creates... its own demand' (Mill, 1844). Say had the insight that all productive activity creates demand along with supply, and Mill added his no less important caveat that while production creates *specific* supplies, and investment creates *specific* productive capacities, the income they generate creates *general* demand, which then is distributed over many goods. Accordingly, for the structure of additional productive capacities to match the structure of additional demand, investment would have to proceed simultaneously in the economy's various sectors and industries in the same proportions in which the buying public apportions the expenditure of its additional income among the outputs of those sectors and industries. That implies a faster growth of sectors and industries for whose output the income elasticities of demand are high and a simultaneous but slower growth of those for whose products income elasticities of demand are low. Such is the meaning of balanced growth. A simplified version of balanced growth, *proportional* growth of all outputs, recurs in John von Neumann's celebrated growth model (Von Neumann, 1945).

On its customary nationalistic interpretation, the argument for balanced growth calls for inward-looking development policies: investment in productive capacities to match the expansion of *domestic* demand. It then conflicts with Ricardo's doctrine of comparative advantage, which says that rather than produce everything at home, each country does better if it specializes in the goods it is best at producing and trades its excess output of them for imports of those commodities in whose production it would have a comparative disadvantage. Moreover, the argument for nationally balanced growth also conflicts with the argument for exploiting economies of scale, whenever a country's domestic market for a particular good is too small to absorb the minimum output that is economical to produce. For in such cases, it is cheaper either to import that good from high-volume low-cost producers abroad, or to produce it at home on a large enough scale to render its cost competitive in world markets and export the surplus.

To resolve those conflicts, growth would have to be balanced, not on a national but on a world scale. Each country would then specialize in areas where its comparative advantage and economies of scale are the greatest, but they would have to keep their borders open to trade and let market forces assure the balanced growth of the world economy as a whole, in the sense of balancing each country's lopsided growth against the complementary lack of balance in the rest of the world's growth. For example, the fast expansion of Great Britain's economy during her industrial revolution consisted in unbalanced growth in the direction of her comparative advantage to a degree that greatly increased her dependence on imports of food and primary products and her need of foreign markets for her exports with which to pay for those imports. To make that work, however, the developing world (which then was much larger) had to grow in an offsettingly unbalanced fashion by specializing on *its* comparative advantages in agricultural production, and also by growing at a much slower rate, given the much lower income elasticity of demand for food than for industrial products.

All this has long been known and more or less taken for granted by most economists; but the new problems and new thinking of the mid-20th century gave new prominence to the argument for nationally balanced growth. To begin with, the break-up of the colonial empires after World War II created many new, independent countries, all of them poor, undeveloped and anxious not only to grow but to catch up with the advanced industrial countries if possible. That brought the problem of accelerating economic development to centre stage and made the developing countries reluctant to acquiesce in their traditional role of primary producers, which, in a system of universal growth balanced on a worldwide scale, would have kept their growth rates well below those of the advanced countries (owing to the much lower demand elasticities for their exports), thereby further widening the gap between rich and poor countries.

Secondly, the Keynesian revolution stressed the importance of effective demand, and that, in the development context, was translated into a new emphasis on matching the structure of supply to the structure of demand. Thirdly, the successful industrialization of Germany and the United States behind the shelter of protective tariffs led to the realization that a country's comparative disadvantage in some sectors is seldom unalterable but usually something that can be remedied through learning by doing; and that realization in turn greatly diminished the importance attached to the conflict between the doctrines of comparative advantage and nationally balanced growth. Finally, the dismal economic performance and protectionist stance of the industrial countries during the great depression of the 1930s led many economists, including some of the most distinguished and influential among them, to believe that, even apart from the argument of the previous paragraph, the developing countries would be well advised to limit their dependence on trade with the advanced countries and not make their own development contingent on the latter's parallel development.

All the above considerations contributed to making many, perhaps most, development economists advocate that the developing countries go their own separate ways, taking the route either of nationally balanced growth or of growth balanced for the developing world as a group, specializing among themselves in the framework of customs unions. Paul Rosenstein-Rodan was the first to advocate such a course in a celebrated article proposing a Danubian federation (Rosenstein-Rodan, 1943); but the foremost and most influential advocate of balanced growth was Ragnar Nurkse, who put the argument in the following way:

> The case for international specialization... is as strong as ever,... but if development through increased exports to the advanced industrial centers is... retarded or blocked, there arises a possible need for promoting increases in output that are diversified in accordance with domestic income elasticities of demand so as to provide markets for each other locally (Nurkse, 1953).

Widespread agreement on the desirability of matching the structure of output to the structure of domestic demand contrasted with widespread disagreement as to the best way to achieve that goal. Nurkse and some others believed that, in poor countries, the market left to itself perpetuates poverty, because to emerge from it would require investment in increasing productivity, which is impeded not only by the low saving of the poor but even more by the lack of profit incentive to build high-productivity plants when the already existing local market for their output is too small. As a means of escaping that vicious circle of poverty, some favoured the central planning of investment to overcome the lack of private incentive; others (including Nurkse) believed that even indicative planning would provide enough additional incentive, especially when aided by tariff protection, tax concessions or cheap credit.

Albert Hirschman and his followers showed more faith in market forces but stressed the virtual impossibility of balanced growth in the narrow literal sense of the simultaneous establishment of many industries all at the same time. He pointed out (Hirschman, 1958) that most poor countries lack the resources for investing in more than one or very few modern projects at any given time, and therefore can aim at balanced growth only in the long run, through a sequential process of building first one then another plant, with each step correcting the worst imbalance in order to approach a more balanced structure gradually. He called that process 'unbalanced growth' and argued that market forces are likely to aid it, because imbalances create shortages, whose impact on prices render their relief or elimination more profitable. Note that Hirschman's unbalanced growth is the distribution over time of individual investment projects whose cumulative long-run aim and effect is still to balance and keep in balance the structure of domestic productive capacities and outputs.

Although the shortcomings of balanced growth were not forgotten (Scitovsky, 1959), it had become the fashionable doctrine of development economists in the period following World War II. The policy-makers of developing countries were influenced by it to the extent of drawing up Three-, Four- or Five-Year Plans to coordinate investment; but they paid more lip service than serious attention to the doctrine of balanced growth. The fashionable policy was import-substituting industrialization, all too often centred on the most highly automated and therefore most prestigious industries. In consequence, the growth of many developing countries not only remained unbalanced but became unbalanced in the wrong direction, in favour of sectors with the country's greatest comparative *dis*advantage. Industry was favoured to the neglect of agriculture; automobiles, large kitchen appliances and petrochemicals were favoured to the neglect of the simpler manufactures and processed foods on which most of the newly generated income of the emerging urban working classes was spent. The unbalanced nature of such development manifested itself in the chronic underutilization of the new modern plants side by side with excess demand for food and its consequences, increasing imports and inflationary pressures. The disappointing record of import-substituting development in many countries led to a gradual shift towards export-led growth, which was equally unbalanced but in favour of industries with a comparative advantage.

Export-led growth therefore was much more successful, especially as long as it was favoured by expanding world trade. Nationally balanced growth continues to remain a theoretical doctrine more than a tried practical policy.

Mention should also be made in this connection of 'harmonic growth', a related but different concept, introduced by Janos Kornai and mainly applied, together with its opposite, 'rushed growth', to the growth policies of socialist countries (Kornai, 1972). Harmonic growth is a planner's value judgement of what list of things and in what proportions a country's growth policy ought to encompass. One of its elements, the balanced satisfaction of all the needs of the consuming public, corresponds to balanced growth; but most of its other elements go beyond a concern with market goods alone and call for such things as a parallel growth of public and private goods, an increase in leisure along with the increased availability of goods, an equitable distribution of income, a steady rate of growth over time, and the free unfolding of talents, which implies adequate and equal access to education, full employment, and matching the training of specialists to the economy's demand for them. The opposite of harmonic growth, rushed growth, is the neglect or sacrifice of some of those or similar elements for the sake of the faster growth of the remainder. An obvious example is the policy of many socialist countries to ignore the housing shortage, neglect residential construction and use the resources so saved for a faster expansion of manufacturing capacity.

BIBLIOGRAPHY

Hirschman, A. 1958. *The Strategy of Economic Development.* New Haven: Yale University Press.

Kornai, J. 1972. *Rush versus Harmonic Growth.* Amsterdam: North-Holland.

Mill, J.S. 1844. *Essays on Some Unsettled Questions of Political Economy.* London: London School of Economics, 1948; New York: A.M. Kelley, 1968.

Neumann, J. von. 1945–6. A model of general equilibrium. Trans. G. Morgenstern, *Review of Economic Studies* 13, 1–9.

Nurkse, R. 1953. *Problems of Capital Formation in Underdeveloped Countries.* Oxford: Basil Blackwell; New York: Oxford University Press.

Rosenstein-Rodan, P.N. 1943. Problems of industrialization of Eastern and South-Eastern Europe. *Economic Journal* 53, June-September, 202–11.

Scitovsky, T. 1959. Growth – balanced or unbalanced? In *The Allocation of Economic Resources,* ed. M. Abramovitz et al., Stanford: Stanford University Press.

Bauer, Peter Tamas

A.A. WALTERS

Born in Hungary in 1915, Bauer became a fellow of Gonville and Caius College, Cambridge, from 1946 and Professor of Economics in the University of London at the London School of Economics from 1960 until he retired as Professor Emeritus in 1983. The earliest and most distinguished critic of development economics, he launched is research with a classic study of the rubber industry (1948), where he showed that the very rapid growth was a consequence of voluntary responses, usually of illiterate peasants, to expanded opportunities due largely to contacts with the West. In *West African Trade*, he showed that, contrary to the views of development economists and the evidence of official statistics, the extensive system of traders was efficient in providing production for the market and for expanding material welfare. State intervention in the form of marketing boards was shown to be a mechanism for exploiting monopsony power to the detriment of producers, particularly the small farmers, and to the benefit of the rulers. Stabilization of farm incomes did not require state marketing; it could be achieved by the farmers themselves.

Bauer's empirical studies and further reflection on the role of the state in development led him to challenge the widespread belief, urged most eloquently by Myrdal, that comprehensive central planning, together with substantial aid from the governments of industrialized countries, was needed to overcome the vicious circle of poverty, low savings and low investment. Bauer pointed out that virtually all the rich countries had emerged from poverty without the supposed benefits of central planning or aid, and that even in very poor countries, provided there was security and suitable motivations, people saved and invested considerable sums efficiently. With central planning, on the other hand, investment was undertaken primarily for political motives and was much more likely to result in economic waste, such as premature industrialization behind high trade barriers. Bauer showed that aid was not a necessary condition of development and, since it reinforced government's grip on the economy, aid frequently inhibited material progress. He stressed the corrosive and corrupting politicization of economic life with its stultifying effects on development.

The meticulous scholarship and historical depth of Bauer's work was unusual if not unique in development studies. The veracity of Bauer's ideas and the poverty of development economics have become increasingly apparent in the 1970s and 1980s. In 1983 his elevation to the peerage as Baron Bauer of Market Ward in the City of Cambridge recognized his outstanding contributions to scholarship.

SELECTED WORKS

1948. *The Rubber Industry*. Cambridge, Mass.: Harvard University Press.
1954. *West African Trade*. Cambridge: Cambridge University Press.
1972. *Dissent on Development*. Cambridge, Mass.: Harvard University Press.
1984. *Reality and Rhetoric: Studies in the Economics of Development*. Cambridge, Mass.: Harvard University Press.

Colonialism

M. ABDEL-FADIL

Everywhere do I perceive a certain conspiracy of rich men seeking their own advantage under the name and pretext of the commonwealth (Sir Thomas More).

Modern colonialism, as a historical phenomenon of territorial expansion, is intimately entwined with the rise and expansion of the modern capitalist world system. So colonialism is entwined with the history, economics, politics and ruling ideas of the modern capitalist society. On the other hand, and to avoid any terminological confusions, the term *imperialism* should be reserved to designate the new nexus of financial and technological dependency relations and arrangements marking the new distinct stage of mature capitalism (Magdoff, 1970).

During the modern colonial period (1870–1945) colonialism has emerged as a general description of the state of subjection – political, economic and intellectual – of a non-European society as a result of the process of colonial organization (Fieldhouse, 1981).

THE AGE OF COLONIALISM: HISTORICAL BACKGROUND. The age of colonialism began about 1500, following the European discoveries of a sea route around Africa's southern coast (1488) and of America (1492). Colonialism thus expanded by conquest and settlement after a period of extensive exploration. The improvement in navigational instruments helped a great deal to make substantial progress in the discovery of new geographical territories.

Portugal emerged as the leading nation in such process of overseas expansion. 'The search for wealth in the form of gold, ivory, spices and slaves spurred the Portuguese and may have been the strongest motivating force behind the colonization drive of the Portuguese during the 16th century' (*Encylopaedia Britannica*, 1977, Vol. 4, p. 881).

The old colonial period, which lasted nearly three centuries, following the major Portuguese and Spanish conquests, may be viewed largely as a commercial venture. The Spaniards and the Portuguese resorted to their warships, gunnery and seamanship to keep the main trade routes open. The Spanish sovereigns created in 1504 the House of Trade (Casa de Contracion) to regulate commerce between Spain and the New World. Their purpose was to establish state monopoly over overseas trade, and thus pour the maximum amount of bullion into the royal treasury.

The old colonial system was disrupted in the 18th century as new contradictions developed due to the rapid advance of the Industrial Revolution in England, and by the progressive control England was able to exercise over world shipping. Such new developments led to a policy of opening the American ports to international trade, a policy at variance with the type of colonial relations prevailing between Spain, Portugal and their colonies. These relations were organized exclusively around the exploitation of precious metals (Furtado, 1970, p. 20).

The century between the 1820s and the outbreak of the World War I saw the establishment of the modern colonial order. For during that period European countries had achieved complete dominance over world trade, finance and shipping. On the other hand, the political and military authority of the European conquerors was backed by superiority in technology, applied science, organization and information systems (Bagchi, 1982).

Between the late 1870s and World War I (1914–18), the colonial powers added to their possessions an average of about 240,000 square miles (620,000 sq. km.) a year, while during the first 75 years of the 19th century the rate of increase in new territories acquired by colonial powers averaged about 83,000 square miles (215,000 sq. km.) a year. By the year 1914, the colonies extended over approximately 85 per cent of the surface of the globe.

Against this historical background, John Hicks establishes a useful distinction between two types of colony: colonies of settlement and trading-post colonies (Hicks, 1969, p. 51). A third type of colony was identified as 'the plantation colonies'. In such case, the colony which started as a colony of settlement was gradually transformed into a trading colony (ibid., p. 53).

THE COLONIZATION DEBATE. While there is a strong connection between mercantile expansion and colonization, it would be a mistake to emphasize the crude economic interpretation of colonialism by narrowing down colonialism to the process of control of supplies of raw materials, mineral resources and markets in underdeveloped and precapitalist regions. In fact, such a narrow economistic approach eliminates a vital aspect of colonialism relating to political activity and the drive for dominance over the daily lives of the people of the colonized regions (e.g. French colonialism).

Nonetheless, colonialism must be viewed, dialetically, as a complex phenomenon of capitalist expansion, operating in terms of time and space. To illustrate this point, S.H. Frankel described such a process as a *disintegrating* but also a *formative* process, a unique process in the history of mankind (Frankel, 1953). Some other writers justified colonial rule on the ground that 'Colonialism was a necessary instrument of "modernization" which would help other peoples to do what they could not have done, or have done as well, by themselves' (Fieldhouse, 1981, p. 43). At the other end of the spectrum, radical theorists, notable among them Walter Rodney, claim that under colonialism 'the only things that developed were dependency and underdevelopment' (Rodney, 1972, p. 256).

One of the most articulate arguments put forward in defence of the colonial rule in underdeveloped areas is that of Lord Bauer, who contends that:

> The colonial governments established law and order, safeguarded private property and contractual relations, organized basic transport and health services, and introduced some modern financial and legal institutions. This environment also promoted the establishment or extension of external contacts, which in turn encouraged the inflow of external resources, notably administrative, commercial and technical skills as well as capital.
>
> These contacts also acquainted the population with new wants, crops, commodities and methods of cultivation and opened new sources of supply of a wide range of commodities. These changes engendered a new outlook on material advance and on the means of securing it: for good or evil these contacts promoted the erosion of the traditional values, objectives, attitudes and customs obstructing material advance (Bauer, 1976, p. 149).

This argument only confirms the deep-seated Western biased view, claiming that material progress and advance can only be achieved by eroding the traditional values, customs and production structures of pre-capitalist and primitive societies. Rosa Luxemburg (1913) would see in Lord Bauer's view an eloquent proof of her radical contentions about colonialism and territorial expansion, by the emerging capitalist nations.

But what is at issue is not the possibility or not of achieving material progress or advancement, but the terms on which these transformations in the material and socioeconomic structures were operated. From our viewpoint, what needs to be stressed is the loss of sovereignty which the process of European colonization entailed for practically all colonized peoples. In Africa, for instance, European colonizers often crushed, repressed or amalgamated states at will. In most instances, the direct colonial rule was designed to direct and reorder the day-to-day lives of the African peoples (Ajayi, 1969).

Seen in a radically different light, thinkers such as Albert Memmi, Jean-Paul Sartre and Franz Fanon placed greater emphasis on the ideological implications and the socio-psychological consequences of the process of colonization. According to Fanon, colonialism tended not only to deprive a society of its freedom and its wealth, but of its very character, leaving its people intellectually and morally disoriented (Fanon, English edition, 1966).

PATTERNS OF COLONIAL TRADE. Historians tend to agree that the conquest of colonies was designed to the economic advantage of the European conquerors.

Some historians (e.g. E.J. Hobsbawm) would go as far as to claim that the Industrial Revolution in England would not have been accomplished without the conquest and penetration of 'underdeveloped' markets overseas (Hobsbawm, 1968, p. 54).

In fact, the primary aim of all European states was to use commercial regulations to maximize their share of colonial trade in both directions and the profits they made from it. The English Navigation Acts, dating from the 1650s, may be taken as typical in this respect. According to these Acts, all colonial trade must be carried in British-owned and registered ships. All goods imported to the colonies must either be the product of Britain or be transhipped and pay duty there. Any colonial exports so 'enumerated' must be carried direct to a British port in the first instance (Deane, 1965, p. 204). The aim of such rules and regulations was to give British shipowners, merchants and manufacturers an assured benefit from colonial commerce and to enable the government to tax colonial trade. This clearly indicates the close association between the process of colonization and the rise of various foreign-trade monopolies held by the charted colonial companies.

Hence, against all claims of the 'Free-Trade' school, the British cotton industry did not rely on its competitive superiority, but relied heavily on the monopolistic practices embodied in colonial trade-regulations, and enforced by the British commercial and naval supremacy (Hobsbawm, 1968, p. 58). On the other hand, the terms of trade between the colonized areas and the metropolitan countries had a tendency to deteriorate steadily over time, so that the primary producers in colonized areas tended to obtain proportionally less with their labour than they could have done had they concentrated on producing food or other subsistence crops for their own use or for the home market (Fieldhouse, 1981, p. 78). This may be characterized, in modern terminology, as 'unequal exchange', which emphasizes once again the exploitative nature of colonial trade.

THE INTERNAL CONTROL OF THE COLONIAL ECONOMY. The key to understanding colonialism as a historical phenomenon lies in analysing the mechanism of the internal control of the colonial economy. In this connection, one has to answer two fundamental questions. Why did the Western countries spend so much energy, blood and money in seeking to procure colonial possessions? What are the direct and indirect economic benefits of colonialism?

In the colonial economy, top priority was given to infrastructure investment: railways, harbours, telegraphs, rivers and roads, since it was believed that these constitute the prerequisites of a modern economy, making it possible to link internal areas of production to the world commodity markets. In the agricultural sector, it is still an open question whether plantations, owned and run by foreigners, made any significant contribution to the development of the colonial economy. On the positive side, they served as the main vehicle of introducing new crops, attracting foreign capital, expanding the base of the cash economy and the wage-labour force, and increasing agricultural productivity. On the negative side, the crops of such plantations were subject to severe fluctuations on the international commodity markets, thus subjecting the colonial economy to severe cyclical fluctuations.

In matters of industrialization, many observers tend to agree that the colonial powers did not positively encourage industrialization in their dependencies, and in many instances their basic policies led to some sort of de-industrialization (Bagchi, 1982). In this respect, many writers invoke the record of colonization in India from the days of the East India Company. For the balance of historical evidence points to the fact that up to the 18th century the economic conditions of India were relatively advanced, and Indian methods of industrial production were comparable with those prevailing in any other advanced part of the world (Baran, 1957, p. 144).

On the other hand, Bill Warren has offered a neo-Marxist view, opposed to the 'Dependency School', regarding the effects of colonialism on the development of productive forces in Third World countries. His main argument runs as follows: 'Direct Colonialism, far from having retarded or distorted indigenous capitalist development that might otherwise have occurred, acted as a powerful engine of progressive social change' (Warren, 1980).

Nonetheless, Warren's positive account of the effects of colonialism on the process of capitalist development in Third World countries tends to be rather unitary in spirit. For the pattern of resource allocation in colonial territories had been shaped and administered largely by foreign investors, bankers and merchants. According to Paul Baran, the principal impact of foreign enterprise on the development of the underdeveloped and precapitalist regions 'lies in hardening and strengthening the sway of merchant capitalism, in slowing down and indeed preventing its transformation into industrial capitalism' (Baran, 1957, p. 205).

This very nature of the process of capitalist development under colonialism led some authors, such as H. Alavi, to offer the highly controversial concept of the 'colonial mode of production'. This concept was offered as a theoretical construction designed to allow for a variety of relations other than those which characterize the 'capitalist mode of production', as experienced in the advanced capitalist economies of the 'centre' (Alavi, 1975). In this respect, Alavi and company established the distinctive features of the 'colonial mode of production' on the basis of empirical investigation of the circuits of capital and forms of labour recruitment of what comes to be called by other authors (i.e. Samir Amin and Gunder Frank) 'colonial capitalism' or 'peripheral capitalism' (Booth, 1985, p. 169). Yet the difficulties and confusions surrounding the concept of a 'colonial mode of production', as a distinct mode of production, remain formidable.

DECOLONIZATION AND NEOCOLONIALISM: TWO SIDES OF THE SAME COIN. The drive towards decolonization in the post-World War II period was a response to the economic crisis of an ageing colonial system. This colonial system was found to involve considerable, and sometimes unacceptable, financial costs to the metropolis. Moreover, colonialism had become increasingly discredited among the people of the colonizing nations themselves, just as the emotional strains of suppressing nationalistic movements in colonized regions had become largely intolerable for public opinion (Fieldhouse, 1981, p. 24).

Nonetheless, the process of decolonization proved to be a nominal process in the sense that the formal end of colonial rule did not necessarily result in genuine economic independence for the former colonies. There is now a community of view among left-wing economists and writers that decolonization took place when and because foreign monopoly capital felt confident that the colonial society and economy had been so restructured that their interests could be preserved without direct political control. In other words, colonialism had been merely transmitted into perpetual neocolonialism (Baran, 1957).

The term 'neocolonialism', which has gained wide acceptance since the mid-1950s, is meant to designate a state of affairs characterized by a structure of dependency relationships whereby the former colonial territories are kept in their subordinate place within the imperialist system. This is maintained and sustained by means of chronic and structural balance of payments difficulties, arising from the trade, aid and investment relationships with their former or new metropolitan countries (Warren, 1973, p. 35).

In sum, colonialism may be seen in a historical perspective as one decisive and dramatic stage in the evolution of international economic relationships. The establishment of colonial rule constituted an arbitrary break in the normal course of history, splitting up regions and creating new artificial entities, transplanting new alien values and institutions into colonized societies. One may finally wonder whether it would not have been better for the people of the colonized regions to remain autonomous until certain indigenous forces could gain momentum and generate new conditions for socioeconomic development and material progress.

BIBLIOGRAPHY
Ajayi, J.F. 1969. Colonialism: an episode in African history. In *Colonialism in Africa 1870–1960*, ed. L.H. Gann and P. Duignan, vol. 1, London: Cambridge University Press.
Alavi, H. 1975. India and the colonial mode of production. In *The Socialist Register, 1975*, ed. R. Miliband and J. Saville, London: Merlin Press.
Bagchi, A.K. 1982. *The Political Economy of Underdevelopment*. London and New York: Cambridge University Press.
Baran, P. 1957. *The Political Economy of Growth*. New York: Monthly Review Press.
Bauer, P.T. 1976. *Dissent on Development*. London: Weidenfeld & Nicholson; Cambridge, Mass.: Harvard University Press.
Booth, D. 1985. Marxism and development sociology: interpreting the impasse. *World Development* 13(7), 761–87.
Deane, P. 1965. *The First Industrial Revolution*. London: Cambridge University Press.
Encyclopaedia Britannica. 1977. 5th edn, Vol. 4.
Fanon, F. 1966. *The Wretched of the Earth*. New York.
Fieldhouse, D.K. 1981. *Colonialism, 1870–1945: An Introduction*. London: Weidenfeld & Nicolson.
Frankel, S.H. 1953. *The Economic Impact of Colonialism on Under-Developed Societies*. Oxford: Basil Blackwell.
Furtado, C. 1970. *Economic Development of Latin America*. London: Cambridge University Press.

Hicks, J. 1969. *A Theory of Economic History*. Oxford: Clarendon Press.

Hobsbawm, E. 1968. *Industry and Empire*. London: Weidenfeld & Nicholson.

Luxemburg, R. 1913. *The Accumulation of Capital*. London: Routledge & Kegan Paul, 1951; New Haven: Yale University Press.

Magdoff, H. 1970. Is imperialism really necessary? *Monthly Review*, Part I, 22(5), October, 1–14; Part II, 22(6), November, 1–11.

Rodney, W. 1972. *How Europe Underdeveloped Africa*. London: Bogle.

Warren, B. 1973. Imperialism and capitalist industrialization. *New Left Review* No. 81, September-October, 3–44.

Warren, B. 1980. *Imperialism*: *Pioneer of Capitalism*. London: New Left Books.

Colonies

DONALD WINCH

The economic advantages and disadvantages of colonies, the best means of establishing them and ensuring their development, and the principles that should govern trade and other relations with the mother country, have persistently served as fertile topics for policy and theoretical debate in the history of political economy. The treatment given here will be confined to the British debate on colonies from late 18th to the first decades of the 20th century.

The British empire was composed of colonies and ex-colonies which had differing histories of acquisition and varying political and economic relationships with the mother country. It follows that the problems which they posed were equally diverse, as illustrated by the differences between the economies of the British West Indies before and after slavery was abolished, the question of public land disposal and emigration to Canada, Australia and New Zealand, and the tasks of administering an Indian sub-continent with a largely peasant population living close to minimum subsistence levels. To this list can be added the problems of integrating Scotland and Ireland into the English economy and polity after the respective Acts of Union in 1707 and 1808, where 'colonial' issues – in a technical rather than emotive sense – were often at stake, even if the term was not used to describe them. Indeed, Ireland and India as subsistence farming economies posed similar problems to British administrators, despite major differences in their cultural backgrounds and political status within the empire. For that matter, even the United States after independence could for some purposes be treated as having a 'colonial' relationship with Britain, largely because it remained a major outlet for British capital and labour.

The sheer magnitude of the problems of empire and their changing nature over more than two centuries would guarantee that they bulked large in the minds of British economists. A few strategic examples will show that there has always been a fairly intimate relationship between economics, economists, and empire. Adam Smith may well have advised the imposition of the Townshend duties on

North America in 1763, and he was certainly involved in advising the British government on the consequences of American break-away when these earlier attempts to exert fiscal control led to successful revolt. Malthus held the first Chair of political economy in Britain at an educational institution at Haileybury established to train the servants of the East Indian Company; and James and John Stuart Mill together devoted nearly 40 years to the service of the Company. The younger Mill was also a consistent supporter of schemes involving the 'systematic colonization' of Australia and New Zealand, as well as taking a major interest, along with most of his classical predecessors and successors, in the problems of the Irish economy. The controversy over imperial preference at the turn of the 20th century underlined the gulf that existed between historical or institutionalist economists and their more orthodox opponents, led by Alfred Marshall, who believed that the increasing challenge to Britain's industrial hegemony did not justify abandonment of deductive methods of economic reasoning or those cosmopolitan free trade principles which had spurred British prosperity earlier. Finally, of course, there is Keynes, whose first employment as a civil servant was within the India Office, and whose first major economic work was a treatise on *Indian Currency and Finance* (1913) – a work which attempted to do for its day what Sir James Steuart had done when he wrote *The Principles of Money Applied to the Present State of the Coin of Bengal* in 1772.

A treatment based on chronology and recurring themes seems the best way of dealing with the diversity of Colonies as a topic of economic interest, though it should be remembered that colonies and empire was never treated solely as *economic* problems, even after the inauguration, largely under Marshall's auspices, of a measure of professional distance in these matters.

The initial and longest period in the history of colonial policy began in England during Elizabethan times and effectively ended with the dismantling of what had become known as the 'old colonial system' in the 1820s. This system was loosely based on the amorphous doctrines which Adam Smith subjected to attack in the *Wealth of Nations* as a central part of his condemnation of the 'mercantile system' (later known as Mercantilism). During this mercantile period colonies generated a large body of literature which reflected the overwhelming concern with national power and economic self-sufficiency as the prime objectives of state intervention. Thus colonies not only served direct strategic purposes as naval or military bases, they were also treated as sources of precious metals, and of strategic and other raw materials necessary to Britain's early manufacturing industries – of particular value when carried in British ships and bought through monopolistic arrangements at prices lower than could be obtained on the world market. Colonies were variously regarded as protected export markets, outlets for surplus population, and sources of tribute, in addition to serving occasionally as prison settlements. Although the development of free trade doctrines, together with associated monetary ideas on specie-flow mechanisms, eventually succeeded in undermining many of the arguments in favour of colonial possessions and regulations, economic nationalism and neo-mercantilistic ideas and policies have always exerted a powerful attraction, especially in countries that were industrial later-comers or anxious to overcome the problems of underdevelopment by means of import-substitution and/or export promotion.

During the 18th century, the established wisdom on the subject of colonies came under question largely because the supposed benefits of trade controls to the mother country were connected with the growing cost to Britain of defending and governing her North American colonies. Among the earliest critics of the colonial system from this point of view was Josiah Tucker, who argued that existing benefits in the form of export markets and imported goods would accrue to Britain under free trade, and without the attendant military and economic burdens of empire. Provoked by David Hume's essays on commerce and money, Tucker also engaged in an important dispute with Hume on the question of whether trade relations between rich and poor countries could be considered as equalizing or not, and if so, by what process – perhaps through rising labour costs and prices in the richer trading partner, or through some other mechanisms of stimulus and emulation in the poorer country. The dispute was of relevance to free-trade relations between England and Scotland after Union, and of potential relevance to Britain's relations with Ireland and other 'colonies', whether acknowledged as such or not. Indeed the Hume–Tucker debate was an early example of recognition of the essential similarities between international and interregional trade in a world in which currencies were linked through the gold standard. It also concerned relative rates of growth and the respective merits of agriculture and manufacturing as the basis for a nation's wealth and prospects for economic development. Would those who had the advantages of an early start acquire world dominion and monopoly; and hence would poorer and later starters in the race be forced to employ protective measures to establish and maintain their infant industries? If noticed, the debate would have foreshadowed later issues raised by Friedrich List and Henry Carey with Germany and the United States in mind, as well as other questions such as 'free trade imperialism', the 'permanence' of the dollar problem after World War II, and the debate on 'dependency' and the development of post-colonial underdevelopment in the 1960s and 1970s.

Smith's extensive treatment of colonies in the *Wealth of Nations* (especially Book IV, chapter 7) became the *locus classicus* of the anti-mercantile position, where much of his discussion was interwoven with an account of the founding of the European colonies which brought matters up to the present, namely to the issues underlying Britain's dispute with its American colonies. Whereas Edmund Burke had advocated the relaxation of trade controls and taxation as a means of preserving the political status quo, Smith maintained that Britain's pretensions to empire would remain those of a shortsighted shopkeeper unless some system could be found whereby the debts and current burdens of empire could be shared by the colonies themselves; and he emphasized the point by closing the *Wealth of Nations* with a warning about the potential long-term effects on British growth prospects of existing arrangements. Hence the elaborate scheme he advanced for an imperial (Anglo-American) free trade zone, with provision for complete fiscal harmonization and legislative union. However, since he regarded this proposal as utopian, its purpose was chiefly to underline the precise conditions under which the burdens of empire could be made acceptable. Much the same result could be achieved through free trade and a treaty of friendship, without provision for imperial government.

Smith's close dissection of the various gains and losses involved in maintaining the monopoly of colonial trade employed a quasi-mercantilist idea of 'vent for surplus', as well as other arguments about the effects on profits of colonial markets which could not be squared with later Ricardian orthodoxy on the doctrine of comparative costs, capital accumulation, Say's Law, and the permanent causes of declining profits. Ricardo also pointed out circumstances in which it was possible for the mother country to so regulate the trade of a colony as to make it less beneficial to the colony, and more advantageous to the mother country than free trade – an early version of the terms-of-trade argument for tariffs (not meant for use) which in the hands of Robert Torrens was to blossom into a case for an imperial *Zollverein* a few years later.

With the support of most political economists, however, the system of colonial preferences was gradually and unilaterally dismantled, beginning with the efforts of Huskisson and Robinson in the 1820s. The views of special interest groups, especially those connected with shipping and the West Indies, which Smith had expected to prevail, were outflanked by an uncertain combination of intellectual argument, political opportunism, and a general realization that Britain's industrial dominance meant that mutual restrictions merely restricted the dominant partner without conferring equivalent benefit. A similar combination involving humanitarian arguments prevailed on the related matter of West Indian slavery and the slave trade. The keystone of Britain's rather isolated status as a free-trading nation was installed with the abolition of the Corn Laws in 1846, a policy that had considerable long-term significance for British agriculture and Britain's relationship to colonial suppliers of food and raw materials, including the United States as well as colonies of recent settlement.

During the 1830s and 1840s public debate on colonies and colonization was dominated by the activities of Edward Gibbon Wakefield and the colonial reformers, a group of radicals dedicated to the revival of 'the lost art of colonization'. Their programme entailed the creation of self-governing colonies as outlets for Britain's surplus capital and labour, avoiding the evils of simply 'shovelling out paupers', abolishing penal settlements, and creating 'civilized' communities enjoying the benefits of free trade and high rates of growth. Wakefield's diagnosis of the simultaneous existence in Britain of surplus capital and labour, and the consequent need for new fields of employment abroad, was developed in opposition to Ricardian orthodoxy on the wage fund and Say's Law. His ideas on the optimal economic development of colonies also conflicted with Smith's view that countries of European settlement enjoying an abundance of land were likely to make rapid economic progress. The key to high rates of growth lay in achieving the correct balance between capital, labour, and their 'field of employment' by restricting access to land. This could be achieved by setting a price on land sufficient to delay dispersal of the wage-labour force, and by using the proceeds of land sale for the purpose of bringing in new immigrants. This policy meant that public land disposal and immigration had to remain an imperial rather than purely local concern, thereby creating scope for conflict when colonies achieved self-government. The Wakefield policy came to be seen as a symbol of imperial oppression, an attempt to place colonial development within a straitjacket designed with European conditions in mind. It also entailed loss of freedom in disposing of one of the main sources of revenue available to self-governing colonies. The colonial reformers' hopes of establishing an empire in which free trade ruled were another casualty of self-government when it led to tariffs being raised by Canada and Australia against British and other goods.

What now seems remarkable is the rapidity and extent of influence exerted over British colonial policy by Wakefield's untried theories, though modern development economics may yield comparable examples. He was also highly successful in convincing a number of leading political economists, not least John Stuart Mill, that his ideas deserved to form the basis for future policy. Mill gave prominence to Wakefield's ideas in his *Principles of Political Economy* and other writings by consistently championing 'systematic colonization' as a solution to Britain's population difficulties; and by treating its application to new countries as a valid exception to the general principle of *laissez faire*, namely as a case where the self-interest principle acting under competitive conditions would lead to a sub-optimal result as far as the community was concerned. As part of his general modification of Ricardo's assumptions concerning capital scarcity and the distant prospect of the stationary state, Mill also endorsed the conclusions of Wakefield's heterodox diagnosis of Britain's economic condition, while denying that it was in conflict with Say's Law and other received Ricardian doctrines. By acknowledging the importance to Britain of the export of capital and labour to colonies, Mill not only removed an obstacle to support for colonization, and hence to the extension of empire, he opened up a major exception to the comparative cost doctrine as an interpretation of Britain's trading pattern: the trade with colonies now became akin to interregional trade. It should also be noted that Mill, confirming the tradition that the only new economic arguments for protection have been advanced by those who favour free trade as a general rule, gave a cautious endorsement to the infant industry case for tariffs.

India was never a colony in the same sense that North America, Australia and New Zealand were British colonies. Attempts were often made to prevent or discourage European colonization before 1830, and until 1858 India was governed by the East India Company acting on a renewable Charter granted by Parliament. The Company had been subjected to closer government control in the late 18th century, deprived of its commercial monopoly in 1813, and finally ceased trading altogether in 1833 when it lost its exclusive privileges over the China trade. These developments represented another victory for the forces of free trade, and they blunted the force of Smith's criticisms both of monopolies and government by trading companies. As we have seen in the case of Tucker, free trade ideas could be associated with a case for complete 'emancipation' (Bentham's term) of all colonies. (It was an association of free trade with anti-imperialism which was an invitation for revisionist historians to counter with a neat, perhaps over-neat, inversion by drawing attention to 'free-trade imperialism'.) But there were fewer spokesmen for such ideas in relation to India, where other notions of European superiority and responsibility held sway, along with more mundane considerations connected with the retention of investment, employment, and trading opportunities.

India had provided Smith with a prime example of a stationary or declining state, something that could either be attributed to the deficiencies of its system of government and taxation, or to those of a backward people whose culture constituted a barrier to economic progress, though usually to a combination of both. In addition, criticism from divergent quarters was made of the flow of tribute leaving India for Britain, much of it financed by exports of textiles that competed with domestic industry: Indian commerce came in conflict with British manufacturing interests, which were placated by the imposition of duties on Indian imports. But with the reorganization of the Company, especially after 1813, came new priorities and opportunities for those with ambitions to bring the light of post-Smithian, and more especially, Ricardian political economy to bear on the problems of Indian administration. Such a task proved highly congenial to James Mill, a critic of the Company's monopoly powers who was appointed by the Company in 1819 and rose to the rank of Chief Examiner in charge of political, judicial, and fiscal correspondence with India. It was largely through Mill's efforts, later endorsed by his son, John Stuart Mill, that the Ricardian rent doctrine came to play such a large part in the conduct of Indian affairs. It provided the basis for the *ryotwari* system of land tenure, whereby the state became the sole landlord and met its revenue needs by levying *ryots* or peasant-farmers according to Ricardian principles of pure rent. By confining the state's exactions to rent it was thought that the peasant farmer would enjoy normal profits and wages, and the state would eliminate an intermediary or landowning class of *zemindars* or rent-receivers. The system embodied action according to a clear analytical proposition, antagonism to rent as a form of private income, and a view of the prospects for Indian economic development that treated the peasant proprietor as a capitalistic entrepreneur, feed from the arbitrary exactions of landowners and responding to market incentives – which is not to say that the application of these Western economic ideas to Indian conditions was any more successful than the *zemindari* alternative.

In Ireland, where similar economic conditions of a growing population dependent on a backward agriculture obtained, it proved more difficult to bypass the Irish landowner in order to grant the kind of security of tenure to the peasant proprietor than either existed or was the aim of administrators in India. Indeed, the initial view of economists during the early classical period was unsympathetic to the preservation of peasant proprietorship in Ireland. The favoured solution was consolidation of tenant-holdings as a preliminary to the creation of a capitalistic form of farming employing agricultural wage-labour along English lines, together with emigration or absorption of the displaced population into alternative employment. Before, but especially after the Great Famine of 1846, emigration, largely unplanned, was the only part of this programme that operated. Under the leadership of John Stuart Mill, J.E. Cairnes, W.T. Thornton and Henry Fawcett, the earlier diagnoses and remedies were entirely recast; a more positive evaluation of the possibilities of transforming cottier tenants into peasant proprietors enjoying security of tenure was registered and advocated as the basis for a solution to Irish problems. It was a position that ran directly counter to English property ideas and involved recognition of the role of custom as opposed to contract in designing policies and institutions for societies that did not conform to the English model.

Mill's deployment of a more relativist approach in policy matters was later to be seen as a welcome, though incomplete concession to a succeeding generation of more full-blooded historical and institutionalist critics of deductive economic theory, with its built-in bias in favour of rational economic man – a creature originally invoked by Mill to underline the contrast with societies where custom prevailed. Such critics were more numerous and vocal after 1870, and the resulting split within the economists' ranks coincided with a campaign for 'fair trade' in the 1880s which blossomed into Joseph Chamberlain's scheme of tariff reform along imperial preference lines – an unwitting return to Torren's imperial *Zollverein*. The historical economists, led by William Cunningham and W.J. Ashley, had already followed Schmoller and other German exemplars in according a more positive valuation to Mercantilism, and this presaged their endorsement of tariff reform as an imperial remedy for Britain's declining competitiveness. At the price of forsaking free trade, Britain could offer preferential treatment to imperial food and raw materials in return for similar preferences in the markets of her ex-colonies. There had already been a revival of interest in imperial federation, which could be portrayed, as it was by John Shield Nicholson, as a return to Adam Smith's project of empire. While much of this belongs to the larger subject of imperialism, a term which has always carried more nationalistic and ideological oxygen, the episode is chiefly of interest here because it was the occasion for a major challenge to economic orthodoxy. Chamberlain's use of arguments supplied by such economists as W.A.S. Hewins brought Marshall into the professional and political fray with his *Memorandum on Fiscal Policy of International Trade* (1908), a work which is still perhaps the best brief restatement of the free trade position based on a combination of neoclassical trade theory and an empirical analysis of contemporary conditions in the colonies as well as in Britain.

Marshall's pupil, John Maynard Keynes, was not as impressed by his master's memorandum when he looked back on it from the vantage point of 1930. At this time Keynes had decided that a revenue tariff was an acceptable policy for Britain to follow, though not for reasons connected with imperial solidarity. Thus when Neville Chamberlain achieved his father's goal with the passage of the Import Duties Act in 1931, followed by the Ottawa Agreements which began the period of imperial preference, Keynes withdrew his support for tariffs. Nevertheless, any account of the revolution associated with Keynes's name is likely to be incomplete without some reference to the ending of free trade in Britain, coupled as it was with the inauguration of an era in which external monetary constraints on British domestic policy were weakened. Of more long-term significance to imperial policy in the interwar period, however, was the revival of interest in state-assisted settlement in the white dominions and the new emphasis on colonial development, with Africa as well as India now assuming a larger role in official, if not professional, economic thinking. At this point colonies and colonial policy become something else, the beginnings of modern development economics.

BIBLIOGRAPHY

Ambirajan, S. 1978. *Classical Political Economy and British Policy in India*. Cambridge: Cambridge University Press.

Barber, W.J. 1975. *British Economic Thought and India, 1600–1858*. Oxford: Clarendon Press.

Black, R.D.C. 1960. *Economic Thought and the Irish Question, 1817–1870*. Cambridge: Cambridge University Press.

Black, R.D.C. 1968. Economic policy in Ireland and India in the time of J.S. Mill. *Economic History Review* 21, 321–36.

Drummond, I.M. 1974. *Imperial Economic Policy, 1917–1938*. London: Allen & Unwin.

Knorr, K. 1944. *British Colonial Theories, 1570–1850*. Toronto: Toronto University Press.

Semmel, B. 1970. *The Rise of Free Trade Imperialism*. Cambridge and New York: Cambridge University Press.

Stokes, E. 1959. *The English Utilitarians and India*. Oxford: Clarendon Press.

Winch, D. 1965. *Classical Political Economy and Colonies*. London: Bell & Sons; Cambridge, Mass.: Harvard University Press.

Wood, J.C. 1983. *British Economists and the Empire*. London: Croom Helm; New York: St. Martin's Press.

Cost-benefit Analysis

SUKHAMOY CHAKRAVARTY

Cost-benefit analysis is a widely used technique of applied welfare economics, which is used to throw light on the *social* desirability of undertaking an economic project. A project can be defined as an act of investment, introduction of a new commodity or a change in policy. Its analytical foundations go back to Dupuit (1844) who in his classic paper on 'consumers' surplus' can be said to have laid the foundations which in modified forms still inform a great deal of contemporary work. In an operational sense, there may be some justification for dating it back to the US Flood Control Act of 1936, as mentioned by Eckstein (1959). In postwar years, considerable impetus was imparted by the growth of a considerable literature on development programming where choice of investment projects figured very prominently. Tinbergen (1956, 1967) was amongst the first set of influential economists who strongly recommended the use of 'accounting prices', subsequently often referred to as 'shadow prices' for the appraisal of social worthwhileness of investment projects. Influential contributions were made in the 1960s by Little and Mirrlees (1969, 1974) which can be directly related to the work done by Tinbergen (1967). Marglin (1963) and Sen (1968) have provided major inputs into the discussion at different stages and were responsible along with P. Dasgupta in propounding a system of guidelines for project appraisal. The Little–Mirrlees work which was sponsored by the OECD has often been compared with the work done by Dasgupta, Marglin and Sen under the auspices of the United Nations through its specialized office at Vienna (UNIDO).

The leading idea behind cost-benefit analysis is that prevailing market prices involve significant distortions. These prices include the interest rate, the wage rate as well as the rate of foreign exchange. These distortions can arise from market imperfections of one sort or another. In addition, because of the presence of external effects, there may be an insufficiency of markets which make usual private profitability calculations misleading/inadequate as indicators for judging the desirability of introducing a specific *change* in the economic situation.

Cost-benefit analysis does not question the fundamental theorems of welfare economics, rigorously worked by Barone (1935), Lange (1942) and Arrow (1951). It is believed that if *suitable corrections* are made to the prices of goods and factors, including the adoption of an appropriate rate of time discount, a 'proper' measure of the benefit-cost ratio for a project can be obtained for purposes of ranking investment projects. For analytical reasons, the criterion generally adopted involves maximization of discounted present value of net benefits at an appropriately chosen rate of social discount rather than maximization of the 'internal rate of return', even though practising project planners often compute internal rates of return as the appropriate social rate of discount is often a matter of dispute.

1. In the literature on cost-benefit analysis, there are broadly speaking two major approaches which have been deployed by recent writers. One line goes back to the Marshallian surplus analysis as revived by Hotelling (1938) and by Hicks (1941). Despite the highly negative comments by Samuelson (1947), the appeal of the 'surplus' approach has proved very strong for certain economists for estimating the net loss to an economy because of the pressure of various distortions. Harberger (1971) has, in particular, argued the case for using the 'surplus approach' probably more forcefully than any other economist. More recently, Willig (1976) has argued that the Marshallian measure which is strictly valid only on the assumption of the 'constancy of the marginal utility of money' can serve as a good enough approximation even when this assumption is not strictly valid. Willig has obtained bounds on the 'error' likely to be committed in the general case, the bounds being dependent on the parameters of the demand function. There is probably enough justification to describe the approach as a 'partial equilibrium' approach even though Harberger (1971) has questioned it and a formal extension to the n-commodity case had been worked out by Hotelling as early as 1938. Hotelling's extension depends on a mathematical theorem which need not be valid *in the large* for a market demand function.

A different approach which may be called the 'programming approach' views the cost-benefit analysis as a part of the decentralized planning procedure, intimately connected with the maximization of an overall social welfare function subject to various side conditions. Social welfare functions can be defined as functionals which include, inter alia, intertemporal extensions as well as distributive judgements. 'Shadow prices' associated with the constrained optimization exercises are treated as the 'correct estimates' of costs and benefits which can be utilized for evaluating a given project. According to this view, the 'plan' itself consists of an ensemble of interlinked projects. Apart from anything else, the validity of this approach rests on the assumption that 'shadow prices' are in some reasonable sense 'stable' which may involve, in particular, the assumption that the project in question is a 'marginal one', although not necessarily.

A variant of cost-benefit analysis is 'cost-effectiveness' analysis which is simpler to carry out. Here benefits are exogenously specified and the problem is to minimize the costs associated with a given profile of 'benefits'. This type of analysis is often applied where some precise, usually, non-pecuniary objective is exogenously stipulated.

2. Following Tinbergen (1967), the planning problem can be broken into three phases. The first and the main phase consists of derivation of an optimum savings path which is characterized by certain associated prices such as the 'wage rate' or the rate of interest or the price of foreign exchange.

At the second stage, the sectoral problems are solved including decisions about how much to produce at home, how much to export, or how much and what to import. This is the sector phase of the planning problem. Tinbergen introduced a distinction between 'tradeables' and 'non-tradeables', a distinction subsequently used by Little and Mirrlees as well. Tinbergen uses for the solution of the 'sector-phase' a method of analysis known as the 'semi-input–output' analysis, which differs from the traditional input–output analysis pioneered by W. Leontief in so far as the inter-industry linkages are confined only to the subset consisting of non-tradeable commodities only. This can lead not merely to reduction of computations but also to savings in 'real resources' as well, especially if the economy is a small open economy where there are no upper bounds on exports.

While the sector phase of the planning problem is connected with problems of export substitution, the third phase which deals with 'project analysis' proper deals with evaluation of issues arising out of a specific act of investment pertaining to a given sector.

The 'three step procedure' is doubtless a convenient one but its validity depends on the assumption that 'feedback effects' are relatively insignificant from one phase to the other. Furthermore, the usefulness of introducing the middle phase depends on the distinction introduced between 'tradeables' and 'non-tradeables'. 'Non-tradeables' are generally defined to include construction, various services, electricity and local transportation activities. The distinction is not entirely independent of policy decisions. Hence, it is possible for two project evaluators to arrive at two independent benefit-cost estimates of a project, depending on which, decisions of the government are to be regarded as part of the 'data' of the problem.

While the three-step decomposition procedure is strongly emphasized by Tinbergen, Little and Mirrlees in their influential manual of industrial project appraisal have chosen to operate basically on a two-stage process treating phases two and three together. They treat foreign exchange as the *numéraire*, compute shadow wage rate and the accounting rate of interest from a macroeconomic optimizing model based on intertemporal utility maximization. Once these basic parameters are obtained, by valuing commodities at their 'border prices', they compute 'benefit-cost' ratios for projects, involving decisions as to which commodities to produce at home or which to import. If non-linearities are present on the export-import side, marginal export revenue and marginal import costs are used instead of fixed 'border' prices. Values of 'non-tradeables' are obtained by a suitable matrix operation which reduces them to an appropriately weighted sum of prices for 'tradeables' and 'labour'. Little and Mirrlees accept that in developing countries there exists an urban-rural wage gap as well as a state of sub-optimality of savings. The corrections to market prices are chiefly designed to correct these 'distortions'. In their analysis, various indirect taxes and subsidies as well as quotas and licences constitute distortion which the project evaluator ought to ignore in arriving at an estimate of 'true' social profitablity.

In contrast with the Little–Mirrlees procedure, the UNIDO approach associated with Dasgupta, Marglin and Sen treats consumption as the *numéraire*, and accordingly estimates a shadow price for foreign exchange along with a shadow price for investment and a shadow wage rate. The authors of the approach show considerable cognizance of various government policy decisions which affect the project choice but are not being evaluated at a given time. Many national governments which take their planning seriously, including desired levels of production of certain specified sectors and related policy decisions on matters of licensing and quotas based on considerations which are socially important even though not entirely price theoretic in character, feel more at home with UNIDO approach. This is particularly true of large size developing countries.

As Sen (1972) has pertinently observed, the question of defining the 'areas of control' is pertinent to cost-benefit computations as one is obliged to deal with a world where various departure from the optimum are the rule. In fact, the whole *raison d'être* of 'cost-benefit analysis' is the very fact that the world is imperfect and suitable corrections are called for in arriving at a proper estimate of how much net benefit accrues to society as a result of committing resources in a specified direction.

3. Important questions arise as to how to value external effects associated with a project. External economies and diseconomies are apt to be very significant in connection with certain types of projects, in the area of irrigation, power, heavy chemicals, steel, etc. The projects in these areas have significant effects on the environment or on the formation of skills in the labour force, etc. It is well known that in these cases a typical price system defined on the space of traditionally 'marketed' commodities cannot capture them. Ad hoc corrections to observed market prices will not do. If external effects are positive and the overall convexity of the feasible set is retained, it may be possible to augment the dimensionality of the commodity space to define magnitudes analogous to prices although their implementation will require complicated tax-subsidy schemes which may be information-intensive, beside being otherwise difficult to implement. With external diseconomies, the assumption of convexity of the production possibility set may cease to hold, making it impossible to implement a plan through price-based decentralized procedures.

4. Large-scale indivisibilities pose well known problems from the point of view of decentralized decision making. Mathematically, the corresponding programming models have mixed integer-linear character, assuming that the objective function is linear. While algorithms exist for solving these problems in the *primal* space,

duality results in the usual sense do not hold even though Baumol and Gomory (1960) succeeded in defining a suitable 'dual' programme for these problems which 'permit the construction of a decentralized decision making arrangement which in principle, will achieve some of the possible efficient allocation of resources'. They also noted some special features which marked these dual prices. Problems posed by indivisibilities for cost-benefit analysis are thus non-trivial. However, when attempting choice of appropriate sites and designs of river valley development schemes, or of a large airport or for that matter setting up a large metal-fuel complex, one cannot avoid having to deal with problems where at least some variables can assume only integer values. While Harberger (1971) will not hesitate to use surplus based arguments even for these large changes, many analysts cannot help having qualms about the ad hoc nature of the estimation of net benefits associated with his procedure. Sectoral programming models based on explicit articulation of inter-industrial linkages, as well as of the spatial distribution of activities along with exogenously given profiles of multiple specified benefits may be the more relevant theoretical approach enabling at least the mapping of relevant trade-offs.

5. An issue on which considerable discussion has taken place is the choice of a social discount rate. Basically, three approaches have been recommended and/or utilized. One is to use as the social discount rate the post-tax real rate of return on risk-free government bonds. This particular choice has been criticized by many economists for ignoring consumption externalities and for giving undue weighting to individual myopia, among others. Marglin (1963a) and Sen (1961) have given persuasive arguments as to why such a procedure may not be appropriate for discounting future benefits associated with public investment decisions. A second approach is to derive from the desired growth rate of the planner the underlying intertemporal substitution rate in consumption. The idea here is that properly specified intertemporal utility maximization exercised subject to production constraints will throw up as a solution the growth path of consumption along which the social rate of discount will equal the marginal rate of transformation through production (Ramsey, 1928). However, this equality will hold only if the government has the capacity to attain the desired rate of savings. Furthermore, such an exercise naturally has to assume that the relevant optimum exists, not an innocuous assumption as the literature on 'optimum savings' has demonstrated.

If, in a mixed economy, there are constraints which do not permit the government to achieve the desired level of investment, one has to take into account the social opportunity cost of capital which measures in terms of consumption, the loss inflicted by preemption of funds from private investment to public investment. Under suitable assumptions, Marglin (1963b) obtained a measure of the social opportunity cost of capital which depends on the social rate of discount (r), the rate of return from private investment in peretuity (p) and a parameter θ_1 representing the amount of public investment displaced by each dollar of public investment ($0 \leqslant \theta_1 \leqslant 1$). Under these assumptions, the social opportunity cost of capital is measured by the expression $[\theta_1 p + (1 - \theta_1)r]/r$ (formula 4 in Marglin, 1963b).

Most developing countries are characterized by substantial amounts of 'structural unemployment'. Furthermore, they suffer from sub-optimality of savings as well. Under these circumstances, even if the opportunity cost of labour employed on industrial or infrastructure projects in terms of output foregone in the rest of the economy is zero, there is likely to be a cost associated with additional consumption that is connected with wage employment. If savings were at an optimal level, such consumption cannot be treated as a social cost. In the presence of government's inability to reach the appropriate level of savings, the 'market wage' will need to be corrected so as to reflect the social cost of employing additional labour, even though such labour would have remained unemployed otherwise. The 'shadow wage' rate which figures in social cost-benefit analysis is then, seen to depend upon three sets of considerations: (a) labour's opportunity cost, which may be zero, if extreme assumptions are made; (b) the industrial wage rate; and (c) the social opportunity cost of capital. Marglin (1976) and Sen (1968) have dealt with this problem in considerable detail.

Opinions are divided amongst economists as to whether cost-benefit analysts should pay explicit attention to considerations posed by income redistribution which are likely to rise in practice whenever an economy policy or an investment project is going to be implemented. Some argue that cost-benefit analysts should concentrate on the 'efficiency related' issues alone and thus ignore distributional considerations. Musgrave (1969) has talked about the pragmatic need for separating 'allocative' objectives from 'distributional' objectives. He has been supported in this case very forcefully by Harberger (1971). On the other side, Eckstein (1959), Marglin (1965) and others have strongly advocated the case for including distributional considerations alongside efficiency considerations. The question of how best to take into account the distributional considerations has also figured in the literature, should it be agreed that cost-benefit analysis cannot ignore these issues.

On the basic question of including distributional judgements explicitly, it would appear that the crucial point is that of identifying the major operative constraints. If the government has available to itself an armoury of non-distortionary taxes and subsidies, there could be pragmatic reason for ignoring distributional considerations. However, this is rarely the case. It would, then be quite appropriate to accord explicit distributional weights depending on the accrual of benefit streams to different classes or sections of society. The relevant issue, then, becomes, how best to express these weights. On this point, it is less easy to recommend any specific procedure although Benthamite and modified Benthamite weighting patterns have been recommended by several economists (Eckstein, 1964).

How do we evaluate the usefulness of cost-benefit analysis as a decision theoretic tool? Kornai (1979) has described cost-benefit analysis as 'enlightened orthodoxy', orthodox because of its adherence to the basic paradigm provided by neoclassical economic theory and 'enlightened' because it does recognize that reality differs in significant respects from the 'wetbild' of the neoclassical economist.

Kornai identifies three major axioms underlying cost-benefit analysis. These are the *existence* of a social welfare function, identification of the objective of decentralized decision makers with the maximization of the *social profit* function and finally the assumptions of *convexity* of production possibility sets along with the concavity of social welfare functions. With good reason, he raises significant doubts about the plausibility of all these three axioms. The important question, however, is whether these doubts invalidate the use of cost-benefit analysis as a practical tool.

Practical planning experience would appear to suggest that cost-benefit analysis has a useful role to play in conjuncction with other instruments of economic policy which help to determine aggregative features of an economy along with the choice of appropriate production and foreign trade structures. If the cost-benefit analysis is viewed as a part of the broader argument for 'planning in stages', some of the criticisms levelled by Kornai would appear as less damaging than otherwise.

This is because such an approach avoids the necessity of viewing the entire planning problem as *one* grand optimization exercise, at one extreme (Frisch, 1976), and the reduction of the national plan to a mere ensemble of projects, on the other (Little and Mirrlees, 1974).

Planning in stages observes the need for devising a coherent macroeconomic policy and planning framework which ensures non-inflationary growth at a desired rate along with balance of payments equilibrium. In the process of implementing this, it also takes into account the indispensible inter-industry links as well. As a part of this procedure, the use of cost-benefit analysis can prove very useful as it avoids wasteful use of resources at the micro level along with preventing the emergence of additional distortions in the process of income generation if suitable distributional weights are allowed for.

More importantly, it forces the collection of relevant data on the project level in a coherent framework. Along with the use of sensitivity analysis with respect to relevant national parameters, it can distinguish between projects which are more 'robust' from the social angle as distinguished from those which are just marginal or highly questionable. Finally, it helps significantly in enhancing the quality of the dialogue between the central planners on the one hand and planners who operate much lower down in the hierarchy of the decision making process.

BIBLIOGRAPHY

Arrow, K.J. 1951. An extension of the basic theorems of classical welfare economics. In *Proceedings of the Second Berkeley Symposium*, Berkeley: University of California.

Arrow, K.J. and Hurwicz, L. 1960. Decentralization and computation in resource allocation. In *Essays in Honor of Harold Hotelling*, ed. R.W. Pfouts, Chapel Hill: University of North Carolina Press.

Barone, E. 1908. The Ministry of Production in the collectivist state. Trans. in *Collectivist Economic Planning*, ed. F.A. Hayek, London: G. Routledge & Sons, 1935.

Baumol, W.J. and Gomory, R.E. 1960. Integer programming and pricing. *Econometrica* 28, July, 521–50.

Dasgupta, P. 1972. A comparative analysis of the UNIDO guidelines and the OECD Manual. *Bulletin of the Oxford University Institute of Economics and Statistics* 34(1), February, 33–51.

Dupuit, J. 1844. *On the Measurement of the Utility of Public Works.* Trans. in *International Economic Papers* No. 2, London: Macmillan, 1952.

Eckstein, O. 1958. *Water Resource Development: The Economics of Project Evaluation.* Cambridge, Mass.: Harvard University Press.

Eckstein, O. 1959. A survey of the theory of public expenditure criteria. In *Conference on Public Finances: Needs, Sources and Utilization,* New York: NBER.

Eckstein, O. 1964. *Public Finance.* Englewood Cliffs: Prentice Hall.

Frisch, R. 1976. *Economic Planning Studies.* Ed. F.V. Long, Dordrecht: Reidel.

Harberger, A.C. 1971. Three basic postulates for applied welfare economics: an interpretative essay. *Journal of Economic Literature* 9(3), September, 785–97.

Harberger, A.C. 1972. Project evaluation. In A.C. Harberger, *Collected Papers,* London: Macmillan.

Layard, R. (ed.) 1976. *Cost-benefit Analysis, Selected Readings.* Harmondsworth: Penguin.

Little, I.M.D. and Mirrlees, J.A. 1968. *Manual of Industrial Project Analysis in Developing Countries.* Vol. II, *Social Cost Benefit Analysis.* Paris: OECD.

Little, I.M.D. and Mirrlees, J.A. 1974. *Project Appraisal and Planning for Developing Countries.* London: Heinemann Educational Books.

Hicks, J.R. 1941. The rehabilitation of consumers' surplus. *Review of Economic Studies* 8, February, 108–16.

Hotelling, H. 1938. The general welfare in relation to problems of taxation and of railway and utility rates. *Econometrica* 6, July, 242–69.

Kornai, J. 1979. Appraisal of project appraisal. In *Economics and Human Welfare,* ed. Michael J. Boskin, New York: Academic Press.

Marglin, S.A. 1963a. The social rate of discount and the optimal rate of investment. *Quarterly Journal of Economics* 77, February, 95–111.

Marglin, S.A. 1963b. The opportunity cost of public investment. *Quarterly Journal of Economics* 77, May, 274–89.

Marglin, S.A. 1967. *Public Investment Criteria.* London: Allen & Unwin; Cambridge, Mass.: MIT Press.

Marglin, S.A. 1976. *Value and Price in a Labour Surplus Economy.* Oxford: Oxford University Press.

Musgrave, R.A. 1969. Cost-benefit analysis and the theory of public finance. *Journal of Economic Literature* 7(3), September, 797–806.

Pigou, A.C. 1932. *The Economics of Welfare.* 4th edn, London: Macmillan; 4th edn, New York: Macmillan, 1938.

Prest, A.R. and Turvey, R. 1965. Cost-benefit analysis: a survey. *Economic Journal* 75, December, 683–735.

Ramsey, F.P. 1928. A mathematical theory of saving. *Economic Journal* 38, December, 543–59.

Sen, A.K. 1961. On optimising the rate of saving. *Economic Journal* 71, September, 479–96.

Sen, A.K. 1968. *Choice of Techniques.* 3rd edn, Oxford: Basil Blackwell.

Sen, A.K. 1972. Control areas and accounting prices: an approach to economic evaluation. *Economic Journal* 82, Supplement, March, 486–501.

Samuelson, P.A. 1947. *Foundations of Economic Analysis.* Cambridge, Mass.: Harvard University Press.

Tinbergen, J. 1958. *The Design of Development.* Baltimore: Johns Hopkins Press.

Tinbergen, J. 1967. *Development Planning*. London: Weidenfield & Nicolson.
UNIDO (United Nations Industrial Development Organisation). 1972. *Guidelines for Project Evaluation*. Authors: P. Dasgupta, S.A. Marglin and A.K. Sen. New York: United Nations.
Willig, R.D. 1976. Consumers' surplus without apology. *American Economic Review* 66(4), September, 589–97.

Countertrade

HELGA HOFFMANN

Countertrade is an international commercial transaction in which the seller agrees to receive goods or services as partial or total settlement for goods or services delivered. In its simplest form, countertrade is a barter or a one-time swap of goods or services without cash payment.

Countertrade has been expanding rapidly since the beginning of the 1980s. But this is not a new phenomenon. Forms of countertrade in Europe can be traced back to before World War II and in the immediate postwar period bilateral trade and payments agreements were widespread among European countries pursuing trade despite non-convertibility of their currencies and/or lack of international liquidity. In Latin America barter-like deals were also common in the immediate postwar period, due to decreasing dollar and gold reserves. Later they receded, when international arrangements favoured a more open multilateral trading system (Outters-Jaeger, 1979, pp. 11–14). Centrally planned economies always favoured countertrade as part of their planning system. Therefore, for some decades, countertrade was typical in East-West trade.

The most common form of countertrade is the *counterpurchase*, in which importation by a firm or country is conditional on its trading partner accepting its exports. Often one side of the deal involves some homogeneous bulk product, agricultural or mineral. Crude oil became the single most important commodity in countertrade in the first half of the 1980s. By mid-decade some 25 per cent of OPEC oil production might have been involved in countertrade, from the settling of outstanding debt for construction work to the purchase of military equipment.

Another form, in which countertrade is in fact used to finance direct investment, is the *buy-back*. In buy-back arrangements, typically, a developed country supplies equipment or a turnkey plant and is paid in the future output of the project. Buy-back is often broader than the exchange of capital goods for resultant products, and might include loans, technology transfer, initial operation of the plant, the establishment of joint ventures and, sometimes, tripartite countertrade arrangements. For example, the Peruvian Government, in the early 1980s, contracted with a French engineering firm to build a petroleum refinery paid partly in refinery products. The French engineering firm, which had built petrochemical plants in Bulgaria, disposed of some of its countertrade obligations from Bulgaria by commissioning a Bulgarian engineering firm to supply and erect the storage tanks for the refinery in Peru.

A common form of countertrade among industrialized countries is the *offset*. Offset is the traditional title of compensatory transactions involving aircraft and military equipment. Offset can be directly related to the equipment sold, as the coproduction or subcontracting of some of the components in the buyer's country, the funding of operations of a joint company or the transfer of technology. But offset might take the form of a commitment to purchase goods and services unrelated to the military equipment sold (indirect offset). Thus, when a United States company sold F-5 fighter aircraft to Switzerland in 1975, the compensatory arrangements included finding export markets for various Swiss products, facilitating Swiss participation in foreign capital projects and assisting with tourist promotion. According to a survey of the US International Trade Commission, military offset represented 80 per cent of United States countertrade sales in 1984 (Group of Thirty, 1985, p. 6).

While at the beginning of the 1970s not much more than a dozen countries, mostly East European, were involved in countertrade, by the middle of the 1980s it had spread to nearly every country in the world. Most of the larger banks and corporations had established specialized countertrade divisions and a whole array of trading companies and law firms were in the business of matching potential countertrade partners (Jones, 1984). Countertrade might have surpassed 10 per cent of world trade in 1985.

Several reasons explain the latest surge in countertrade. The more recent requests came mostly from developing countries and they have been rising parallel to the worsening of the international economic environment for these countries and their mounting balance of payments difficulties (United Nations, 1986). Economic slack through much of the world and a weakening of the relationship between international trade and world output had among its manifestations depressed primary commodities markets and a persistent and fairly generalized decline in commodity prices in the first half of the 1980s. Terms of trade worsened for developing countries, which continued to accumulate debt. Subsequent debt servicing difficulties were followed by a dramatic decline in the flow of finance to developing countries. Demand for countertrade became more evident in developing countries particularly after the drying-up of voluntary bank lending and export credit cover that followed the Mexican debt crisis of 1982 (United Nations, 1986). With export earnings of developing countries falling or growing at a rate below the interest rate of their debt and with a high proportion of their export earnings tied up in debt repayment, countertrade became a way of assuring specific imports. In this sense, countertrade is a form of import finance for developing countries lacking alternative. Many developing countries are resorting to it owing to reciprocal impossibility of cash payments or credit. Thus, South-South trade, which suffered more than proportionately when developing countries had to produce a trade surplus and cut imports to pay their debt service, is gaining new impulse through countertrade.

When access to markets becomes more limited and uncertain, it can be expected that firms or countries will use their import potential as tool to open markets for their exports. In fact, firms from industrialized countries are increasingly offering countertrade as one more competitive peg in the battle for outlets. Countertrade may also be used to circumvent foreign exchange controls. When the import of a product has low priority in the foreign exchange allocations of a developing country, foreign suppliers have discovered that the obtaining of the contract might be quicker if they are willing to accept countertrade. In general, reciprocity demands – and countertrade can be seen as one of them – are tried as means of cutting through trade barriers and they grow with them. Countertrade tended to increase along with the erosion of the international trading system.

Critics of countertrade have argued that it necessarily imposes extra costs. The theoretical argument rests on the inefficiency implicit in arranging the 'double coincidence of wants' which is the prerequisite of any barter deal. The introduction of money reduced the cost of commercial transactions, because the efforts once wasted in trying to match sellers and buyers could be devoted instead to production. Therefore, if money exists as a means of exchange, barter (or countertrade) is irrational. However, the traditional case against barter was presented in the context of a closed economy. The implication of extending the argument to international trade is that all trading partners have equal access to the same monetary instruments. If access to hard currency is not present or is even partial, the theoretical case against barter does not hold, and we are back to the basic tenet that some trade (even barter) is better than no trade at all.

It is no coincidence that countertrade expanded in a period of sluggish world economic growth, of relatively slow growth in international trade and of proliferation of various forms of protectionism. Under these conditions, the observed increase in countertrade arrangements should not be seen in comparison with an ideal trade situation but rather as a pragmatic response to the peculiar conditions now prevailing in the international trading and financial system.

BIBLIOGRAPHY

Group of Thirty. 1985. *Countertrade in the World Economy*. New York.

Jones, S.F. 1984. *North–South Countertrade*. Special report No. 174, London: The Economist Intelligence Unit.

Organization for Economic Co-operation and Development. 1985. *Countertrade: developing country practices*. Paris: OECD.

Outters-Jaeger, I. 1979. *The Development Impact of Barter in Developing Countries*. Paris: Development Centre of the Organization for Economic Co-operation and Development.

UNCTAD. 1986. *Countertrade. Background note by the UNCTAD Secretariat*. New York; UNCTAD.

United Nations. 1986. Countertrade in developing countries. *Supplement to the World Economic Survey 1985–1986*, New York: United Nations (Sales No. ST/ESA/188).

Courcelle-Seneuil,
Jean Gustave

ALBERT O. HIRSCHMAN

French economist and economic adviser. Born in the Dordogne in 1813, Courcelle-Seneuil studied law in Paris, then returned to his native region to manage an industrial firm. At the same time, during the July monarchy, he wrote for Republican newspapers and economic periodicals. After the 1848 Revolution, he held briefly a high position in the Ministry of France. In the following years, he became a frequent contributor to the *Journal des économistes*, and published a successful textbook on banking in 1852. In 1853, the Chilean government contracted him to teach economics at the University of Chile in Santiago, and to be available as official economic adviser; he stayed for ten years, until 1863, when he returned to France. While in Chile, he published his most ambitious work in economics, the *Traité théorique et pratique d'économie politique* (1858), which the Chilean Government arranged to bring out in a Spanish translation. After his return to France, he resumed his activity as prolific writer of books and articles on economic affairs. He also published several works on political and historical topics and translated into French John Stuart Mill's *Principles of Political Economy*, Sumner Maine's *Ancient Law* and William Graham Sumner's *What Social Classes Owe to Each Other*. He was appointed councillor of state in 1879, and three years later was elected member of the Académie des Sciences Morales et Politiques. He died in 1892.

Throughout his life, Courcelle-Seneuil was a stalwart defender of free trade and *laissez faire*. Charles Gide, the co-author (with Charles Rist) of a well-known history of economic doctrines, wrote about him in rather sarcastic terms:

> He was virtually the *pontifex maximus* of the classical school; the holy doctrines were entrusted to him and it was his vocation to denounce and exterminate the heretics. During many years he fulfilled this mission through book reviews in the *Journal des économistes* with priestly dignity. Argus-eyed, he knew how to detect the slightest deviations from the liberal school (Gide, 1895, p. 710).

Courcelle-Seneuil's special interest, starting with the publication of a small book on bank reform in 1840, was the introduction of more freedom into banking or, to use a modern term, the 'deregulation' of this industry. Above all, he advocated the abolition of the Bank of France's exclusive right of issue. According to Gide, Courcelle-Seneuil was more esteemed in England and the United States than in France. In any event, adoption of his monetary and banking proposals was never seriously considered in his own country.

Once in Chile, Courcelle-Seneuil became a powerful policy maker and influential teacher. He arrived at a time when the international prestige of the *laissez faire* doctrine was at its height and when gold booms and subsequent busts in California and Australia caused considerable fluctuations in Chile's agricultural exports to these areas, creating a need for flexible short- and long-term credit facilities. This combination of events, joined with the prestige emanating from the foreign savant, permitted him to obtain in Chile what he had failed to achieve in his own country: under his guidance, the administration of Manuel Montt (1851–61) promulgated a banking law that established total freedom for any solvent person to found a bank and permitted all banks to issue currency subject only to one limitation: the banknotes in circulation were not to exceed 150 per cent of the issuing bank's capital.

Courcelle-Seneuil's advice was also sought in connection with a new customs tariff and here again he achieved substantial change: the level of protection was severly cut back, although some tariffs were retained for revenue purposes.

But the principal influence exercised by Courcelle-Seneuil resided in his forceful teaching: as the University of Chile's first professor of economics, he was apparently successful in instilling doctrinaire zeal in his students, some of whom later became influential policy makers. Thus, Chilean historians have not only traced the abandonment of convertibility in 1878 to the permissiveness of the 1860 Banking Law and the lack of industrial development to the 1864 tariff; they also see Courcelle-Seneuil's indirect influence in the acquisition of the nitrate mines of Tarapacá by private foreign interests after Chile's victory over Peru in the War of the Pacific (1882) had given it title to the mines. Alienation of the mines was indeed recommended by a government committee dominated by Courcelle-Seneuil's disciples, who felt, like their teacher, that state ownership and management of business enterprises was to be strictly shunned. Secular inflation, industrial backwardness, domination of the country's principal natural resources by foreigners – all of these protracted ills of the Chilean economy have been attributed to the French expert.

Since the economically advanced countries were also those where economic science first flourished, they soon produced a peculiar export product: the foreign economic expert or adviser. Courcelle-Seneuil is probably the earliest prototype of the genre and his ironic career in Chile exhibits characteristics that were to remain typical of numerous later representatives. First, the adviser is deeply convinced that, thanks to the advances of economic science, he knows the correct solutions to economic problems no matter where they arise. Secondly, the country which invites the expert looks forward to his advice as to some magic medicine which will work even when (perhaps especially when) it hurts. Some countries seem particularly prone to this attitude. In Chile foreign or foreign-trained experts have played key roles at crisis junctures, from Courcelle-Seneuil in the mid-19th century to Edwin Kemmerer in the 1920s, the Klein–Saks Mission in the 1950s, and finally to the 'Chicago boys' in the 1970s. Thirdly, the influence of the adviser derives not only from the intrinsic value and persuasiveness of his message, but from the fact that he usually has good connection in his home country and can therefore facilitate access to its capital market. Courcelle-Seneuil, for example, suspended his university courses in 1858–9 to accompany a Chilean financial mission that travelled to France in search of a railroad construction loan. Fourthly, the foreign adviser is often criticized for wishing to transplant the institutions of his own country to the country he advises, but his real ambition is more extravagant: it is to endow the country with those ideal institutions which exist in his mind only, for he has been unable to persuade his own countrymen to adopt them. Fifthly, history in general, and nationalist historiography in particular, is likely to be unkind to the foreign adviser. In retrospect he can easily become a universal scapegoat: whatever went wrong is attributed to his nefarious influence. This demonization is more damaging than the adviser himself could possibly have been: it forestalls authentic learning from past experience.

SELECTED WORKS

1840. *Le crédit et la Banque.* Paris.
1858. *Traité théoretique et pratique d'économie politique*, 2 vols, Paris: Amyot.
1867. *La Banque libre.* Paris: Guillaumin.

BIBLIOGRAPHY

Encina, F. 1951. *Historia de Chile.* Santiago: Nascimiento, Vol. 18, ch. 58.
Fuentealba, H.L. 1946. *Courcelle-Seneuil en Chile*: errores del liberalismo económico. Santiago: Prensas de la Universidad de Chile.
Gide, C. 1895. Die neuere volkswirtschaftliche Litteratur Frankreichs. *Schmollers Jahrbuch.*
Hirschman, A.O. 1963. *Journeys toward Progress.* New York: Twentieth Century Fund, 163–8.
Journal des économistes. July 1892. Obituary [of M. J.G. Courcelle-Seneuil].
Juglar, C. 1895. Notice sur la vie et les travaux de M. J.G. Courcelle-Seneuil. Académie des Sciences Morales et Politiques. *Compte Rendu*, 850–82.
Pinto, S.C. 1959. *Chile, un caso de desarrollo frustrado.* Santiago: Edit. Universitaria.
Will, R.M. 1964. The introduction of classical economics into Chile. *Hispanic-American Historical Review* 44(1), February, 1–21.

Dependency

J.G. PALMA

The general field of study of dependency analysis is the development of peripheral capitalism. Its most important contribution is its attempt to analyse it from the point of view of the interplay between internal and external structures. Its most well-known feature is the internal debate about whether capitalism remains 'historically progressive' in the Third World (i.e. capable of developing the productive forces of these societies and thus able to lead them towards socialism).

With the necessary degree of simplification which every classification of intellectual tendencies entails, one can distinguish four major approaches – not mutually exclusive from the point of view of intellectual history – in dependency analysis: (i) dependency as a theory of 'inhibited' capitalist development in the periphery; (ii) dependency as an analysis of concrete processes of development; (iii) dependency as a theory of the 'development of underdevelopment'; (iv) dependency as a reformulation of the structuralist analysis of Latin American development. The first two have in common the fact that they analyse the process of capitalist development in the periphery as historically progressive, but do so in a different way from the one predicted by Marx and Engels (for the classical marxist view on capitalist development in the periphery, see Palma, 1978). The main difference between these two first approaches to dependency lies in the fact that each has a different reason for their disagreement with classical marxist analysis. While one approach departs from it mainly arguing changes in 'circumstances' – the world capitalist system has been transformed in such a way that the industrialization of the periphery cannot take place in the way predicted by Marx and Engels – the other puts the emphasis on changes in 'diagnosis'; Marx's analysis is itself over-optimistic regarding the possibilities of industrialization in the backward areas of the world.

The other two approaches have in common their extreme scepticism regarding the possibilities of industrialization in the periphery – a postulate that goes against the spirit and the letter of Marx's writings. The main difference between these two second approaches is that while for one not only is there no possibility of capitalist development in the periphery at present, but there has never been one and there will never be one (i.e. there is no escape from the 'development of underdevelopment' within this system); for the other approach there are still certain alternatives to this supposed 'accumulation of backwardness'.

DEPENDENCY AS A THEORY OF 'INHIBITED' CAPITALIST DEVELOPMENT IN THE PERIPHERY. Ever since the end of the 19th century (the period of the 'Classics of Imperialism') Marxist analysis has put emphasis in the necessity of a 'bourgeois democratic revolution' as an essential requirement for any backward society to be able to embark in a process of capitalist development proper. In the words of Rosa Luxemburg '[bourgeois] revolution is an essential for the process of capitalist emancipation. The backward communities must shed their obsolete political organizations, and create a modern State machinery adapted to the purpose of capitalist production' (1913, p. 395). The main intellectual and political concern of this approach to dependency analysis is an attempt to explain why this 'bourgeois-democratic' revolution has not taken place as expected after the process of political independence in the Third World, and how this is inhibiting their process of capitalist development.

In the Marxist literature, the 'bourgeois democratic' revolution is defined as a revolt of the forces of production against the old outmoded relations of production. In this way the structure of the old political and legal system would be broken and a new economic expansion would be expected to take place. This revolution would be based on an alliance between the bourgeoisie and the proletariat; the principal battle line would be between bourgeoisie and the traditional oligarchies, between industry and land, capitalism versus pre-capitalist forms of monopoly and privilege; because it is the result of the pressure of a rising class whose path is being blocked in economic and social terms, the revolution would bring not only political emancipation but economic progress as well (i.e. it could be seen as a 'supply side' explanation to the obstacles to economic development in the Third World).

Nevertheless, the political independence of the backward nations has not been followed by these developments, contrary to the expectations of the 'Classics of Imperialism'. Even more, in the case of most of the periphery it is precisely in the post-colonial period that the development of individual nations (with the due economic and political variations) has taken upon itself the articulation with the advanced capitalist countries which the classical writers on imperialism noted in the colonies – the growth of their productive sectors concentrated on primary products, whether mineral or agricultural; the limited degree of industrialization; and financial dependence. For this reason, this group of dependency writers attempt to explain why the 'bourgeois-democratic' revolution is being hindered and what the consequences of this are. Their main argument is that the process of industrialization in the backward countries is contradictory not only with some internally dominant groups, but also with imperialism. For this reason, the ability of the incipient national bourgeoisies to develop in the post-colonial phase would depend upon their political capacity to assert themselves over these two groups. This double contradiction in capitalist development in the periphery (particularly in the process of industrialization) would tend to be transformed into a single contradiction through the alliance of the groups in question (the so-called 'feudal-imperialist alliance'). This type of approach to dependency figures prominently in the political and economic analysis of large sectors of the Latin American left (including some Communist parties of the subcontinent). Further-more, it seems to have had an important influence – albeit an unacknowledged one – upon the original ECLA analysis of the obstacles facing Latin American development (*see* STRUCTURALISM).

DEPENDENCY AS AN ANALYSIS OF CONCRETE PROCESSES OF DEVELOPMENT. The two main characteristics of this approach to dependency are, first, that it does not take classical marxist theory of development as a mechanical continuum of discrete stages through which each backward society must pass, not least because when this theory was formulated it was not based on any concrete experience of capitalist development in the periphery (although when it was formulated there were already several experiences of it, particularly in Latin America), but mainly on an extrapolation of the experience of Western Europe. Secondly, from a methodological point of view, it does not aspire to build an alternative mechanico-formal theory of development applicable to all the periphery and at all times, but to concentrate on the study of what have been called 'concrete situations of dependency'. In the words of F.H. Cardoso,

> The question which we should ask ourselves is why, it being obvious that the capitalist economy tends towards a growing internationalization, societies are divided into antagonistic classes, and that the particular is to a certain extent conditioned by the general, with these premises we have not gone beyond the partial – and therefore abstract in the Marxist sense – characterization of the Latin American situation and historical process (1974, pp. 326–7).

Briefly, this second approach to the analysis of dependency (which emerged with the publication of Cardoso and Faletto, 1967) can be expressed as follows:

(i) In common with the other approaches to dependency, this second approach sees the peripheral economies as an integral part of the world capitalist system, in a context of its increasing internationalization; it also argues that the central dynamic of that system lies outside the peripheral economies and that therefore the options which lie open to them are limited (but not determined) by the development of the system at the centre; in this way the particular is in some way conditioned by the general. Therefore, a basic element for the understanding of these societies is given by the 'general determinants' of the world capitalist system, which is itself changing through time; the analysis therefore requires primarily an understanding of the contemporary characteristics of the world capitalist system. One characteristic of this approach to dependency, and one which has been widely recognized, has been to incorporate more successfully into its analysis of Latin America development the transformations which are occurring and have occurred in the world capitalist system, and in particular the changes which became significant towards the end of the 1950s in the rhythm and the form of capitalist movement, and in the international division of labour, one of the most important being the emergence of the so-called multinational corporation which progressively transformed centre-periphery relationships, and relationships between countries of the centre. As foreign capital has increasingly been directed towards manufacturing industry in the periphery, the struggle for industrialization, which was previously seen as an anti-imperialist struggle, in a way has become increasingly the goal of foreign capital. Thus dependency and industrialization cease to be 'contradictory' and a path of 'dependent development' becomes possible.

(ii) Furthermore, this approach not only accepts as a starting point and improves upon the analysis of the location of the economies of the periphery in the world capitalist system, but also accepts and enriches their demonstration that these societies are structured through unequal and antagonistic patterns of social organization, showing the social asymmetries and the exploitative character of social organization which arise from its socio-economic base; it also gives considerable importance to the effect of the diversity of natural resources, geographical location, and so on, of each economy, thus extending significantly the analysis of the 'internal determinants' of the development of the peripheral economies.

(iii) But while these improvements are important, the most significant feature of this approach is that it goes beyond these points, and insists that from the premises so far outlined one necessarily arrives at a *partial, abstract* and *indeterminate* characterization of the peripheral historical process, which can only be overcome by understanding how the 'general' and 'specific' determinants interact in particular and concrete situations. It is only by understanding the specificity of the movement in these societies as a dialectical unity of both, and a synthesis of these 'internal' and 'external' factors, that one can explain the particularity of social, political and economic processes in the dependent societies.

DEPENDENCY AS A THEORY OF THE 'DEVELOPMENT OF UNDERDEVELOPMENT'. This approach to dependency analysis was first developed at the end of the 1950s, and took off with the publication of Paul Baran's *Political Economy of Growth* (1957). It is characterized by the acceptance, almost as an axiomatic truth, of the argument that no third world country can now expect to break out of a state of economic dependency and advance to an economic position closest to that of the major capitalist industrial powers. This is a very important proposition since it not only establishes the extent to which capitalism remains historically progressive in the modern world, but also thereby defines the economic background to political action. Yet, too often, the question is ill defined; it is not at all self-evident; its intellectual origins are obscure; and its actual foundations are in need of a fuller analysis.

Starting out with this 'stagnationist' analysis, André Gunder Frank (1967) attempted to develop the thesis that the only political solution is a revolution of an immediate socialist character, totally de-linked from the world capitalist system for within its context there could be no alternative to underdevelopment. Although Frank did not go very far in his analysis of the capitalist system as a whole, its origins and development – and why it could only offer destruction to the periphery – Immanuel Wallerstein tackled this tremendous challenge in his remarkable book (1974).

The central line of Frank's analysis regarding the complete lack of historical progressiveness of capitalism in the third world is continued (among many others) by Dos Santos (1970), Marini (1972), Caputo and Pizarro (1974), and Hinkelamert (1970). This type of approach to dependency analysis has been criticized from all sides, and on almost every point in their analysis: see Laclau (1971), Brenner (1977), Cardoso (1974), Warren (1980) and Palma (1978).

DEPENDENCY AS A REFORMULATION OF STRUCTURALIST ANALYSIS OF LATIN AMERICAN DEVELOPMENT. Towards the middle of the 1960s the UN Economic Commission for Latin America (ECLA) analyses were overtaken by gradual decline, in which many factors intervened. The statistics relating to Latin American development in the period after the Korean War presented a gloomy picture which was interpreted in different ways as indicating the failure of the policies ECLA had been proposing since its foundation. Furthermore, the first attempts to introduce into the traditional ECLA analysis a number of 'social aspects' (Prebisch, 1963) far from strengthening the analysis, revealed its fragility (see Cardoso, 1977). One of the results of the relative decline in their influence of ECLA's analysis was the emergence of an attempt to reformulate its thought.

This attempt took place just at the time when an important sector of the Latin American left was breaking with the first approach discussed above (capitalist development was both necessary and possible but hindered by the 'feudal-imperialist alliance') and moving towards the third one ('development of underdevelopment'). Not only did the different processes of reformulation take place at the same time, but they had an extremely important element in common: *pessimism* regarding the possibility and viability of capitalist development in the periphery.

The irony was that while both groups were busy writing and publishing different versions of stagnationist theories which did not take into account the cyclical pattern characterist of capitalist development (the most sophisticated perhaps being Furtado, 1966), international trade was picking up, the terms of trade were changing in favour of Latin America, and some countries were able to take advantage of the favourable situation and accelerated rapidly the rhythm of their economic development. Thus, as Cardoso (1977, p. 33) remarks, 'history has prepared a trap for pessimists'.

But if the attempt at reformulation which followed the crisis in ECLA school of thought did not succeed in grasping the transformations which were occurring at that moment in the world capitalist system, it did in time produce together with the abandonment of stagnationist theories, a movement towards a more structural-historical analysis of Latin America (of the type discussed in the second approach above). The first substantial critique of stagnationist theories came from Tavares and Serra (1970); see also Pinto (1965 and 1974), Sunkel and Paz (1970) and Cariola and Sunkel (1982) among others.

BIBLIOGRAPHY

Amin, S. 1972. Underdevelopment and dependence in Black Africa: origins and contemporary forms. *Journal of Modern African Studies* 10, 503–25.

Amin, S. 1973. *Neocolonialism in West Africa*. Harmondsworth: Penguin.

Amin, S. 1976. *Unequal Exchange*. Brighton: Harvester.

Baran, P.A. 1957. *The Political Economy of Growth*. New York: Monthly Review Press.

Brenner, R. 1977. The origins of capitalist development: a critique of neo-Smithian Marxism. *New Left Review* 104, 25–93.

Caputo, O. and Pizarro, R. 1974. *Dependencia y relaciones internacionales*. San José, Costa Rica: Editorial Universitaria Centroamericana.

Cardoso, F.H. 1972. Dependency and development in Latin America. *New Left Review* 74, 83–95.

Cardoso, F.H. 1976. The consumption of dependency theory in the US. *Latin America Research Review* 12, 17–24.

Cardoso, F.H. and Faletto, E. 1979. *Dependency and Development in Latin America*. Trans. by Marjory Mattingly Urquidi, Berkeley: University of California Press. (A translation and revision of *Dependencia y desarrollo en América Latina*, Mexico: Siglo Veintiuno Editores, 1971; first version, 1967).

Cariola, C. and Sunkel, O. 1982. *Un Siglo de Historia Económica de Chile, 1830–1930*. Madrid: Ediciones Cultura Hispanica. Also in *The Latin American Economies: growth and the export sector, 1880–1930*, ed. R. Cortez Conde and S.J. Hunt, New York: Holmes and Meier.

Dos Santos, T. 1969. The crisis of development theory and the problems of dependency in Latin America. In *Underdevelopment and Development*, ed. H. Bernstein, Harmondsworth: Penguin.

Dos Santos, T. 1970. The structure of dependency. *American Economic Review, Papers and Proceedings* 60, 231–6.

Frank, A.G. 1967. *Capitalism and Underdevelopment in Latin America. Historical Studies of Chile and Brazil*. New York, London: Monthly Review Press.

Frank, A.G. 1977. Dependency is dead, long live dependency and the class struggle: an answer to critics. *World Development* 5, 355–70.

Furtado, C. 1966. *Subdesarrollo y Estancamiento en América Latina*. Buenos Aires: Editorial Universitaria de Buenos Aires.

Hinkelamert, 1970. *El Subdesarrollo Latinoamericano: un caso de desarrollo capitalista*. Santiago: Ediciones Nueva Universidad, Universidad Catolica de Chile.

Laclau, E. 1971. Feudalism and imperialism in Latin America. *New Left Review* 67, 19–38.

Lenin, V.I. 1899. *The Development of Capitalism in Russia*. Moscow: Progress Publishers, 1964.

Luxemburg, R. 1913. *Die Akkumulation des Kapitals, ein Beitrag zur ökonomischen Erklärung des Imperialismus*. Berlin: P. Singer. Trans. by Agnes Schwartzschild as *The Accumulation of Capital*, London: Routledge and Kegan Paul, 1951; New Haven: Yale University Press.

Marini, R.M. 1972. Brazilian sub-imperialism. *Monthly Review* 9, 14–24.

O'Brien, P. 1975. A critique of Latin American theories of dependency. In O. Oxaal, T. Barnet and D. Booth, *Beyond the Sociology of Development*, London: Routledge & Kegan Paul.

Owen, R. and Sutcliffe, B. 1972. *Studies in the Theory of Imperialism*. London: Longman.

Palma, J.G. 1973. *La Via Chilena al Socialismo*. Mexico: Siglo XXI Editores.

Palma, J.G. 1978. Dependency: a formal theory of underdevelopment or a methodology for the analysis of concrete situations of underdevelopment? *World Development* 6, 881–924.

Pinto, A. and Knakel, J. 1972. The centre-periphery system 20 years later. In *International Economics and Development: Essays in Honour of Raul Prebisch*, ed. L.E. di Marco, New York and London: Academic Press.

Prebisch, R. 1963. *Hacia una dinámica del desarrollo latinoamericano*. Mexico: Fondo Cultura Económica. Trans. as *Towards a Dynamic Development Policy for Latin America*. New York: United Nations.

Rodriguez, O. 1980. '*La Teoria' del Subdesarrollo de la CEPAL* Mexico: Siglo XXI Editores.

Serra, J. 1974. *Desarrollo Latinoamericano: Ensayos Criticos*. Mexico: Fondo de Cultura Economico.

Sunkel, O. 1973. Transnational capitalism and national disintegration in Latin America. *Social and Economic Studies* 22, 132–76.

Sunkel, O. and Paz, P. 1970. *El subdesarrollo latinoamericano y la teoria del desarrollo*. Mexico: Siglo XXI Editores.

Tavares, M.C. and Serra, J. 1970. Mas allá del estanciamento. In Serra (1974).

Walicki, A. 1969. *The Controversy Over Capitalism*. London: Oxford University Press.

Wallerstein, I. 1974a. *The Modern World-System: Capitalist Agriculture and the Origins of the European World-Economy in the Sixteenth Century*. New York: Academic Press.

Wallerstein, I. 1974b. Dependency in an interdependent world: the limited possibilities of a transformation within the capitalist world-economy. *African Studies Review* 17, 1–26.

Warren, B. 1973. Imperialism and capitalist industrialization. *New Left Review* 63, 3–44.

Warren, B. 1980. *Imperialism: Pioneer of Capitalism*. Ed. John Sender, London: Verso.

Development Planning

AMIYA KUMAR BAGCHI

Conscious plans for development of the economy as a whole over an extended period (say, five or ten years) were drawn up for the first time in the Soviet Union in the 1920s. The socialist countries of Eastern Europe, and the People's Republic of China have since then been the most consistent practitioners of development planning. However, the practice of drawing up development plans soon spread from the Soviety Union to non-socialist countries and some of the plans promulgated by the respective governments were also implemented, with different degrees of success.

In socialist countries, the broad outlines of the development plan have to be approved by the highest authority, which may be the praesidium of the supreme legislative and executive body or the Party Congress convened for the purpose. However, the political and administrative authorities at the lower levels of administration, such as the county or the province, transmit information upwards regarding both the availability of resources and the felt needs of development. The actual implementation of the plan and the detailing of the outputs to be produced and the inputs to be used for executing the plan are delegated to the lower level authorities. As we shall see later, in socialist countries an almost continuous debate has been conducted regarding the degree of devolution of administrative authority and decentralization of economic decision-making. By and large, the central leadership in socialist countries has taken the decisions regarding the strategic and long-term variables, such as the rate and sectoral composition of investment, the degree of openness of the economy, and the allocation of resources as between different regions, while leaving the tactical or short-run production decisions to the lower-level authorities.

Long-term development plans have to be based on a depiction of the structure of the economy and its probable evolution under the influence of different types of intervention by the government. In the Soviet Union in the 1920s, inspiration for the construction of models of a planned economy was drawn mainly from the works of Karl Marx. (For an anthology of translations of Soviet writings on the subject, see Spulber, 1964.) In particular, by drawing on the schemes of expanded reproduction constructed by Marx (1893 and 1894), G.A. Fel'dman constructed a two-sector model of development by assuming the economy to be closed and dividing it into two vertically-integrated sectors, one producing capital goods and the other consumer goods (Fel'dman, 1928 and Domar, 1957). Fel'dman assumed that capital goods were the only limiting factor of production. An analytically equivalent model was constructed by P.C. Mahalanobis (1953). One interesting result of the Fel'dman–Mahalanobis model is the demonstration that given a constant technology and a constant capital–output ratio, the long-term rate of growth of the economy is determined by the proportion of investment devoted to the expansion of the capital goods sector.

In Fel'dman's model, the capital goods sector included all the intermediate goods needed for producing the final goods, as did the consumer goods sector. But the actual calculation of the output of a particular intermediate good needed to sustain a desired level of a particular capital good or consumer good could be made only after all the direct and indirect uses of the corresponding intermediate good had been traced. In trying to solve this problem, the Soviet planners early evolved the method of the material balances, under which, once, let us say, a given volume of output of finished steel had been decided upon, all the inputs directly and indirectly needed to sustain that level of output in the way of iron ore, coal, limestone, blast furnace and steel-smelting facilities, transport services and power would be worked out. This would generally involve several iterations until the demands and supplies of the different inputs converged. These exercises would be carried out for all the major items entering planning – and these could run to several hundred items (Montias, 1959).

Wassily Leontief later worked out what has come to be known as the input–output method of analysis, which can be regarded as the logical completion of the method of material balances. (For a succinct summary of the available elaborations of the input–output models used in plan exercises, see Taylor, 1975.)

In the Soviet Union and other socialist countries, considerable attention was paid to the use of mathematical methods for solution of large-scale planning problems and for finding out least-cost methods of carrying out given projects or programmes. The Russian mathematician L.V. Kantorovich has been credited with the discovery of the method of linear programming though the first convenient algorithm for solving such a programme was invented by G.B. Dantzig (Kantorovich, 1965). However, the real problems of planning in the Soviet Union and other socialist economies have centred on questions of the use of prices or simulation of planning by markets, on the degree of decentralization of decision-making, and on the level and composition of maintainable investment, rather than on questions of which techniques to use to draw up plans.

Socialist economies such as the Soviet Union and China, soon after the beginning of planning, attained very high rates of investment: the rate of investment during the first five-year plan in Russia went up, for example, from 15 per cent to 44 per cent of national income between 1928 and 1932 (Ellman, 1975). In China the ratio of investment to national income went up to 25 per cent at the end of her first five-year plan (1953–7), and in the 1970s the investment–income ratio generally stayed above 30 per cent. One result of the drive to raise the rate of investment and construction was that the huge labour surpluses in these countries which had been prevalent in pre-revolution days were mopped up after the first few years of planning.

The problems that the socialist countries typically faced were well summed up by Mao Zedong in his famous talk on the ten major relationships (Mao, 1956). According to Mao, in the context of Chinese development, maintenance of a balance was crucial in the relationships (i) between heavy industry, light industry and agriculture; (ii) between industry in coastal regions and industry in the interior; (iii) between civil investment and defence construction; (iv) between the state, the units of production and the actual producers; (v) between the central and local authorities; (vi) between Han, that is, the majority nationality, and the minority nationalities; (vii) between Communist Party authorities and cadres and non-members of the Party; (viii) between different policies fostering revolution rather than counter-revolution; (ix) between rewarding the correct policy-executors and punishing the wrongdoers; and (x) between China and the foreign countries. The relations (vi), (vii), and (ix) are political questions of broad importance involving socialist legality, the correct treatment of counter-revolutionary elements, but also questions with a mainly Chinese orientation. But the other relations involve mainly questions of economic strategy and have appeared in many different contexts. It has been felt in many socialist countries that not enough attention was paid until recently to the aim of raising the standards of living of the people. Too many resources were devoted to the development of heavy industry and too few to the growth of light industries catering for mass consumption (cf. Kalecki, 1969).

It was also felt that because of the highly centralized character of management, the stress on investment and a general atmosphere of scarcity within which managers were to achieve certain quantitative goals, there is a tendency at the enterprise level in a socialist economy to hoard resources and to invest too much (Kornai, 1980). Moreover, it was thought that in the drive to raise the rate of industrialization, while keeping prices stable by ensuring the supply of an adequate quantity of agricultural goods at fixed prices to the non-agricultural sector, plans had tended to discriminate against the rural producers. The allegation that Soviet industrialization was mainly financed by Russian peasants has been called into question by recent research (Ellman, 1975; Vyas, 1979). However, in many socialist countries, including China, moves have been made in recent years to increase the incomes of agricultural producers significantly and prices of agricultural products have been raised drastically with the same end in view. In China, deliberate attempts have also been made to bring down the ratio of accumulation (investment) to national income, to increase the rate of growth of light industry, and to provide greater incentives to peasants and industrial enterprises to change their product mix in response to changing demand patterns, to economize on scarce resources and to bring about a greater degree of flexibility of management (Ma Hong, 1983, and Xue Muqiao, 1981). But the chief instruments of adjustment and reform have been changes in prices paid to producers of specified goods, especially agricultural commodities, and political and administrative decentralization, rather than allowing producers to change their prices or their investment patterns independently of political authorities. The main underpinnings for an egalitarian distribution of income in the shape of a comprehensive public distribution and social security system and of stability in consumer prices have so far been maintained in all socialist economies. One reason for this is that there is no simple way in which an economy-wide reform can be instituted so that prices either equal prices of production or equalize supplies and demands in all markets but do not bring about other undesirable side-effects in the form of an increase in inequality of income distribution or unemployment.

Socialist economies have been concerned in recent years with making a transition from a regime of extensive to one of intensive growth, that is, from one where economic growth is accelerated by raising the rate of investment or the application of labour to one where it can be raised by increasing the productivity of agents of production. Economic reforms are seen as one means of doing this. Increasing the rate of innovation and adaptation and absorption of imported technology are seen as other means of doing this. It is in the latter area that the relations between socialist countries and advanced capitalist economies become crucial. Socialist economies are striving to import improved technologies from the USA, the EEC countries and Japan without becoming dependent on them or becoming heavily indebted to them. On the other side, the advanced capitalist countries are trying to increase their markets in socialist countries without selling them technologies which could make them economically or militarily stronger than the capitalist countries in the future.

The problems that the non-socialist countries have faced in formulating credible development plans have been far more complex than those discussed above and their success in implementing them has been far more mixed.

While the Soviet theorists and Mao took a socialist system to be the environment in which a development plan was to be located, most other theorists were not explicit about the kind of system they had in mind when they proposed specific plans for development of the underdeveloped economies. Paul Rosenstein-Rodan's pioneering attempt to formulate appropriate plans for development of the Eastern European countries after World War II can be taken to be the genesis of what came to be known as the 'balanced growth' doctrine (Rosenstein-Rodan, 1943). Ragnar Nurkse (1953) developed some of these ideas further in his writings. According to these theorists, in a poor underdeveloped economy, a credible development plan would have to consist of a programme for a simultaneous and balanced development of all the important sectors in the economy, so that expanding demands are met by matching supplies, and vice versa. Moreover, this process of balanced growth would lead to the realization of internal economies of scale and external effects arising from learning processes, and a decline in uncertainty faced by buyers, sellers and investors (see, in this connection, Dobb, 1960, ch. 1). Maurice Dobb (1951), Nurkse and Lewis (1954) all stressed the necessity and possibility of mobilizing underemployed and unemployed labour for the purpose of capital formation in underdeveloped economies.

The balanced growth doctrine has the advantage that it can be embodied in specific development plans elaborated out of the Fel'dman–Mahalanobis models, and the input–output models devised by Leontief and his co-workers and later followers. But even before such models had been elaborated to take account of all the interconnections involved in a dynamic income generation process, it was clear that in a non-socialist economy, a development plan, however well-formulated, was likely to run into problems because of the lack of concordance between planners' goals and private sector goals and lead to political side-effects which could derail it before it had really had time to run its course.

It is useful to analyse some of these problems by using the four-sector model of development which Mahalanobis (1955) used as the scaffolding for drawing up the draft second five-year plan of India. In this model, the economy is divided into four vertically integrated sectors, the first producing capital goods by factory methods, the second producing consumer goods by factory methods, the third producing consumer goods by handicraft methods and the fourth producing services by labour-intensive methods. The idea behind this classification was that a designated proportion of the output of capital goods industries would be devoted to their own expansion in order to promote growth, while the handicraft and service sectors would meet much of the demand for consumer goods and services generated by increasing incomes and at the same time mobilize underemployed and unemployed labour, thus minimizing the need to divert investible resources to the factory sector for production of more consumer goods.

However, one of the basic conditions for employment of more labour would be that the new workers can be fed and clothed (Nurkse, 1953; Lewis, 1954). It cannot be assumed that some automatic mechanism would spring up for diverting food from the farms to factories in urban or rural areas. Kalecki (1955) was one of the first to emphasize the importance of ensuring a smooth supply of wage goods and keeping the rate of saving high by curbing consumption for financing development in Third World countries.

Most Third World countries were, however, characterized by various kinds of landlordism or other semi-feudal constraints such as debt bondage, the use of non-market coercion, etc., limiting farm output. The failure to carry out thorough-going land reforms which would vest the ownership and management of the land in the hands of the actual cultivators also meant that traders and moneylenders could continue to prosper by exacting extortionate margins on goods sold or bought and charging usurious interest rates on loans to the poor in the countryside. These conditions also facilitate political coalitions between landlords, traders and moneylenders blocking the process of reforms to endow the peasants with the incentive and wherewithal to produce more and meet the needs of industrialization.

As Kalecki (1955) realized, if the marketed surplus fails to go up, an increase in the rate of investment as envisaged by all development plans would soon meet an inflation barrier (since the income elasticity of the demand for food is high and its price elasticity is low). A rising output of farm products does not in itself guarantee a rising volume of marketed surplus. If the consumption of the supplier of farm products rises proportionately more than farm output, then the marketed surplus will fall. With a landlord-dominated farm sector, traders and landlords generally command enough credit and other assets to ensure that the rest of society pays a stiffly rising price for farm products whenever the output of agriculture falters (say, because of adverse weather conditions or floods or pests). If the government can be persuaded to run a procurement programme so that it is committed to buying up any agricultural supplies coming on the market at a minimum price, but cannot force the landlords or traders to deliver the grain (or cotton or oilseeds) at that price, then a ratchet is put under the prices of farm products. Thus the physical rate of growth of farm output puts only an outside limit on the rate of growth of non-agricultural output: the actual limit (which is lower) is set by the ownership pattern of agricultural assets and by the conditions of sales of agricultural commodities. When the farm sector is dominated by landlords, the rate of growth of agricultural output interacts with such factors as luxury consumption of the rich, the tendency to speculation whenever the harvest is poor, the extremely skewed distribution of credit, and public support for farm prices to produce a constricting limit on industrial growth. In a socialist economy, with fixed prices of food grains, a comprehensive public distribution system and the abolition of speculation, a similar rate of agricultural growth would be consistent with a much higher rate of industrial development. (A non-socialist economy with a relatively egalitarian distribution of landholdings would pose lesser problems for growth than a landlord-dominated society.) Thus, referring back to the four-sector Mahalanobis model, it can be seen that mobilization of labour to produce labour-intensive consumer (or capital) goods would require as a precondition a durable solution of the problem of supply of the needed foodgrains and other agricultural goods.

It can also be seen that stepping up the rate of investment in the economy would require stepping up the rate of savings to an equivalent amount. Such a stepping up of saving would not normally occur on a voluntary basis in an underdeveloped economy which had been stagnating before the onset of development planning. So the government would have to tax the rich in order to release the necessary resources for investment and keep the demand for foodgrains and other goods with inelastic supplies within reasonable bounds (compare Kalecki, 1955).

However, in a non-socialist economy the government generally fails to curb the increase in the purchasing power in the hands of the rich to an adequate extent. The rich then not only demand and commandeer more of the scarce resources which should go into investment, they also do not purchase sufficient amounts of the handicrafts or the labour-intensive consumer goods which, in the four-sector Mahalanobis model, are supposed to satisfy the increasing demands released in the economy. Thus excess capacity emerges (or continues) in many sectors of the economy (including capital goods turned out by government and private factories), with attendant unemployment, even while there is excess demand in other sectors (see Bagchi, 1970). In particular, the rich generally demand newer types of luxury goods produced in the advanced capitalist countries. If these cannot be produced at home, they will be imported from abroad. Since the failure to step up the rate of aggregate saving to an adequate extent or channel investment into the sectors which accelerate the growth of the economy lead in any case to balance of payment deficits, most Third World countries attempting to plan their development will also have foreign trade regimes characterized by exchange controls, high tariffs on permitted imports, and quantitative restrictions on imports and exports. Under these circumstances, restricted importables will normally fetch high premia in domestic currency and it will be profitable to smuggle them in or produce them behind the walls of the high tariffs and quantitative restrictions of various kinds, thus leading to further division of resources.

Some of the difficulties underdeveloped countries faced in obtaining enough foreign capital inflows for financing development were approached via the so-called 'two-gap' models of aid, trade and development (Chenery and Bruno, 1962; Manne, 1963; and McKinnon, 1964). In these models, on plausible assumptions about the desired rate and pattern of growth, a gap between *ex ante* exports and imports and a parallel gap between *ex ante* investment and savings are estimated. Since exports of most underdeveloped primary-commodity-producing countries are price and income-elastic, and many of them also face non-price barriers in trade, whereas their planned investment is often relatively import-intensive, it was often found that the *ex ante* trade gap was larger than the *ex ante* investment–saving gap (Landau, 1971). It was argued then that the planning authorities of the country concerned should plan to borrow or canvas for aid to cover the larger of the two gaps, and then development could proceed as planned.

Few countries, however, were in the happy position of being able to borrow or receive as aid whatever foreign capital inflow the planning exercises indicate as the optimum amount, even in the days when official grants and loans were less niggardly than they have become in the last decade or more. Moreover, the two-gap models themselves did not indicate the desirable or the feasible method of adjustment of the two gaps to each other *ex post*, and to the amount of foreign capital actually received. Even if the foreign aid or loans equalled the larger of the two gaps, the planning authorities could not leave the adjustment process to autonomous market forces, but had to adopt specific policies to bring about an appropriate adjustment process (Vanek, 1967, ch. 6). When the foreign trade gap is dominant, for example, it is appropriate to allow savings to go down, in order to make the investment–savings gap rise to the export–import gap rather than stimulate (import-intensive) investment and increase the trade gap further. Under a wide variety of conditions, both policy-induced and market-induced adjustment processes would lead to a rise in consumption and a slowing down of investment (because of the uncertainty as regards the availability of imports and because of inventory accumulation as a result of excess capacity in import-constrained sectors). Thus where foreign capital inflows are a binding constraint, a negative relation may well be observed between inflows of aid and domestic savings effort (Rahman, 1968; Griffin, 1970).

Moreover, with overvalued foreign exchange and with a perceived disadvantage in investing in fields requiring new, foreign-controlled technology, there may also be hidden outflows of domestic capital to safe havens of hoarding or investment even while a substantial amount of foreign capital is coming in under official auspices.

Besides two-gap models, there were other advances in the understanding of development plans. It was realized that where the supply of foreign exchange was a constraint, planners might try to build up intersectoral linkages so as to provide for machines to produce machines or produce higher-order intermediate goods, and so attempt to accelerate economic development to the maximum possible extent (Raj and Sen, 1961). Optimizing exercises involving time-lags could be carried out with the same class of models. However, the implementation of the indicated development plans by non-socialist developed countries would founder on their inability (a) to buy the technology, which was often patented or otherwise owned by transnational corporations, on reasonable terms, (b) to devise appropriate social and organizational mechanisms for absorbing and diffusing the technology, and for exacting the needed savings and allocation of investment out of the economy (see Bagchi, 1982, ch. 9).

In the field of application of input–output analysis and social accounting matrices to development plan models there have also been significant advances. Although it was sometimes suggested that different clusters of industries of the economy (such as heavy industry, light industry and agriculture) could grow at very different rates, because the current input–output flow system regularly displayed gaps between some sectors and close ties as between others (Manne and Rudra, 1965), it was realized that the flows of demands generated by the planning process would tie the growth patterns of different sectors tightly together, as we have already seen. Significant advances have been made in applying the social accounting matrices to plan models, and the implicit multipliers relating the growth of particular sectors or factor incomes to the rest of the economy have been utilized to predict the income generation and distributional implications of different patterns of plan expenditures (Pyatt and Round, 1979; Taylor, 1979).

However, it is one thing to devise models for development and another thing to implement them in underdeveloped countries with big landlords, propertied classes which are divided among themselves and which are continually attracted to the metropolitan centres by the lure of more modern life styles, safety of investments against threats of revolutions, and other considerations. Rosenstein-Rodan (1943) had conceived of the development plan as being carried out by a 'trust' which could internalize all external effects and all secondary effects of investment. In actual fact the limits of organization either through the market or in firms or governmental organizations, and the temptation to resort to opportunistic behaviour to the detriment of the collective good have been far more prevalent in non-socialist underdeveloped countries than in the socialist economies. The propertied, or more narrowly, capitalist groups have found it very difficult to evolve codes of cooperation without which confidence in the future and long-term investment become very fragile plants (see Axelrod, 1984).

Even while the balanced growth doctrine was being evolved, Albert Hirschman had proposed exploiting the profitability-signalling property of disequilibrium situations to recommend a path of development along which imbalances were deliberately engineered (Hirschman, 1958). In fact, as it turned out, capitalists more often reacted the 'wrong' way to disequilibria, by cornering scarce commodities, using political levers to raise barriers against entry into their favoured pastures, playing intertemporal arbitrage games to defeat the planners' intentions (see Bagchi, 1966; Hirschman, 1968). The obstacles to the execution of development plans in non-socialist countries had been foreseen in the 1950s by many Marxists, of whom Paul Baran was the most prominent (Baran, 1952, 1957), and by other social scientists such as Gunnar Myrdal (1957). In the general atmosphere of crisis in the world economy, there is sometimes an agreement between proponents at both extremes of the political spectrum that development planning is impossible in Third World countries. What both experience and analysis indicate, however, is that the implementation of development plans is likely to be fraught with contradictions. There will be imbalances between regions, increasing differentiation of peasantry, tensions between development of the public and private sectors, conflicts between interests of local development and interests of transnational corporations and their local collaborators, and questions will be raised and often resolved through bloody confrontations regarding the appropriate political regimes. It is through the mobilization of ordinary people to tackle these manifold contradictions and to fight the vested interests blocking the progress of development programmes that further advances will be made. National planning, in that sense, has been and will always be, intimately tied up with politics. But for most Third World countries development planning remains an essential part of the programme for charting their own future.

BIBLIOGRAPHY

Axelrod, R. 1984. *The Evolution of Cooperation.* New York: Basic Books.

Bagchi, A.K. 1966. Shadow prices, controls and tariff protection in India. *Indian Economic Review*, New Series, 1(1), April, 22–44.

Bagchi, A.K. 1970. Long-term constraints on India's industrial growth 1951–8. In *Economic Development in South Asia*, ed. E.A.G. Robinson and M. Kidron, London: Macmillan.

Bagchi, A.K. 1982. *The Political Economy of Underdevelopment.* Cambridge and New York: Cambridge University Press.

Baran, P.A. 1952. The political economy of backwardness. *Manchester School of Economic and Social Studies* 20(1), January, 66–84.

Baran, P.A. 1957. *The Political Economy of Growth.* New York: Monthly Review Press.

Chenery, H.B. and Bruno, M. 1962. Development alternatives in an open economy: the case of Israel. *Economic Journal* 72, March, 79–103.

Dobb, M.H. 1951. *Some Aspects of Economic Development.* Delhi: Delhi School of Economics.

Dobb, M.H. 1960. *An Essay on Economic Growth and Planning.* London: Routledge & Kegan Paul; New York: Monthly Review Press.

Domar, E. 1957. A Soviet model of growth. In E. Domar, *Essays in the Theory of Economic Growth*, New York: Oxford University Press.

Eckstein, A. 1977. *China's Economic Revolution*. Cambridge: Cambridge University Press.

Ellman, M. 1975. Did the agricultural surplus provide the resources for the increase in investment in the USSR during the first five year plan? *Economic Journal* 85, December, 844–63.

Fel'dman, G.A. 1928. K teorii narrodnogo dokhoda. *Planvoe khoziaistvo* 11, 12. Trans. as 'On the theory of growth rates of national income', I and II, in Spulber (1964).

Griffin, K. 1970. Foreign capital, domestic savings and economic development. *Bulletin of the Oxford University Institute of Economics and Statistics* 32(2), May, 99–112.

Hirschman, A. 1958. *The Strategy of Economic Development*. New Haven: Yale University Press.

Hirschman, A. 1968. The political economy of import-substituting industrialization in Latin America. *Quarterly Journal of Economics* 82(1), February, 1–32.

Kalecki, M. 1955. The problem of financing economic development. *Indian Economic Review* 2(3), February, 1–22.

Kalecki, M. 1969. *Introduction to the Theory of Growth in a Socialist Economy*. Oxford: Basil Blackwell.

Kantorovich, L.V. 1965. *The Best Use of Economic Resources*. Oxford: Pergamon.

Kornai, J. 1980. *Economics of Shortage*. 2 vols, Amsterdam: North-Holland.

Landau, L. 1971. Saving functions for Latin America. In *Studies in Development Planning*, ed. H.B. Chenery et al., Cambridge, Mass.: Harvard University Press.

Lewis, W.A. 1954. Economic development with unlimited supplies of labour. *Manchester School of Economic and Social Studies* 22, May, 139–91.

Lockett, M. and Littler, C.R. 1983. Trends in Chinese enterprise management 1978–1982. *World Development* 11(8), August, 683–704.

McKinnon, R.I. 1964. Foreign exchange constraints in economic development and efficient aid allocation. *Economic Journal* 74, June, 388–409.

Mahalanobis, P.C. 1953. Some observations on the process of growth of national income. *Sankhya* 12(4), September, 307–12.

Mahalanobis, P.C. 1955. The approach of operational research to planning in India. *Sankhya* 16(1 and 2), December, 3–130.

Ma Hong. 1983. *New Strategy for China's Economy*. Beijing: New World Press.

Manne, A. 1963. Key sectors of the Mexican economy. In *Studies in Process Analysis*, ed. A. Manne and H.M. Markowitz, New York: John Wiley.

Manne, A. and Rudra, A. 1965. A consistency model of India's Fourth Plan. *Sankhya*, Series B 27(1 and 2), September, 57–144.

Mao Zedong. 1956. On the ten major relationships. In *Selected Works of Mao Tse-tung*, Vol. V, Peking: Foreign Languages Press, 1977.

Marx, K. 1893. *Capital: A Critique of Political Economy*, Vol. II. Trans. from the 2nd German edn of 1893, ed. F. Engels, Moscow: Foreign Languages Publishing House, 1957.

Marx, K. 1894. *Capital: A Critique of Political Economy*, Vol. III. Trans. from original German edn of 1894, ed. F. Engels, Moscow: Foreign Languages Publishing House, 1966.

Montias, J.M. 1959. Planning with material balances in Soviet-type economies. *American Economic Review* 49, December, 963–85.

Myrdal, G. 1957. *Economic Theory and Underdeveloped Regions*. London: Duckworth.

Nurkse, R. 1953. *Problems of Capital Formation in Underdeveloped Countries.* Oxford: Basil Blackwell; New York: Oxford University Press.

Nuti, D.M. 1981. Socialism on earth. *Cambridge Journal of Economics* 5(4), December, 391–403.

Pyatt, G. and Round, R.I. 1979. Accounting and fixed price multipliers in a social accounting matrix framework. *Economic Journal* 89(356), December, 850–73.

Rahman, M.A. 1968. Foreign capital and domestic savings: a test of Haavelmo's hypothesis with cross-country data. *Review of Economics and Statistics* 50, February, 137–8.

Raj, K.N. and Sen, A.K. 1961. Alternative patterns of growth under conditions of stagnant export earnings. *Oxford Economic Papers* 13(1), February, 43–52.

Rosenstein-Rodan, P.N. 1943. Problems of industrialisation of eastern and south-eastern Europe. *Economic Journal* 53, June–September, 202–11.

Spulber, N. (ed.) 1964. *Foundations of Soviet Strategy for Economic Growth: Selected Soviet Essays, 1924–1930.* Bloomington, Indiana: Indiana University Press.

Taylor, L. 1975. Theoretical foundations and technical implications. In *Economy-Wide Models and Development Planning*, ed. C.R. Blitzer, P.B. Clark and L. Taylor, London: Oxford University Press.

Taylor, L. 1979. *Macro Models for Developing Countries.* New York: McGraw-Hill.

Vanek, J. 1967. *Estimating Foreign Resource Needs for Economic Development: Theory, Method and a Case Study of Colombia.* New York: McGraw-Hill.

Vyas, A. 1979. Primary accumulation in the USSR revisted. *Cambridge Journal of Economics* 3(2), June, 119–30.

Xue Muqiao. 1981. *China's Socialist Economy.* Beijing: Foreign Languages Press.

Disguised Unemployment

AMIT BHADURI

Marx set out the notion that a 'reserve army' of unemployed labour is more or less continuously maintained in the course of capitalistic development. In the initial phases, this reserve army may be created through the destruction of the pre-capitalistic modes of production, while in later phases, a systematic bias in favour of labour-displacing innovations could serve the same purpose. This entails a broad vision of capitalistic development under extremely elastic supply conditions for labour where the actual level of wage employment is usually demand-determined. This means that the supply of labour tends to adjust to its demand through various routes, such as higher participation rate (e.g. as more married women join the labour force or the average schooling period is shortened), interregional and international migration of labour etc., all this taking place against the background of continuous induced innovations. Under these circumstances, it is not very useful to think of a 'natural' rate of growth, set by the growth of labour force and of labour productivity, as the maximum feasible growth rate of a capitalist economy (Marglin, 1984, pp. 103–8).

The elastic nature of the labour supply and its adjustability to the level of demand entail the existence of open or disguised unemployment as an untapped reservoir of labour in the normal course of capitalist development. However, such disguised unemployment, although real, is a somewhat amorphous phenomenon in an advanced capitalist economy for two distinct reasons. First, under normal circumstances, many potential entrants (e.g. married women, late school-leavers, young people on the farm) may not actually even try to enter the labour market unless demand is seen to be high with all sorts of job vacancies exceeding their corresponding numbers in registered unemployment. Second, the economic nationalism in the richer countries often takes the form of strictly regulating the migration of 'guest-workers' so that open unemployment in the (potentially) labour-exporting countries, rather than disguised unemployment in the advanced capitalist countries, becomes the normal pattern. And yet, prolonged stagnation in economic conditions in an advanced capitalist country may make this phenomenon of disguised unemployment more visible, as the redundant workers either seek various forms of self-employment with virtually no invested capital or try to sell their labour services directly as porters, odd-jobmen, domestic servants, farm-hands etc. (Robinson, 1956, pp. 157–8). Their earnings in these peripheral jobs would then become the 'reservation price' of this marginalized labour force. When unemployment dole and social security set a higher reservation price, some of this unemployment may come out in the open instead of being disguised. In this sense, it is probable that the growth of the welfare state may openly register as unemployed some who would have been otherwise unemployed in a disguised fashion earlier. And, the reverse could happen if the social security measures are cut by the government.

The existence of such disguised unemployment on a significant scale is usually accommodated by a secondary or informal labour market mostly in the service sector. This is much more easily visible in the phenomenon of massive migration to urban centres from rural areas in many developing countries. While all such migrants from rural areas aspire to limited job opportunities in organized industries located in urban areas, only a small fraction among them are actually able to find proper jobs at any given point of time. The rest spend their time waiting in search of appropriate jobs. In the meantime, they somehow manage to disguise their unemployment either by self-employing themselves with tiny amounts of invested capital (e.g. polishing shoes, cleaning cars etc.) or by selling their labour services directly in odd jobs or simply taking recourse to the support of the elaborate kinship system in more traditional societies, e.g. by living off better-placed relatives and migrant workers from their home areas. Thus, the phenomenon of disguised unemployment in the urban areas of many developing countries becomes closely linked with the massive migration from rural areas during the course of industrialization.

A distinguishing feature of disguised unemployment in such an informal sector is the irregular and often long hours of work per day. This is evident enough in the case of most self-employed persons in the informal sector; but even those who are employed on a wage-labour basis usually have highly flexible wage contracts in many respects (e.g. domestic servants, odd-jobmen, etc.). Partly the explanation lies in the lower unionization of this sector. However, a deeper explanation lies in the fact that most self-employed persons as well as workers paid at the piece-rate have to work extended hours per day simply to make a livelihood. But this also could have a limited advantage for some of them insofar as the entire family can participate in the work (e.g. traditional carpet making, weaving and other types of artisan work are often done by many members of the family working together). In this context, we have to make a sharp distinction between labour-service and the labourer providing such service: the same amount of labour service (say, 18 hours per day) may be spread out over several family members working as labourers (say, three). In some cases, each family member (labourer) may on an average have a lighter work load (of only six hours) per day compared to an average worker in the organized industry. This brings us to a somewhat different analytical dimension of disguised unemployment: some person may be unemployed in a disguised manner not only in the sense of having a very low earning rate, i.e. *income-wise* unemployment, but also in the sense of relatively light work-intensity per day, i.e. *time-disposition-wise* unemployment. And, unless one believes in the neoclassical proposition that income necessarily reflects the marginal product, one would have to devise a third (and separate) criterion of disguised unemployment in terms of abnormality low *productivity* of labour. However, given the structure of reward in a capitalist economy, one needs to be careful in applying these concepts. Thus, an 'important person' belonging to the board of directors of several large corporations, may be making a well-above-average income by attending only a couple of board meetings per month. Such a person may very well be considered to be disguised unemployed by the time-disposition criterion and even perhaps by the labour-productivy criterion, although he cannot by any means be considered unemployed, disguised or not, by the income criterion! Also recall in this context that 'unproductive labour' was a common category used in the classical tradition of political economy and all those engaged in unproductive labour (e.g. 'priests, prostitutes and professors' according to a picturesque phrase employed by Rosa Luxemburg) could be considered to be disguised unemployed by the productivity criterion.

In the normal organization of factory work under the capitalist system, the threefold distinction between income-wise, time-wise and productivity-wise disguised unemployment may not be particularly relevant. Thus, an unemployed industrial worker is both income- and time-wise unemployed and of course, he does not have much of a chance to be productive either. However, such a distinction can be highly relevant in the context of traditional family-based agriculture, especially for characterizing such phenomena as rural poverty or the existence of surplus labour. Consider for example a typical rural woman in the poorest strata: in addition to all her other work inside and outside the house, she may have to spend long hours collecting wood for fuel and carrying water home from a distance. Although she has exceptionally hard and long working hours every day and must be considered time- and disposition-wise fully employed and certainly productive in every normal sense of the term, in keeping her family going under most difficult circumstances, in all probability she would *not* be classified as 'gainfully employed' by the income criterion. Indeed her case is the opposite of that our 'important person' who has a high income by attending a couple of board meetings every month. It is to be noted that the worst kind of rural poverty is often concentrated among people who are fully employed by the time-disposition criterion, but may be described as disguised unemployed by the income criterion, because of their miserably low earning rate per hour of work. After all, this is what the phrase 'eking out a living' usually means.

There can hardly be any serious doubt that in the backward agriculture of many populous countries (e.g. in South Asia), a high proportion of the population engaged in cultivation have extremely low income, and in this sense suffers from disguised unemployment by the income-criterion. Nevertheless, it is far more problematic to identify what such disguised unemployment by the income criterion implies in terms of either the time-disposal or the productivity criterion.

If one were to believe in the ideologically potent neoclassical slogan that all 'factors of production' including labour always tend to get paid according to their marginal product even in pre-capitalist, backward agriculture, then that proportion of population with extremely low income could be said to be rather unproductively engaged in agriculture. Their low income would be the 'evidence' of their low productivity which in turn would imply a corresponding level of disguised unemployment in agriculture. But this would involve implicit theorizing based on the dubious assumption that income (earning) is always positively associated with productivity, even in traditional agriculture.

Such implicit theorizing apart (a sophisticated example of which is the so-called 'efficiency wage' hypothesis e.g. Bliss and Stern, 1978) the important question remains as to whether there is any meaningful sense in which one can argue about the existence of significant surplus labour and disguised unemployment in backward agriculture, judged by the productivity criterion. This would imply that some surplus labour can be withdrawn from agriculture without adversely affecting the level of agricultural output. Or, in more textbookish jargon, 'at the margin' labour contributes nothing to output, so that the marginal product of labour is zero in such agriculture.

Put in such general terms, the formulation is too fuzzy to be useful. For instance, if by 'margin' one means the *intensive* margin of higher labour input per unit of land, then considerable empirical evidence exists, at least in India, to suggest that the smaller-sized land holdings usually use family labour more intensively. both in current agricultural operations *and* in direct investment of labour for improving land quality. As a result, the total output, taking all crops together over the year, tends to be higher per unit of land on smaller holdings (Bharadwaj, 1974, chs. 2, 3 and 7 provide an excellent account). This tendency towards an *inverse* relation between farm size and productivity per acre in traditional agriculture would tend to cast doubt on the simple-minded proposition that the 'marginal' product of labour is zero, especially if the notion of intensive margin is used.

Without going into such finer points of intensive and extensive margin, Schultz (1964, ch. 4) proposed the 'epidemic test': the 1918–19 influenza epidemic in India killed 6.2% of the 1918 population and 8.3% of the working population in agriculture (the latter according to Schultz's estimate). Schultz found that, although the weather conditions were roughly similar in 1916–17 and in 1919–20, in the latter year agricultural output was lower by about 3.8%, providing circumstantial evidence that withdrawal of labour from agriculture did affect output level. However, apart from many statistical and conceptual problems (e.g. the relation between acrage change in the sense of extensive margin and output change which is a resultant of both extensive and intensive margin in his macro-level statistical investigation), this 'epidemic test' must be deemed to be over-simplistic despite its apparent ingenuity. At best, it showed that a *random* $x\%$ withdrawal of labour from cultivation did affect the acrage and/or output level. But it does in no way establish the impossibility of *selectively* withdrawing $x\%$ labour through suitable reorganization of agricultural production at the family and regional level (e.g. Sen, 1967). And yet, most of the important initial proponents of the 'surplus labour' doctrine had in mind such selective (but not random) withdrawal of labour that may be induced by industrialization and expansion in urban employment opportunities (Nurkse, 1953; Lewis, 1954). And, once it is recognized that such withdrawal of labour from agriculture can be accompanied by reorganization of labour in the family farm through adjusting the hours of work of the family members staying back on the farm or through higher availability of land per cultivating family, it seems plausible to argue analytically (e.g. Takagi, 1978) as well as empirically that labour can usually be released from agriculture without adversely affecting the level of agricultural output. Indeed, post-revolutionary experiences of agrarian reorganization in China and Vietnam demonstrated the possibility of using surplus labour to improve the quality of land through better drainage and irrigation without a significant drop in short-run agricultural output, despite all the serious problems of lack of adequate incentive to private production in cooperative and collective agriculture.

BIBLIOGRAPHY

Bharadwaj, K. 1974. *Production Conditions in Indian Agriculture* (A study based on farm management surveys). Occasional Paper 33, Department of Applied Economics, Cambridge: Cambridge University Press.

Bliss, C. and Stern, N. 1978. Productivity, wages and nutrition, Parts I and II. *Journal of Development Economics* 5(4), 331–98.

Lewis, W.A. 1954. Economic development with unlimited supplies of labour. *Manchester School of Economic and Social Studies* 22, May, 139–91.

Marglin, S.A. 1984. *Growth, Distribution, and Prices.* Cambridge, Mass.: Harvard University Press.

Nurkse, R. 1953. *Problems of Capital Formation in Underdeveloped Economies.* Oxford, Clarendon Press; New York: Oxford University Press.

Robinson, J. 1956. *The Accumulation of Capital.* London: Macmillan Homewood, Ill.: R.D. Irwin.

Schultz, T.W. 1964. *Transforming Traditional Agriculture.* New Haven: Yale University Press.

Sen, A.K. 1967. Surplus labour in India: a critique of Schultz's statistical test. *Economic Journal*, 154–60.

Takagi, Y. 1978. Surplus labour and disguised unemployment. *Oxford Economic Papers* 30(3), November, 447–57.

Dual Economies

R. KANBUR AND J. McINTOSH

The concept of a 'dual economy' relates to various asymmetries of production and organization that exist in developing countries. The term was originally coined by Boeke (1953), in the context of his socioeconomic studies in Indonesia, to represent an economy and a society divided between the traditional sectors and the modern, capitalist sectors in which the Dutch colonialists operated. This organizational asymmetry also turns out to be a significant feature of the classic Lewis (1954) model of development. However, the notion of 'dualism' goes wider than asymmetry between a modern and traditional sector. A number of models have appeared in the literature, since Lewis's celebrated paper, which employ or emphasize asymmetries and rigidities of different types. Our object is to view these contributions as equally valid representations of dualism, and to compare and contrast their findings with those of earlier writers.

Dual economy models are a subclass of two-sector models of growth. They are intended to capture particular features of developing countries so as to enable a more accurate analysis of development paths and policies. The famous two-sector model of Uzawa (1961–3), for example, would *not* be regarded as a dual economy model. In that model product and factor markets clear instaneously across sectors, and although the two sectors each produce a commodity which is different with respect to input requirements and consumption characteristics, this is where the 'asymmetry' between the two sectors stops. Both sectors use capital and labour (although with different production functions) and production decisions in both sectors are characterized by profit maximization.

The 'asymmetry' in the Uzawa model is, of course, the minimal necessity to make a two-sector model interesting – without asymmetry in production or consumption we would be back to a one-good world. However, the various dual economy models can be seen as departures from this minimal asymmetry; different models introduce different types of asymmetries, in different combinations, to highlight different points of interest.

In comparison with the Uzawa model, the Lewis model displays several types of asymmetries. In the former, there are two factors of production, capital and labour. Both factors are used in each sector, and factors are perfectly mobile between the two sectors. The Lewis model has three factors of production – land, labour and capital – and the two sectors are agriculture (or the traditional sector) and manufacturing (or the modern sector). But agriculture uses no capital and manufacturing uses no land while both sectors use labour. One way of viewing this asymmetry in production is as extreme factor immobility of two of the factors of production across the two sectors, and we will return to the factor mobility assumptions in dual economy models presently. However, attention has focused on yet another asymmetry in the Lewis model, and it is to this that we now turn.

In the Lewis model, manufacturing sector production decisions are made with the objective of maximizing profits, while in the agricultural sector the distribution of product is according to 'conventional norms' rather than marginal products. This is precisely what is meant by duality in the mainstream of development thought. As Little (1982) observes:

> Duality can be defined in many ways. But a useful analytic institutional definition would seem to be that an economy is dualistic when a significant part of it operates under such a paternalist or quasi-feudalist regime, while another significant part operates under a system of wage employment – which may be capitalist or socialist (if state capitalism is regarded as a variety of socialism). Surplus labour may exist in such a situation, but not necessarily so.

Little's final comment introduces the notion of 'surplus labour', and highlights the fact that this is in principle independent of the organizational asymmetry which lies at the heart of dualism. If by surplus labour is meant that the marginal product of labour is close to zero, then a competitive allocation of product is not possible in the agricultural sector – the wage so determined would be too low for survival. It is in such a situation that distribution of product according to norms may arise. However, the use of norms may be present even when the marginal product of labour is positive and sufficiently large.

What the conventional norms are matters for the Lewis story. If, for example, the traditional sector consists of family farms and distribution is according to average product, the consequences are different from the case where the traditional sector consists of landlords who maintain a work force at some income level above marginal product. In the latter case, when a worker leaves for the modern sector the landlords appropriate his income. In the former case, as one worker leaves, the average product rises and affects the supply price of the remaining workers.

From the point of view of static analysis, dual economies give rise to economic inefficiency. For maximization of national output what is required is that the marginal product of each factor be equalized across the two sectors. But the production asymmetry means that capital is not used at all in agriculture and land is not used at all in industry, while the organizational asymmetry means that even when returns to labour are equalized across the sectors by labour

115

mobility, it is not the marginal products of labour in the two sectors which are so equalized.

In fact, in comparison with a neo-classical model it is clear that the agricultural sector is too large and the manufacturing sector is too small relative to the efficient outcome. In this sense accumulation of capital plays a double role – not only does it increase the level of national output, but it also moves the composition of national output in the direction of the efficient outcome. For Lewis, however, the role of accumulation and growth of the modern sector with unlimited supplies of labour at a fixed real wage was to demonstrate how the savings ratio could increase rapidly under such dualistic development, it being assumed that the only saving was undertaken by capitalists in the modern sector.

Jorgenson's (1961) model has many similarities with the Lewis model. The feature of the model emphasized by Jorgenson is production asymmetry between the two sectors:

> Productive activity in each sector may be characterized by a function relating output to each of the factors of production – land, labour and capital. The special character of the theory of development of a dual economy is a certain asymmetry in production relations. If the two production functions were essentially symmetric, that is, if each function included all three productive factors, the resulting model would be suited to the problems of industrial balance in an advanced economy or to dynamic problems in the theory of international trade. In the theory of a dual economy the output of the traditional or agricultural sector is a function of land and labour alone; there is no capital accumulation.... Land does not appear as a factor of production in the manufacturing sector; the level of manufacturing output is a function of capital and labour alone.

Jorgenson also introduces organizational asymmetry:

> While it is not unreasonable to assume that profits are maximized in the advanced sector, there seems to be much less reason for making such an assumption for the agricultural sector.... It is assumed through the analysis that follows that the classical model applies.

Jorgenson's model is that of a closed economy, in which the terms of trade between agriculture and manufacturing determine accumulation and the rate of growth, and these terms of trade are themselves determined by the balance of supply and demand. Lewis (1954) considers both the closed and the open economy model, and discusses how accumulation may run into food-supply problems in the former case. Thus both the models are distinguished by an inefficient sectoral allocation of labour owing to organizational asymmetry, by a focus on the rate of profit in manufacturing as the engine of growth given the production and savings assumptions, and by a recognition of the role of food supply in permitting growth to continue in the closed economy context. The model of Fei and Ranis (1964) also has similar characteristics (see Dixit, 1973, for a comparison of the behaviour of the Jorgensen and Fei–Ranis models).

The Lewis (1954) and Jorgenson (1961) models are not the only ones in the development literature that depart from the symmetry of two sector neo-classical models of growth. A number of more recent papers in the literature emphasize other asymmetries, and we wish to incorporate these into our overview of dual economy models. The celebrated model of Harris and Todaro (1970) is one such example. In fact, accumulation barely makes an appearance in this model. It is a standard, two-sector neo-classical model except for one particular asymmetry – the wage in manufacturing is above the market clearing level. Otherwise, and in contrast to the models of Lewis and Jorgenson, both sectors use capital and labour and the labour market in agriculture is competitive. In common with Lewis and Jorgenson, capital is immobile between the two sectors, and it is labour which is the equilibrating flow. The sectoral allocation of labour equilibrates at that value which equalizes the agricultural wage with the manufacturing wage times the employment rate in the manufacturing sector. The terms of trade can be taken as endogenous or, in the small open economy case, as exogenous. The key feature is the inefficiency caused by the fact that the marginal products of labour in the sectors are no longer equal. The literature contains many papers which consider policy responses to this inefficiency, such as Bhagwati and Srinivasan (1974), and others which modify the capital mobility assumptions, such as Corden and Findlay (1975). But the family resemblance between the Harris–Todaro model and the Lewis and Jorgenson models should be clear. In all models, marginal products of the mobile factor are not equalized across the sectors because of an institutional asymmetry in the manner in which returns to the factor are determined in each sector. In the Harris–Todaro model it is manufacturing that departs from marginal product pricing of labour; in the Lewis–Jorgenson models this role is played by agriculture.

In all three models discussed so far, it is assumed that product markets are perfectly competitive – the focus of the asymmetry is the determination of the returns to factors. However, a class of models has recently been developed by Taylor (1983) and associates which introduces a non-clearing product market for the output of one of the sectors, manufacturing. Together with a non-clearing labour market, this introduces Keynesian features into the dual economy. Implicit in the models of Taylor is a 'sink' into which unsatisfied purchasing power goes, and out of which it can be attracted by means of government policy. In contrast to these Keynesian features of the manufacturing sector, with its output being demand constrained, the agricultural sector output is modelled as having a flexible price which adjusts to equate supply and demand. The asymmetry attempts to capture the stylized facts that agricultural commodity markets are largely competitive while manufacturing product markets are oligopolistic. Such dualism is a departure from the earlier models of Lewis, Jorgenson and Harris–Todaro, but it is an asymmetry that needs to be investigated more closely. In particular, the different models each highlight a particular asymmetry but do not bring this together in a way that can pinpoint the contribution of each – this we would consider to be an important area of research.

Asymmetries of factor and product markets are certainly a major distinguishing feature of various dual economy models. However, there is another strand running through these models and that is the different assumptions regarding *factor mobility*. In the Uzawa two-sector model, the two factors are perfectly mobile between the sectors. In effect, therefore, there is a unified market for each factor across the two sectors. The various dual economy models make different assumptions with regard to different factors. As already noted, in the Lewis model capital is used only in the manufacturing sector (and land is only used in the agricultural sector), which can be treated as a production asymmetry or as an extreme assumption of the mobility of the two factors – they are perfectly immobile. This is similarly true of the Jorgenson model. But in both the Lewis and Jorgenson models, it is assumed that there is a (constant) wage differential between the two sectors. Two interpretations are given for this differential. One is simply in terms of compensating differences – the urban wage is higher to compensate for the disadvantages of the urban lifestyle (for a model which incorporates this explicitly, see McIntosh, 1975). The other seems to be more akin to a statement that the differential is an equilibrium phenomenon, generated by less than perfect mobility of labour across the two sectors. While the two interpretations may be indistinguishable as equilibrium phenomena, whether or not labour (or any other factor) is instantaneously mobile affects the *dynamics* of the model significantly, as is shown in Kanbur and McIntosh (1985). The long run stability and time path of a model can be altered radically depending on whether or not intersectoral factor movements are assumed to be fast relative to the rate of accumulation.

A similar situation arises in the Harris–Todaro model with respect to speeds of adjustment of the labour force across the two sectors. In the original paper the labour migration process and equilibrium is analysed *conditional* on a given capital stock. In other words, they assume this adjustment to be infinitely fast relative to the rate of accumulation. This seems an implausible specification, but it would not matter if the nature of the specification were irrelevant to the dynamics and the equilibrium of the model. However, as Bartlett (1983) has shown, allowing sectoral labour adjustment to occur at a speed commensurate with the rate of capital accumulation can introduce instability into the model with important consequences.

Thus the implications of alternative assumptions on the speed of intersectoral reallocation of factors in dual economy models, especially for the dynamic behaviour of these models, remains an extremely important area of analysis. The variety of time paths generated by different assumptions should alert us to their critical importance. However, there is another aspect of long run analysis that needs to be discussed. If dualism is to do with asymmetrics and factor immobilities, is not the end of dualism to do with the end (or a severe diminishing) of these asymmetrics and immobilities? Given their particular definition of dualism, and their particular specification of intersectoral factor movement speeds, the models discussed here all trace out the consequences of accumulation with unchanged assumptions. But none of the models surveyed here, and indeed none of the models we are aware of, incorporates the end of dualism itself as a long run outcome. Even in the Lewis model, the end of the surplus labour phase may or may not herald the end of organizational asymmetry between the two sectors. There is, thus, a gap in the literature; there are dual economy models of development, and there are non-dual economy models of growth but there are no models which treat the degree of factor immobility and asymmetry as endogenous and, hence, there are no models which analyse the path of dualism itself. This is clearly a major area for further research.

So far we have interpreted dualism to mean intersectoral asymmetries at the national level. However, in the wake of the policy debates on the new international economic order, there has developed a class of 'North–South' models which can essentially be viewed as models of dualism on the international scale. So far as asymmetries are concerned, these models share many of the features of standard dual economy models. As Findlay (1984) notes: 'I use the term "North–South" model to refer to any model in which there is some basic asymmetry related to the stage of development between the two regions.' Findlay (1980) has himself explored asymmetries in the operation of factor markets, with 'surplus labour' in the South and neo-classical conditions in the North. Taylor (1983) has modified this to make the North Keynesian by introducing non-clearing factor and product markets.

As in standard dual economy models, factor mobility assumptions are crucial to models of international dualism. All of the best known North–South models share the feature that labour is immobile between the regions (although international migration models tackle this aspect, they are not in an explicitly 'North–South', i.e. asymmetry based, framework). In this North–South models differ from single economy models because in many ways the essence of the latter is the shift of labour from the traditional to the modern sectors. However, recent models in the North–South genre focus on *capital mobility* (e.g. Burgstaller and Saavedra-Rivano, 1983), and in this way they differ again from standard models, which on the whole disregard capital mobility across sectors.

As with standard dual economy models, North–South models do not entertain to any great extent the end of dualism itself as the world economy progresses. However, an equally obvious problem is that at the level of global interaction a two-sector classification is perhaps too coarse to capture some basic questions of interest. In particular, the neglect of OPEC and COMECON as trading blocks in the world is difficult to justify empirically, and it is difficult to see how the special features of these blocks can be fitted into a two-region framework. Surplus labour is hardly a characteristic of OPEC, and they do not produce a manufactured product. Some attempts have been made to build a Three Regions Model of Global Interaction incorporating North, South and OPEC (Gonzalez-Romero and Kanbur, 1986; Taylor, 1983; and van Wijnbergen, 1985), but much more work is needed here, and the incorporation of COMECON is still an open question.

The need for a finer level of disaggregation at the world level raises the question of whether the two-sector classification is adequate at the economy level. Of course, it depends on the questions being asked. As Sen (1975) observes, 'A million × million matrix is not a joy to handle.' Thus, there are costs to disaggregation and the optimal level of disaggregation depends on the purpose at hand. But it can be argued that for some purposes the dual structure may not be adequate, in particular where the nature of dualism is changing and the economy is characterized, for example, by an advanced capitalist sector which produces goods for export, an intermediate manufacturing sector which produces non-traded goods for domestic consumption, and a traditional agricultural/ urban-informal sector. In these cases the insights of dual economy models need to be extended in order to shed light on the development process.

BIBLIOGRAPHY

Bartlett, W. 1983. On the dynamic instability of induced-migration unemployment in a dual economy. *Journal of Development Economics* 12, 85–95.

Bhagwati, J. and Srinivasan, T.N. 1974. On reanalyzing the Harris–Todaro model: policy rankings in the case of sector-specific sticky wages. *American Economic Review* 64, 502–8.

Boeke, J.H. 1953. *Economics and Economic Policy of Dual Societies as Exemplified by Indonesia.* New York: Institute of Pacific Relations.

Burgstaller, A. and Saavedra-Rivano, N. 1983. Capital mobility and growth in a North–South model. Columbia University Economics Department Discussion Paper No. 111.

Corden, W.M. and Findlay, R. 1975. Urban unemployment, intersectoral capital mobility and development policy. *Economica* 42, 59–78.

Dixit, A.K. 1973. Models of dual economies. *Models of Economic Growth*, ed. J.A. Mirrlees and N.H. Stern, New York: John Wiley & Sons, 325–57.

Fei, J.C.H. and Ranis, G. 1964. *Developmment of the Labour Surplus Economy: Theory and Policy.* Homewood: Irwin.

Findlay, R. 1980. The terms of trade and equilibrium growth in the world economy. *American Economic Review* 70, 291–9.

Findlay, R. 1984. Growth and development in trade models. In *Handbook of International Economics*, Vol. 1, ed. R.W. Jones and P.B. Kenen, Amsterdam: North-Holland, 187–232.

Gonzalez-Romero, A. and Kanbur, S.M.R. 1986. Oil and the North-South terms of trade. University of Essex Discussion Paper.

Harris, J.R. and Todaro, M.P. 1970. Migration, unemployment and development: a two-sector analysis. *American Economic Review* 60(1), March, 126–42.

Kanbur, S.M.R. and McIntosh, J. 1986. Dual economy models: retrospect and prospect. University of Essex Discussion Paper.

Jorgenson, D.W. 1961. The development of a dual economy. *Economic Journal* 71, 309–34.

Lewis, W.A. 1954. Economic development with unlimited supplies of labour. *Manchester School of Economics and Social Studies* 22, 139–91.

Little, I.M.D. 1982. *Economic Development: Theory, Policy, and International Relations.* New York: Basic Books.

McIntosh, J. 1975. Growth and dualism in less developed countries. *Review of Economic Studies* 42, 421–43.

Sen, A.K. 1975. *Employment, Technology and Development.* Oxford and New York: Oxford University Press.

Taylor, L. 1983. *Structuralist Macroeconomics.* New York: Basic Books.

Uzawa, H. 1961–3. On a two-sector model of economic growth. *Review of Economic Studies*, Pt. I, 29, October 1961, 40–47, Pt. II, 30, June 1963, 105–18.

van Wijnbergen, S. 1985. Interdependence revisited: a developing countries perspective on macroeconomic management and trade policy in the industrial world. *Economic Policy* 1, November, 81–317.

Famine

A.K. GHOSE

Attempts to formulate a precise definition of famine are fraught with difficulties. In commonsense terms, a famine refers to a sudden event involving large-scale deaths from starvation within a short period. In reality, the existence of starvation has been and remains a persistent characteristic of many societies. This means that a famine has to be defined in terms of a significant deviation from a 'norm' and it is hard to avoid ambiguities in such an enterprise. Moreover, in many situations, it is virtually impossible to distinguish between deaths from starvation and those from disease. Since starvation reduces the human body's resistance to disease, deaths from starvation can be easily confused with deaths from disease and famines are typically accompanied by epidemics. In spite of these difficulties of definition, however, a famine, when it occurs, rarely fails to be recognized. There is usually a sudden increase in mortality and there are obvious signs (e.g. begging, eating of inedibles, food riots, sharp increase in petty crimes, unusual scales of migration, etc.) of a desperate search for food by a sizeable section of the population.

In recorded history, nearly all societies have periodically suffered the devastating consequences of famines. The earliest recorded famine, which occurred in ancient Egypt, dates back to the fourth millennium BC. The most recent famines occurred in Ethiopia and Sudan as late as 1985–1986. While a complete list of famines is unlikely ever to be compiled, even an incomplete reckoning strongly suggests that very few societies managed to escape them (see the list provided in the 1985 edition of the *Encyclopedia Britannica*, vol. 4, p. 675).

Unfortunately, in spite of its ubiquity in human history, famine remains a misunderstood or at best an inadequately understood phenomenon. It is true, of course, that some societies (e.g. the European countries) which repeatedly suffered famines in the past are now free of this threat. But this should be seen as a fortuitous result of varied historical processes rather than as an outcome of purposive endeavours. For misconceptions about the causes of famine persist and hinder scientific investigations into past famines even today. The fact that many societies do not as yet possess the ability to anticipate, prevent or even adequately respond to famine is in part attributable to the wide acceptance of views based on such misconceptions.

In section 1, the most influential of these views are briefly discussed and are confronted with factual evidence drawn from some of the major famines of the past. Apart from highlighting some common fallacies with respect to causation, this discussion also brings into focus some important facts which a theory of famine must seek to explain. An approach to famine analysis is then outlined in section 2. Finally, some policy measures needed to counter the threat of famine in contemporary developing countries are briefly discussed in section 3.

1. THE QUESTION OF CAUSATION. If wars are not taken into account, it would be true to say that natural disasters, principally droughts and floods, preceded most of the major famines in known history (the exceptions are the Bengal famine of 1943 which was not preceded by any natural disaster and the Irish famine of the 1840s where the precipitating factor was a plant disease in the form of potato blight). This fact gave rise to a remarkable fallacy of the *post hoc ergo propter hoc* type. Until very recently, the major famines were widely believed to have been caused by food shortages generated by natural disasters (see, for example, Masefield, 1963 and Aykroyd, 1974). Thus famines were viewed as natural rather than social phenomena. Descriptions of famine as the 'extreme and persistent shortage of food' (1985 edition of the *Encyclopedia Britannica*, vol. 4, p. 674) abound in the literature on the subject.

The proponents of the 'food shortage' hypothesis sometimes sought support in simple-minded interpretations of Adam Smith's view that market forces achieved the best results in social production and distribution and of Malthus's view that famines constituted a 'positive check' on population growth. If market forces indeed ensure the optimal production and distribution of food in all situations, then famines must imply food shortages due to natural calamities. Alternatively, if it is societies' failure to keep population growth in line with growth of food supply which invites nature's wrath in the form of famine, food shortages are again implied.

The view that famines are caused by food shortages was held with such certainty that some observers, when confronted with evidence that food was not in short supply during certain famines, suggested that famines were partly explained by people's reluctance to change their food habits even in times of scarcity. Thus one commentator on the Irish famine insinuated that the Irish people's refusal to eat anything other than potatoes had worsened the situation (C.E. Trevelyan quoted in Woodham-Smith, 1962). Another commentator on the Bengal famine of 1943 suggested that many Bengalis could in fact have saved their lives had they been prepared to eat wheat (Moraes, 1975). Yet, it has been reported time and again that during famines people eat all sorts of inedibles including human flesh (*Encyclopedia Britannica*, vol. 4, p. 675; Mallory, 1926).

On reflection, the emphasis on food shortage in explaining famine appears rather puzzling. For, even on purely logical grounds, it is implausible to suppose that famines are universally caused by food shortages. While most famines were indeed preceded by reductions in food output, it cannot be deduced that such reductions necessarily led to food shortages. And while food shortages can certainly cause famines, it does not follow that all famines must necessarily be caused by food shortages. Famine implies that some people do not have adequate access to food, it does not imply that food itself is in short supply.

The explanation of the puzzle may well lie in the fact that habits of thought often fail to change *pari passu* with changing reality. It is possible to imagine situations where famines must necessarily be caused by food shortages. In a country where transport systems and trade relationships are undeveloped, a localized crop failure can cause a localized famine even though there may not be a serious food shortage in the country as a whole. Some of the famines of the remote past were undoubtedly of this type. Such circumstances, however, have long ceased to exist. The development of transport systems and trade relationships has virtually eliminated the possibility of localized crop failures generating localized food shortages.

It is arguable, however, that famines are to be explained not in terms of food shortages but in terms of 'food availability decline'. In a society with a given pattern of distribution of food among the population, a certain level of food supply is required to ensure that even the most disadvantaged sections do not starve. If the food supply falls below this level, the poorest must starve unless the decline in the food supply itself leads to a reduction in the inequality of food distribution. Since it can be plausibly argued that a decline in food supply typically leads to a worsening of food distribution, reductions in food supply can clearly cause famine. But, firstly, it still cannot be argued that famines are necessarily caused by reductions in food supply. Secondly, since changes in food distribution in consequence of reductions in food supply are of crucial importance in determining the overall effects, reductions in food supply in themselves do not have much predictive power. A ten per cent decline in food supply may lead to a major famine in one situation but to only a minor squeeze on some people's food consumption in another.

It is useful, at this point, to look at some facts. A careful scrutiny of the available evidence from some of the major famines of the past yields the following conclusions. First, some major famines were not in fact preceded by any significant decline in food production or availability. The outstanding example is the Bengal famine of 1943, but there are others (Sen, 1981). Second, many of those famines which were preceded by food availability decline did not in fact involve absolute shortages of food. The examples include the Indian famines which occurred between 1860 and 1910 and the Irish famine of the 1840s (Ghose, 1982; Woodham-Smith, 1962). Third, even during severe famines, food was often exported not only from the countries concerned but also from the famine-affected regions themselves. For example, throughout the period 1860–1910, when twenty major famines and scarcities were experienced, India was a signficant net exporter of food-grains; moreover, there is evidence to show that some of the regions worst affected by famines exported food in the famine years (Ghose, 1982). Ireland also was a net exporter of food during the 1840s (Woodham-Smith, 1962). Fourth, only the people belonging to particular social classes died of starvation during famines. In India, for example, landlords and merchants often prospered during famines while agricultural labourers, artisans, barbers, washermen, etc. died in their thousands (Ghose, 1982; see also Alamgir, 1980; Sen, 1981; Woodham-Smith, 1962 for further evidence).

These facts argue strongly against the 'food shortage' hypothesis. The 'food availability decline' hypothesis does much better, but even this fails to explain a number of major famines. Clearly, famines do not have a single cause. A recognition of this helps focus attention on the determinants of people's access to food. Food supply may indeed be one of these determinants, but it certainly is not the only one.

2. FAMINE AND ECONOMIC ANALYSIS. Perhaps because famines were believed to be caused by natural disasters, economists had rarely concerned themselves with famine analysis; this was left, until very recently, largely to journalists, administrators and historians. The classical economists noted the distressing poverty of the labouring classes; Malthus and Marx in particular attempted to identify the causes of persistent misery and provided some valuable insights (Malthus, 1798 and 1800; Marx, 1867, ch. 25). But Malthus negated his own insights by insisting that famines constituted a 'positive check' on population growth and Marx was primarily concerned with the long-term dynamic of capitalist economies. On the whole, analysis of poverty and famine remained outside the framework of classical political economy. The neoclassical framework of general equilibrium analysis, currently in vogue, assumes away possibilities of starvation; it supposes that individuals possess adequate resources to survive above starvation levels even without entering exchange relations (Koopmans, 1957). Even the early development theorists did not concern themselves with problems of starvation and famines (consider the works of Mandelbaum, Nurkse and Lewis).

In the early 1970s, the problems of poverty and malnutrition in developing countries began to attract economists' attention. Subsequently, following the pioneering work of Sen (1977), famine analysis was brought into the domain of economists' interests. Much remains to be done and, in particular, famine analysis is yet to be integrated into the body of development theory. But a new approach to famine analysis has emerged and this is outlined below.

A household's (or an individual's) access to food is determined, firstly, by its asset-holding and, secondly, by the possibilities of transforming assets into food. The universally held asset is labour. But households may hold, in addition, land, other instruments of production or special skills. The transformation possibilities depend both on the employability of the assets for production (including production of services) and on the exchange ratios between assets and food or between yields of assets and food. At the level of individual households, employability of assets is not always guaranteed; labour may remain unemployed, artisanal products may remain unsold and services may not be demanded. Exchange ratios can be complex and unstable. For a peasant household which owns land and produces its own food requirements, productivities of land and labour are the relevant exchange ratios and these obviously depend on the quality of land as well as on weather conditions. For a peasant household which produces a non-food crop, an additional relevant exchange ratio is that between the non-food crop and food. For a landless labourer, the ratio of exchange between labour and food may be direct (when wages are paid in food) or indirect (when wages are paid in money). A variety of other institutional arrangements such as tenancy and credit relations may have important consequences for the ratio of exchange between labour and food for both peasants and landless labourers. The important point to note in all this is that assetholding, employability of assets and exchange ratios, which determine individual households' access to food, are subject to rules set by societies.

It takes only a small step to see that in any society, the distribution of food among the population depends on the distribution of productive assets (in the case of agrarian societies, on the structure of property rights in land), on the rules governing their employability and on a host of exchange relations and ratios. Changes in one or more of these parameters and variables imply changes in the distribution of food and may mean a drastic reduction in some people's access to it. Depending upon the particular characteristics of a society, such changes can be caused by a variety of factors including reductions in food output due to natural disasters. A serious analysis of famine requires an adequate understanding of the relevant institutional and economic characteristics of the society in question as well as identification of those variables which are liable to drastic changes.

To see these arguments in more concrete terms, consider an agrarian society which is composed of three classes: food producers (i.e. landowners), agricultural labourers and other workers (artisans and service workers such as barbers, washermen, etc.). Food flows principally from the landowners to the other classes in exchange for labour, non-food products and services, and these exchanges are mediated by money. Thus the ability of the non-landowners to acquire food depends on three types of variables: the landowners' demand for labour, non-food products and services; the prices of these items and the price of food. A crop failure may affect all these variables: the landowners' demand for agricultural labour, artisanal products and services may decline and the relative prices of these items vis-à-vis food may decline simultaneously. A crop failure can thus lead not only to a decline in food supply but also to a more unequal distribution of the available food. But the relative prices of labour, artisanal products and services vis-à-vis food can decline for other reasons too, as a consequence of a sharp rise in the government's demand for food, for instance. Thus even when food supply remains unaltered, inequality of food distribution may sharply rise leading to a famine. A focus on employment and prices is adequate for analysing both of these cases; a focus on food supply is both inadequate and misleading.

There is in fact something more to the story. In the situation described above, it has been supposed that the landowners produce only food, but they may be producing both food and non-food crops in some combination. In general, the cropping pattern depends in an important way on the structure of landownership. For example, other things being equal, food production is likely to be more emphasized in a situation where a majority of the landowners are peasant proprietors than in a situation where a majority are larger landlords. The level of food production itself is in part socially determined. This also means that the extent of decline in food production in the wake of a natural disaster is not independent of the structural characteristics of an economy. While in one situation, all efforts may be made to limit the damage to food crops, such efforts may well be directed largely to limiting the damage to non-food crops in another situation.

In short, famine fundamentally is a social phenomenon which can be understood only by focusing on the institutions and arrangements which determine the access to food of different classes and groups in a society. In this perspective, the links between persistent mass poverty and periodic famines are rather obvious. The same set of forces generate mass poverty over time and famines in certain periods. Mass poverty results from long-term changes in social production and distribution mechanisms; famines result from violent short-term changes in the same mechanisms. Growth or mass poverty increases vulnerability to famine through raising the percentage of population surviving on the margin of subsistence in normal periods. Famine increases mass poverty by permanently altering the distribution or productive assets in favour of the richer section of the population (see Ghose, 1982 for some evidence). Emphasis on such simple indicators as food supply frustrates efforts to develop effective policies and instruments for combating both mass poverty and the ever-present threat of famine in the less developed parts of the world.

3. FAMINE AND STATE POLICY. In societies where universal social security systems are unlikely to be in place for a long time to come, anticipation, relief and prevention of famine must be among the central objectives of state policy. And it is absolutely essential to ensure that state policy is based on sound judgements. The potential cost of judgemental error is high; millions of lives may be at stake. These, of course, are normative statements. It certainly cannot be assumed that governments everywhere will adopt policies whose desirability is manifest from a humanitarian standpoint. It is naive to suppose that many of the past famines would not have occurred had a correct theory existed; saving lives was not always a high priority for governments. This, however, is no place to dwell on these issues.

As already noted, the index traditionally used to anticipate famine has been per capita food output (or availability). It should be clear from the arguments presented above that this index is quite inadequate for the purpose and can be totally misleading. In fact, no single index is adequate. For correct anticipation, changes in the pattern of asset distribution, in employment possibilities, in wages and prices and in per capita food output must all be carefully monitored.

As for famine relief, strictly non-interventionist policies were sometimes advocated in the past. During the Indian famines of the 19th century and the Irish famine of the 1840s, the colonial administrators invoked Adam Smith's doctrines to justify non-interventionist policies (Ambirajan, 1978; Aykroyd, 1974; Rashid, 1980; Woodham-Smith, 1962). Repeated failures of the market forces to cure famines eventually proved to be persuasive arguments in favour of intervention. For some time now, the standard method of intervention has been free distribution of food to the famine-affected population. This undoubtedly is the best option once a famine is already in course. If, however, an approaching famine can be anticipated well in advance, implementation of appropriately designed and timed food-for-work programmes is a far better method. This is not only because assets can be created at the same time as starvation deaths are prevented, but also because this method allows people to retain their dignity.

For either of these methods of intervention to be feasible, food must be available. It has been argued above that famines generally do not involve food shortages. It would be wrong to suppose, however, that governments can acquire enough food for purposes of relief through purchases from the market or that relief can be provided in the form of cash payments. Governments' attempts to purchase food from the market in the pre-famine or famine periods will increase the relative price of food and thus risk worsening the situation. Relief in the form of cash payments will also increase the relative price of food and is most likely to redistribute food among the poor. For effective relief, governments must either drawn upon accumulated food stocks or stop food exports or increase food imports. A viable policy of stock management in food is an essential weapon in the fight against famine.

Elimination of the threat of famine calls for policies which are essentially the same as those needed to eradicate mass poverty. These policies fall into two categories: those designed to improve the security of access to food of the vulnerable groups and those designed to reduce the dependence of food output on the forces of nature. The first category includes such policies as agrarian reforms, creation of stable employment outside agriculture, promotion of effective organizations of the poor, development of state-sponsored social security systems for the poorest, etc. The second category includes measures to improve technological conditions of production in the food sector (e.g. development of effective irrigation and drainage systems). However, though conceptually it is convenient to separate them, the two types of policies are interactive in practice. Implementation of agrarian reforms, for example, often facilitates the development of irrigation and drainage systems. Improvement in the security of access to food of the vulnerable groups and reduction in the degree of dependence on nature generally reinforce each other.

The entire discussion in this essay has been concerned with economic processes and policies within countries. These certainly should be accorded primacy, but it needs to be recognized that they are not altogether independent of the nature and dynamics of international economic relations. To take an example, the policy of encouraging production of export crops to the neglect of food crops (a policy which has relevance for food security issues), pursued in many developing countries, is directly linked to the nature of their involvement in international economic relations. From another standpoint, it can be said that the international economy displays certain features which are remarkably similar to those observed in national economies. The level of food production in the world today is such that there need be no starvation and famine in any part of the globe. But just as adequate food availability in a country does not guarantee access to adequate food for all, the existence of food surplus at the global level does not do much to resolve food security problems in individual countries. The causes are similar and so are the remedies.

BIBLIOGRAPHY

Alamgir, M. 1980. *Famine in South Asia: Political Economy of Mass Starvation.* Cambridge, Mass.: Oelgeschlager, Gunn and Hain.

Ambirajan, S. 1978. *Classical Political Economy and British Policy in India.* Cambridge: Cambridge University Press.

Aykroyd, W.R. 1974. *The Conquest of Famine.* London: Chatto & Windus; New York: Readers Digest Press, 1974.

Ghose, A.K. 1982. Food supply and starvation: a study of famines with reference to the Indian sub-continent. *Oxford Economic Papers* 34(2), July, 368–84.

Koopmans, T.C. 1957. *Three Essays on the State of Economic Science.* New York: McGraw-Hill.

Mallory, W.H. 1926. *China: Land of Famine.* New York: American Geographical Society.

Malthus, T.R. 1798. *An Essay on the Principle of Population.* London. Harmondsworth: Penguin, 1970.

Malthus, T.R. 1800. *An Investigation of the Cause of the Present High Price of Provision.* London.

Marx, K. 1867. *Capital* Vol. 1. Reprinted, Harmondsworth: Penguin, 1976; New York: International Publishers, 1967.

Masefield, G.B. 1963. *Famine: Its Prevention and Relief.* Oxford: Oxford University Press.

Moraes, D. 1975. The dimensions of the problem: comment. In *Hunger, Politics and Markets: The Real Issues of the Food Crisis,* ed. S. Aziz, New York: New York University Press.

Rashid, S. 1980. The policy of laissez-faire during scarcities. *Economic Journal* 90, September, 493–503.

Sen, A.K. 1977. Starvation and exchange entitlements: a general approach and its application to the Great Bengal Famine. *Cambridge Journal of Economics* 1(1), 33–59.

Sen, A.K. 1981. *Poverty and Famines: An Essay on Entitlement and Deprivation.* Oxford: Clarendon Press.

Woodham-Smith, C. 1962. *The Great Hunger: Ireland 1845–49.* London: Hamish Hamilton.

Fiscal and Monetary Policies in Developing Countries

ÉPRIME ESHAG

Economic development is a highly complex process involving not only economic but also social, political, cultural and technological changes. But here it is more narrowly defined as the process of increasing the utilization and improving the productivity of available resources, a process which stimulates the growth of national income and results in an increase in the economic welfare of the community.

A person's economic welfare can roughly be measured by his income and consumption. For individuals in different income groups it is assumed, in line with the 19th-century English Utilitarians, that the amount of economic welfare, or utility, derived from a given increment in income will be larger for those in the lower than in the higher income groups. As Marshall put it, 'A shilling is the measure of less pleasure, or satisfaction of any kind, to a rich man than to a poor one' (Marshall, 1920, p. 19). This means that in assessing the pace of development one must take into account the distribution of national income; the larger the share of the lower income groups, which constitute the bulk of the population in LDCs, in any given increment of national income, the greater the increase in the economic welfare of the community and hence the higher its rate of development.

The two most striking characteristics of LDCs, which largely account for their low per capita income, are the underutilization and the inferior productivity of their land and labour resources. These characteristics are primarily due to the inadequacy of their capital equipment in relation to the size of their labour forces and to the available area of cultivable land. An additional reason is that their technology is generally backward and their labour force often lacks technical, administrative and organizational skills and suffers from poor health. Both these deficiencies can be remedied only through investment – investment in capital equipment, including infrastructure, and in human resources through education, health care and new skills.

From another point of view, LDCs can be seen as 'supply-determined', in that it is the productive capacity rather than demand that generally limits the level of their activity. This means that the long-run rate of growth in them is determined by the rate at which their productive capacity grows as a result of net investment in the economy. Leaving aside the question of the capital intensity of production, the larger the share of investment in GNP, the greater the rate of growth of productive capacity. An acceleration in the rate of growth of productive capacity and GNP will require an increase in the share of investment in GNP (Kalecki, 1976, pp. 100–103).

The role of fiscal and monetary policies and instruments in development in the non-socialist economies dealt with here is discussed under two broad headings: (I) Financing of Investment and (II) Pattern of Investment; the use that can be made of these instruments in demand management and in dealing with short-term internal and external imbalances (Eshag, 1983, pp. 41–50 and ch. 6) is not considered. The discussion will cover both the *potential* of fiscal and monetary instruments for promoting development and the *actual* use made of them by developing countries. The potential is determined by assuming that the governments of LDCs are genuinely committed and give the highest priority to the promotion of development, as defined above. This assumption is not entirely realistic: in each country there are a number of classes and income groups, often with diverging interests, exercising different degrees of influence on governments, which cannot therefore be expected to act neutrally in the interest of the economic welfare of the community as a whole. Moreover, one must take into account the relative weakness and unreliability of the administrative machinery of most LDCs, which in practice constrains their freedom of choice of policy instruments (Eshag, 1983, pp. 23–6).

I. FINANCING OF INVESTMENT. The total resources available to a country for financing domestic investment is equal to the sum of national savings and net capital receipts from abroad. The inflow of foreign capital into LDCs is determined by a number of political and economic factors in which fiscal and monetary policies play a relatively minor role; the discussion can, therefore, be confined to the use of these policies to promote savings.

Of the two sets of instruments, fiscal and monetary, it is the former that can play a significant role in determining the shares of savings and consumption in GNP. The *direct* impact of monetary measures on consumption is largely confined to sales made under hire-purchase or consumer credit schemes, which represent a relatively small proportion of total consumption in LDCs. The neoclassical assumption that a rise in the real rate of interest would have a significant positive effect on private propensity to save and vice versa is of doubtful validity (Eshag, 1983, pp. 44–6). The propensity to save is determined by a large number of factors in which the interest rate plays a relatively minor role (Keynes, 1936, ch. 8–9). Moreover, such correlation as may exist between the rate of interest and private propensity to save is as likely to be negative as positive.

Since savings equal national income *less* consumption, it follows that measures which succeed in restraining the growth of government and private consumption, without at the same time retarding the growth of production, will also raise the share of savings in national income. To ensure that the growth of production is not retarded, the authorities must be willing to offset the contractionary impact of curbing consumption by an adequate increase in public investment.

Of the various categories of *government consumption*, the one that can be reduced in most LDCs – namely, those that do not face a serious threat of external aggression – without hindering their development, is expenditure on defence. A significant part of the increment in savings resulting from a cut in defence outlay will be in the form of scarce foreign exchange resources used to import military equipment.

In a study of defence expenditure of a random sample of 24 developing countries outside the region of the Arab-Israeli conflict, it was found that the unweighted arithmetic average of the ratio of their defence expenditure to GNP between 1974 and 1978 was of the same order of magnitude as that of nine members of NATO, and some 50 per cent greater than that of four neutral European countries. This ratio was particularly high for the eight Asian countries included in the sample, which together accounted for almost two-thirds of the population of LDCs; it amounted to about 4.5 per cent, compared with a ratio of 3 per cent for NATO members and 2 per cent for the neutral countries. Moreover, in almost all LDCs, expenditure on defence was higher than on health and, in some, even larger than combined outlay on education and health. The reasons for this economically wasteful pattern of expenditure, which remains unchanged to date, include the use of military force to suppress political opposition; armament races between countries involved in territorial disputes, often of little or no economic significance; and, at times, display of sophisticated modern weapons for prestige (Eshag, 1983, pp. 81–8).

Taxation. Apart from rationing, the chief instrument for increasing savings by restraining the growth of *private consumption* is taxation. Both direct and indirect taxes have the effect of reducing the purchasing power of the private sector's real disposable income and consumption. Because private consumption accounts for a considerably larger share of GNP than investment, any reduction in its rate of growth is calculated to raise the pace of expansion of savings and investment by a much higher percentage; this explains the important role generally assigned to taxation in development.

To ensure its effectiveness in promoting development, a taxation system should possess certain basic characteristics. First, the system should ensure that the burden of taxation is primarily borne by the higher income groups; the higher the per capita income of a group, the larger its contribution to tax revenue as a proportion of its income should be. This requires the implementation of a progressive system of direct taxation on income and wealth. It also implies that indirect taxes levied for revenue purposes, should be imposed mainly on 'luxuries' – namely, goods and services largely consumed by the higher income groups – rather than on those consumed by the bulk of population, 'necessities'.

Second, taxation measures should, whenever possible, be so devised as to stimulate production and, in any case, should not significantly reduce material incentives. For this reason, in two important sectors in LDCs, agriculture and small businesses, a system of progressive lump-sum taxation is preferable to taxation of production, income or profits. In neither of these two sectors is it possible in practice to enforce a dependable system of bookkeeping which could be used for the assessment of the taxpayers' income even with an efficient and reliable fiscal machinery, which is rarely to be found among LDCs. A system of 'taxation by area', under which tax rates per acre are fixed for different regions of a country on the basis of *potential* land yields and are graduated according to the taxpayers' aggregate landholding, has the advantage of being simple and is also calculated to stimulate production. Similar advantages can be derived in the taxation of small businesses from a system of 'licence fees', under which the fees are varied according to some concrete and well-defined criteria, such as the location of a business and its size (Eshag, 1983, pp. 108–112).

Third, the taxation system should be simple and readily understood by both collectors and payers of taxes, even if simplicity is achieved at the cost of some inequity in the distribution of the tax burden.

Fourth, to permit a faster growth in investment than in consumption, tax revenue should be income-elastic. In addition to implementing a progressive system of direct taxation, lump-sum taxes, such as those proposed for agriculture and small businesses, should be raised periodically in line with inflation and growth of potential land yields.

Fifth, to ensure that total tax revenue is not subject to violent fluctuations, tax sources should be diversified. The need for stability in tax revenue is a further reason for taxation of the agricultural sector along the lines suggested, rather than through export taxes or commodity boards (Eshag, 1983, pp. 104–6).

Very few developing countries have to date made adequate use of taxation policy to restrain the growth of private consumption. 'Tax ratio', which measures the ratio of tax revenue to GNP, provides a rough indication of governments' efforts to restrain private consumption and of their success in doing so. In a study covering a random sample of 27 LDCs, it was found that in the first half of the 1970s the unweighted arithmetic mean of their tax ratio was about 14 per cent, of which less than one-third was received from direct taxes. This compared with a tax ratio of almost 40 per cent, in which about two-thirds represented direct tax revenue, for a sample of thirteen industrial countries (Eshag, 1983, pp. 92–7).

The pronounced difference between the tax ratios of LDCs and developed economies, which persists to date, can be explained only partly by the lower per capita income of the former. The large inequality of income distribution in LDCs suggests that their taxation potential is significantly higher than is indicated by their per capita income. That per capita income by itself does not provide a sufficient explanation of the low tax ratios in LDCs is clearly demonstrated by the fact that the average tax ratio among the nine African countries was appreciably higher than that for the eight Latin American countries included in the above sample, although the average per capita income of the former was about 60 per cent lower than the latter. The available evidence shows that the unwillingness and inability of governments in LDCs to tax the richer strata of the community, who exercise a substantial influence on the formulation and implementation of tax measures, goes a long way to explain their low tax ratios. The influence of big landlords, for example, is largely responsible for the use of out-of-date land and rental valuations as a basis of tax assessments and thus for allowing inflation to erode the real value of land taxes in many countries.

II. PATTERN OF INVESTMENT. Market forces would inevitably tend to pull a large proportion of investment resources to 'inessential industries', namely those that cater to the relatively strong demand of higher income groups. This would stimulate the production of luxuries at the expense of necessities, and produce a 'lop-sided' development. Selective fiscal and monetary measures can be used to influence the allocation of resources in a way which discourages this type of development. Such measures should be directed at (a) promoting 'essential industries', which produce necessities, in order to prevent a rise in the price of wage goods, which generally results in the redistribution of income in favour of higher income group, and (b) ensuring a balanced sectoral and regional growth, so as to reduce production bottlenecks and regional inequalities of income.

It is clear that the formulation of a meaningful and coherent investment policy can only take place within the framework of a development plan. As a minimum, the plan should provide a rough outline of projected movements in the volume and pattern of production and demand as well as of requirements for productive capacities, including labour and raw materials inputs.

In most LDCs, the public sector accounts for a significant proportion (varying between about 30 and 50 per cent) of total investment. The pattern of this investment is determined by governments themselves and does not require the employment of fiscal and monetary instruments whose efficacy in influencing the allocation of resources can rarely be predicted accurately. Since the value of public investment is equal to the government's savings plus its net borrowing, it follows that, *ceteris paribus*, a rise in tax ratio would increase the share of public investment in the total. Thus, taxation, apart from raising the share of investment in GNP by restraining consumption, contributes to the efficacy of the policies concerned with regulating the pattern of investment.

Fiscal instruments. Historically, *import tariffs* have been the most popular fiscal instrument used to promote industrial development. Because the protection afforded to domestic industries by tariffs cannot be accurately estimated, they have at times been reinforced by *import quotas*. Although these protectionist policies have played an important role in encouraging import substitution in LDCs since the Great Depression of the 1930s, the pattern of industrialization induced by them has in most countries failed adequately to conform to their development needs. This is largely explained by the absence of an investment licensing system that could effectively discourage the flow of resources into inessential industries; these have thrived, often with the aid of foreign investment, behind the protective barriers of tariffs and quotas. The reason for this is to be found partly in the weakness of the administrative machinery responsible for implementing investment regulations and partly in the political influence exercised by the richer classes in the formulation of such regulations; what is a 'luxury' for the poor is often regarded as a 'necessity' by the rich.

Tax concessions and *multiple exchange rates* are two other instruments employed to influence the allocation of resources, although these, like tariffs and quotas, have in practice largely served to foster industrialization in general rather than to direct resources into essential industries. Tax concessions are provided in the form of temporary exemption from profit taxes (tax holidays) for certain new industries, and of tariff concessions on industrial inputs. Under the multiple exchange rates system differential exchange rates are applied to foreign-exchange transactions to encourage the production and export of industrial products.

Apart from credit subsidies, discussed below, a number of other *subsidies* are often used to encourage the export of manufactures and to stimulate agricultural production. The latter subsidies usually take the form of the provision of agricultural inputs to farmers at subsidized prices and/or of guaranteed price schemes under which the prices paid to farmers exceed world prices.

Monetary instruments. Although monetary instruments play no signficant role in directly increasing savings and investment, they can be used to influence the pattern of investment. In theory, this can be done through the operation of special *development banks* which are charged with the provision of cheap, or subsidized, credit to selected industrial establishments and to the agricultural sector. According to the OECD, there were about 340 such banks operating in some 80 developing countries in the mid-1960s; indications are that their number has significantly increased since that date. Over half the banks were state-owned and funded by the exchequer; the remainder had a mixed ownership or were private. Mixed and private banks are given governmental subsidies to enable them to earn a normal rate of profit (Eshag, 1983, pp. 186–92).

In addition to advancing loans to selected private enterprises, *industrial development banks* also help to promote new industrial ventures, directly or in partnership with private firms, and provide technical assistance to their clients. Formally, these banks are supposed to attach a greater weight to the development implications of their investments than to profitability, although in practice this is generally true only of some state-owned banks (Eshag, 1983, pp. 193–6). On the whole, the primary function of the banks, like that of the fiscal instruments discussed above, has been to promote industrialization, without much discrimination between essential and inessential industries.

Officially, the principal function of the *agricultural development banks*, most of which are state-funded, is to advance credit, at subsidized interest rates, to the agricultural sector, in particular to 'small farmers', namely those who cultivate relatively small plots of land with little fixed capital and with backward technology and who are, in consequence, very poor. Owing to their low credit rating, small farmers have virtually no access to commercial banks and have to meet the bulk of their credit requirements by borrowing from non-institutional sources, notably professional moneylenders, landlords and merchant middlemen, at rates of interest which far exceed those charged by commercial banks. The subsidized credit provided by development banks can thus, in theory, contribute to development in two important ways: (a) to improve the lot of small farmers by reducing the cost of their borrowing; and (b) to stimulate agricultural production by financing the modernization of cultivation techniques, especially among small farmers.

The operation of agricultural development banks during the early 1970s has been studied by the World Bank, FAO and many agricultural economists (Eshag, 1983, pp. 196–203, footnotes). Almost all these studies indicate that very few countries have in practice made full use of the developmental potential of these banks. It is estimated that in most countries less than 30 per cent of subsidized credit was allocated to small farmers, the remainder being appropriated by medium and large landlords. According to the World Bank, between 70 and 80 per cent of small farms had commonly no access to institutional credit. Indications are that to date no significant change has taken place in the above picture of credit distribution, which has contributed to a growing inequality of income and wealth between the rich and poor farmers and has hindered agricultural production. In the opinion of most writers, including the FAO and World Bank, the primary explanation for this is to be found in the political and social influence of big landlords, which enables them to appropriate the bulk of subsidized credit (Eshag, 1983, pp. 203–7).

CONCLUSION. Three broad conclusions emerge: (a) fiscal and monetary policies have the potential to make a significant contribution to development; (b) LDCs have so far failed adequately to exploit this potential; and (c) the principal cause of this failure has been the institutional obstacles to development, largely of socio-political nature, of which the system of land tenure deserves a special mention.

BIBLIOGRAPHY

Eshag, E. 1983. *Fiscal and Monetary Policies and Problems in Developing Countries.* Cambridge: Cambridge University Press.

Kalecki, M. 1976. *Essays on Developing Economies.* Brighton: Harvester Press.

Keynes, J.M. 1936. *The General Theory of Employment Interest and Money.* London: Macmillan; New York: Harcourt, Brace.

Marshall, A. 1920. *Principles of Economics.* 8th edn. London: Macmillan, 1964.

Foreign Aid

HOLLIS CHENERY

Foreign aid originated from the disruption of the world economy that followed World War II. Before the system of international trade and capital movements could be restored, the economies of the industrial countries had to be rebuilt and their ties with former colonies replaced by multilateral arrangements. Until these structural changes could be brought about, much of the world depended on the United States for essential imports.

Postwar reconstruction was greatly facilitated by the willingness of the United States to finance its large surplus of exports over imports on highly concessional terms under the European Recovery Program, generally known as the Marshall Plan. This arrangement was the forerunner of aid programmes for developing countries. It was built around the concept that American loans and grants could be more efficiently utilized in the context of an overall analysis of European trade and development. The Organization for European Economic Cooperation (OEEC), which was set up to administer the Marshall Plan, formulated principles and procedures that have been used in administering foreign aid programmes ever since.

The European Recovery Program had two main objectives: to restore the economies of its member countries as rapidly as possible and to develop a viable pattern of trade that would not require further concessional loans. Most participating countries achieved these objectives over the five-year period 1948–53. During this period the transfers from the United States in the peak years amounted to 2–3 per cent of total US GNP – ten times the current US aid levels (Price, 1955). Since its objectives were achieved on schedule, the Marshall Plan has generally been considered a great success. This performance cannot be taken as a precedent for aid programmes for less developed countries, however, without examining the differences in their objectives and initial conditions.

As Western Europe recovered and its former colonies became independent, the OEEC was transformed into an organization for coordinating the bilateral aid programmes and trade policies of its member countries, becoming in 1961 the Organization for European Cooperation and Development (OECD). At the same time, the International Bank for Reconstruction and Development (World Bank) was shifting from reconstruction loans to industrial countries to long-term loans to developing countries. This shift was accelerated by the establishment in 1959 of a fund for soft loans to the poorest countries (the International Development association or IDA) as an affiliate of the World Bank. This was followed by the creation of regional development banks for Latin America, Asia and Africa. By the early 1960s, therefore, the present institutional framework for government transfers of resources to less developed countries was largely in place.

PRINCIPLES OF INTERNATIONAL AID. What is foreign aid? In common usage it includes governmental resource transfers to poor countries that are mainly for development purposes; it excludes quasi-commercial transactions ('hard loans') such as export credits whose benefits to the lender approximate their cost. For most purposes, it also excludes public transfers for non-developmental objectives, such as military assistance, and private charity (Bhagwati, 1969). To be more precise, foreign aid is usually discussed using definitions adopted by the OECD, which are based on the grant element of loans for development purposes.

International aid is customarily measured in two ways: by indices of its cost to the donor country, such as the share of its GNP; and by indices of the amount of resources transferred to the recipients, such as the percentage of their imports or investment that it finances. Several of these measures are shown in Table 1 for different groups of donor countries and periods.

Although there is no general theory of international aid, there is a set of questions that regularly arises in discussing this topic. What are the benefits and costs of concessional loans and grants? How are they affected by different forms of resource transfer or by the economic structures of the participants? Is there an overall gain or loss to the world economy? While these questions must be looked at separately from the standpoint of the donor and the recipient, it is useful to start with the potential gain to the system as a whole.

If the world economy were characterized by competitive equilibrium in all countries and markets, the benefits to aid recipients would be approximately offset by costs to donors; the only net gain from aid would lie in improving income distribution (Little and Clifford, 1965, ch. 3). In the opposite case of prevailing disequilibrium in commodity and factor markets – illustrated by postwar Europe – the prevalence of bottlenecks created the possibility of achieving large increases in production in relation to the resources transferred with little reduction in consumption in the donor country. In fact, the more rapid growth of the European market for US exports over a 10 year period may well have offset most of the original cost of the Marshall Plan to the United States.

The typical conditions under which the transfer of aid to developing countries takes place lie somewhere between these two extremes. There are many instances of foreign exchange bottlenecks whose elimination makes aid more productive, but most of them are the result of mismanagement of trade and investment

Table 1 *Aid by Major Donors* (Official Development Assistance)

Donor	ODA Volume (1983 $ billion) (Share of World Total)				ODA as Per Cent of Donor GNP			
	1950–55	1960–61	1970–71	1983–84	1950–55	1960–61	1970–71	1983–84
United States	$4.0	8.7	7.0	8.2	0.32	0.56	0.31	0.24
	(50)	(46)	(31)	(22)				
European	$3.7	6.5	7.1	11.8	0.52	0.64	0.42	0.52
Community	(47)	(35)	(31)	(32)				
Japan	$0.1	0.6	1.6	4.0	0.04	0.22	0.23	0.34
	(1)	(3)	(9)	(11)				
Other OECD	$0.1	0.6	2.1	4.3	—	0.18	0.36	0.43
	(1)	(3)	(9)	(12)				
Total OECD (%)	7.9	16.3	17.8	28.4	0.35	0.52	0.34	0.36
	(100)	(88)	(79)	(77)				
OPEC (%)	—	—	1.1	5.0	—	—	0.78	0.95
			(5)	(13)				
E. Europe (%)	—	1.9	2.6	3.1	—	—	0.15	0.21
		(10)	(11)	(9)				
Other (%)	—	0.4	1.1	0.3	—	—	—	—
		(2)	(5)	(1)				
TOTAL WORLD	7.9	18.8	22.8	37.0	0.30	0.41	0.33	0.37
	(100)	(100)	(100)	(100)				

Source: OECD, *Twenty-five Years of Development Cooperation*, 1985, Table III.

policies that could well have been avoided. One situation in which the Marshall Plan analogy has some validity was the world oil crisis of 1973, when concessional lending to oil importing developing countries made it possible to sustain higher rates of growth by the lenders as well as the borrowing countries.

The main objective of international aid programmes is long-term economic development, which requires transforming the structure of production and trade (Chenery and Strout, 1966). Recently the distributional aspects of this process have been stressed by both donors and recipients, implying that greater weight should be given to the reduction of poverty than to the mere growth of total income. This shift in emphasis makes the design of aid programmes more complex and increases the need for coordination of donor activies.

Since the time of the Marshall Plan the general concepts of international aid and the effectiveness of specific approaches have been the subject of controversy. The neoclassical critique objects to the implied interference with market forces and the possibility that aid may perpetuate inefficient policies (Johnson, 1967). The radical critique objects to the external control or 'conditionality' that can be exerted by the major donor agencies as a group and their tendency to resist radical change. These criticisms will be addressed in the course of considering the aid process in more detail, first from the recipient and then from the donor point of view.

THE RECIPIENT VIEW. Recipients and donors can agree on the broad objectives of international aid: long-term development and efficient use of resources. These can be achieved more readily if donors and recipients collaborate in the design and execution of aid programmes. Disagreements arise over the magnitude of aid provided, its allocation among countries and the ways in which the resource transfer is made.

In macroeconomic terms foreign aid performs two functions: it adds to the resources available for investment and it augments the supply of foreign exchange to finance imports. Although additional aid serves both these purposes, their relative importance varies according to the economic structure of the recipient. Since many of the goods that are critical to development must be imported – machinery, fuels, and raw materials – a shortage of foreign exchange can become a bottleneck when the cost of imports increases more rapidly than export earnings.

Two major techniques of aid administration have been designed to fit the different conditions under which aid is provided. The first, project aid, is designed to increase output and efficiency in specified productive units. The magnitude of external loans is related to the import of capital goods and other inputs required to carry out the project: disbursement takes place over the period of five years or more required to design and construct the physical plant. In addition, technical assistance to improve the design and operation of projects – or even of whole sectors – has increasingly become an integral part of the project aid package.

The second major technique of aid administration is programme lending, which is designed to support the recipient country's macroeconomic policies and particularly its increased need for foreign exchange during a period of structural change. Although a programme loan may be based on the imports needed by particular sectors, the fungibility of resources requires an assessment of policies related to the balance of payments as a whole. Programme loans are typically disbursed much more rapidly than projects and are preferred by borrowers for this reason.

During periods of stability in the world economy, such as the 1960s, an aid system based largely on project lending can function relatively efficiently since the long-term factors of investment and productivity growth are the dominant problems. However, in times of disequilibrium and rapid change, such as the early 1950s and, again, the 1970s, the need for foreign exchange to maintain imports and support structural adjustment becomes more important. In recent years, this need for 'structural adjustment loans' has been one of the principal issues between borrowers and lenders. Although donors tend to prefer project loans because they are more easily monitored, the recipient's need for imported materials to run existing plants may be greater than its need for additional productive capacity.

THE DONOR VIEW. Although virtually all the objectives of aid recipients can be included under the heading of development, the motives of donors are more complex. To a greater or lesser degree they regard foreign aid as an instrument of foreign policy, which affects both the allocation of bilateral aid among countries and the choice between the more visible project aid and the less visible programme aid. Most donors also use aid as a means of supporting national producers by limiting eligible goods procured with aid funds.

The principal economic distortion in the aid system is the common practice of tying procurement to the donor country. This issue has been attacked with some success by the OECD, most of whose members have agreed to extend procurement to developing countries as well (see OECD, 1985, ch. 10). It has been estimated that the practice of tying bilateral aid reduces its value by 25 per cent or more as compared to the system of competitive bidding that is followed by the World Bank and other multilateral agencies. On the other hand, some donors argue that this support to domestic exporters is a political cost that must be incurred in order to secure parliamentary approval of aid appropriations.

The collective views of the donor countries are expressed in the recommendations of the OECD Development Assistance Committee and in the discussions of the World Bank and International Monetary Fund. In general these agencies have tried to secure larger volumes of aid, more efficient means of transferring resources, and larger allocations to the neediest countries. For example, the Commission on International Development appointed by the World Bank recommended that the share of aid channelled through international institutions be substantially increased from its level of ten per cent in order to secure more equitable use of available funds (Pearson Commission Report, 1969). This shift has been successfully accomplished: in 1985 the multilateral share of OECD aid stands at 30 per cent, of which the World Bank accounts for more than half.

The growth of multilateral lending has made it possible to address more effectively the issue of allocation among countries. Although economists are reluctant to make interpersonal or international comparisons of the marginal utility of income, there is widespread support among the donor countries for allocating aid on the basis of need, which is equated with low per capita income. This principle conflicts with allocation on the basis of efficiency in the use of external resources, which tends to be higher in middle-income countries than in the poorest. A compromise has been reached by reserving the most concessional loan terms for very poor countries while allowing for variation within this category according to the efficiency of use. However, this is still a substantial political element in most bilateral aid programmes.

The growth of multilateral aid has had indirect benefits to both donors and recipients. Perhaps the most important is the extension of arrangements for aid coordination to most aid recipients. The original pattern was established in the early 1960s in the aid consortia set up for India, Pakistan, and Turkey by the World Bank and the OECD. These arrangements included the evaluation of aid needs, government policies and donor pledges of future aid. Subsequent consultative groups under the World Bank have moved toward less formal arrangements aimed at agreement on the diagnosis of country economic needs and the coordination of project and programme lending from many donors.

In the turbulent economic conditions that have prevailed since 1973 the importance of collaboration among donors and recipients has increased. For many countries the traditional form of project lending is no longer the most effective approach to restructuring the economy, and new procedures for structural adjustment lending have had to be developed. These involve greater coordination between the short-run approach of the IMF and the medium- to long-term analysis of the World Bank. The need for new approaches has been particularly acute in sub-Saharan Africa, where the combination of external shocks and inefficient internal policy responses has led to a general decline in per capita incomes (World Bank, 1984, 1985).

PERFORMANCE OF THE INTERNATIONAL AID SYSTEM. Over the past quarter century the transfer of concessional aid from richer to poorer countries has become an established part of the world economy. Although donors and recipients have somewhat different political and social objectives, there is a core of agreement that the main purpose of this transfer is to promote long-term development. Development is now understood to mean not only increasing per capita income but also reducing poverty and the structural changes needed to sustain these processes.

How well does the system work? Since aid is only one of a number of influences on development, the answer can be only partial. However, it is possible to compare the role of aid in the 1960s, when the international economy as a whole was functioning quite well, to the more recent periods in which the strains on the international system were much greater.

In retrospect the period 1960–73 appears as an episode of high and relatively stable growth in both the advanced and developing countries. As shown in Table 1, Official Development Assistance (ODA), as measured by the OECD, rose from 0.35 per cent of the GNP of the advanced countries in the early 1950s to 0.52 per cent in the early 1960s. This level of aid was equivalent to about 20 per cent of the investment of the recipient countries, although increased aid was offset to some extent by increased consumption.

For a low-income country, borrowing of this magnitude would permit a rise in investment – in physical and human capital – of perhaps 15 per cent and a corresponding increase in the rate of growth. While this is consistent with the observed increase in aggregate growth of developing countries from under five per cent in the 1950s to nearly six per cent in the 1960s, it can only be said that aid was one of several important factors contributing to this result.

On the foreign exchange side, aid added a margin of some 20 per cent to export earnings in the 1960s. This was particularly important to countries – perhaps a third of the total – in which the inability to expand exports constituted an important limitation to accelerating growth (see Chenery and Strout, 1966). Aid was a critical factor in countries such as Korea, Taiwan, Greece and Israel in supporting the reorientation of their trade policies from import substitution to export expansion. The importance of this contribution was shown by counterfactual simulations of the development of these countries with less aid than was actually received.

By 1970 the system of international aid was being criticized for being excessively oriented toward growth and not paying sufficient attention to the distribution of its benefits (Faber and Seers, 1972). Poverty alleviation was adopted by most donors and recipients as a primary objective of the aid process. Subsequent studies have shown that while there may be political resistance to this objective, there is no necessary economic conflict between poverty alleviation and growth; in the long run the two are likely to be mutually reinforcing by producing a more productive labour force.

The instability of the world economy following the oil crisis of 1973 has had a large impact on the design and performance of the international aid system. The worsening in terms of trade of oil-importing developing countries in 1973–5 and again in 1980–82 involved larger transfers than the total of concessional aid, and they had to be financed mainly by borrowing on commercial terms. The poorest countries, whose debt servicing capacity is limited, had to restrict their imports to fit the volume of aid available, which in many African countries led to the reduction of economic growth below the rate of population increase. Many middle income countries with more diversified economies – particularly in East Asia – were able to restructure their economies and limit their borrowing to fit the growth of export earnings. The net effect has been to increase the gap between sub-Saharan African and other developing countries.

Although energy markets have now moved closer to equilibrium conditions, the decade of adjustment 1974–84 has had a lasting effect on the foreign aid system. Even though the traditional OECD donors plus the new oil surplus countries financed a modest increase in concessional aid (from 0.33 to 0.37 per cent of their GNP), it fell far short of the amounts needed to sustain the growth of the poorest countries (see World Bank, 1984 and 1985). While borrowing from private banks at low real interest rates offset this shortage for the more creditworthy countries in the 1970s, it also led to the debt crisis of the early 1980s, in which the recession in the advanced countries made economic restructuring and export expansion more difficult.

PROSPECTS FOR FOREIGN AID. In the forty years since the start of the Marshall Plan, the international aid system has performed an increasing variety of functions:

(1) Aid accelerated the structural changes required by postwar reconstruction and performed a similar – but more limited – function in adjusting to the energy crisis.

(2) A cooperative model of international support for development was perfected in the 1960s and functioned fairly effectively at relatively low levels of concessional aid so long as world trade expanded rapidly.

(3) A shift in emphasis from growth to poverty reduction was attempted in the 1970s, but its impact was limited by the overriding requirements to readjust the production and trading structure of the oil-importing countries.

Although the volume of aid has failed to grow rapidly enough to meet the demands of the past decade, there are several aspects of the present system that make it more durable than it appeared to be in the early 1960s. In the first place, while the reduction in the US share from 50 to 22 per cent of the total (shown in Table 1) has lowered the rate of growth, the present system is less vulnerable to changes in American foreign policy and the whims of the US congress. While it would be rash to predict much of an increase in the overall Aid/GNP ratio, it should be easier to maintain the existing share.

Secondly, as per capita incomes of aid recipients have risen, a considerable number of the more successful countries have graduated from concessional to commercial borrowing, particularly in East Asia and Latin America. Continuation of this trend would make it possible to concentrate the aid system increasingly on the more intractable development problems of sub-Saharan Africa and South Asia, which contain most of the absolute poor.

Finally, the most enduring aspect of aid is likely to be the discovery and dissemination of knowledge to fit the development needs of poor countries. A notable success has been the joint sponsorship of agricultural research by multilateral and bilateral aid agencies over the past fifteen years. Knowledge is a classic case of the economist's 'public good', and the expansion of this aspect of the international aid system should command wide support.

BIBLIOGRAPHY

Bhagwati, J.N. 1969. *Amount and Sharing of Aid*. Overseas Development Council Monograph No. 2, Washington, DC.

Chenery, H.B. and Strout, A.M. 1966. Foreign assistance and economic development. *American Economic Review* 56, September, 679–733.

Faber, M., and Seers, D. (eds) 1972. *The Crisis in Planning*. London: Chatto & Windus.

Johnson, H.G. 1967. *Economic Policies Toward Less Developed Countries*. Washington, DC: Brookings.

Little, I.M.D. and Clifford, J.M. 1965. *International Aid*. Chicago: Aldine.

Organization for Economic Cooperation and Development. 1985. *Twenty-Five Years of Development Cooperation*. Paris: OECD.

Pearson, L.B. 1969. *Partners in Development: Report of the Commission on International Development*. New York: Praeger.

Price, H.B. 1955. *The Marshall Plan and its Meaning*. Ithaca: Cornell University Press.

World Bank. 1984. *World Development Report*. New York: Oxford University Press.

World Bank. 1985. *World Development Report*. New York: Oxford University Press.

Gerschenkron, Alexander

ALBERT FISHLOW

Gerschenkron was born in Odessa in 1904 and died in Cambridge, Massachusetts, in 1978. He left Russia in 1920 and settled in Austria. In 1938, a decade after receiving the degree of *doctor rerum politicarum* from the University of Vienna, he emigrated to the United States and spend the next six years at Berkeley. After a short period at the Federal Reserve Board, he went to Harvard in 1948 to teach both economic history and Soviet Studies. His passion for the former dominated, and he flourished there as the *doyen* of economic history in the United States. He influenced a generation of Harvard economists through his required graduate course in economic history and attracted several to his seminar and the field. His erudition and breadth were legendary, and defined an indelible, if unattainable, standard of scholarship for his colleagues and students.

Gerschenkron's principal contribution to economics was the elaboration of a model of late-comer economic development. Its central hypothesis is the positive role of relative economic backwardness in inducing systematic substitution for supposed prerequisites for industrial growth. State intervention could, and did, compensate for the inadequate supplies of capital, skilled labour, entrepreneurship and technological capacity found in follower countries. Thus the German institutional innovation of the 'great banks' provided access to needed capital for industrialization, even while greater Russian backwardness required a larger and more direct state role.

Gerschenkron's analysis is consciously anti-Marxian: it rejected the English Industrial Revolution as the normal pattern of economic development and deprived the original accumulation of capital of much of its conceptual force. Elements of modernity and backwardness could survive side by side, and did so in a systematic way. Apparent disadvantageous initial conditions of access to capital could be overcome. Success was rewarded with proportionately more rapid growth, signalled by a decisive spurt in industrial expansion.

This model, first presented in 1952 in an essay entitled 'Economic Backwardness in Historical Perspective' (reprinted in 1962), underlay Gerschenkron's extensive research into the specific developmental experiences of Russia, Germany, France, Italy, Austria and Bulgaria. Out of those historical studies emerged a comparative, all-encompassing European picture. 'In this fashion, the industrial history of Europe is conceived as a unified and yet graduated pattern' (Gerschenkron, 1962, p. 1). In turn, his hypotheses became progressively more precise. They may be summarized as follows:

(1) Relative backwardness creates a tension between the promise of economic development, as achieved elsewhere, and the reality of stagnancy. Such a tension motivates institutional innovation and promotes locally appropriate substitution for the absent preconditions of growth.

(2) The greater the degree of backwardness, the more interventionist was the successful channelling of capital and entrepreneurial guidance to nascent industries. Also, the more coercive and comprehensive were the measures to reduce domestic consumption.

(3) The more backward the economy, the more likely were: an emphasis upon producers' goods rather than consumers' goods; use of capital intensive rather than labour intensive methods of production; emergence of larger rather than smaller units of both plant and enterprise; dependence upon borrowed, advanced technology rather than indigenous techniques.

(4) The more backward the country, the less likely was the agricultural sector to provide a growing market to industry through rising productivity, and the more unbalanced the resulting productive structure of the economy.

The considerable and continuing appeal of the Gerschenkron model derives from its logical and consistent ordering of the process of European development, the conditional nature of its predictions and its generalizability to the experience of the late late-comers of the present Third World. His formulation rises above other theories which emphasize stages of growth both because of its attention to historical detail and its insistence upon the special attributes of late-comer development that cause differential evolution. In Gerschenkron's own hands, his propositions afforded an opportunity to blend ideology, institutions and the historical experience of industrialization, especially that of Russia, in a dazzling fashion. For others, his approach has proved a useful starting point for the discussion of non-European late-comers, including Japan and the newly industrializing countries.

The model is, of course, not without its limitations. History, even of Europe alone, does not in every detail bear easily the weight of such a grand design. In other parts of the world, as might be expected from a concept rooted in the special features of the historical European experience, larger amendments are frequently required. And somewhat surprisingly, in view of Gerschenkron's own pathbreaking essay in political economy, *Bread and Democracy in Germany*, there is too little attention to the domestic classes and groups whose interests the interventionist state must adequately incorporate if it is to play the central role required. Backwardness too easily becomes an alternative, technologically rooted explanation, distracting attention from the state rather than focusing upon its opportunities and constraints.

Still, the concept of relative backwardness, and Gerschenkron's always insightful and rich elaborations in so many national contexts, represent a brilliant and original contribution to economic history for which he is justly celebrated. It is not the only one. The 'Gerschenkron effect', arising from the difference between calculated Paasche and Laspeyre indexes of Soviet machinery output (1951), also commemorates him. Current price weights will tend to underestimate the extent of growth because prices and quantities are negatively correlated, just as base year weights exaggerate it. The larger is the difference between the alternatively constructed quantity indexes, the greater is the degree of structural change. Again, divergence rather than uniformity is the source of useful information about historical processes.

Alexander Gerschenkron has few peers, past or present, in his command of comparative economic history. Scholarly interest in contemporary economic development has brought him an increasing following. His insights thus continue to influence a new generation of scholars and guarantee him a central place in any assessment of the evolution of the discipline of economic history.

SELECTED WORKS

1943. *Bread and Democracy in Germany.* Berkeley: University of California Press.

1951. *A Dollar Index of Soviet Machinery Output.* Santa Monica: Rand Corporation.

1962. *Economic Backwardness in Historical Perspective.* Cambridge, Mass.: Harvard University Press.

1968. *Continuity in History and Other Essays.* Cambridge, Mass.: Harvard University Press.

1970. *Europe in the Russian Mirror.* London: Cambridge University Press.

1977. *An Economic Spurt That Failed.* Princeton: Princeton University Press.

Harris–Todaro Model

M. ALI KHAN

The replacement of the equality of wages by the equality of expected wages as the basic equilibrium condition in a segmented, but homogeneous, labour market has proved to be an idea of seminal importance in development economics. Attributed originally to Todaro (1968, 1969) and Harris–Todaro (1970), and commonly referred to as the Harris–Todaro hypothesis, the idea was very much in the air around the late 1960s as can be seen from the contemporaneous writings of Akerlof–Stiglitz (1969), Blaug et al. (1969) and Harberger (1971), among others.

The motivation for the Harris–Todaro hypothesis lies in an attempt to explain the persistence of rural to urban migration in the presence of widespread urban unemployment, a pervasive phenomenon in many less developed countries. It is natural to ask why such unemployment does not act as a deterrent to further migration. According to the Harris–Todaro hypothesis, the answer lies in the migrant leaving a secure rural wage W_r for a higher expected urban wage W_u^e even though the latter carried with it the possibility of urban unemployment. The expected wage is computed by using the rate of urban employment as an index for the probability of finding a job. Thus

$$W_u^e = W_u(L_u/(L_u + U)) + 0(U/(L_u + U))$$
$$= W_u(1/(1 + U/L_u)) = W_u(1/(1 + \lambda)) \tag{1}$$

where W_u is the urban wage, L_u is the number of urban employed, U the number of urban unemployed and λ the rate of urban unemployment. Thus, the Harris–Todaro hypothesis is precisely formulated by the equilibrium condition

$$W_r = W_u^e \Leftrightarrow W_u = W_r(1 + \lambda). \tag{2}$$

Once the Harris–Todaro equilibrium condition is embedded in a two-sector, so-called general equilibrium model (see Johnson, 1971), we obtain the Harris–Todaro model. However, it should be noted that the Harris–Todaro hypothesis introduces a further unknown, namely the equilibrium rate of unemployment, and thus, in contrast to the standard two-sector model, the Harris–Todaro model must be buttressed by a theory of urban wage determination. The simplest setting

148

is the one originally adopted by Harris–Todaro and subsequently by Bhagwati–Srinivasan (1973, 1974, 1977), and others. This work assumes the urban wage to be an exogenously given constant and typically rationalizes it as a consequence of government fiat.

In the 1970s, however, several theories of endogenous urban wage determination were proposed. Foremost among these is the work of Joseph Stiglitz who provides a microfoundation for the urban wage in terms of labour-turnover (Stiglitz, 1974) or in terms of biological efficiency considerations (Stiglitz, 1976). One may also mention in this context the work of Calvo (1978), who sees the equilibrium urban wage as an outcome of trade union behaviour; and of Calvo–Wellisz (1978), who see a higher urban wage as a consequence of costly supervision. At this stage of the development of the literature, each theory of urban wage determination led to a particular version of the Harris–Todaro model and the common structural similarities were obscured.

In Khan (1980a), the elementary observation is made that all these variants of the Harris–Todaro model could be studied under one rubric if the determination of urban wages is seen in a somewhat more abstract way, i.e.,

$$W_u = \Omega(W_r, \lambda, R, \tau) \tag{3}$$

where R is the rental on capital and τ a shift parameter. This led to the, so-called, generalized Harris–Todaro (GHT) model whose importance lay not so much in synthesizing the several variants of the Harris–Todaro model but in emphasizing the points of contact of this literature with the trade theory literature. In particular, when (3) collapses to

$$W_u = W_r \tag{4}$$

that is, when the elasticities of the omega function with respect to λ, R and τ are all zero, we obtain the Heckscher–Ohlin–Samuelson (HOS) model in the case when capital is intersectorally mobile or the Ricardo–Viner model in the case when it is not (for details on these basic constructions of trade theory, see, for example, Caves–Jones, 1985).

Let us now consider in some detail the GHT model in the case when capital is intersectorally mobile. Let a country consist of an urban and a rural sector, indexed by u and r respectively, and be endowed with positive amounts of labour L and capital K. Let the ith sector produce a commodity i in amount X_i in accordance with a production function

$$X_i = F_i(L_i, K_i) \qquad i = u, r, \tag{5}$$

which is assumed to exhibit constant returns to scale and is twice continuously differentiable and concave. The allocation of labour and capital, L_i and K_i, is determined through marginal productivity pricing. Thus, we have

$$P_r F_r^K = R = P_u F_u^K \tag{6}$$

$$P_r F_r^L = W_r \qquad \text{and} \qquad P_u F_u^L = W_u \tag{7}$$

where F_i^j is the derivative of $F_i (i = u, r)$ with respect to j ($j = L, K$). The country is considered too small to influence the positive international prices of the two commodities, P_u and P_r. On rewriting the equilibrium condition (2) in a slightly more general form,

$$W_u = \rho W_r(1 + \lambda); \qquad \rho \text{ a shift parameter,} \tag{8}$$

(5), (6), (7) and (8), along with the material balance equations below, complete the specification of the model.

$$K_r + K_u = L \qquad \text{and} \qquad L_r + L_u(1 + \lambda) = L. \tag{9}$$

The first point to be noticed about this model is a *decomposability property* whereby the factor prices, W_u, W_r and R and the unemployment rate λ are independent of the endowments of labour and capital and depend solely on P_u, P_r and the shift parameters τ and ρ. This can be seen most easily if we subsume the marginal productivity conditions (6) and (7) into price equal unit cost equations

$$P_i = C_i(W_i, R) \qquad i = u, r. \tag{10}$$

This allows one to decompose the model into a subsystem comprising equations (8) and (4) along with (10).

This basic observation leads to several interesting characteristics of the equilibria of the GHT model. First, the market rural wage and market rental correctly measure the social opportunity cost of labour and capital if we use the international value of GNP as the relevant measure of social welfare. Second, despite the presence of a distorted labour market, there is no possibility of immiserizing growth. Third, an increase in capital (labour) increases the output of the capital (labour) intensive commodity and decreases the output of the labour (capital) intensive commodity provided the intensities are measured in *employment adjusted* terms, that is

$$\frac{k_u}{1 + \lambda} = \frac{K_u}{L_u(1 + \lambda)} \gtreqless \frac{K_r}{L_r} = k_r. \tag{11}$$

This third property is an analogue of the Rybczynski property of the HOS model. Not surprisingly, we also obtain an analogue of the Stolper–Samuelson property whereby the effect of changes in international prices on factor returns depends on factor intensities, provided these are now measured in *elasticity adjusted* terms. The urban sector is said to be capital intensive in elasticity adjusted terms if

$$\theta_{rL}(\theta_{uK}(1 - e_\lambda) + \theta_{uL}e_R) > \theta_{uL}\theta_{rK}(e_W - e_\lambda) \tag{12}$$

where θ_{ij} is the share of the jth factor $(j = K, L)$ in the ith sector $(i = u, r)$, and e_i is the elasticity of the $\Omega(\cdot)$ function with respect to the relevant variable.

In the setting where e_w equals unity and e_λ, e_R and e_τ are all zero, (11) and (12) collapse to the conventional physical and value intensities of Magee (1976) and Jones (1971) for the HOS model with proportional wage differentials. Under the further specialization that ρ in (8) equals unity, there is no difference between these two kinds of intensities and a perfect correspondence between the Rybczynski and Stolper–Samuelson theorems.

The appearance of the physical and value intensities of the wage-differential model leads us to inquire into the possibility of downward-sloping supply curves of X_r and X_u. This is indeed possible and a sharp generalization is available in the result that there are perverse price-output responses in the GHT model if and only if the employment adjusted factor intensities do not conflict with the elasticity adjusted intensities; see Kahn (1980b) for details.

Another direct consequence of the decomposability property of the model is a generalization of the Bhagwati (1968), Johnson (1971), Brecher–Alejandro (1977) paradox. This states that capital inflow in the presence of a tariff and with full repatriation of its earnings is immiserizing if and only if the imported commodity is capital intensive in employment adjusted terms. This result is independent of the various mechanisms for the determination of urban wages. For details, see Khan (1982a).

The results that we have presented so far have a trade-theoretic flavour but one question that has remained in the forefront of analytical work on the Harris–Todaro model relates to the effect of urban wage subsidies on urban unemployment and urban output. A seminal result here is the Corden–Findlay (1975) paradox which draws attention to the fact that urban employment and urban output could rise if the urban wage is increased. This question has now been resolved by Khan (1980b) and Neary (1981).

So far we have focused on the comparative-static properties of the Harris–Todaro equilibrium. It is also worth emphasizing that the actual existence of the Harris Todaro equilibrium cannot be taken for granted and must be proved. In the original Harris–Todaro model with an exogenously given rigid wage, equilibrium exists if and only if the rural sector is more capital intensive in employment adjusted terms; see Khan (1980a). Furthermore, following Neary's (1978) lead for the wage differential model, one can present 'reasonable' adjustment processes of the Marshallian type under which the Harris–Todaro equilibrium is locally asymptotically stable if and only if the employment adjusted factor intensities do not conflict with the elasticity adjusted intensities. Since the elasticity adjusted intensities of (12) collapse to $\theta_{rL}\theta_{uK}$ in the Harris–Todaro model with a rigid wage, we have the satisfying result that the criteria for the existence of equilibrium and its stability coincide.

There are several aspects of the Harris–Todaro model that we have not covered. In particular, we have confined our attention to the version with intersectorally mobile capital. In many ways, the case of sector-specific capital is more difficult and also more interesting. In addition, even for the version that we have discussed, several substantive questions of interest have not been touched on. These relate to gains from trade which now depend on the asymmetric nature of the model and as to whether the rural or the urban commodity is being exported as in Khan–Lin (1982); to the possibility of underemployment as in Bhagwati–Srinivasan (1977); to the possibility of educated unemployment as in Chaudhuri–Khan (1984); to the consequences of a distorted capital market as in Khan–Naqvi (1983); to the interaction of ethnic groups as in Khan (1979) and Khan–Chaudhuri (1985); to the introduction of an informal sector as in Fields (1975) and Stiglitz (1982); to cost-benefit analyses as in Srinivasan–Bhagwati (1975) and Stiglitz (1977, 1982). However, what we have hoped to show is that the GHT model is a versatile and useful analytical tool for a variety of questions arising in international and development economics.

BIBLIOGRAPHY

Akerlof, G. and Stiglitz, J.E. 1969. Capital, wages and structural employment. *Economic Journal* 79, 269–81.

Bhagwati, J.N. 1968. Distortions and immiserizing growth. *Review of Economic Studies* 35, 481–5.

Bhagwati, J.N. and Srinivasan, T.N. 1971. The theory of wage differentials: production response and factor price equalization. *Journal of International Economics* 1, 19–35.

Bhagwati, J.N. and Srinivasan, T.N. 1973. The ranking of policy interventions under factor market imperfections: the case of sector-specific sticky wages and unemployment. *Sankhya*, Series B, 35(4), December, 405–20.

Bhagwati, J.N. and Srinivasan, T.N. 1974. On reanalyzing the Harris–Todaro model: policy rankings in the case of sector-specific sticky wages. *American Economic Review* 64, 502–8.

Bhagwati, J.N. and Srinivasan, T.N. 1977. Education in a job ladder model and the fairness-in-hiring rule. *Journal of Public Economics* 7(1), 1–22.

Blaug, M., Layard, P.R.G. and Woodhall, M. 1969. *The Causes of Graduate Unemployment in India*. London: Allen Lane.

Brecher, R.A. and Diaz-Alejandro, C.F. 1977. Tariffs, foreign capital and immiserizing growth. *Journal of International Economics* 7, 317–22.

Calvo, G.A. 1978. Urban unemployment and wage determination in LDC's: trade unions in the Harris-Todaro model. *International Economic Review* 19, 65–81.

Calvo, G.A. and Wellisz, S. 1978. Supervision, loss of control and the optimum size of the firm. *Journal of Political Economy* 86, 943–52.

Caves, R.E. and Jones, R.W. 1985. *World Trade and Payments*. 4th edn, Boston: Little, Brown & Co.

Chaudhuri, T.D. and Khan, M. Ali. 1984. Educated unemployment, educational subsidies and growth. *Pakistan Development Review* 23, 395–409.

Corden, W.M. and Findlay, R. 1975. Urban unemployment, intersectional capital mobility and development policy. *Economica* 42, 59–78.

Fields, G.S. 1975. Rural-urban migration, urban unemployment and job-search activity in LDCs. *Journal of Development Economics* 2, 165–87.

Harberger, A.C. 1971. On measuring the social opportunity cost of labour. *International Labour Review* 103, 559–79.

Harris, J.R. and Todaro, M. 1970. Migration, unemployment and development: a two sector analysis. *American Economic Review* 40, 126–42.

Johnson, H.G. 1971. *The Two-Sector Model of General Equilibrium*. Yrjö Jahnsson Lectures, Chicago: Aldine-Atherton.

Jones, R.W. 1971. Distortions in factor markets and the general equilibrium model of production. *Journal of Political Economy* 79, 437–59.

Khan, M. Ali. 1979. A multisectoral model of a small open economy with non-shiftable capital and imperfect labor mobility. *Economic Letters* 2, 369–75.

Khan, M. Ali. 1980a. The Harris–Todaro hypothesis and the Heckscher–Ohlin–Samuelson trade model: a synthesis. *Journal of International Economics* 10, 527–47.

Khan, M. Ali. 1980b. Dynamic stability, wage subsidies and the generalized Harris–Todaro model. *Pakistan Development Review* 19, 1–24.

Khan, M. Ali. 1982a. Social opportunity costs and immiserizing growth: some observations on the long run returns versus the short. *Quarterly Journal of Economics* 96, 353–62.

Khan, M. Ali. 1982b. Tariffs, foreign capital and immiserizing growth with urban unemployment and specific factors of production. *Journal of Development Economics* 10, 245–56.

Khan, M. Ali. and Chaudhuri, T.D. 1985. Development policies in LDCs with several ethnic groups – a theoretical analysis. *Zeitschrift für Nationalökonomie* 45, 1–19.

Khan, M. Ali and Lin, P. 1982. Sub-optimal tariff policy and gains from trade with urban unemployment. *Pakistan Development Review* 21, 105–26.

Khan, M. Ali and Naqvi, S.N.H. 1983. Capital markets and urban unemployment. *Journal of International Economics* 15(3–4), 367–85.

Magee, S.P. 1976. *International Trade and Distortions in Factor Markets*. New York and Basle: Marcel-Dekker.

Neary, J.P. 1978. Dynamic stability and the theory of factor market distortions. *American Economic Review* 68, 672–82.

Neary, J.P. 1981. On the Harris–Todaro model with intersectoral capital mobility. *Economica* 48, 219–34.

Srinivasan, T.N. and Bhagwati, J. 1975. Alternative policy rankings in a large open economy with sector-specific minimum wages. *Journal of Economic Theory* 11, 356–71.

Srinivasan, T.N. and Bhagwati, J. 1978. Shadow prices for project selection in the presence of distortions: effective rates of protection and domestic resource costs. *Journal of Political Economy* 86, 91–116.

Stiglitz, J.E. 1974. Alternative theories of wage determination and unemployment in LDC's. the labor-turnover model. *Quarterly Journal of Economics* 88, 194–227.

Stiglitz, J.E. 1976. The efficiency wage hypothesis, surplus labor, and the distribution of income in the LDCs. *Oxford Economic Papers* 28, 185–207.

Stiglitz, J.E. 1977. Some further remarks on cost-benefit analysis. In *Project Evaluation*, ed. H. Schwartz and R. Berney, Washington, DC: Inter-American Development Bank.

Stiglitz, J.E. 1982. The structure of labor markets and shadow prices in LDCs. In *Migration and the Labor Market in Developing Countries*, ed. R.H. Sabot, Boulder: Westview Press.

Todaro, M.P. 1968. An analysis of industrialization: employment and unemployment in LDCs. *Yale Economic Essays* 8, 329–492.

Todaro, M.P. 1969. A model of labor migration and urban unemployment in less developed countries. *American Economic Review* 59, 138–48.

Hill, Polly

C.A. GREGORY

Polly Hill was born on 10 June 1914 into a remarkable Cambridge family that includes Nobel Prize winning physiologist A.V. Hill (her father) and J.M. Keynes (her mother's brother) among its many distinguished members. She graduated from Cambridge in 1936 with a degree in economics.

Her first job upon leaving university was with the Royal Economic Society as an editorial assistant, a position she held for two years (1936–8). Her next appointment was a once year (1938–9) research position with the New Fabian Research Bureau (which almost immediately re-amalgamated with the Fabian Society) where she wrote her first book *The Unemployment Services* (1940). This book was concerned to expose the inefficiency and inhumanity of the system of unemployment relief and to make constructive proposals. Polly Hill's commitment to social justice has not waned: economic inequality is the central theme of all her books.

At the outbreak of the war she was obliged, as an unmarried young woman, to become a temporary civil servant. She worked first, briefly, in the Treasury, then for a long time in the Board of Trade and finally in the Colonial Office. She resigned in 1951. After a period of unemployment she became a journalist for the weekly *West Africa*. She married in 1953 and moved to Ghana with her husband where, at the age of forty, she began her academic career. The academic posts she held there involved no teaching and she was able to become, as she has put it, 'a pupil of the migrant cocoa farmers of southern Ghana'. She began her fieldwork as an economist and collected data using the questionnaire method, producing her second book, *The Gold Coast Cocoa Farmer: A Preliminary Survey* (1956) with characteristic speed and efficiency. The prevailing orthodoxy had it that sedentary food farmers in southern Ghana had suddenly taken up cocoa farming at the end of the 19th-century with such a degree of success that cocoa exports had risen from nil to over 50,000 tons by 1914 – the largest quantity for any country. Polly Hill had uncritically accepted this orthodoxy and her subsequent realization that most farmers appeared to be migrants who had bought their land was to have a profound effect upon her intellectual methods. She abandoned the questionnaire method of data collection in favour of one that sought to develop generalizations on the basis of: (1) detailed fieldwork in one village; (2) fieldwork done by others elsewhere; (3) archival sources. She also began a lifelong struggle with development economists and other purveyors of orthodoxies based on casual empirical observation and 'commonsense'. She drifted towards anthropology and history where the qualities of her empirical findings were recognized for what they were: revolutionary. She spent three and a half years collecting detailed evidence to substantiate her claim that the cocoa farmers were migrants and made many fascinating discoveries in the process. For example, she found that the matrilineal farmers adopted an entirely different mode of migration from patrilineal farmers: the former bought family lands with the aid of their kin, and were prepared to grant usufructural rights to their male and female kinsfolk; the latter clubbed together in so-called 'companies', groups of non-kin, the land being divided into strips from a base line, according to the contribution each had made, with subsequent division on inheritance always being longitudinal. Upon hearing of this Professor Meyor Fortes, then Professor of Social Anthropology at Cambridge, encouraged her to apply for a Smuts Visiting Fellowship. This enabled her to write *The Migrant Cocoa-Farmers of Southern Ghana: A Study in Rural Capitalism* (1963) which is now widely regarded as a classic. (She was awarded a PhD in social anthropology from Cambridge under new special regulations in 1966 on the basis of it.) Mainstream writers on development have by and large ignored the book even though it contains telling criticisms of aspects of W.A. Lewis's work.

Following more fieldwork in Ghana, Nigeria and India she produced a further stream of books (1970a, 1970b, 1972, 1977, 1982, 1985, 1986) and many articles of outstanding quality which established her reputation as the world's foremost economic anthropologist. She was appointed a Fellow of Clare Hall in Cambridge in 1965 (a position she still holds) and subsequently to the prestigious Smuts Readership in Commonwealth Studies (1973–9). Her publications document in painstaking detail the complexity of agrarian relations in the tropical regions of the world in which she was worked. The books as a whole constitute an encyclopaedia of knowledge on the socio-economic conditions of poverty and economic inequality and her work ranges in scope from 'agrestic servitude' to 'zamindars'. Her oeuvre is much more than a compilation of facts though. Her own data and that of others is presented in a theoretical context which has broadened as her own field experience has widened. She has been unrelenting in her empirically based critiques of development economists and her latest book (1986) is a concerted attempt to make them see the error of their ways.

SELECTED WORKS

1940. *The Unemployment Services.* London: Routledge.

1956. *The Gold Coast Cocoa Farmer: A Preliminary Survey.* Oxford: Oxford University Press.

1963. *The Migrant Cocoa-Farmers of Southern Ghana: A Study in Rural Capitalism.* Cambridge: Cambridge University Press.

1970a. *The Occupations of Migrants in Ghana.* Ann Arbor: University of Michigan Press.

1970b. *Studies in Rural Capitalism in West Africa.* Cambridge: Cambridge University Press.

1972. *Rural Hausa: A Village and a Setting.* Cambridge: Cambridge University Press.

1977. *Population, Prosperity and Poverty: Rural Kano 1900 and 1970.* Cambridge: Cambridge University Press.

1982. *Dry Grain Farming Families: Hausaland (Nigeria) and Karnataka (India) Compared.* Cambridge: Cambridge University Press.

1985. *Indigenous Trade and Market Places in Ghana, 1962–64.* Jos Oral History and Literature Texts, University of Jos, Nigeria.

1986. *Development Economics on Trial: The Anthropological Case for a Prosecution.* Cambridge: Cambridge University Press.

Hirschman, Albert Otto

M.S. McPHERSON

Hirschman was born on 7 April 1915 in Berlin. After attending the Sorbonne and the London School of Economics he obtained a doctorate in economic science from the University of Trieste in 1938. His early career was dominated by the struggle against fascism in Europe (Coser, 1984). He actively supported the underground opposition to Mussolini while in Italy in the mid-1930s, fought with the Spanish Republican Army in 1936 and later with the French Army until its defeat in June 1940. He stayed on in Marseilles six months more, engaging in clandestine operations to rescue political and intellectual refugees from Nazi-occupied Europe. He avoided arrest by leaving France for the United States in January 1941. There he produced his first book, *National Power and the Structure of Foreign Trade* (1945), which introduced some of the main themes of what is now called 'dependency theory'.

After the war he served as an economist in the Federal Reserve Board until 1952, when he left for Colombia where he stayed four years. Beginning in 1956 he held professorships successively at Yale, Columbia and Harvard, and in 1974 was appointed professor at the Institute for Advanced Study in Princeton.

Hirschman has been a leading figure in economic development since the publication in 1958 of his second book, *The Strategy of Economic Development*. Hirschman's analysis grew out of extensive practical experience in Colombia as an adviser both to its government and to private firms. Characteristically, Hirschman dissented from orthodox views of both right and left, arguing that neither *laissez faire* nor 'rational' economy-wide planning made sense for poor countries. Government needed to encourage 'unbalanced growth', deploying its scarce decision-making capacities strategically to set up disequilibria that would stimulate effort and mobilize hidden and underutilized resources. Targeting development efforts on key industries with strong 'linkages' to other parts of the economy could stimulate a favourable dynamic.

Hirschman later provided the label 'possibilism' (1971) for the outlook that shaped much of his thought on development and on which he elaborated in many further books and articles. When social science focuses exclusively on the search for general laws, it obscures the irreducible role of the unique and the unpredictable in human affairs. This causes progress to be viewed either as ensured by the application of general rules or thwarted by the presence of inescapable obstacles. But history reveals that actual social change often follows paths that are *a priori* quite unlikely, turning obstacles into opportunities and confounding rules with unanticipated consequences. From this starting point, Hirschman has cultivated an approach to development problems which embodies respect for complexity and openness to the possibility of genuine novelty – what he once called the discovery of 'an entirely new way of turning a historical corner' (1971, p. 27).

Since 1970, Hirschman has been bringing his possibilist approach to bear on broader problems of social theory. His slim volume, *Exit, Voice, and Loyalty* (1970) revealed the unexpected richness to be found in comparing the implications of dissatisfied clients alternatively *exiting* from an organization or giving *voice* to their complaints. This volume, like Hirschman's more recent work (1982b) on the forces that propel individuals and societies into and out of periods of intense political involvement, explores issues on the borderline between economics and politics. But unlike most economists with an interest in 'public choice', Hirschman shows no inclination to reduce politics to economics. Indeed, both works stress that standard models of economic behaviour fail to make sense of familiar forms of 'public-minded' behaviour such as voicing one's convictions on public matters, participating in demonstrations or working to support candidates for office.

Hirschman's propensity to devise analytical formulations that express rather than conceal the complexities of human motivations and institutions is evident also in his studies of historical views of capitalism (1977, 1982a). Hirschman shows that capitalism has been seen as a powerful civilizing influence and alternatively as a destroyer of the moral and social fabric; still other views have portrayed capitalism, for better or worse, as too feeble to overcome the restraints of preceding social forms. These competing ideological views have evolved, Hirschman notes, in total isolation from one another. A fuller view would recognize that all these contradictory tendencies are present at once, but to recognize this truth would be highly inconvenient, making it 'much more difficult for the social observer, critic, or "scientist" to impress the general public by proclaiming some inevitable outcome of current processes' (1982a).

'But', Hirschman concludes, in a question that captures well his own unique stance in modern social science, 'after so many failed prophecies, is it not in the interest of social science to embrace complexity, be it at some sacrifice of its claim to predictive power?' (1982a, p. 1483).

SELECTED WORKS

1945. *National Power and the Structure of Foreign Trade.* Berkeley and Los Angeles: Bureau of Business and Economic Research, University of California.
1958. *The Strategy of Economic Development.* New Haven: Yale University Press.

1970. *Exit, Voice, and Loyalty*: *Responses to Decline in Firms, Organizations, and States*. Cambridge, Mass.: Harvard University Press.

1971. Introduction: political economies and possibilism. In A.O. Hirschman (ed.), *A Bias for Hope*: *Essays on Development and Latin America*, New Haven: Yale University Press.

1977. *The Passions and the Interests*: *Political Arguments for Capitalism Before Its Triumph*. Princeton: Princeton University Press.

1982a. Rival interpretations of market society: civilizing, destructive, or feeble? *Journal of Economic Literature* 20, December, 1463–84.

1982b. *Shifting Involvements*: *Private Interest and Public Action*. Princeton: Princeton University Press.

1986. *Rival Views of Market Society and Other Essays*. New York: Viking-Penguin International.

BIBLIOGRAPHY

Coser, A. 1984. *Refugee Scholars in America*: *Their Impact and Their Experiences*. New Haven: Yale University Press.

Industrialization

AMIYA KUMAR BAGCHI

Industrialization is a process. The following are essential characteristics of an unambiguous industrialization process. First, the proportion of the national (or territorial) income derived from manufacturing activities and from secondary industry in general goes up, except perhaps for cyclical interruptions. Secondly, the proportion of the working population engaged in manufacturing and secondary industry in general also shows a rising trend. While these two ratios are increasing, the income per head of the population also goes up, except again for temporary interruptions (Datta, 1952; Kuznets, 1966, 1971; Sutcliffe, 1971). There are cases in which the per capita income goes up, income derived from secondary industry per head of the population also goes up, but there may be little growth either in the proportion of income derived from the secondary sector or in the ratio of the working force engaged in that sector. Such cases, except when they are observed for a highly developed country, not only make the unambiguous labelling of the process of development as industrialization difficult; they also pose questions regarding the sustainability of the process that has been observed.

Other characteristics are also often associated with industrialization or a more general process of what Kuznets has called 'modern economic growth' (Kuznets, 1966, ch. 1). These include a narrowing and ultimate closing of the gap between productivity per head in the secondary sector and in the primary sector (that is, agriculture, forestry and fishing), continual changes in the methods of production, the fashioning of new products, rise in the proportion of population living in towns, changes in the relative ratios of expenditures on capital formulation and consumption and so on.

Most of these associated characteristics were derived from the experience of Great Britain, or more narrowly, England and Wales, which was the first country to industrialize. That experience has remained unique in many ways. But since England was the original centre for diffusion of the economic and technical changes associated with the industrialization process, it is important to understand what happened in that country.

At least since the days of Karl Marx, England has been known as the first country in which feudalism broke down, and capitalism brought the economy under its sway (Dobb, 1946). This meant that all means of production came to be owned by a small group of property-owners called capitalists, and the rest of the working people became free wage-workers who earned their livelihood by selling their labour power to the capitalists (Dobb, 1946). It has been claimed that while serfdom broke down all over western Europe, England was the only country where a group of landlords managed to concentrate most of the land in their hands and prevent the consolidation of a free peasantry which could be used by an absolutist state to defeat the rise of capitalist agriculture (Moore, 1967, ch. 1; Brenner, 1976). It has been further claimed that economic individualism which has been taken as the hallmark of the motivation of an entrepreneur in capitalist society, goes back in England to the 12th–13th centuries, so that capitalism went through a long process of birth in the first industrializing nation (Macfarlane, 1978, chs 5–7). By the time of the first industrial revolution, England was a society in which the abiding interest of the rulers was to make money from agriculture, trade and industry, and in which the rulers were prepared rationally to order the affairs of the state so as to enable the entrepreneurs to conquer foreign countries and markets, by the force of arms if need by and had the financial and military might to carry out those plans. England had also become the leader in trade and finance among the countries of western Europe, after the decline of Amsterdam (Braudel, 1984).

The English industrial revolution is traditionally associated with the rise of machine-based industry powered by steam (Marx, 1887, chs XIV and XV; Mantoux, 1928). Certainly the classic age of British dominance of world industry, which is roughly the period from the end of the Napoleonic wars up to 1870, was characterized by the conquest of production methods by machines with moving parts of iron and steel, powered by steam, and operated by scores or even hundreds of operatives concentrated in single factories. However, what is becoming apparent is that for practically the whole of the eighteenth century, traditional techniques and materials (such as wood), and traditional sources of power such as muscles of men, women and children, animals, and water and wind, were responsible for growth and spread of factory industry (Musson, 1972; Von Tunzelmann, 1978; Crafts, 1985).

The experience of England lends credence to the postulation of a stage of 'industrialization before industrialization' or 'proto-industrialization' (Mendels, 1972). This has been defined as 'the development of rural regions in which a large part of the population lived entirely or to a considerable extent from industrial mass production for inter-regional and international markets' (Kriedte, Medick and Schlumbohm, 1981, p. 6). The growth of industry in England was spearheaded by an explosion in the development of cotton spinning; and the cotton mills which utilized the new spinning machines sought out suitable sources of water power and labour – mostly in the rural areas or small towns. Steam engines were an element in the industrial revolution, but they did not come into their own as the major prime movers in manufacturing industry until perhaps the second quarter of the nineteenth century.

In England, cotton textiles were a relatively new industry; and they grew at first by redressing the balance of labour power needed in traditional spinning methods, so that no major displacement of labour took place within the system of proto-industrialization, in the 18th century. But machine spinning stimulated handloom production, and handloom weavers were pauperized even in England when powerlooms displaced handlooms (Bythell, 1969). In other countries, where traditional handicrafts were displaced by the new machine-made fabrics, and because of political or internal social factors they were not replaced, or not replaced quickly enough, by any considerable growth of machine industry, pauperization and de-industrialization were widespread and in some cases they became endemic phenomena (Bagchi, 1976; Kriedte, 1981). So Ricardo's worries about the possible employment-displacing effects of machinery were justified after all (Ricardo, 1821, ch. 31; see also Hicks, 1969). But in Britain, continued growth of external trade and the coming of the railway age helped in overcompensating the labour-displacing effects. Not all countries had the same advantages.

The proto-industrialized order was succeeded in England by the system of machine manufacture perhaps because the former faced its severest crisis there: social relations there had already been transformed in a fully capitalist mould by the time smallscale manufacture reached its fullest development. Developments in science, technology and statecraft almost certainly helped resolve the crisis in favour of a higher stage of industrial development.

The fact that England had a decisive lead in the use of machine manufacture and steam power, and had formal or informal colonies where she could ignore barriers erected by the USA or Continental European countries made her the supreme industrial nation of the world for almost three-quarters of a century (cf. Robinson, 1954).

Once the revolution in textiles and steam power had been pioneered in England it could, however, be diffused to other countries, provided the latter possessed suitable political and social conditions. It is on the basis of the timing, speed and social mechanism of diffusion of the industrial revolution that we can distinguish three clusters of countries which have gone through an unambiguous process of industrialization. The first is the cluster of countries on both sides of the North Atlantic seaboard and overseas colonies with populations of predominantly European origin; the second consists of Japan and the four islands of industrialization in the Far East, viz., South Korea, Taiwan, Hong Kong and Singapore, and the third is the cluster of socialist counries led by the Soviet Union. The rest of the world are still struggling, with only varying degrees of success, to get a sustained process of industrialization going (Bagchi, 1982).

The English industrial revolution was, to start with, very much a matter of textiles; it was only in the 19th century that it affected other industries, especially iron and steel and mechanical engineering in general, on a large scale. The uniqueness of England, with all the advantages of a first start (Robinson, 1954) allowed her to expand her markets overseas in an almost unrestrained manner until the USA and other western European countries expanded their home production, not only of textiles, but also of other manufactures, often behind walls of protection against the English manufactures. The west European industrialization was helped very much by the nearness of England: from Britain flowed information about the new inventions, machines, men and capital, although there was for a time an attempt to restrict the exports of new machinery from England (Landes, 1965). Capital flows from England and to a lesser extent from France, were particularly important in supporting the movement of European populations to the USA, Canada, Australia, South Africa, New Zealand and Argentina (Kuznets, 1971; Bagchi, 1972; Edelstein, 1982).

Yet despite more active support by politically independent governments, the spread of industrialization to western Europe took a surprisingly long time to get going (Lewis, 1978, chs. 7 and 8; Crafts, 1985, ch. 3). One set of reasons had to do with political, social and structural factors. The French needed a major revolution before the bourgeoisie could take possession of the state apparatus. Even then, the entrenchment of peasant agriculture in the countryside probably delayed the full conversion of the primary sector to capitalist relations. In other countries, even the 1848 revolution did not complete the process of capitalist take-over. Associated with these lags went the fact that by English standards, too high a proportion of population continued to depend on agriculture and a large gap between agricultural and industrial productivity continued to persist down to the eve of World War I. Such political and social lags, of course, even more impeded the process of industrialization in the countries of central, southern and eastern Europe down to the period between the two world wars. We will have to pay separate attention to the case where the logjam in the process of industrialization was only broken with the Bolshevik Revolution, with most other countries of eastern Europe following after World War II (Berend and Ranki, 1982).

As the process of industrialization spread, the supply of importable technologies and the financial requirements for implementing such technologies both increased. According to one estimate, gross domestic investment as a proportion of GDP in Great Britain increased from around 4 per cent in 1700 to 5.7 per cent in 1760, 7.9 per cent in 1801 and 11.7 per cent in 1831 (Crafts, 1983), and remained between 10 and 12 per cent between 1831 and 1860 (Feinstein, 1978, p. 91). By contrast in countries such as Germany, Sweden or Denmark the rate of investment in their phase of industrialization (after 1860) often reached 15 per cent and more of GDP. In the USA the social preconditions for industrialization were much more favourable than in most European countries, and the export of capital from Europe considerably aided her industrialization process until she in turn became a creditor nation around the turn of the 19th century.

The latecomers among the western European countries, and Japan on the other side of the world, used state intervention on a much wider scale and much more purposively than Britain did. This intervention did not take the same form in all countries: in a country such as Germany, financing of industry was far more widely supported by the state and by new instruments of finance created for the purpose than, say, in Italy. It is doubtful whether a general pattern of successful state intervention to overcome economic backwardness can be discerned from the historical experience as has sometimes been claimed (Gerschenkron, 1962). What can be asserted is that state intervention in industry was much more likely to succeed in countries where capitalist relations had advanced far than where intervention from the top was used as a substitute for social change which might upset the balance of class forces among the rulers (cf. Berend and Ranki, 1982).

The example of Russia is especially instructive in showing the limits of state action in a society where capitalist relations had taken root only to an imperfect degree. In Russia serfdom had been consciously introduced in the 17th century, and the system bore particularly heavily on regions producing grain which was a major export of eastern European lands. The so-called village communes (*obschina*) produced both agricultural products and handicrafts. Beginning around the 1830s modern machinery was employed in the processing of beet sugar and in the spinning of cotton yarn. Even after the abolition of serfdom in 1861, handicrafts remained predominant (Crisp, 1978), but later on, the system of domestic production and production by handicrafts became more and more integrated into the system of capitalist production (Lenin, 1898). It was only in the 1880s that large-scale industry employing modern machines experienced an accelerated growth in Russia (Lyaschenko, 1949; Crisp, 1978).

The development of modern industry and capitalism in general in Russia gave rise to a vigorous debate which still has contemporary relevance in many countries of the third world. Some of the Russian Populists (*Narodniks*) contended that the development of capitalist industry was impossible in a backward country such as Russia. They argued that modern machine-based industry destroys handicrafts and small peasant agriculture, the incomes of people dependent on them consequently shrink, and thus modern industry faces a severe – indeed insurmountable – realization problem. Countering this argument, Lenin pointed out that capitalism created its own markets by converting goods produced within a household or barter economy into tradeable commodities and by continually generating new methods of production. The latter in their turn create demands for new equipment and materials (Lenin, 1897, 1899). Lenin did not deny that capitalism needed foreign markets. But at that stage he attributed the need not to the impossibility of realizing the surplus value but to intercapitalist competition and the continuous drive of capital towards expansion. In the process of discussing the analytical issues involved Lenin enunciated a law of development of capital, namely, that 'constant capital grows faster than variable capital, that is to say, an ever larger share of newly-formed capital is turned into that department of the social economy which produces means of production' (Lenin, 1897, pp. 155–6).

While markets expanded in Russia with state support for development of railways and war-related industries, the process of industrialization before the Revolution of 1917 remained ridden with numerous contradictions. Before the

Stolypin reforms (which were initiated after the abortive revolution of 1905) the spread of individual ownership in agriculture was held up by numerous restrictions on peasant mobility and on the transferability of land. Even after the Stolypin reforms (or reaction) landlords' social and economic power continued to limit the development of capitalism in agriculture (see, e.g., Lenin, 1912). A substantial proportion of growth in the industrial capital stock was financed by foreign banks and foreign entrepreneurs (McKay, 1970). Large-scale industry was regionally and sectorally concentrated (Portal, 1965) and the proportion of the working force engaged in industry (including construction) was only 9 per cent in 1913; it was only after the Bolshevik Revolution and the implementation of the two Five Year Plans that there was a decisive change in the occupational structure. The proportion of the working force engaged in industry and construction climbed to 23 per cent in 1940 and 39 per cent in 1979; correspondingly the proportion engaged in the agriculture and forestry declined from 75 per cent in 1913 to 54 per cent in 1940 and 21 per cent in 1979 (Sarkisyants, 1977, p. 180; see also Kuznets, 1966, p. 107).

In Japan, the course and the pattern of industrialization differed considerably from the sequence witnessed in western Europe and the USA, and also from that followed in socialist countries. Under Tokugawa rule, Japan was characterized by was has been called 'centralized feudalism' (Ohkawa, 1978, p. 140) with the *shogun* exercising supreme power through the *daimyos* and a rigid hierarchy going down to the village level. But the increasing use of money for the payment of taxes, countrywide transactions in money required to support the *daimyos'* and their retainers' expenditures in their travels to the capital and back, and the increasing indebtedness of many *daimyos* to merchants enhanced the power of the latter. The merchants' ambitions, the peasants' discontent and the frustrations of many of the feudal lords in the face of the increasing threat posed by the military and technological advance of the Western powers ultimately led to the end of the shogunate and the restoration of the Meiji emperor. The fierce nationalism bred among the nobility under the isolation enforced on the country earlier by the shogunate led them to define their objectives in the image of the activities of the Western imperialist powers (Beasley, 1963; Norman, 1943; Smith, 1961).

While abolishing many of the privileges of the warrior class the new Japanese rulers held on to the rigid rules of hierarchal control descending from the emperor through the nobility and the higher ranks of merchants to the village headmen, and down to the peasants working in the fields. The rigid subjugation of family members, especially of women, to the patriarch and the use of communal ties to enforce authoritarian rule continued unabated, and was adapted to the requirements of modern industry (Morishima, 1982). A high level of land taxes imposed on the peasantry financed much of the economic growth in Japan which accelerated from the 1880s. Young women, more or less bonded to the factories by their fathers or other family heads provided cheap labour. The first steps in the industrialization process were taken under the guidance of the state which built or financed shipyards, telegraph lines, railways and armament works

(Lockwood, 1968). The actual pace-setter in the industrialization process, in Japan as in Britain, was textiles, and for a long time, handicraft methods continued to be used alongside of machine methods in producing Japan's industrial goods. Silk, indemnities from foreign conquest, and exports of cotton yarn and cotton goods allowed Japan to do without much foreign investment in her drive towards industrialization. As in Britain, so in Japan, external markets and imperial conquest played an important role in the rise of modern industry (Lockwood, 1968).

Japan's industrial growth was already impressive in its diversity and sophistication during the interwar years. But it is since World War II that her growth has surpassed earlier historical standards (Ohkawa, 1978; Armstrong, Glyn and Harrison, 1984). The reserve army of labour in agriculture was finally exhausted there under the dual impact of land reforms imposed by the American occupation authorities and rates of industrial growth that often exceeded 15 per cent per year. Accompanying the Japanese growth was domination of trade and industry by a handful of giant conglomerates, the *zaibatsu*, giant firms and general trading corporations or *soga soshas*, acting in close collaboration with the Ministry of International Trade and Industry, and the subjugation of the labour movement to company objectives. It is these characteristics combined with a systematic exclusion of foreign capital from practically all fields that led observers to use the phrase 'Japan Inc.' to characterize the Japanese system of management. Japan eventually surpassed all capitalist countries except the USA in the value of her industrial production and in her technological advance.

While the countries on the two sides of the north Atlantic seaboard were industrializing and Japan was slowly emerging as a challenger to the industrial and political supremacy of the Western powers in the Far East, the majority of the people living in Asia, Africa and Latin America hardly experienced any positive process of industrialization. The movement of neither capital nor labour favoured such a process in China, India, Egypt, Peru, Brazil or Mexico, even in the exceptional days of massive British investments overseas that enriched the USA, Australia or Canada with men or materials (Edelstein, 1982; Davis and Huttenback, 1985). Only a small fraction of foreign investment made by Britain and France went to the non-white, dependent colonies, or formally independent, but effectively dependent countries peopled by non-white populations. These investments went generally into plantations, mines, railways rather than manufacturing industries. While the British dominions such as Canada or Australia pursued their economic policies largely independently of metropolitan control and protected their nascent industries, India, Egypt or even China and Turkey were forced to pursue *laissez faire* policies under the pressure of the metropolitan powers. The small flows of foreign investment into the colonies were swamped in the case of India, West Indies or even Brazil by the outflow of capital to the metropolitan countries (and thence to their colonies of settlement) as political tribute, and profit on external trade, foreign exchange transactions or plantation and railway enterprises (Bagchi, 1982, chs 3 and 4).

Policies of free trade or state intervention in favour of metropolitan trade and industry generally led to a decline in handicrafts and domestic industry on a large scale in such countries as India, China and Turkey. This erosion of proto-industrial output and employment was only very inadequately compensated by the rise of modern industry. Colonial rule also led in many cases to the strengthening of ties of bondage of various kinds in the rural areas. When migration occurred on a large scale from these countries, it was often organized by the merchants from the metropolitan countries, and the migrants often entered into a semiservile condition in the plantations of Assam (India), Trinidad, Guyana, or mines of South Africa. The effective control of modern plantation and mining enterprises and many areas of trade, especially wholesale internal and external trade by merchants from metropolitan countries, policies of free trade and processes of de-industrialization retarded the development of an indigenous mercantile community in most of the dependent colonies and often delayed the onset of any process of industrialization until the 1950s.

In many Latin American countries industrialization was quickened in the 1930s as a result of import restriction policies forced on the governments by the deep depression, especially in primary commodity exports, and attendant balance of payments crises. Following on from this experience, many of them adopted industrialization as a strategy of development and the basic objective of planning. The Prebisch–Singer thesis of a secular decline in terms of trade of primary products provided the rationale for such a strategy in Latin America (Prebisch, 1950; Singer, 1950; Spraos, 1982). Elsewhere, the success of the Soviet experiment provided an inspiration for planning.

However, after some initial successes, in most countries of the third world, the process of industrialization was caught up in multiple contradictions. In few countries were there land reforms conferring the right of ownership and control on the cultivating peasantry. This failure rendered the supply of food grains and other farm products inelastic and enabled the entrenched landlords and traders to speculate in these commodities. As a result, any stepping up of investment through governmental efforts soon met inflation barriers and balance of payments crises. The latter were aggravated by a tendency to import newer and newer consumer goods for the upper and the middle classes, by an inability to bargain from a position of strength with the suppliers of technology, and by the oversell practised by many of the aid-givers wanting to tie the loans or grants to purchases of goods from the donor country. In many Latin American countries, threats of social revolution were met by imposition of authoritarian regimes, generally with US connivance or assistance. The case of Chile where a popular government under the presidentship of Salvador Allende was replaced by a brutal military dictatorship is perhaps the most glaring example of this tendency, but Argentina, Brazil and Uruguay all fitted the same pattern. The primary commodities boom in the early 1970s, rise in oil prices in 1973–4 and 1978–9, along with attraction provided to transnational corporations by explicit policies of wage repression and labour regimentation, boosted the rate of industrial growth in countries as widely dispersed as Brazil and Iran. However, in most of these countries, including some oil-exporters such as Mexico and Nigeria, astronomically large external debts and debt servicing charges put a stop to most development efforts by the early 1980s.

A few economies in east Asia, more specifically the two enclaves of Hong Kong and Singapore, and the two medium-sized economies of South Korea and Taiwan went through a process of successful industrialization. In South Korea and Taiwan, radical land reforms, partly brought about through the defeat of the Japanese in 1945 who had been major land-holders in these two provinces, and partly imposed by the US authorities fearing a Communist revolution in emulation of the People's Republic of China, enormously speeded up the movement of trading capital into industry, increased the elasticity of supply of farm products and widened the market for basic consumer and producer goods. Chinese overseas capital had for a long time dominated trade and money-lending in many countries of east and south-east Asia. Communist take-over of mainland China drove out a sizeable section of big mercantile capital. The newly migrating and old Chinese overseas capital then turned to industrial investment in many of these countries. Increased US military activities in the region, attempted economic blockade of Communist China by the Western capitalist countries and the large expenditures attending US military aggression in Vietnam provided multiple opportunities to the traders and industrialists in the region for capital accumulation and expansion. Many Japanese, American and western European transnational corporations found Singapore, Hong Kong, Taiwan and South Korea useful as export platforms since these four economies provided the attraction of low wages, a disciplined (and regimented) labour force and privileged access to US, EEC and Japanese markets.

However, despite the fact that many Asian economies have continued to experience positive growth in a period of global recession, it cannot be said yet that the east Asian experience is catching or easily diffusible. Most of Africa is experiencing negative growth, and large clusters of population are caught there in the clutches of famine. Most Latin American economies are yet to get out of the debt trap. The only other countries which are still experiencing a positive process of industrialization to a greater or lesser extent are the socialist countries which have embraced some variant of Marxism as their guiding ideology. The share of industry in GNP rose steeply in most of these countries and often exceeded 40 per cent. The high rate of economic growth in these countries was financed by the confiscation of rent incomes from land, by the channelling of all surpluses into investment and by allowing only a moderate rise in real wages until an acceptable level of GNP was reached (cf. Ellman, 1975; Lippit, 1974). One feature that has distinguished socialist industrialization is that usually the share of services in GNP and employment has been lower than in most non-socialist economies. In a country such as China, the abnormally low share of services has been seen as a defect associated with the phase of extensive growth.

Most of the socialist countries are also now grappling with problems of lower productivity growth. Effective decentralization of planning processes, increased responsiveness to changes in relative scarcity and signalling of such changes through changes in relative prices and provision of adequate incentives to managers and workers have been generally seen as the answer to these problems. Increased imports of technology from the OECD countries and their effective absorption are also seen as part of the answer, but the successful pursuit of such strategies is intertwined with the issue of economic reforms on the one hand and geopolitical manoeuvring between the two blocks on the other.

One problem that will continue to bedevil industrialization strategies in most large third world countries for a long time is the very high ratio of the working population engaged in agriculture to the total working force. Even in a country such as China, which has experienced a trend rate of industrial growth of more than 10 per cent over the years since the Communist revolution in 1949, and where the share of industry in national income went up to 42.2 per cent in 1982, agriculture and forestry continued to employ 71.6 per cent of the labour force in the same year (China, 1983, pp. 24, 121). It is only some medium-sized economies with a high rate of industrial growth such as South Korea and Taiwan that have experienced any major shift in the population balance towards industrial employment.

The experience of the structural changes within the east Asian group of capitalist economies shows that under favourable circumstances, it is possible for the less industrialized economies to grow at high rates if there is a sustained shedding off of the lower-productivity sectors by the more advanced regions and the grafting of the shedded output on to the structures of the less developed economies (Yamazawa, Taniguchi and Hirata, 1983). The process is very similar to that observed in western Europe in the early part of the 19th century, except that the role of migration of population to countries outside the region (such as the USA in the case of western Europe) in easing population pressure has been minimal. But the roles of direct investment by Japanese and other OECD firms and of privileged access to extra-regional markets have been more significant than in the case of western Europe. (It could, of course, be argued that western European countries had a privileged access to markets in their dependent colonies.)

The general developments in the advanced capitalist bloc of countries (within which Japan occupies a unique position because of her maintenance of moderate to high rates of growth and near full employment and her large trade surpluses with most other countries), however, preclude the replication of the east Asian pattern in the rest of the third world. Most of them are afflicted by high rates of unemployment – exceeding levels witnessed since the end of the 1930s. Some countries such as the UK experienced an absolute decline in manufacturing (Singh, 1977). These developments aggravated protectionism in these countries, thus creating barriers against the expansion of exports from the third world countries, while the OECD group of countries continued to constitute the biggest market for manufactured goods in the world. Developments in microelectronic technology posed major threats to the further expansion of labour-intensive textile products and clothing exports from the third world to the OECD countries (UNCTAD, 1981). More generally, the spread of microelectronic technologies embracing whole branches of manufacture are threatening to remove many assembly operations which the OECD-based transnational corporations had earlier found it profitable to subcontract to the favoured export enclaves including the east Asian group of newly industrializing countries (Kaplinksky, 1984).

Within the OECD group, the USA has become the biggest magnet for capital flows from all over the world. The high interest rate and large budget deficits maintained by the US government have forced most other OECD governments to pursue deflationary policies within their borders. There is little sign as yet that such trends will be reversed. The Japanese, who have run up large trade surpluses (exceeding US $40 billion) with the USA have proceeded to invest most of their export surplus in the US. Thus the diffusion that is borne on the backs of foreign investment within the order of capitalism has been severely hampered by these developments.

The only alternative that is left for most third world countries is to rely on building industries on the basis of domestic resources and domestic markets. But the guidelines laid down by the International Monetary Fund seeking to impose severely deflationary policies on most countries applying for its assistance in meeting their debt problems, the power exerted by OECD-based transnational corporations in effectively restricting the flow of technology, and the internal social structures in most of these countries blocking the spread of literacy and accrual of purchasing power to common people are likely to hamper the feeble efforts at industrialization on a self-reliant basis. The other path of industrialization, building on growing exports and expanding international investment flows, would appear also to be beset with dangerous pitfalls for most of the poor countries of the world. Thus the spread of industrialization in the near term to the poorer countries is likely to be very slow compared with the speed witnessed between, say, 1950 and 1978. At the other end of the spectrum, in countries such as the USA and UK, services and finance have gained tremendously at the expense of manufacturing industry, and it is through the use of financial instruments as much as advanced technology in manufacturing (including armaments production) and services that the USA dominates the economies of most of the capitalist countries. But as Japan continues to forge ahead even in frontier technologies such as the mass production of semiconductor chips for use in the most advanced microelectronic processes (cf. Gregory, 1985), a change in the balance within the capitalist order is very likely. In the meanwhile continued growth in the socialist world will also affect the global balance in manufacturing and economic power.

BIBLIOGRAPHY

Armstrong, P., Glyn, A. and Harrison, J. 1984. *Capitalism since World War II: The Making and Breaking of the Great Boom*. London: Fontana.

Bagchi, A.K. 1972. Some international foundations of capitalist growth and underdevelopment. *Economic and Political Weekly* 7(31–33), Special Number, August, 1559–70.

Bagchi, A.K. 1976. De-industrialization in India in the nineteeenth century: some theoretical implications. *Journal of Development Studies* 12(2), January, 135–64.

Bagchi, A.K. 1982. *The Political Economy of Underdevelopment*. Cambridge and New York: Cambridge University Press.

Bairoch, P. 1975. *Economic Development of the Third World since 1900*. London: Methuen.

Beasley, W.G. 1963. *The Modern History of Japan*. New York: Praeger.

Berend, I.T. and Ranki, G. 1982. *The European Periphery and Industrialization 1780–1914*. Cambridge: Cambridge University Press.

Blackaby, F. (ed.) 1979. *De-industrialization*. London: Heineman.

Braudel, F. 1984. *The Perspective of the World: Civilization & Capitalism, 15th–18th Century*. London: Collins; New York: Harper & Row.

Brenner, R. 1976. Agrarian class structure and economic development in pre-industrial Europe. *Past and Present* 70, February, 30–75.

Bythell, D. 1969. *The Handloom Weavers: A Study in the English Cotton Industry during the Industrial Revolution*. Cambridge: Cambridge University Press.

China. 1983. *Statistical Yearbook of China 1983*. Hong Kong: State Statistical Bureau PRC and Economic Information Agency.

Crafts, N.F.R. 1983. British economic growth, 1700–1831: A review of the evidence. *Economic History Review* 36(2), May, 177–99.

Crafts, N.F.R. 1985. *British Economic Growth during the Industrial Revolution*. Oxford: Clarendon Press.

Crisp, O. 1978. Labour and industrialization in Russia. In Mathias and Postan (1978).

Datta, B. 1952. *The Economics of Industrialization*. Calcutta: World Press.

Davis, L. and Huttenback, R.A. 1985. The export of British finance, 1865–1914. *Journal of Imperial and Commonwealth History* 13(3), May, 28–76.

Dobb, M. 1946. *Studies in the Development of Capitalism*. London: Routledge & Kegan Paul; New York: International Publishers, 1947.

Edelstein, M. 1982. *Overseas Investment in the Age of High Imperialism; The United Kingdom 1850–1914*. London: Methuen.

Ellman, M. 1975. Did the agricultural surplus provide the resources for the increase in investment in the USSR during the first five year plan? *Economic Journal* 85, December, 844–63.

Feinstein, C.H. 1978. Capital formation in Great Britain. In Mathias and Postan (1978).

Gerschenkron, A. 1962. *Economic Backwardness in Historical Perspective*. Cambridge, Mass.: Harvard University Press.

Gregory, G. 1985. Chip shop of the world. *New Scientist*, 15 August, 28–31.

Habakkuk, H.J. and Postan, M. (eds) 1965. *The Cambridge Economic History of Europe*. Vol. VI: *The Industrial Revolution and After*, Pts 1 and 2, Cambridge: Cambridge University Press.

Hicks, J. 1969. *A Theory of Economic History*. Oxford: Clarendon Press.

Hilton, R. (ed.) 1976. *The Transition from Feudalism to Capitalism*. London: New Left Books.

Kaplinsky, R. 1984. The international context for industrialization in the coming decade. *Journal of Development Studies* 21(1), October, 75–96.

Kriedte, P. 1981. The origins, the agrarian context, and the conditions in the world market. In Kriedte, Medick and Schlumbohm (1981).

Kriedte, P., Medick, H. and Schlumbohm, J. 1981. *Industrialization before Industrialization: Rural Industry before the Genesis of Capitalism*. Cambridge and New York: Cambridge University Press.

Kuznets, S. 1966. *Modern Economic Growth: Rate, Structure and Spread*. New Haven: Yale University Press.

Kuznets, S. 1971. *Economic Growth of Nations: Total Output and Production Structure*. Cambridge, Mass.: Harvard University Press.

Landes, D. 1965. Technological change and development in Western Europe 1750–1914. In Habakkuk and Postan (1965).

Lenin, V.I. 1897. A characterisation of economic romanticism (Sismondi, and our native Sismondists). Trans. from Russian in Lenin, *Collected Works*, Vol. 2, Moscow: Foreign Languages Publishing House, 1963.

Lenin, V.I. 1898. The handicraft census of 1894–95 in Perm Gubernia and general problems of handicraft industry. Trans. from Russian in Lenin, *Collected Works*, Vol. 2, Moscow: Foreign Languages Publishing House, 1963.

Lenin, V.I. 1899. *The Development of Capitalism in Russia*. Text of the 2nd edn of 1908, trans. from Russian in Lenin, *Collected Works*, Vol. 3, Moscow: Progress Publishers, 1964.

Lenin, V.I. 1912. The last valve. Trans. from Russian in Lenin, *Collected Works*, Vol. 18, Moscow: Progress Publishers, 1968.

Lewis, W.A. 1978. *Growth and Fluctuations 1870–1913*. London: Allen & Unwin.

Lippit, V.D. 1974. Land reform and economic development in China. *Chinese Economic Studies* 7(4), Summer, 3–181.

Lockwood, W.W. 1968. *The Economic Development of Japan*. Princeton: Princeton University Press.

Lyaschenko, P.T. 1949. *History of the National Economy of Russia to the 1917 Revolution*. London and New York: Macmillan.

Macfarlane, A. 1978. *The Origins of English Individualism*. Oxford: Basil Blackwell.

McKay, J.P. 1970. *Pioneers for Profit: Foreign Entrepreneurship and Russian Industrialization*. Chicago: University of Chicago Press.

Mantoux, P. 1928. *The Industrial Revolution in the Eighteenth Century*. London: Jonathan Cape.

Marx, K. 1867–94. *Das Kapital*. Trans. by S. Moore and E. Aveling as *Capital: A Critical Analysis of Capitalist Production*, Vol. 1. Reprinted, Moscow: Foreign Languages Publishing House, n.d.

Mathias, P. and Postan, M.M. (eds) 1978. *The Cambridge Economic History of Europe*. Vol. VII, *The Industrial Economies: Capital, Labour and Enterprise*, Pts 1 and 2, Cambridge and New York: Cambridge University Press.

Mendels, F. 1972. Proto-industrialization: the first phase of the industrialization process. *Journal of Economic History* 32(1), March, 241–61.

Moore, B. Jr., 1967. *Social Origins of Dictatorship and Democracy: Land and Peasant in the Making of the Modern World*. London: Allen Lane.

Morishima, M. 1982. *Why has Japan 'Succeeded'?* Cambridge: Cambridge University Press.

Musson, A.E. (ed.) 1972. *Science, Technology and Economic Growth in the Eighteenth Century*. London: Methuen.

Norman, E.H. 1943. *Soldier and Peasant in Japan*. New York: Institute of Pacific Relations.

Ohkawa, K. 1978. Capital formulation in Japan. In Mathias and Postan (1978).

Portal, R. 1965. The industrialization of Russia. In Habakkuk and Postan (1965), Pt 2.

Prebisch, R. 1950. *The Economic Development of Latin America and its Principal Problems*. United Nations, New York: Reprinted in *Economic Bulletin for Latin America* 7(1), February 1962, 1–22.

Ricardo, D. 1821. *On the Principles of Political Economy and Taxation*. 3rd edn, reprinted in *The Works and Correspondence of David Ricardo*, Vol. I, ed. P. Sraffa with the collaboration of M.H. Dobb, Cambridge: Cambridge University Press, 1951; New York: Cambridge University Press.

Robinson, E.A.G. 1954. The changing structure of the British economy. *Economic Journal* 64, September, 443–61.

Sarkisyants, G.S. (ed.) 1977. *Soviet Economy: Results and Prospects.* Moscow: Progress Publishers.

Singer, H. 1950. The distribution of gains between investing and borrowing countries. *American Economic Review* 40, May, 473–85.

Singh, A. 1977. UK industry and the world economy: a case of de-industrialisation? *Cambridge Journal of Economics* 1(2), June, 113–36.

Smith, T.C. 1961. Japan's aristocratic revolution. *Yale Review* 50(3), Spring, 370–83.

Spraos, J. 1982. Deteriorating terms of trade and beyond. *Trade and Development. An UNCTAD Review*, No. 4, Paris: UNCTAD.

Sutcliffe, R.B. 1971. *Industry and Underdevelopment*, London: Addison-Wesley.

UNCTAD. 1981. *Fibres and Textiles: Dimensions of Corporate Marketing Structure.* Geneva: United Nations.

Von Tunzelmann, G.N. 1978. *Steam Power and British Industrialization to 1860.* Oxford: Clarendon Press.

Yamazawa, I., Taniguchi, K. and Hirata, A. 1983. Trade and industrial adjustment in Pacific Asian countries. *Developing Economies* 21(4), December, 281–312.

Inequality between Nations

ALBERT FISHLOW

From the origins of systematic economic analysis, differences in national prosperity have been remarked upon. Indeed, Adam Smith's *Wealth of Nations* elaborated the theoretical reasons supporting the contemporary observation that income in Europe varied inversely with the extent of state intervention. But it is to the beginning of sustained economic growth in the 18th century and the wonders of compound interest that we trace the present large differences among national per capita incomes. Countries that followed early in the van of England's industrial revolution could multiply their initial levels of per capita income by factors of ten to twenty times over the course of a century and a half. Those that did not faced ever larger disparities. The World Bank's *World Development Report* in 1985 recorded a range of per capita income from $120 in Ethiopia to $22,870 in the United Arab Emirates and $14,110 in the United States.

Conventional measures on inequality applied to such a distribution of income levels, like the Gini coefficient, show values among nations in excess of 0.7, and thus notably greater than inside even the most unequal of countries. On a global level, half the world population commands little more than 5 per cent of total income, while at the other end, 15 per cent of the population receives something like three-fourths of world income.

These comparisons overstate inequality by reason of the use of market exchange rates to convert national currencies to US dollars. In poorer countries, non-traded goods and some wage goods sell for much less than their exchange rate derived equivalent. Systematic collection and analysis of domestic prices in a number of countries in a study conducted under the direction of Irving Kravis (1982) have provided a more accurate indication of the extent of bias introduced by the use of exchange rates to convert national values to dollars. It is considerable. For the poorest countries, incomes relative to those in the United States are understated by a factor of 2.5; in the richest, overstated by 7 per cent. Thus Malawi's 1975 gross product per capita rises from $138 to $352, while France's falls from $6428 to $5977. Even as adjusted for this bias, international inequality remains extreme: the Gini coefficient exceeds 0.6 and the poorest half of the world's population has access to only 12 per cent of the world's product.

This relative gap between the rich and poor has not narrowed in the post-World War II period, despite the much improved performance of developing countries. Since 1950, although developing country annual per capita income growth has accelerated to almost 3 per cent, the industrialized countries have more than kept pace. Indeed, it is only during the disturbed international economic environment of the 1970s that faltering growth in the industrialized economics enabled developing countries to move ahead more rapidly, and there and signs of reversal in the 1980s. Most troubling is the plight of the low income countries (excluding China). Africa and South Asia have fallen further behind, even as the new industrializing counries of East Asia and some Latin American countries have improved their positions. It has become more common to speak of Third and Fourth Worlds, as increased differentiation has emerged among developing countries. Signs of improved performance in South Asia and China in recent years remain unmatched in Africa.

Attention to this widening relative gap obscures the positive attainments of the developing countries over the last 35 years. Their economic performance, even while many were burdened simultaneously with the task of nation-building as artificial colonial boundaries and status were swept away, exceeds that attained by the present industrialized countries in the past. It is a still greater improvement over the progress of the developing countries before 1950, when their growth was much slower and more erratic.

So long as the differences between industrialized and developing countries are the central issue, the perspective cannot help but be pessimistic. Improvements in relative position still imply a continuous increase in the size of the absolute gap until the time when the ratio of per capita incomes equals the inverse of the ratio of growth rates. For middle-income developing countries, whose income per capita is only about a fourth of the industrialized country level after correction for exchange rates, the absolute difference will continue to widen, because growth rates do not come close to being four times greater. Those select developing countries attaining sustained rates of growth greater than the expansion of the industrialized countries nonetheless confront an absolute gap whose elimination is to be reckoned in units of centuries, and not even decades (Morawetz, 1977, pp. 26–30).

Such arithmetic raises the question of the usefulness of gaps, relative or absolute. Why not opt instead for an absolute criterion analogous to the focus upon poverty within countries? As W.A. Lewis has said: 'What will happen to the gap between the rich and the poor countries?... Since I think what matters is the absolute progress of the LDCs and not the size of the gap, I do not care' (Ranis, 1972, p. 420). With this shift of emphasis, the development problem continues to remain immense. By a World Bank criterion of minimal standard of living, some 40 per cent of the population of developing countries is in a destitute state. Rapid and consistent economic growth, and redistributionist policies, will be required to make a significant dent in the present dismal situation.

But even were such efforts to yield results, concern about inequality between nations will not go away readily. Comparisons will influence economic analysis as well as international policies. The existence of the gap has contributed to new ways of thinking about the process of integration of developing countries into the world economy, as well as inspiring practical efforts to reduce it.

The conceptual issue posed by increasing inequality over the 19th and 20th centuries, despite a more inclusive international economy, is its inconsistency with predictions of convergence inherent in a competitive market framework. Trade, capital flows and migration are all supposed to equalize returns to factors of production, and thereby to diminish national differences. The apparent failure to do so on a global scale has led to a group of theories emphasizing the opposite: the adverse effects of developing country integration in the world economy through declining terms of trade, backwash and demonstration effects, unequal exchange, technological dependence and domestic disintegration. These theories, and the experience of the Great Depression, reinforced an inward, interventionist and industrialization orientation to development efforts in most developing countries in the postwar period.

That point of view, despite its critical reception in industrialized countries, continues to be influential in developing countries, not least among policy makers. From intellectual origins at the Economic Commission for Latin America in the 1940s, this criticism of an asymmetrical international order led to the first UNCTAD conference in 1964 and its continuing service as a permanent forum for the discussion of relationships between developing countries. On that first occasion and at subsequent meetings, the South, united politically, sought to extract aid concessions and preferential trade access from the North. The principal harvest was the eventual acceptance of a Generalized System of Preferences, and thus a modest discrimination in favour of developing countries. The Third World was very much in the role of supplicant in behalf of a limited agenda.

It was not until after the oil crisis and price rise in 1973 and an enhanced sense of commodity power, that developing countries, backed by OPEC, extended their demands and elevated their voices on behalf of a more comprehensive New International Economic Order. The UN General Assembly, in a Sixth Special Session convened in April 1974, concluded its deliberations by committing itself 'to work urgently for the establishment of a new international economic order [NIEO] ... which shall correct inequalities and redress existing injustices, make it possible to eliminate the widening gap between the developed and developing countries'. The range of concrete proposals included stabilization of commodity prices at more favourable levels; enhanced regulation of foreign investment and technology transfer; new rules for the international monetary system, including a linkage of IMF special drawing rights to development finance; enhanced official aid and a debt moratorium for some hard-pressed developing countries; and greater participation in the decision structure of the multilateral economic institutions, the IMF, World Bank and GATT (Fishlow, 1978).

For a brief moment, North-South economic relations stood centre stage in the traditional pride of place of East-West strategic concerns. New international negotiating structures were created. More conciliatory stands on some issues were taken by the industrialized countries, including agreement in principle on a modest commodity stabilization effort. A new international commission under the leadership of Willy Brandt submitted an action report (Independent Commission, 1980). Even a summit meeting was eventually held in 1981. But the sense of urgency and the faith in negotiation of extensive international economic reforms had already receded by that time.

The limited progress did not owe itself simply to the radicalism of the demands. Despite occasional rhetorical flourishes, the platform of the NIEO was reformist, and accepting of the importance of the international economy for the prospects of developing countries. Indeed, emphasis was placed upon a competitive international order, in which developing countries could exploit their new-found comparative advantage. The self-reliance, or delinking, advocated by some Third World spokesmen was implicitly rejected. Many of the specific proposals had been aired before. Yet in their totality, there was also a clear commitment to discrimination and non-reciprocity, a tendency toward intervention in market processes, and demands for a redistribution of resources and power that industrialized countries found objectionable. The more conservative political tide of the late 1970s and early 1980s in the industrialized countries reinforced this opposition even as it became clearer that the feared capacity of developing countries to restrict supply to needed raw materials had been overstated.

But the NIEO agenda also lapsed because of the relative gains experienced by many developing countries in the 1970s as international trade expanded and capital flows increased in unanticipated fashion. Oil exports clearly gained from their improved terms of trade. The East Asian newly industrializing countries did likewise by exporting manufactured products at a rate that compensated for their worsened terms of trade. Even under the old order it was possible for some countries to make it. This differentiation among developing countries reduced their political coherence and unity. Commodity agreements might help some, but they also could harm others increasingly dependent upon primary imports. The emergence of the newly industrializing countries and their penetration of developed country markets, defined another path to success.

Nor did the slowing of growth of many of the heavily indebted developing countries in the early 1980s owing to higher oil prices, interest rates and industrialized country recession stimulate a renewed cry for a new order, although some leaders tried. Debt problems, and their remedies, tended to be specific to particular countries. The critical element of Third World unity was largely absent, despite some common origins in external economic circumstances.

Although Latin America was especially afflicted by a debt problem, it involved oil exporters as well as importers. Africa also faced a problem, but of a different kind. Mounting debt service payments on official debt, rather than private, were the proximate source of import compression. Each region sought to mobilize relief for its difficulties, but in different ways. At the same time, a large East Asian debtor like Korea managed to avert reduced growth in part because its low debt-export ratio permitted continuing creditworthiness. Low income China and the countries of the Indian sub-continent, virtually unencumbered by debt, experienced much improved economic performance in the early 1980s.

Yet it would be a mistake to dismiss the efforts of the developing countries in the name of the NIEO as of no practical value. Even in the absence of fully effective political pressure, they have kept alive a concern with the consequences of industrialized country policies. Present opposition to protectionism owes itself in part to the constant vigilance of developing countries. They have also kept in the forefront the need for greater coordination of macroeconomic policy among the developed countries themselves, since they bear many of the consequences of its inadequacy. And they have been instrumental in seeking to increase the role for official flows to finance medium term, rather than immediate, adjustment to changes in the world economy. In regional forums, developing countries have sometimes been more successful in achieving practical cooperation.

Although the focus on the gap between rich and poor nations has faded in recent years compared to its ascendance in the 1970s, the great and persistent inequality between developing and developed countries remains. It is difficult to imagine that there will not be a resurgence in political attention when circumstances again seem more propitious. Redistributionist reforms on a global scale – even when efficiency enhancing and mutually beneficial – will not prove easy, however. In the last analysis, the moral and ethical sense inherent in community that informs national policies to deal with internal inequality is less evident at the international level. Vague, and sometimes even concrete, threats to international order do not fully substitute as a compelling and continuing impulse to action. In a world of sovereign states, the primary burden for relative and eventual absolute reduction of the gap falls upon national development strategies.

BIBLIOGRAPHY
Fishlow, A. et al. 1978. *Rich and Poor Nations in the World Economy*. New York: McGraw-Hill.
Independent Commission on International Development Issues. 1980. *North-South: A Program for Survival*. Cambridge, Mass.: MIT Press.
Kravis, I. et al. 1982. *World Product and Income. International Comparisons of Real Gross Product*. Baltimore: Johns Hopkins Press.
Morawetz, D. 1977. *Twenty-five Years of Economic Development, 1950 to 1975*. Washington, DC: The World Bank.
Ranis, G. (ed.) 1972. *The Gap Between Rich and Poor Nations*. London: Macmillan; New York: St. Martin's Press.

International Migration

M.P. TODARO AND L. MARUSZKO

The literature on international migration from developing countries has expanded considerably in recent years. Much of it tends to be empirical and policy-oriented with the majority of studies seeking to estimate the magnitude of inter-country migration flows and the associated benefits and costs. However, unlike the ever more abundant literature on the theoretical determinants and consequences of internal migration in developing nations, the literature on international migration is notable for its absence of theoretical models designed to analyse the causes and consequences of migration across borders. As a result, policy prescriptions for promoting or regulating international flows are often made without any underlying conceptual framework.

In part, the problem arises from the institutional context in which international migration occurs – placing legal, physical and cultural constraints on the unfettered locational choices of individual workers. The theoretical work to date, based mostly on neoclassical trade theory, skirts this difficulty by focusing on international migration in aggregate terms. By doing so, it has ignored the underlying basis for mass movements of labour – the individual migrant's decision-making process.

Furthermore, these economic models usually examine international migration within a perfect world of full employment, flexible wages and full factor mobility. Traditional trade theory views migration as a simple disequilibrium phenomenon in which labour seeks to equalize returns across countries. As long as real returns to labour are unequal, the models suggest that international migration will persist in the absence of physical constraint by governments. Only after factor returns are equalized will migration cease.

This view of international migration is implicit in many of the trade models ranging from the earlier simple neoclassical framework of Grubel and Scott (1966) to the more elaborate trade models of Berry and Soligo (1969), Rivera-Batiz (1982) and Ethier (1985), among others. Moreover, under the perfect world assumptions, these models often generate results that are not applicable to the not-so-perfect world of international migration. In the absence of an acceptable theoretical framework, therefore, most researchers have turned their attention to quantifying the direct benefits and costs of migration by focusing on the most obvious and easily obtainable information. Unfortunately, this approach has serious pitfalls, as the less obvious and indirect benefits and costs are typically overlooked.

A basic methodological requirement for theorization about international migration, therefore, is to include both macro- and micro-level factors and relationships within a single frame of reference. This essay will be a step in that direction. In presenting a model of the individual worker's decision to emigrate, it will lay a foundation for the neoclassical trade model which explains the mass migration of labour across borders as an attempt to equalize returns to factors. However, in contrast to traditional trade models, in our model, international migration will be shown to cease long before actual returns to labour are equalized across countries – i.e., it will cease when 'expected' returns are equalized. Perhaps, more importantly, by focusing simultaneously on three sectors – the domestic rural, the domestic urban and the foreign – our model will attempt to incorporate both internal and international migration choices within a single decision theoretic framework.

MIGRATION AND DOMESTIC UNEMPLOYMENT. One of the major purported benefits of organized, short-term labour emigration is that it contributes to the relief of unemployment in the labour-exporting country. This view will be disputed in the model to be presented here. While it may be true that labour emigration contributes to the relief of overall domestic unemployment, it will be shown that this favourable effect may be offset by a costly rise in urban unemployment provoked by increased rural–urban migration. Perhaps the most significant policy implication of this result is that policies designed to encourage labour exports in an effort to eliminate unemployment at home may be, in fact, exacerbating the domestic urban unemployment problem and increasing the rate of urbanization. The analysis also suggests that the promotion of labour exports may impose a significant cost on the rural sector as well. Such costs arise in the situation in which the rural sector does not possess a surplus of labour but large expected income differentials induce out-migration which, in turn, lowers rural output. In sum, our model of international migration suggests that the benefits and costs of labour exports must be examined and weighed more carefully than in previous studies, with particular emphasis on secondary and tertiary effects.

A preliminary review of empirical studies, both at the macro and micro level, suggests that the key variables underlying the decision to emigrate are the prospects for obtaining employment and the wage differentials between the country of immigration and that of emigration. Five well-known studies illustrate this point.

On a macro level, Hietala (1978) examined the labour flows between the Nordic countries in 1963–75 and found migration to be highly correlated with unemployment and wage differentials in almost all cases. This econometric study is particulary significant because it examined international migration in the absence of the usual physical and institutional constraints on migration – the Nordic countries have had a common labour market since 1954. Stahl (1984), in a major study of the current volume and characteristics of international migration in several ASEAN countries, also argued that wage differentials played a major role in the out-migration of workers from the leading labour-exporting countries.

On a micro level, Ulgalde (1979), in a survey of migrants from the Dominican Republic, found that 30% migrated because of unemployment and another 30% migrated in search of higher wages. Castano (1984), in a field study of Colombian workers migrating to Venezuela, found that 36% migrated in search of higher wages while another 26% cited the lack of jobs as their primary reason for moving. Finally, in a survey of Mexican migrants to the US, Cornelius (1978) found that 30% migrated due to the lack of jobs while another 31% went in search of higher wages.

Our model of international migration will therefore focus both on wage differentials and employment probabilities and thus will also be useful in analysing another type of major labour flow occurring in the world today – the flow of temporary workers, particularly from several Asian and a few Arab nations, to the oil-producing Persian Gulf countries. The prospect of substantial foreign exchange earnings, combined with the potential for reducing the high unemployment rates that often characterize the labour-sending countries, has led many developing countries to actually promote the export of their labour. The model will examine the various economic consequences of labour-export promotion policies and offer some insight into their possible costs.

A THREE-SECTOR MODEL OF LEGAL INTERNATIONAL MIGRATION. A major purported benefit of international migration is that it reduces the often high rates of unemployment in labour-exporting countries. While it may be true that labour emigration contributes to the relief of overall unemployment, one possibility ignored in the literature is that this favourable effect may be offset by a costly rise in urban unemployment provoked by increased rural–urban migration. For example, a number of studies have noted that labour export promotion has increased rural–urban migration and accelerated urbanization in several Asian and a few Arab labour-exporting countries. Stahl (1984) observed this effect in his study of the ASEAN countries, particularly with regard to the Philippines, Thailand and Indonesia, which export labour to the Middle East. The Population Information Center (1983) stated that the migration of skilled and semi-skilled Jordanian workers to Saudi Arabia and Kuwait opened up many jobs in the cities and provoked internal rural–urban migration to fill them. Finally, the United Nations Department of International Economic and Social Affairs (1982) declared that urbanization had been accelerated by emigration in Pakistan, also a major exporter of labour to the Middle East.

This is precisely the situation which arises when individuals seeking employment abroad must first come to their domestic urban areas in order to obtain foreign jobs. In many labour-exporting developing countries, such workers must register with urban modern-sector recruitment agencies (private or government run) which provide contracts with specific employers for employment abroad. Moreover, potential international migrants coming from outside the city must not only come to the urban centre to register for foreign jobs, they must also wait there in order to maximize their opportunity for foreign employment.

In a study of the major labour-exporting ASEAN countries, Stahl (1982) observed that recruiters, with registrants far in excess of the number of foreign jobs available, chose only those workers immediately present as delays in post and travel made it difficult to call in registrants residing outside the city. Under such circumstances, workers seeking foreign employment must migrate to the city and wait some period of time, usually in the informal sector, before obtaining a foreign job. For example, Martin (1984) noted that recruitment is concentrated in urban centres in the labour-exporting countries. Moreover, he argued that most potential international migrants enter the informal sector of the urban economy while waiting for the opportunity to migrate.

If one examines this situation within the context of a Todaro-type model of migration (Todaro, 1969; Harris and Todaro, 1970) then the offer of relatively higher-paying foreign jobs from recruiters in urban areas should increase the economic attractiveness of the urban economy and, hence, increase the rate of rural-urban migration and possibly also the rate of urban unemployment.

This section examines the effect of international labour emigration on the urban unemployment rate by extending the Todaro model of internal migration to rural-urban-international migration. In doing so, we arrive at a three-sector model of international legal migration based on assumptions that are in keeping with the observations made by researchers studying the major labour-exporting countries. Moreover, the model is unique within the current theoretical work on international migration because it focuses on the individual's decision to migrate.

The model. The model examines the behaviour of three types of migrants: rural workers seeking urban modern sector jobs; rural workers seeking foreign jobs; and urban employed workers seeking foreign jobs.

As within the framework of the original Todaro (1969) model, it is assumed that the decision to migrate depends on the expected relative income differential between the place of origin and the foreign destination. The expected income diffential, in turn, depends on actual income differentials, the cost of migration and the probability of employment.

It is assumed that rural workers seeking urban jobs must wait in the informal sector some period of time before obtaining an urban modern-sector job. Those seeking foreign jobs must also come to the city in order to obtain those jobs. Furthermore, they must wait in the informal sector some period of time before obtaining foreign employment. Urban employed workers seeking forcign jobs are assumed to continue their employment in the urban sector until they have obtained jobs abroad.

For simplicity, it will be assumed that the natural rate of increase of the urban labour force is zero. Hence, any change is due to rural-urban migration and labour out-migration. This implies that at any point in time, the urban labor force consists of (1) rural immigrants looking for urban jobs, (2) rural immigrants looking for foreign jobs, with both groups residing in the informal sector of the urban economy, and (3) urban workers who are already employed in the modern sector of the economy. Under the assumption of a zero natural rate of increase, the employed 'urban' workers are actually former rural residents who have managed to obtain urban modern-sector jobs. Some of these urban employed will continue their jobs while others seek foreign employment. In terms of this analysis, it is the urban employed workers desiring foreign jobs that are important as their emigration affects the probability of employment of groups (1) and (2). Including a natural rate of increase of the urban labour force in the model would not change the results.

Formally, the model can be expressed as:

(I) IN-MIGRATION OF RURAL WORKERS. As in Todaro (1969), rural–urban migration of workers seeking domestic employment is a function (f) of the expected relative rural–urban income differential, ($\alpha^e_{r,u}$):

$$f(\alpha^e_{r,u}(t)), \qquad f < 1, \quad f' > 0 \tag{1}$$

which depends on the discounted value of average earnings in the rural and urban sectors (Y_r and Y_u, respectively), the probability of having an urban job (P_u), and the initial cost of migrating to the urban sector (C_u) such that:

$$\alpha^e_{r,u}(0) = \int_{t=0}^{t=n} P_u(t)[(Y_u(t) - Y_r(t))/Y_r(t)] e^{-rt} dt - C_u(0). \tag{1a}$$

By extending this framework to deal with international migration, rural–urban migration is also now a function (g) of the expected relative rural–foreign income differential ($\alpha^e_{r,f}$):

$$g(\alpha^e_{r,f}(t)), \qquad g < 1, \quad g' > 0 \tag{2}$$

which depends on the discounted value of average earnings in the rural and foreign sectors (Y_f), the probability of having a foreign job (P_f), the cost of migrating to the urban sector in order to find a foreign job (C_u), and the cost of migrating abroad (C_f) such that:

$$\alpha^e_{r,f}(0) = \int_{t=0}^{t=n} P_f(t)[(Y_f(t) - Y_r(t))/Y_r(t)] e^{-rt} dt - C_u(0) - C_f(0). \tag{2a}$$

Since individuals obtain foreign jobs through recruiters and other foreign employment contacts in the urban sector, the probability of finding a foreign job is actually the probability of being selected for a foreign job by the recruiter with which the potential international migrant is registered. This probability corresponds to the random selection process described in Todaro (1969) and is less than one, since recruitment agencies have registrants in excess of the number of foreign jobs available.

It is assumed that once an individual succeeds in finding a foreign job through one of these domestic channels, he is guaranteed employment upon arrival at the foreign destination. In other words, upon having found a foreign job in the urban sector, the individual faces a probability equal to one of being employed in the country of immigration. This assumption seems reasonable in light of the fact that recruiters usually provide fixed time period employment contracts with specific employers in the labour importing country.

The cost of migrating abroad (C_f) may include recruiter's fees as well as transportation costs or any other costs associated with migrating abroad, including psychological costs. The important point is that in deciding whether to migrate, the individual must charge the cost to himself as if it were to apply the day that he leaves his rural home. In other words, the individual must have the amount C_f before leaving the rural sector as he will be unemployed some period of time before going abroad. The cost of migrating to the urban sector (C_u) is included in the potential migrant's calculations as he must go to the city in order to find a foreign job.

(II) OUT-MIGRATION OF URBAN EMPLOYED WORKERS. The rate of emigration of employed urban workers (h) is a function of the actual, rather than the expected, relative urban-foreign income differential $(\alpha_{u,f})$:

$$h(\alpha_{u,f}(t)), \qquad h < 1, \quad h' > 0 \tag{3}$$

which depends on the discounted value of average income in the foreign and urban sectors less the costs of migration such that:

$$\alpha_{u,f}(0) = \int_{t=0}^{t=n} [(Y_f(t) - Y_u(t))/Y_u] e^{-rt} dt - C_f. \tag{3a}$$

The intuition behind this formulation is that if, for example, the potential international migrant from the urban modern sector faces a one in three chance of finding a foreign job once he has decided to migrate, he will continue employment in the urban sector for three years prior to emigration. Thus, at the time of emigration, his expected income differential will be the same as his actual income differential.

(III) EXPLICIT EXPRESSIONS FOR THE PROBABILITIES OF EMPLOYMENT. In (Todaro, 1969), the probability of a rural–urban migrant being selected for an urban modern sector job in any given period is defined as the ratio of urban modern sector job openings relative to the number of urban unemployed. However, in this version of the model, the probability of being selected for a modern sector job is also affected by the emigration of employed modern sector workers which creates an additional flow of job openings. This probability can be expressed as:

$$\Pi_u(t) = (\gamma(t)N(t) + h(t)S(t))/(S(t) - N(t)) \tag{4}$$

where $\gamma(t) = \dot{N}(t)/N(t)$ is the rate of urban job creation due to growth in modern sector output minus the growth of labor productivity. $N(t)$ is modern sector employment. $S(t)$ is the total urban labour force. Hence, $S(t) - N(t)$ is the number of unemployed in the urban sector (the informal sector).

The probability of a rural–urban migrant being selected for a foreign job is also affected by the emigration of employed modern sector workers who take some of the available foreign jobs:

$$\Pi_f(t) = (k(t)S(t) - h(t)S(t))/(S(t) - N(t)) \qquad (5)$$

where, $k(t)$ is the rate of foreign job creation and $k(t)S(t)$ yields total emigration opportunities for both employed modern sector workers and unemployed rural–urban migrants.

This formulation recognizes the fact that modern sector workers have an advantage over unemployed workers in obtaining foreign employment due to their work experience, wider contacts, and higher wage incomes to sustain themselves while waiting for the opportunity to emigrate. Thus, rural individuals seeking foreign jobs look at the net foreign jobs available after employed modern-sector workers have emigrated. To insure that net emigration opportunities are available for rural–urban migrants, we assume $k > h$.

In calculating the probability of obtaining urban (or foreign) jobs, rural individuals are assumed to compare the number of urban (or foreign) jobs available with the total number of urban unemployed $(S(t) = N(t))$ rather than with the number of urban unemployed workers seeking urban jobs (or the number of urban unemployed workers seeking foreign jobs). This assumption seems more realistic from a behavioural point of view since rural individuals living in different locations would have great difficulty estimating the total number of urban (or foreign) jobs available with the total number of urban unemployed $(S(t) - N(t))$ rather than with the number of proxy for the number of other individuals seeking the same type of employment.

It is assumed further that the number of foreign jobs available grows with the size of the urban labour force $(S(t))$. This assumption stems from observations that the accumulation of a growing number of workers in the urban sector creates more opportunities for foreign employment as recruiters, employment agencies, and other traffickers in manpower expand to meet the growing demand for foreign jobs from domestic workers. The value of k, however, is a policy parameter, since governments may encourage or discourage labour export efforts.

(IV) URBAN LABOUR SUPPLY FUNCTION. The urban labour supply function in its most general form can be expressed as:

$$\frac{\dot{S}(t)}{S(t)} = f(\alpha_{r,u}^e(t)) + g(\alpha_{r,f}^e(t)) - k(t). \qquad (6)$$

For more explicit results and in keeping with Todaro (1969), a definite form of the labour supply function is assumed – that it is separable in income differentials (adjusted for the costs of migration) and the probability of employment. We also assume a one-period time horizon which allows us to treat the various income differentials as fixed. The basic results are unaffected by this assumption.

Letting $\alpha_{r,u} = (Y_u - Y_r)/Y_r$ and $\alpha_{r,f} = (Y_f - Y_r)/Y_r$, the labour supply function can now be expressed as:

$$\frac{\dot{S}}{S} = \Pi_u f(\alpha_{r,u}) + \Pi_f g(\alpha_{r,f}) - k. \tag{6a}$$

Assuming that the f, g and h functions are continuous and monotonically increasing in their respective percentage real income differentials, we get unique values for these functions for any given set of differentials. Substituting for

$$\Pi_u \quad \text{and} \quad \Pi_f$$

from section (III) into the above equation, the urban labour supply finally becomes:

$$\frac{\dot{S}}{S} = \left(\frac{\gamma N + hS}{S - N}\right)f + \left(\frac{kS - hS}{S - N}\right)g - k. \tag{6b}$$

This equation simply says that the rate of increase of the urban labour force ($\dot{S}/S$) is equal to rate of in-migration of rural workers seeking urban jobs in response to a given percentage rural–urban income differential (f) adjusted for the probability of finding an urban job (($\gamma N + hS)/(S - N)$) plus the rate of in-migration of rural workers seeking foreign jobs in response to a given percentage rural–foreign income differential (g) adjusted for the probability of finding a foreign job (($kS - hS)/(S - N)$) less the rate of emigration of both employed and unemployed workers from the urban sector.

(V) EQUILIBRIUM CONDITIONS. The equilibrium condition for our model is defined as the urban employment rate (E) such that:

$$\frac{\dot{E}}{E} = \frac{\dot{N}}{N} - \frac{\dot{S}}{S} = 0. \tag{7}$$

Substituting for $\dot{N}/N$ from section (III) and $\dot{S}/S$ from the final labour supply function into the above equation, we obtain the condition:

$$\gamma + k = \left(\frac{\gamma N + hS}{S - N}\right)f + \left(\frac{kS - hS}{S - N}\right)g. \tag{8}$$

Thus, the equilibrium urban employment rate is one in which the total flow of migrants is just sufficient to fill the new modern sector jobs being created, replace the job vacancies left by emigrating employed workers, fill the emigration opportunities for unemployed workers and provide a net addition to the urban unemployed (in light of the higher modern sector employment). Dividing the numerator and denominator of the right hand side of the above equation by

S, substituting $E = N/S$ and then solving for E we obtain:

$$E = \frac{\gamma + k + hg - kg - hf}{\gamma + k + \gamma f}.$$ (9)

Taking the case where $\gamma > k > h$, we recall that: γ is the rate of urban job creation; k is the rate of foreign job creation, or total rate of emigration from the urban sector; f is the rate of in-migration of rural workers seeking urban jobs in response to a given rural-urban income differential; g is the rate of in-migration of rural workers seeking foreign jobs in response to a given rural–foreign income differential; h is the rate of out-migration of urban employed workers workers obtaining foreign jobs in response to a given urban–foreign income differential.

For meaningful results, it must be true that the equilibrium employment rate is positive and less than one. For $E > 0$, it must be true that:

$$\gamma + k + hg > kg + hf$$

and it is, since $k > kg$ and $\gamma > hf$. The condition for $E > 1$ is:

$$hg < \gamma f + hf + kg$$

which holds since $k > h$.

(VI) EFFECT OF AN INCREASE IN THE RATE OF FOREIGN JOB CREATION.

$$E_k = (\mathrm{Dem}(1 - g) - \mathrm{Num}(1))/\mathrm{Dem}^2$$ (10)

where 'Dem' is the denominator of equation (9) and 'Num' is its numerator.

The effect of an increase in emigration opportunities on the equilibrium urban employment rate depends on the relative values of f and g for a given γ and h. In the case where the value of g is such that:

$$g > f\frac{(\gamma + h)}{\gamma + h + \gamma f}$$ (10a)

an increase in foreign job creation will lower the equilibrium rate of urban employment, or equivalently, it will raise the urban employment rate. That is, in the situation where g is sufficiently large (i.e. meets the above condition), the creation of additional emigration opportunities for unemployed workers will draw proportionately more rural individuals seeking foreign employment into the urban centre than is required to match emigration opportunities and hence, result in an increased urban unemployment rate. This implies that under such circumstances policies designed to eliminate unemployment through the promotion of labour exports will meet with increasing frustration, unless there is a simultaneous concentrated effort to raise rural incomes and hence, lower real income differentials.

187

(VII) EFFECTS OF INCREASED PROPENSITIES TO MIGRATE.

$$E_f = (\text{Dem}(-h) - \text{Num}(\gamma))/\text{Dem}^2 \qquad (11)$$

$$E_g = (\text{Dem}(h - k) - \text{Num}(0))/\text{Dem}^2 \qquad (12)$$

Equation (11) is clearly negative and since Dem > Num and $k > h$, equation (12) is also negative. Thus, an increased propensity to migrate on the part of rural workers seeking either urban or foreign jobs will raise the equilibrium rate of urban unemployment.

$$E_h = (\text{Dem}(g - f) - \text{Num}(0))/\text{Dem}^2 \qquad (13)$$

The net results depends on the relative values of (f) and (g). On one hand, the increased emigration of employed workers (h) creates more urban job opportunities as these workers leave and thereby raises the in-migration of rural workers seeking urban jobs via its impact on their probability function. On the other hand, it lessens emigration opportunities for rural workers seeking foreign jobs and hence lowers their migration into the urban sector. If f is greater than g, then the urban unemployment rate will rise. The urban unemployment rate rises because the increase in the flow of rural workers seeking urban jobs outweighs the decrease in the flow of rural workers seeking foreign jobs.

Recall that we are treating the percentage income differentials as given in this analysis. Hence, we are examining the effect of an increased desire to migrate reflected in an increase in f, g or h. This increased desire to migrate could be the result of any number of influences suggested by the literature including such non-economic factors as more information about working abroad from friends or relatives and hence, less insecurity on the part of the individual to emigrate or perhaps the result of 'modernized' tastes and hence, the desire to acquire foreign goods or perhaps the result of job frustration due to underemployment or even an attraction to 'city lights'. However, keeping in mind the results of this section and recalling that f and g respond positively to increases in income differentials, it is immediately evident that if rural incomes fall, the values of both f and g will be larger in response to the larger rural–urban and rural–foreign income differentials, respectively, and the equilibrium rate of urban unemployment will be higher. Similarly, if foreign earnings rise, the values of both g and h will be larger in response to the larger rural–foreign and urban–foreign income differentials, respectively, and in the situation where $f > g$, the equilibrium rate of unemployment will be also higher.

(VIII) POLICY IMPLICATIONS. Most of the major labour-exporting countries are contending with the dual problems of rapid urbanization and high overall rates of urban unemployment. In light of our results, their efforts to lower the overall rates of unemployment through the promotion of labour exports (raising k) will increase rates of urbanization and urban unemployment in cases where the propensity to migrate of rural workers seeking foreign jobs (g) is sufficiently high. This implies that policy-makers will have to examine the benefits and costs of labour-export promotion more carefully. The social costs associated with rapid urbanization and high urban unemployment may offset to a considerable extent the benefits associated with increased foreign exchange earnings when one considers that in addition to the social costs of increased unemployment are the enormous costs of providing housing, education, health facilities, sanitation and public transportation for the new urban dwellers.

Moreover, as migration networks mature, one can expect an increase in the desire to migrate as individuals obtain more information about working abroad and become exposed to foreign consumption patterns from friends and relatives who have lived overseas. As was shown earlier, any increased propensities to migrate on the part of rural workers seeking foreign jobs (g), given existing income differentials, will result in higher urban unemployment rates. Furthermore, if one considers the trend of widening income differentials between the more advanced developing countries which are usually the labour-importers and the less developed countries which usually export labour, there exists the strong possibility that the urban unemployment problem will worsen as more individuals flock to the city to seek both the higher paying foreign jobs and the urban jobs that native emigrants leave behind.

Another implication of our model is for the rural sector. Although the impact of labour-export promotion on the rural sector was not examined directly, the model does show that the rate of out-migration from the rural sector would rise with increased opportunities for foreign employment. In the situation where the rural sector does not have a surplus of labour, this higher rate of out-migration may cause a decline in rural output. Another possible outcome is a costly rise in mechanization, which has already occurred in Jordan. Both possibilities would further exacerbate problems of urbanization and underemployment, the first by widening the rural–urban income gap and the second by displacing rural jobs and pushing more migrants toward the city.

As Stahl (1982 and 1984) has noted, one possible measure that policy-makers could take to mitigate this induced rural–urban migration effect is to disperse recruitment agencies throughout the country so as to give rural workers the opportunity to seek foreign employment without having to come to urban centres to obtain a foreign job. However, in cases where much of the recruitment is done through private agencies, it would be difficult to force private recruiters to relocate the areas that would be clearly inefficient from their point of view. The government might instead require that private recruiters obtain workers from a government-run central office that keeps files on registrants from various parts of the country (i.e., among those who have registered for foreign jobs at their local government foreign recruitment office) and draws on the available pool of registrants according to whatever criteria has been developed. However, as Stahl has pointed out, this measure may be also insufficient to deal with the problem due to the widespread existence of unlicensed recruitment offices which would be virtually impossible to regulate.

Perhaps the most important implication of the model arises out of the welfare evaluation of the foreign exchange remittances sent home by international migrants. Most researchers have concluded that the sheer size of these remittances indicates a large positive benefit for the labour-exporting nation, even in cases where remittances are used primarily for conspicuous consumption and/or real estate speculation. However, our model underlines an important negative element in the welfare equation that has been typically overlooked – namely, the social and private costs of increasing urban unemployment and possibly declining agricultural output generated by the induced migration of additional rural workers now seeking both modern sector and foreign higher wage jobs. Balancing these added costs against the presumed benefits of foreign remittances could conceivably tip the scales against the widespread belief in the positive association between increased international short-term migration and local economic gains.

BIBLIOGRAPHY

Berry, A.R. and Soligo, R. 1969. Some welfare aspects of international migration. *Journal of Political Economy* 77(5), September-October, 778–94.

Birks, J.S. and Sinclair, C.A. 1980. *International Migration and Development in the Arab Region*. Geneva: International Labor Office.

Castano, G.M. 1984. Migrant workers in the Americas: a comparative study of migration between Colombia and Venezuela and between Mexico and the United States. Center for U.S.-Mexican Studies, New York.

Cornelius, W.A. 1978. Mexican migration to the United States: causes, consequences, and U.S. responses. Migration Study Group, Massachusetts Institute of Technology.

Ethier, W.J. 1985. International trade and labor migration. *American Economic Review* 75, September, 691–707.

Grubel, H. and Scott, A. 1966. The international flow of human capital. *American Economic Review* 56, May, 268–74.

Harris, J. and Todaro, M.P. 1970. Migration, unemployment and development: a two sector analysis. *American Economic Review* 60(1), March, 126–42.

Hietala, K. 1978. Migration flows between Nordic countries in 1963–75. In International Union for the Scientific Study of Population, *Economic and Demographic Change: Issues for the 1980's*. Liège: IUSSP.

Martin, P.L. 1984. The economic effects of temporary workers. Mimeo, University of California, Davis, March.

Population Information Center, The Johns Hopkins University. 1983. *Population Report*, October.

Rivera-Batiz, F. 1982. International migration, non-traded goods and economic welfare in the source country. *Journal of Development Economics* 11(1), 81–90.

Stahl, C. 1982. *International Labor Migration and International Development*. Geneva: International Labour Organization.

Stahl, C. 1984. *International Labor Migration and the ASEAN Countries*. Geneva: International Labour Organization.

Todaro, M.P. 1969. A model of labor migration and urban unemployment in less developed countries. *American Economic Review* 59(1), March, 138–48.

Todaro, M.P. 1970. Labor migration and urban unemployment: reply. *American Economic Review* 60(3), September, 187–8.

Ulgalde, A.F. 1979. International migration from the Dominican Republic. *International Migration Review* 13(2), Summer, 235–54.

United Nations, Department of International and Social Affairs. 1982. International migration: policies and programs. *Population Studies* No. 80, New York: United Nations.

Labour Surplus Economies

GUSTAV RANIS

The distinguishing feature of a labour surplus economy is that it is dualistic in the sense that there exists heterogeneity among the sectors, mainly in terms of differences in organizational behaviour. While the physiocrats were the first to emphasize the special role of agriculture and to place two interacting sectors within one macroeconomic framework, the classical school, specifically Ricardo, utilized the assumption of the near fixity of land, combined with Malthusian population pressures on the land and the notion of an institutionally determined real wage in agriculture, to construct the first model of a labour surplus economy. Unfortunately, his was a static analysis, weak on inter-sectoral interactions and devoid of technology change in agriculture; it was left to the post-Keynesian revival of the labour surplus model, by Lewis (1954), Fei and Ranis (1964), among others, to present the complete model and apply it to the Third World's postwar development effort. In section I we present this modern version of the labour surplus economy, while in section II we examine the conditions for the successful evolution over time of that economy into neoclassical homogeneity between the sectors en route to successful modern growth.

I. THE ANALYTICS OF THE LABOUR SURPLUS ECONOMY MODEL. The modern version of the labour surplus economy is based on the existence of a particular kind of asymmetry among sectors of a developing economy. Specifically, one or more of the major production sectors is characterized by the absence of clearance in its labour market. Such a condition of 'labour surplus' may exist in large portions of the agricultural sector, as well as in some non-agricultural activities such as services and even in a portion of small-scale industry. The crucial distinguishing characteristic is that in such sectors or subsectors the neoclassical wage, i.e. a marginal product equal to the wage, does not obtain. This is because the initial endowment conditions, an abundant labour supply relative to scarce cooperating factors such as land, would drive the full employment marginal product of labour below an acceptable or survival level of income. The coexistence of neoclassical (or commercialized) and non-neoclassical (or non-commercialized) sectors and their interaction lies at the heart of the labour surplus model's analytical power. Success in development can then be defined as the achievement of the end of the labour surplus condition via the gradual reallocation over time of a growing population from the non-commercialized to the commercialized sector.

We begin by describing the structural characteristics of each of these two sectors taken individually and then proceed to examine the nature of their interaction in the context of the development process. Concentrating initially on the non-commercialized sector which may, for purposes of convenience only, be assumed to have agricultural product characteristics, it is here that, given its relatively large size and dispersed economic actors, the foundation for any vigorous, sustained growth of the system as a whole must be located.

The initial state of 'over-population' means that, under conditions of stationary technology, with land very intensively cultivated, the workings of the law of diminishing returns result in extremely low marginal increments of output to additions in the labour force. These production conditions, including the existing initial endowment and state of the arts, yield a production function as represented in Figure 1a. The factors of production used as inputs are labour, measured on the horizontal axis, and land, measured on the vertical axis, with the production contour lines represented by the curves indexed by M, M' and M''. Under the usual assumptions about constant returns to scale, we can identify two ridge lines, OV^* and OU^*, marking off the region of factor substitutability; for example, below the ridge line OV^*, the production contours become either perfectly horizontal (or could even bend backwards), indicating that, with land held constant, further increases of labour input beyond that point would render the factor redundant, i.e. of zero (or even negative) marginal product in terms of its impact on output. (The region above OU^* where land is redundant would be quite symmetrical but irrelevant to the labour surplus economy.) If total cultivable land is essentially fixed, say at Ot units, i.e. it cannot be increased without substantial investment of capital, the amount of labour which can be absorbed without becoming fully redundant can then be determined by the ridge line, i.e. ts units. The more interesting question, however, is not the existence of a substantial portion of the total labour force which, under conditions of constant technology, has a zero or negative marginal product – an unlikely event – but that, in these non-commercialized sectors substantial inputs of labour are likely to be applied to work yielding a marginal product below the institutional or living wage.

To demonstrate that point more precisely, let us, in Figure 1b, show the total product curve for a given, fixed amount of land and, for convenience only, assume that the institutional wage is equal to the average product, i.e. the slope of OM in Figure 1b, or the height of Ow in Figure 1c in which the marginal product of labour curve is also shown. Under these conditions we can locate the proportion of the total agricultural labour force OP which is disguisedly unemployed, PP', i.e. point R in Figure 1b marks off the region to the right where the wage lies above the marginal product; similarly, in Figure 1a $R'e$ units of labour are

192

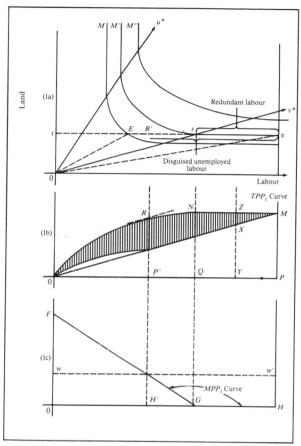

Figure 1   Production Conditions in the Agricultural Sector

disguisedly unemployed, equal to *PP'* units in 1b or *HH'* units in 1c. This is the static concept of disguisedly unemployed or underemployed labour which is viewed as a statistically important phenomenon in the labour surplus economy, with its eradication over time both a primary objective of development and a primary source of finance for its achievement.

It should be noted that the argument that the marginal product of labour may be driven to zero, which has occupied a good deal of the literature on the labour surplus economy, is really quite subsidiary and only used for convenience. What is crucial is the notion that there exists an institutional wage in the non-commercialized sector or sectors lying above the marginal product of labour, which is low due to the heavy endowment of labour relative to land, the cooperating factor. The notion of an institutional real wage does not require that any of the agricultural labour force be redundant in the sense that it can be removed under assumptions of constant technology without affecting agricultural output adversely (*es* in Figure 1a) – only that some portion of the agricultural population recieve food allotments in excess of their marginal product. It is only in this sense that organizational dualism is an important feature of the labour market in the labour surplus economy. Given the abundance of labour and the relative scarcity of cooperating factors, this is what is meant by underemployment i.e. employment is limited not by a lack of effective demand but by technological and resource constraints. The only assertion is that wage determination in the non-commercialized sector contains a strong dosage of sharing, a function of the fact that people cannot be readily dismissed when households and production units coincide and/or when decisions are still made on a collective rather than an individual profit-maximizing basis.

The magnitude of such an institutional wage by definition cannot be determined by the usual tools of economic analysis. Like other bargaining wages, it depends on social attitudes and the nature of the sharing nexus at a relatively early stage of development. In fact, it is really not a wage in the usual sense of the word but a consumption or income standard which determines the non-commercialized reservation price of labour. In a socialist system the state might set the consumption standard, with the central government providing food subsidies, if necessary. In the more relevant, mixed developing economy case it is the landlord or the head of the family or the village which provides such a subsidy since they are unwilling to dismiss or starve their tenants, relatives or members.

This abandonment of the marginal productivity theory of wage determination in agriculture is clearly controversial (see Binswanger and Rosenzweig, 1984). It essentially asserts that where an already relatively abundant agricultural labour force is being augmented by rapid population increase, the agricultural real wage is likely to rise only gradually, lagging behind productivity increase, an empirically verifiable phenomenon in many parts of the developing world.

The existence of substantial disguised unemployment in the non-commercialized sector is significant because it represents a population which is consuming output but unable to make a commensurate contribution to it. Thus the major problem, as well as opportunity, in the labour surplus economy consists in the reallocation of such relatively parasitic portions of the labour force into alternative employment where they are able to make a commensurate contribution to total output.

The commercialized sector of the labour surplus economy, in contrast, behaves neoclassically or, if you will, conventionally. The only thing that really distinguishes it from the familiar one-sector commercialized economy is that the supply of labour is determined by conditions in the non-commercialized sector. However, given the special characteristics of the labour market in the labour surplus economy, special attention must be given to the significance of such linkages between the sectors. These may be classified into three main types, i.e. the inter-sectoral labour market, the inter-sectoral commodity market, and the inter-sectoral financial market.

Given the 'unlimited supply of labour' condition in the non-commercialized sector of the economy, the unskilled wage in the commercialized or industrial sector will tend to be tied to, though certainly not equal to, the non-commercialized real wage. This wage gap for unskilled labour between the two sectors is required to induce the typical agricultural worker to overcome his attachments to soil and family, partly to meet transport costs, and partly as a consequence of such institutional factors as minimum wage legislation, unionization, etc., which usually do not extend beyond the commercialized sector. Consequently, the existence of a relatively constant or gently upward sloping real wage over time in both sectors, with a gap between them, can be expected to induce labour-intensive technology choices and, more importantly, labour-using technology change over time in both the non-commercialized and commercialized sectors of the labour surplus economy. Both wages may be expected to rise in part because, as we have noted, as agricultural productivity increases, there may be an upward adjustment of the institutional wage, in part because the wage gap itself may rise as a consequence of a change in the extent of intervention by minimum wage legislation, unionization, etc. But once these two wage levels are given within a general equilibrium context, the release of labour by the non-commercialized sector and its absorption by the commercialized sector represents an essential ingredient of balanced growth within the labour surplus economy.

Secondly, an understanding of the workings of the inter-sectoral commodity market is required for an assessment of the contribution of the non-commercialized sector to the rest of the economy. This can be seen in terms of the net real resources transferred, i.e. the difference between the shipments of food and raw materials delivered to the industrial sector and the shipments of industrial goods sent in the opposite direction. The agricultural sector's export surplus may thus be viewed as the domestic contribution of that sector to both the labour reallocation and industrialization process over time.

The participants in the dualistic commodity market are, on one side, the owners of the agricultural surplus and, on the other, the newly allocated industrial workers who may be thought of as owning wage income in the form of non-agricultural goods and anxious to trade some of it for the food 'left behind'. Once this transition is completed, the newly allocated industrial worker finds himself in possession of the same agricultural goods needed at least to maintain his consumption standard. In this fashion the dualistic commodity market is indispensable for transforming the consumption bundle of the agricultural labour force into a wages fund for the newly allocated non-agricultural workers. At the same time the owners of the agricultural surplus, for example, the landlords, obtain ownership of (or a claim against) a portion of the newly formed industrial capital stock.

Thirdly, the financial counterpart of the real resources contribution of the agricultural to the non-agricultural sector over time is affected through the workings of the inter-sectoral financial market. The savings of the agricultural sector become a claim against non-agriculture, the magnitude of which is determined by the size of its export surplus with non-agriculture. These savings must somehow be channelled into non-agricultural investment, i.e. what is left of the agricultural surplus that is not siphoned off by consumption or intermediate input requirements must find its way into capital formation in the rest of the economy. The only other contributors to investment, probably minor at this early stage, are industrial profits, in the closed economy, and foreign capital, in the open economy.

The inter-sectoral financial intermediation network, either formal or informal, which matches up savers and investors and thus finances the investment goods, represents a crucial link in the development chain. In the beginning, channelization within the extended family is likely to be most prominent. Over time, as the availability and diversity of the financial intermediation network grows, an increased separation of ownership and control is made possible, with claims maintained in the form of savings, bank deposits, postal savings, stocks and bonds, etc. If we maintain the simplifying assumption that land and labour represent the only factors of production in agriculture, and capital and labour the only factors in non-agriculture, industrial capital goods are destined for investment back in the industrial sector. In the beginning, agricultural savings are likely to constitute the major source of the economy's total investment fund, dwarfing savings of the non-agricultural sector which in turn are likely to become more important later on.

II. THE DYNAMICS OF DEVELOPMENT IN THE LABOUR SURPLUS ECONOMY. The heart of the development problem in the labour surplus economy may thus be seen as the ability of the two sectors, the agricultural or non-commercialized and the non-agricultural or commercialized, to move together in a sufficiently balanced and rapid fashion to eliminate the dualistic characteristic of the economy, i.e. to eliminate the labour surplus condition. More precisely, the agricultural sector must yield sufficient increases in productivity, hence surpluses, and preserve a sufficiently large part of such surpluses for investment in non-agriculture, with the help, mainly, of technology change; simultaneously, the non-agricultural sector's productivity, with the help, again, of technology change, as well as capital accumulation, must grow fast enough to absorb the labour thus being reallocated. Taking investment and technology efforts together, what results is a balance between increases in productivity in agriculture and non-agriculture approaching the notion of 'balanced growth'. Such 'balance' has two dimensions: one, the volume of agricultural workers freed up through productivity increase in the agricultural sector must not be too far out of line with the new employment opportunities created in the non-agricultural sector; and two, the markets for the goods of the agricultural and non-agricultural sectors must clear without a major change in the inter-sectoral terms of trade. Moreover, such balanced growth must proceed, over time, at a pace in excess of the additions to the population or labour force which may be viewed as simultaneously adding to the pool of the underemployed or disguisedly unemployed.

As we have already noted, the entire process must, moreover, not only be balanced but also proceed at a pace in excess of population growth if the initial reservoir of surplus labour is ultimately to be exhausted, labour to become a scarce commodity, and neoclassical wage determination to take over. Furthermore, even if balanced growth, as indexed by the rate of labour reallocation, substantially exceeds the rate of population growth, the excess must be sufficient so that the length of time it takes to arrive at that turning point, marking the end of dualism, is also socially and politically acceptable.

Balanced growth as an analytical concept in the dual economy context thus addresses itself to the identification of a set of necessary and sufficient conditions. The real world, of course, never functions smoothly and in a fully 'balanced' fashion. 'Unbalanced' growth is likely to exhibit itself via relative agricultural neglect and a rise in food prices which may or may not be self-correcting. We have chosen to focus on the more or less synchronized real resources functions which need to be performed by both sectors, if 'success' defined as the end of labour surplus is to be ultimately achieved. Once balanced growth has proceeded long enough and fast enough, labour shortage will appear in both sectors, with the marginal productivity calculus of wage determination taking over everywhere. At this point organizational dualism disappears, and, given considerable increases in per capita incomes and the workings of Engel's Law, agriculture gradually becomes an appendage to the economy, i.e. just another smooth, symmetrical sector within the system's total input–output matrix. Increasingly the economy is now ready to perform according to the rules of modern economic growth as described by Simon Kuznets (1966).

Thus far we have examined development of the labour surplus economy in the closed economy context. The open economy or trade-related dimensions of development in the labour surplus economy are, of course, important enough to warrant substantial amendment of the analysis presented here. During the early colonial, or open agrarian, phase of development the economy may well be tied to foreign markets by virtue of some of the labour force being weaned away from food production and into land-based export-oriented activity, for example, minerals and other primary products of interest to the foreigners. This typically leads to a triangular relationship among the cash-crop export sector, the foreign sector, and the food-producing domestic agricultural sector. But once the economy moves out of its colonial or 'overseas territory' phase and into a national development-oriented effort, our analysis must be amended to take 'openness' into account.

To do so, we must first recognize that the export-oriented cash-crop agricultural sub-sector continues to generate foreign exchange earnings, but that these are now used to assist in the construction of a new, domestically oriented, industrial sector producing previously imported non-durable consumer goods, i.e. to fuel so-called primary or 'easy' import substitution. These exports now provide a second source of agricultural surplus which, converted into industrial capital goods imports, and possibly supplemented by the inflow of foreign savings, help finance non-agricultural growth in the balanced growth context. In this way a new triangular relationship between two kinds of commercialized acivities, one agricultural and one non-agricultural, and the food-producing non-commercialized agricultural hinterland replaces the colonial triangle.

What happens at the end of this primary import substitution phase is critical, i.e. once domestic markets for the easy or non-durable consumer goods are exhausted, it is apparent that the relatively natural resources rich labour surplus countries have a tendency to continue on with import substitution, now shifting from labour-intensive light industries to the more capital-intensive durable consumer goods, the processing of raw materials, and the production of capital goods. At the same time, in the minority of countries which have a relatively poor natural resources base, we observe a shift from a domestic to an export market orientation for the same labour-intensive non-durable consumer goods. In that case the export sector now constitutes a powerful new production function available to the economy, through which traditional and, later, non-traditional exports can be converted into imported capital goods and raw materials. Second, the openness of the economy now permits foreign capital to provide additional finance in support of the balanced growth process. Finally, an important potential advantage of the economy's openness is, of course, the whole range of additional technological alternatives now made available, which, hopefully with modifications and adaptations, can help increase the speed of the balanced growth process.

The open economy, in other words, not only permits the labour surplus economy to harvest the normal gains from trade, to benefit from the vent for surplus of previously underutilized resources – in this case both raw materials and unskilled labour – but also, dynamically, to affect the direction of technology change and thus introduce competitive forces and ideas from abroad which permeate the entire economy and are undoubtedly of great importance in determining the overall success of the labour system's balanced growth efforts.

Needless to say, the graduation from the labour surplus condition is easier in a relatively small economy, *ceteris paribus*, where the discipline of the international marketplace can play a somewhat larger role and the reliance on balanced domestic growth, away from the competitive influences of the international market, needs to be relatively smaller. But while the two strands, i.e. domestic balanced growth and labour-intensive industrial exports, may have a different weight in different typological contexts, they must complement each other if the transition to modern growth is to be achieved over a reasonable span of historical time.

BIBLIOGRAPHY

Binswanger, H. and Rosenzweig, M. (eds) 1984. *Contractual Arrangements, Employment and Wages in Rural Labor Markets in Asia.* New Haven: Yale University Press.

Fei, J. and Ranis, G. 1964. *Development of the Labor Surplus Economy: Theory and Policy.* Homewood, Ill.: Irwin.

Kuznets, S. 1966. *Modern Economic Growth: Rate, Structure and Spread.* New Haven: Yale University Press.

Lewis, W.A. 1954. Economic development with unlimited supplies of labour. *Manchester School of Economics and Social Studies* 22, May, 139–91.

Land Reform

E.V.K. FITZGERALD

The redistribution of land property titles by the state is a key issue in poor agrarian countries where land is both the main productive asset and the basis of survival and accumulation for the majority of the population, and thus land tenure is the foundation of the social structure and political power. 'Agrarian reform', which encompasses the transformation of rural administrative institutions, labour use and markets as well, is the modern form of this concept. Urban land reform is not dealt with here, as it is usually subsumed under housing policy. Historically, while widespread changes of land tenure have been characteristic of social revolutions since ancient times (Tuma, 1965), and classical economic doctrine supported the sweeping away of the feudal land tenure system to permit commercial modernization and stabilize the independent peasantry, the 'agrarian question' only becomes a central issue of political economy in the 19th century (Hussain and Tribe, 1981).

Modern theories of land reform derive from, on the one hand, perceptions of the previous structure of land tenure and production relations; and on the other, the new pattern to be established, intentionally or otherwise. The transition between the two systems can generally be held to involve as central elements both the stabilization of the peasantry and the redefinition of agriculture within the national development model (Ghose, 1983).

In capitalist (or 'mixed') economies during the post-World War II years, possibly inspired by the Japanese experience under US occupation, there flourished a considerable enthusiasm for redistributive land reform, which was seen principally as constituting (or reconstituting) a prosperous small-farmer class on estates expropriated from the aristocracy or foreigners (Warriner, 1969) with a particular function of underwriting democracy (Jacoby, 1971), while responding to the millennarian demands of the peasantry for security (Wolf, 1969). However, the international interest in planned economic development led to a concern with the productive consequences of land reform, in terms of both the benificiaries themselves and urban food supplies; particularly in view of the growing evidence of food output stagnation, underutilized land and rural underemployment (Dorner, 1972). The planners' theoretical views on this can be divided (Lehmann, 1978) into two groups reaching similar conclusions by different routes. First, there is a structuralist approach (Barraclough, 1973; Dorner, 1972), stressing the need for more rapid growth of food output to sustain the growing urban wage-bill, underutilization of large estates by 'traditional' landlords, the lack of internal markets for the new infant industries of the import-substitution era, and the necessity to create more rural employment in order to stem migration towards the cities. Second, there is an essentially microeconomic neoclassical approach (Schultz, 1964; Griffin, 1974; Lipton, 1974), emphasizing the superior efficiency of labour-intensive small farmers in terms of land use and the lack of access by peasants to credit and inputs due to tenure structures which permit capital- (or land-) intensive landlord control of markets, which argues that the situation of underemployment of labour and scarcity of capital could be remedied with increased output by redistribution of land titles and the consequent freeing of factor markets.

Such theoretical approaches have had a considerable effect upon the views of international institutions (UN, 1976; World Bank, 1974) but it would appear that the doctrines applied in practice by governments have been based on objectives more closely related to the maintenance of state power, such as improved supply of cheap food to the towns and the blocking or rural insurgency movements. Land reform projects under these circumstances have involved, at most, the breaking up of large inefficient estates, without affecting commercial farmers (i.e. high land ceilings on owner-cultivated holdings), in favour of individual family farms; with the ultimate purpose of promoting the development of capitalism in agriculture (de Janvry, 1981; Ghose, 1983). Indeed the so-called 'green revolution' (new crop technologies and mechanization) and resettlement schemes (moving the landless to areas recently opened up by irrigation or roads) have since the mid-1970s largely replaced land reform in orthodox doctrine (King, 1977) as a means of attaining the above objectives without further rural upheaval.

The outcome of such capitalist land reform has been surprisingly similar. Ghose (1983) identifies 'unimodal' pre-reform systems in Asia and the Middle East, where landlords (with merchants and moneylenders) extract economic surplus from small tenant farmers: here the initial effect of land reform is to relieve peasants from this burden, without changing production systems. This raises their incomes substantially but reduces the marketed surplus, while efforts to encourage equitable modernization through the creation of producer cooperatives are undermined by market forces, which tend to lead to peasant differentiation, further encouraged by state support of accumulation by the successful farmer (credits, inputs, etc.); eventually polarization between capitalist farmers and landless proletarians results. This transition is more direct in 'bimodal' systems of large commercial estates employing labour from sub-subsistence plots: part of the labour force is 'peasantized' when the land is distributed, but many (particularly migrant labourers) are excluded because there is insufficient land to provide family farms for all, so differentiation starts earlier. A similar polarization occurs in the non-reform sector (de Janvry, 1981), the dynamics of which are as important, if not more so, as those of the reformed portion of the land, usually the lesser part in any case. This polarization probably increases productive efficiency, but continued urban food shortages and narrow domestic markets betray the hopes of structuralist theorists; while the slow growth of production and the continued underemployment belie the hopes of the neoclassicals. Except in particular cases, such as Japan, where the state can subsidize the peasant economy out of a highly productive industrial sector; the liberating effect of such land reforms, as landlords are eliminated, is outweighed as incipient capitalism eventually dispossess the rural poor once more (Ghose, 1983).

Land reform is one of the first acts of post-revolutionary socialist regimes (Wadekin, 1982), which are faced with the strategic problem of not only collectivizing production relations but also of industrializing a predominantly rural economy while meeting the cost of popular claims for basic needs satisfaction and the defence of the new state against external aggression (Saith, 1985). Early socialist thought (Hussain and Tribe, 1981) was agreed on the need to sweep away landlordism but not the form of agrarian enterprise that should emerge; indeed it was supposed that capitalism would already have transformed agriculture so that direct worker control along industrial lines would be possible. The experience of Russia and China, however, revealed the need to secure the support of the peasantry, prevent the re-emergence of capitalism, and extract resources (exports, food and labour) from agriculture to finance industrialization. The canonical works of Lenin, Stalin and Mao on this problem have formed the basis for socialist agrarian reform theory, their major differences being in relation to the political role of the peasantry as a 'revolutionary class' (Saith, 1985). General agreement on the concepts of land nationalization and eventual collectivization as necessary steps in the construction of socialism meant that doctrine on 'primitive socialist accumulation' made the disposition of the surplus, rather than land tenure as such, the central issue (Saith, 1985). This in turn requires a theoretical redefinition of production relations to entail not only the juridical ownership of land as such but also the control over the distribution of its product (Bettelheim, 1975).

Land reform doctrine as applied in socialist countries has also revealed a surprising degree of uniformity (Wadekin, 1982): in Eastern Europe, as in Soviet Russia four decades earlier, land was nominally nationalized almost immediately but large estates were effectively subdivided among the peasantry, only the more modern ones being retained as state farms; the explicit aim being to secure peasant support for the revolution in the first years. While Lenin had felt that the New Economic Policy could be a vehicle to encourage voluntary cooperativization through favourable internal terms of trade, Stalin implemented forced collectivization culminating in the 'Model Charter' of 1935 appropriating all landed property in the state, establishing collective farms where income entitlement and certain assets (i.e. a small plot and some livestock) were vested in the household, but which in effect were equivalent to state farms. This model was also applied extensively in Eastern Europe in the early 1950s, although progress was slower in some cases and in others (e.g. Poland and Yugoslavia) the process was not completed at all. However, the only restriction, apart from the avoidance of political destabilization, was to avoid a decrease in agricultural supplies during the transition. The Chinese land reform did not differ in essence from this model as far as tenure is concerned, the operation of nationalized land being vested in the commune with family plots etc.: the major difference was the attention paid to industrial supply to the countryside, and the political emphasis on the transformation of production relations within the collective farm (Lardy, 1983).

The more recent attempts to increase rural productivity by various forms of 'liberalization' of socialist agriculture have not involved significant changes in land tenure, but can be termed a 'third agrarian reform' none the less, because they do affect entitlements to the surplus generated on that land, generally in favour of the direct cultivator. In this sense, they can be seen as a 'repeasantization' of agriculture (Saith, 1985). At the same time, the experience of the newer socialist states in the Third World has indicated a need to regard export agriculture, rather than food, as the main generator of surplus, because capital equipment and producer goods are mainly imported. These two theoretical advances permit an articulation between various property forms in agriculture where state control is exercised through exchange relations rather than land ownership (FitzGerald, 1985).

In sum, we may conclude that modern land reforms 'liberate' the peasantry in their initial stage, strengthening thereby the logic of the peasant economy. Capitalist and socialist land reforms differ in their degree of imposed collectivization and the extent of surplus extraction; but they share the common criterion of planned modernization and thus the ultimate destruction of the peasant economy. Subsequent developments depend upon the national model of accumulation within which agriculture is then inserted. The key factor is not the form of land tenure as such, but rather the use of the economic surplus generated; its retention promotes agrarian capitalism, while its extraction foments peasant resistance.

BIBLIOGRAPHY

Barraclough, S. 1973. *Agrarian Structure in Latin America.* Lexington, Mass.: Heath.
Bettelheim, C. 1975. *The Transition to Socialist Economy.* Brighton: Harvester.
de Janvry, A. 1981. *The Agrarian Question and Reformism in Latin America.* Baltimore: Johns Hopkins Press.
Dorner, P. 1972. *Land Reforms and Economic Development.* Harmondsworth: Penguin.
FitzGerald, E.V.K. 1985. The problem of balance in the peripheral socialist economy. *World Development* 13(1), 5–14.
Ghose, A.K. (ed.) 1983. *Agrarian Reform in Contemporary Developing Countries.* London: Croom Helm.
Griffin, K. 1974. *The Political Economy of Agrarian Change.* London: Macmillan; Cambridge, Mass.: Harvard University Press.
Hussain, A. and Tribe, K. 1981. *Marxism and the Agrarian Question.* London: Macmillan; Atlantic Highlands, N.J.: Humanities Press.
Jacoby, E.H. 1971. *Man and the Land.* London: Deutsch.
King, R. 1977. *Land Reform: a Survey.* London: Bell.

Lardy, N. 1983. *Agriculture in China's Modern Economic Development.* Cambridge: Cambridge University Press.

Lehmann, D. 1978. The death of land reform: a polemic. *World Development* 6(3), 339–45.

Lipton, M. 1974. Towards a theory of land reform. In *Agrarian Reform and Agrarian Reformism*, ed. D. Lehmann, London: Faber.

Saith, A. (ed.) 1985. *The Agrarian Question in Socialist Transition* London: Cass.

Schultz, T.W. 1964. *Transforming Traditional Agriculture.* New Haven: Yale University Press.

Tuma, E.H. 1965. *Twenty-six Centuries of Agrarian Reform.* Berkeley: University of California Press.

United Nations. 1976. *Progress in Land Reform: Sixth Report.* New York: United Nations.

Wadekin, K.E. 1982. *Agrarian Policies in Communist Europe.* Dordrecht: Martinus Nijhoff.

Warriner, D. 1969. *Land Reform in Principle and Practice.* Cambridge: Cambridge University Press.

Wolf, E. 1969. *Peasant Wars in the Twentieth Century.* New York: Harper & Row.

World Bank. 1974. *Land Reform.* Washington, DC: International Bank for Reconstruction and Development.

Latifundia

E.V.K. FITZGERALD

The *latifundium* first appears extensively during the later Roman empire as a type of large agricultural enterprise which obtained labour services from a resident workforce (*coloni*) in return for the temporary use of a plot of land, when the slaves on the estates created from the land of conquered communities became too costly. As the Empire declined, the latifundia also became local centres of economic and political power, absorbing the free peasantry into villein or 'servile' status, and providing the foundation for the manorial system of rural organization in the Middle Ages (Tuma, 1965). Labour shortages and urban growth led to an abandonment of this form of direct exploitation of labour in Western Europe by the 15th century in favour of more flexible rental agreements in kind, and eventually in money; though serfdom persisted in Eastern Europe and Russia well into the 19th century, and became a central theme in the 'agrarian question' (Hussain and Tribe, 1981).

The reconquest of Spain in the 15th century had confirmed the latifundium as an effective means of territorial and labour control based on large land grants to military leaders, so the system was logically extended to Latin America, where the *hacienda* (or large autonomous landed estate) became the cornerstone of colonial policy (Florescano, 1984). In the 17th and 18th centuries, hacienda autonomy was strengthened by the weakness of colonial administration from the cities. After Independence in the early 19th century, the agrarian structure of Latin America was perpetuated for over a hundred years by the central economic role of raw material exports produced by large landowners, and the lack of access to political power of the peasantry on sub-subsistence plots, known as *minifundio* (Barraclough, 1973).

Detailed historical research (reported in Duncan and Rutledge, 1977) reveals the enormous variety of *latifundio* arrangements for securing labour by ceding subsistence plots, and conflicts with neighbouring Indian communities over such land rights. It has also shown that these enterprises were generally market-oriented and guided by a profit motive, although there are close parallels with the manorial system (Kay, 1974). Nonetheless, the archaic and feudal nature of the latifundio has traditionally been seen (from Mariategui, 1928 to Furtado, 1970) as an obstacle to economic development, engendering a theoretical debate as to whether Latin American agriculture should be seen as capitalist because of its mercantile relationship with the national and world economy (Frank, 1967) or as feudal because of its labour relations (Laclau, 1971).

In political doctrine, the latter view has tended to prevail, and latifundia have been the main target of land reform in Latin America as involving inequitable social relations and inefficient use of land. Occupying up to half the farmed area as recently as World War II, they are now almost extinct. The latifundio was not a feature of the rest of the Third World (except the Philippines) where large estates are usually organized as plantations or on a sharecropping basis, although in ancient and colonial times various forms of obligatory labour contributions from the peasant communities were common.

In underdeveloped areas, income cannot be realized from land without intensive labour use, so any pattern of distribution of property rights is necessarily accompanied by a system of interpersonal and intergroup relationships governing the application of labour to land. The historical survival of the 'servile' system in various forms has lead to a reassessment of its economic logic, particularly in comparison to the large 'commercial' farm employing exclusively wage labour (de Janvry, 1981). The cost of such servile labour power is less than the price of proletarian labour power (i.e. the free market wage) because the opportunity cost to the owner of the ceded plot is less than the value of production the labourer can generate on it through the use of family labour. The extensive use of land on the latifundio means a low opportunity cost of marginal plots and its denial to independent smallholders; while the lack of alternative occupations means that the labour power of *colono*'s family has a near-zero opportunity cost as well. To be effective, the local hacienda system must thus prevent outward migration by mechanisms of a legal or traditional nature: it is characteristic of a situation where there is a scarcity of rural labour and landlord dominance of local society. The system should also be seen in the context of widespread reciprocal labour agreements and payments in labour time (for rent, use of draught animals, etc.) between peasant farmers themselves (Pearse, 1975). From the landowner's point of view, therefore, the latifundio system can be a profit-maximizing solution, and in a situation where labour rather than land (despite appearances) is really the scarce resource, it may be a relatively technically efficient (albeit not socially desirable) solution for a capitalist economy as a whole.

In a situation of relative labour surplus (commonly associated with early industrialization, population transition and the modernization of agriculture itself), the 'semi-proletarian' settled outside the estate becomes an even cheaper and more flexible source of labour power, as labour is only used and paid seasonally, while the minifundio, now producing for subsistence and even some marketed surplus, can deliver cheap labour without reciprocal obligations to the capitalist sector, made up now of latifundia in transition towards commercial farms with mechanization and technical inputs (Goodman and Redclift, 1981).

Although the latifundio as such is becoming a thing of the past, similar systems of rural labour organization persist because the nature of agricultural production itself is such that the need for seasonal labour for large scale-efficient farms coexists with the superior work-intensity of household production. This implies that the articulation of distinct forms of production in a single location is still necessary. The equivalent of the latifundio concept in a post-capitalist context might be detected in the form of state farms or producer collectives established in Eastern Europe, where household labour time is divided between collective enterprise land and the family plot. This ensures the necessary labour supply for harvests etc. on the mechanized collective land, while providing an income incentive for high productivity on labour-intensive individual land. This system need not necessarily be exploitative (in that the profits so generated are not appropriated by a landowner) but apparently must still be maintained by non-market mechanisms such as collective solidarity or restraints on migration.

BIBLIOGRAPHY

Barraclough, S. 1973. *Agrarian Structure in Latin America.* Lexington, Mass.: Heath.

Delgado, O. (ed.) 1965. *Reforma agraria en America Latina.* Mexico City: Fondo de Cultura Economica.

de Janvry, A. 1981. *The Agrarian Question and Reformism in Latin America.* Baltimore: Johns Hopkins Press.

Duncan, K. and Rutledge, I. (eds) 1977. *Land and Labour in Latin America*: *Essays on the Development of Agrarian Capitalism in the Nineteenth and Twentieth Century.* Cambridge and New York: Cambridge University Press.

Florescano, E. 1984. The formation and economic structure of the hacienda in New Spain. In *The Cambridge History of Latin America*, Vol II: *Colonial Latin America*, ed. L. Bethell, Cambridge: Cambridge University Press.

Frank, A.G. 1967. *Capitalism and Underdevelopment in Latin America.* New York: Monthly Review Press.

Furtado, C. 1970. *Economic Development of Latin America.* Cambridge: Cambridge University Press.

Goodman, D. and Redclift, M. 1981. *From Peasant to Proletarian*: *Capitalist Development and Agrarian Transitions.* Oxford: Blackwell; New York: St. Martin's Press, 1982.

Griffin, K. 1981. *Land Concentration and Rural Poverty.* 2nd edn, London: Macmillan.

Hussain, A. and Tribe, K. 1981. *Marxism and the Agrarian Question.* London: Macmillan; Atlantic Highlands, N.J.: Humanities Press.

Kay, C. 1974. Comparative development of the European manorial system and the Latin American hacienda system. *Journal of Peasant Studies* 2(1), 69–98.

Laclau, E. 1971. Feudalism and capitalism in Latin America. *New Left Review* No. 67, 19–38.

Mariategui, J.C. 1928. *Siete ensayos de interpretacion de la realidad peruana.* Lima: Editorial Amauta.

Pearce, A. 1975. *The Latin American Peasant.* London: Cass.

Tuma, E.H. 1965. *Twenty-six Centuries of Agrarian Reform.* Berkeley: University of California Press.

Lewis, W. Arthur

RONALD FINDLAY

W. Arthur Lewis was born on the island of St. Lucia in the British West Indies in 1915. He studied and taught at the London School of Economics before moving to Manchester University, where he did some of his most seminal work on development economics, the 1954 article on 'Economic Development with Unlimited Supplies of Labour' and the 1955 treatise on the *The Theory of Economic Growth*. In the 1950s he was a senior official in agencies of the United Nations, and was for a time Vice Chancellor of the University of the West Indies. He went to Princeton in 1963 where he has remained ever since. He has held many part-time advisory positions with international organizations and governments in developing countries, particularly in West Africa and the Caribbean. He was awarded the Nobel Prize for Economics in 1979, together with T.W. Schultz, for their contributions to economic development.

His earliest original research was on the application of price theory to problems of industrial organization and public utilities. A number of studies published during the forties on 'The Two Part Tariff', 'Competition in Retailing', 'Fixed Costs' and other related topics were brought together in a volume entitled 'Overhead Costs', published in 1949. Two other books published at the same time were *Economic Survey 1919–1939* and *Principles of Economic Planning*. The first of these was an examination of the troubled economic history of the world economy in the inter-war period, notable for the way in which he linked together the experiences of the 'core' industrial countries with those of the primary producing 'periphery' of the world economy. The pessimism about the possibility of international trade to serve as a sustained 'engine of growth' for the developing countries, that has marked his subsequent writings on development economics down to his Nobel Prize Lecture in 1980 (entitled the 'Slowing Down of the Engine of Growth') can perhaps be traced to his study of the interwar period, an interesting parallel with the case of Ragnar Nurkse who also came to the study of development problems after writing his *International Currency Experience* on the breakdown of the international monetary system in the thirties. The book on planning, though written at an introductory level, was an early examination of the problems of coordinating government intervention and the market in a mixed economy.

Lewis's most famous and influential contribution to economics is undoubtedly the 1954 paper on development with 'unlimited supplies' of labour. He presents a stylized model in which the typical poor country is divided into a 'traditional' and a 'modern' sector. The former consists of peasant agriculture as well as self employment of various sorts in urban areas, where the primary objective of economic activity is to maintain consumption. The 'modern' sector comprises commercial farming, plantations and mines and manufacturing, in which there is hired labour and profit is the motive for production organized by a class of capitalists and entrepreneurs. Lewis adopts a strictly classical viewpoint on two crucial features of his model. First, the real wage of unskilled labour in the modern sector is exogenously given, with employment and profits then being determined by the demand for labour corresponding to the fixed stock of capital in the short run. The second classical feature is that the accumulation of capital is governed by saving out of profits. The process of economic development is viewed as the expansion of the modern relative to the traditional sector until such time as the 'surplus labour' pool in the traditional sector is drained and an integrated labour market emerges with a neoclassically determined equilibrium real wage. This model of a 'dual economy' has generated considerable controversy and an extensive polemical literature, to which references can be found in Findlay (1980). The most sophisticated and thorough theoretical defense of the dual economy model is Sen (1966).

Another notable theoretical contribution of this 1954 paper is a model of the terms of trade between manufactures and primary products that is developed further with empirical applications in his 1969 Wicksell Lectures. The key idea is that the relative world prices of manufactures and tropical products such as coffee, tea, sugar, rubber and jute are determined by the relative opportunity costs of labour in food production. The Pittsburgh steel worker's wages are governed by the Kansas farmer's productivity, while the Brazilian coffee plantation wage is determined by the much lower productivity of peasant subsistence agriculture. Lewis applies this model in a very imaginative way to illuminate several key aspects of the history of the world economy, including his most recent major work *Economic Growth and Fluctuations 1870–1913*, published in 1978. This volume pushes his examination of the world economy in the interwar period back to the 'gold age' of 1870 to 1913. Unlike the earlier book, based on secondary sources, this one is a deeply original piece of statistical and historical research in the manner of Schumpeter and Kuznets.

The reader can find an extensive collection of Lewis's articles and shorter monographs in the volume edited by Mark Gersovitz (1983). A measure of his influence on the field of development economics can be gathered from the volume of essays in his honour edited by Gersovitz and others (1982).

SELECTED WORKS

1949a. *Economic Survey 1919–1939*. London: Allen & Unwin.

1949b. *Overhead Costs*. London: Allen & Unwin.

1949c. *The Principles of Economic Planning*. London: Allen & Unwin.

1954. Economic development with unlimited supplies of labour. *Manchester School* 22, May, 139–91.

1955. *The Theory of Economic Growth*. London: Allen & Unwin.

1969. *Aspects of Tropical Trade 1883–1965*. Wicksell Lectures, Stockholm: Almqvist & Wicksell.

1978. *Growth and Fluctuations 1870–1913*. London: Allen & Unwin.

1980. The slowing down of the engine of growth (Nobel Lecture). *American Economic Review* 70(4), December, 555–64.

BIBLIOGRAPHY

Findlay, R. 1980. On W. Arthur Lewis' contributions to economics. *Scandinavian Journal of Economics* 82(1), 62–76.

Gersovitz, M. et al. (eds.) 1982. *The Theory and Experience of Economic Development: Essays in Honour of W. Arthur Lewis*. London: George Allen & Unwin.

Gersovitz, M. (ed.) 1983. *Selected Economic Writings of W. Arthur Lewis*. New York: New York University Press.

Sen, A.K. 1966. Peasants and dualism with or without surplus labor. *Journal of Political Economy* 74, October, 425–50.

Linkages

ALBERT O. HIRSCHMAN

A linkage (or linkage effect) was originally defined as a characteristic, more or less compelling sequence of investment decisions occurring in the course of industrialization and, more generally, of economic development. In putting forward the concept in *The Strategy of Economic Development* (1958, ch. 6), A.O. Hirschman criticized the then dominant Harrod–Domar growth model in which growth depends only on the capital–output ratio and on the availability of capital. More generally, the concept arose from a perspective contesting the conventional representation of an economy where natural resources, factors of production, and entrepreneurship are all available in given amounts and need only be efficiently allocated to various activities for best results. Hirschman contended instead that 'development depends not so much on finding optimal combinations for given resources and factors of production as on calling forth and enlisting for development purposes resources and abilities that are hidden, scattered, or badly utilized' (1958, p. 5). This view led to a search for various inducing and mobilizing mechanisms. The resulting 'strategy of unbalanced growth' values investment decisions not only because of their immediate contribution to output, but because of the larger or smaller impulse such decisions are likely to impart to further investment, that is, because of their linkages. The strategy has important implications for investment planning: it proposes that dynamic considerations, based on the linkages, should be allowed to complement the criterion of static efficiency.

BACKWARD AND FORWARD LINKAGES

In connection with the process of industrialization in countries undertaking to industrialize in the second half of the 20th century, two sequences held promise for generating special pressures toward investment. First, an existing industrial operation, relying initially on imports not only for its equipment and machinery, but also for many of its material inputs, would make for pressures towards the domestic manufacture of these inputs and eventually towards a domestic capital goods industry. This dynamic was called *backward linkage*, since the direction of the stimulus towards further investment flows from the finished article back towards the semi-processed or raw materials from which it is made or towards the machines which help make it.

Another stimulus towards additional investment points in the other direction and is therefore called *forward linkage*: the existence of a given product line A, which is a final demand good or is used as an input in line B, acts as stimulant to the establishment of another line C which can also use A as an input.

The stimuli towards further investment are rather different for backward and forward linkages. The pressures towards backward linkage investments arise in part from normal entrepreneurial behaviour, given the newly available market for intermediate goods. But there may also be resistance against such investments on the part of established industrialists who prefer to continue relying on imported inputs for price and quality reasons. At the same time, state policies often favour backward linkage investments (which hold out the promise of foreign exchange savings and or a more 'integrated' industrial structure) through the promise of tariff protection and through various preferential foreign exchange and credit allocations, particularly in periods of foreign exchange stringency. The pressures towards forward linkage investments come primarily from the efforts of existing producers to increase and diversify the market for their products. In contrast to backward linkage, there will be only whole-hearted support for forward linkage on the part of existing domestic producers. On the other hand, official development policy is not likely to be particularly concerned with promoting forward linkage investments.

The linkage dynamic made it possible to visualize the industrialization process in terms of an input-output matrix, most of whose cells would be empty to start with, but would progressively fill up, in large part because of backward and forward linkage effects. This close connection with Leontief's input–output model, which was being given just then its first practical applications through the computation of input–output tables for various national economies, contributed to the favourable reception of the linkage concept and probably gave it a certain advantage over related attempts at describing the dynamic of industrialization, such as the 'leading sector' (Rostow, 1960), the 'propulsive industry' (Perroux, 1958, vol. II), or the 'development block' (Dahmén, 1950). On the other hand, this connection sometimes made for too mechanistic a concept of the linkage dynamic which is strongly influenced, as already noted, by state policies and other institutional factors (Raj, 1975).

The connection with the input–output model made it appear that measurement of backward and forward linkages would be an easy task, but this was largely an illusion. Input–output analysis is by nature synchronic whereas linkage effects need time to unfold. In a country setting out to industrialize, existing input–output tables cannot reveal which additional industrial branches are likely to be *created* in the wake of industrial investment in a given product line. The input–output framework is even less suited to tracing backward linkage effects towards the machinery and equipment industries. Nevertheless, once a developing country has a fairly broad industrial base so that a given industrial investment leads primarily to the *expansion* rather than to the *creation* of other industries, the measurement of linkage effects through statistical devices based on input–output tables becomes more meaningful.

The technical problems of measurement of backward and forward linkages have been widely debated (see in particular *Quarterly Journal of Economics*, 1976). The most elaborate attempt at measurement has been carried out by economists at the Employment Program for Latin America of the International Labor Office (PREALC) whose primary interest was in the direct and indirect effects of investments in a given industry on *employment*, rather than on industrial expansion in terms of output (García and Marfán, 1982).

Given the difficulties of measurement the linkage concept has been more influential as a general way of thinking about development strategy than as a precise, practical tool in project analysis or planning. In addition, it has contributed to the understanding of the growth process. It clarified the political economy of late industrialization and was also able to shed light on the earlier phase during which the countries of the periphery were integrated into the world economy as exporters of primary products. These two areas of application will be discussed in turn.

LINKAGES AND INDUSTRIALIZATION

Backward linkage and import-substituting industrialization. The backward linkage dynamic is particularly important for the newly industrializing countries of the 20th century because their industrialization has often started with the imparting of 'last touches' to a host of imported inputs and then worked itself backwards, in contrast to the industrialization of the older industrial countries which of necessity had to proceed in a more 'balanced' way, that is, with all industrial stages – finished, semi-processed goods and machinery – being created more or less in tandem (Hirschman, 1968). For the late industrializers of the 20th century, vigorous pursuit of the backward linkage dynamic was therefore essential for achieving an industrial structure of any depth. Industrialization following this sequential, staged path became widely known as Import-Substituting Industrialization.

The centrality of backward linkage in this process had somewhat contradictory social and political consequences. On the one hand, the original entrepreneurs of the process were often erstwhile importers who, in periods of foreign exchange shortage, found it profitable to manufacture from imported inputs the finished articles they could no longer procure from abroad. Hence the importance of traders, frequently recent immigrants, and of foreign firms in the process and among the entrepreneurial groups. The often noted comparative weakness of the 'national bourgeoisie' in the late industrializing countries may in this manner be related to the pattern of industrialization.

But the sequential unfolding of this pattern was also responsible for a rather different characteristic: a good part of the newly emerging industrial establishment is likely to be tightly held by a few large-scale, vertically integrated family firms or 'groups' (Leff, 1978). As long as industries were first established to occupy the last stage of manufacturing, with major inputs being imported, the firms operating in that stage would often be anxious, if only for reasons of quality control, to own the upstream factories that would be founded later to supply those inputs; and they would have the means to do so precisely because, between setting up one stage of manufacturing and the next, considerable time would elapse permitting accumulation of investible funds.

The resulting concentration of part of industrial production in a few vertically integrated 'groups' sometimes coexists with the pre-eminent role played by immigrant minorities or foreigners. These two characteristics have made for a third: in most countries the state assumed a substantial role in the process through public enterprises that were meant to counteract or to pre-empt excessive domination over the industrial establishment either by foreigners and immigrants or by a few powerful private monopolistic groups (Jones, 1982, ch. 2). Another reason for direct state intervention was the frequent preference of private industrialists for continued reliance on foreign suppliers of semi-processed and capital goods – this occasional resistance to backward linkage is yet another characteristic of import-substituting industrialization.

This pattern of industrialization was faulted on two opposite counts: for running out of steam before accomplishing a great deal and for being pushed to uneconomic lengths. Both critiques, originating of course in different camps, arose in the 1960s and have sometimes been made simultaneously, with varying justification. One group of critics posited an early stage which was alleged to be 'easy' in comparison to a later stage when the easy stage has become 'exhausted' and further progress in pushing backward linkage – towards the more 'basic' intermediate or capital goods industries – runs into various obstacles: the size of the market is too small, the capital needed is too large to be raised locally, and the technology is controlled by transnational corporations. If these obstacles effectively stopped further progress, industrialization was denounced as 'stunted' and as 'lacking integration'; alternatively, if it proceeded with foreign capital in key positions, industrialization, originally hailed as a harbinger of national emancipation, was viewed as bringing on a new 'dependency', more insidious and debilitating than the earlier forms this condition had taken. It was also suggested (O'Donnell, 1975) that the problems of transition from the 'easy' to the 'difficult' stage bear some responsibility for the breakdown of democracy and the rise of authoritarian regimes in various Latin American countries during the Sixties and Seventies. Not much of this thesis, however, survived the animated debate to which it gave rise (Hirschman, 1979; Kaufman, 1979; Serra, 1979).

A very different critique of an industrialization that has backward linkage as its principal engine emphasized the danger of doing too much rather than too little, because of the misallocation of resources which the process was believed to entail. This neoclassical critique pointed out, for example, that, given the nature of the process, the *effective* rate of protection granted to domestically produced finished articles was much higher than appeared from the nominal rates, because of the large proportion of the total value of these articles that was imported, usually at much lower or zero rates, as intermediate inputs (Johnson, 1967).

However, those high levels of effective protection are bound to decline once the intermediate inputs are in turn produced in the country and are hence eligible for the level of protection generally available to domestically produced goods (Corden, 1966). The more successful the process of backward linkage, the more likely it was therefore that excessive levels of effective protection would be brought down.

Customs duties were not the only element in the environment of protection that fostered the new import-substituting industries. An important sheltering device was unintended. In the postwar period a number of developing countries experienced inflation. In combination with fixed, hence lagging exchange rates, the inflationary pressures resulted in long periods of overvaluation of the currency that made it necessary to establish quantitative import controls. Such controls generally favoured the new industries with their high requirements of imported inputs and machinery and the arrangement thus served to subsidize industrial investment and expansion. The subsidy was paid, via the overvalued exchange rate, by the exporters of traditional primary products. The resources that were transferred in this roundabout manner from the traditional agricultural or mining sectors to the emerging industrial establishment could not have been mobilized directly. In the industrializing societies of Latin America, for example, the interests tied to the traditional export sectors were still in a highly influential position and it was out of the question to tax them outright (Kafka, 1961; Furtado, 1967).

While ingenious in the short term, the usefulness of the arrangement was bound to decline with time. The discrimination against exports, resulting from the overvalued exchange rate, was not particularly serious during the first stages of industrial development when most new manufacturers had their hands full asserting themselves in their own rapidly growing domestic market. Moreover, in the shorter run, export volume of some of the traditional products – tropical tree crops and minerals from existing installations – did not react adversely to the overvaluation. But conditions changed after a decade or two of the postwar industrialization drive. Exports of industrial products became possible in the conditions of rapidly expanding world trade characteristic of the Sixties and early Seventies. Because of scale economies, some linked industries could only be economically justified if export markets could be found for a portion of their output almost from the start. Finally, the overvaluation interfered with the vigorous pursuit of the backward linkage dynamic itself as long as materials and machinery could be imported at bargain prices. It therefore became desirable to establish realistic exchange rates, to reduce the degree of protection, and to adopt a new set of policies for both continued industrialization and export promotion.

Such a correction of the course of economic policy was not easy to perform. On the one hand, it was resisted by groups that had prospered under the older set of policies. In some countries, such as Chile, on the other hand, the new course was imposed in the form of total reversal of previous policies as though they had been wholly misguided; in the process, considerable damage was caused to the industrial structure that had been built up and unemployment rose to very high levels.

CONSUMPTION LINKAGE. The linkage concept represented an attempt to identify specific powerful pressures towards investment decisions that make themselves felt in a growing economy. Once launched, the concept proved versatile: new types of linkage effects were identified and found useful for the analysis of a wide range of development experiences. The mechanisms of the new linkages were more roundabout than the backward and forward variety. Thus *consumption linkage* is defined as the stimulus towards domestic production of consumer goods that will be undertaken as newly earned incomes are spent on such goods. In an open economy such goods will often be imported at first, but eventually domestic production will become an attractive proposition (Watkins, 1963; Hirschman, 1977).

Consumption linkage is actually the *initial* step in the process of import-substituting industrialization. The backward and forward linkage dynamic can explain the *spread* of industrial activity from an established industrial nucleus, but how to account for a country's first generation of industrial plants? Many of these have typically come into being in the peripheral countries as increasing domestic incomes originating in export agriculture of mining caused imports of various consumer goods to reach a volume that made domestic manufacture economically attractive. Eventually some of these goods would be exported, so that the countries in question 'tend to develop a comparative advantage in the articles they *import*' (Hirschman, 1958, p. 122; for an empirical study, see Teitel and Thoumi, 1986).

Rising imports of consumer goods, such as textiles, into newly developing countries have often been blamed for the decay of local handicraft and artisanal production. It appears that they must be correspondingly credited with laying the groundwork for local industry, through consumption linkages.

The strength of these linkages and their effectiveness in inducing industrial development depend not only on the aggregate income stream to which primary exports give rise, but on many other factors, including the distribution of this income. The more egalitarian the distribution of a given income the larger will be the consumer demand for many typical products of modern industry and the more likely does it become that the domestic market will reach the size at which local production is warranted. The early development of manufactures in the northern United States, in contrast to delayed industrialization in the American South and in Latin America, with their much greater income inequalities, has been explained on these grounds (Baldwin, 1956). The argument that an egalitarian distribution of income is favourable to growth is of course at odds with the more traditional view which emphasizes the need for capital and therefore for savings, most readily accumulated by the rich.

When domestic incomes increase because of a boom in primary exports, a considerable portion of the increase will be spend on food in low-income countries. The concept of consumption linkage must therefore be extended to the additional domestic food production that is induced by the rise in exports. In Chile, for example, the rise in nitrate exports in the decades before World War I made for an expansion of wheat production in the Central Valley (Cariola and Sunkel, 1985). In Ecuador, mounting cocoa exports in the early decades of the century led similarly to an expansion of the production of rice which, once introduced, turned out to be well suited to some of the country's soils and climate, so that rice took over as an important foreign exchange earner when the cocoa plantations were devastated by disease in the Thirties. It may therefore be not just luck if one primary product is rapidly followed by another as a mainstay of a country's exports: consumption linkage will on occasion explain a good part of the story.

Recognition of the importance of consumption linkage has substantial implications for development policy. As long as only backward and forward linkages are taken into account a development strategy that pays attention to the linkage concept is likely to have a pro-industry bias. But this bias disappears when consumption linkages are given their due. Recent reappraisals of development strategy thus invoke the linkage argument while favouring a tilt of investment priorities towards agricultural improvement (Adelman, 1984; Mellor and Johnston, 1984). It is of course ironic that an analytical tool which originally served to justify the building up of industry in less developed areas should later be used for advocating a quite different development strategy. But this very shift testifies to the acceptance the linkage concept had gained: no matter what strategy is advocated, it is now felt necessary to make the case for it in terms of the vigorous linkage effects that would ensue.

FISCAL LINKAGE

Consumption linkage describes a familiar, spontaneous process: incomes are earned in a new activity and are then spent on goods that, while often imported at first, will eventually be produced domestically. One activity induces another through the market. But new activities can also be established by the state as it interferes with such market forces. The state can tap the flow of income accruing to the exporters through various forms of export taxes, or it can impose tariffs on the imported articles on which a good part of the new export-related incomes will be spent. The resulting fiscal receipts can then be used to finance public or publicly supported investment projects. These sequences spell out a new class of *fiscal linkages* (Pearson, 1970). They are again rather roundabout and perhaps unreliable mechanisms compared to backward and forward linkages. Within that category, however, extraction (and subsequent expenditure) of revenue through export taxes has a relatively straightforward character and may be called *direct* fiscal linkage. The raising (and disposal) of fiscal receipts through tariffs on imports involves still more steps and is labelled *indirect* fiscal linkage.

The choice by the state between direct and indirect fiscal linkage has largely depended on the kind of commodity that is being exported. Export taxes (direct fiscal linkage) have been prevalent in the case of primary commodities that were produced in enclave conditions, that is, in geographically isolated, often originally foreign-owned, plantations, mines and petroleum fields. It was the very concentration of production in an outlying area, its ownership by one or a few foreign firms, and the ease with which fiscal control over production and export volume could be established that invited in these cases the use of taxation at the source. When, on the contrary, the export commodity was produced over a wide, centrally located area by numerous small domestic, politically influential producers, as in the case of coffee, cocoa, or other tropical crops, direct taxation was administratively difficult and politically inadvisable. Here the state resorted preferentially to indirect extraction of revenue by imposing tariffs on the imports which would flow into the country as a result of its primary exports.

The idea that the state should take advantage of some existing source of economic growth to stimulate growth elsewhere arose with particular strength in countries where the export product was a clearly *depletable* natural resource such as guano or petroleum. It was supposed that the state had a special responsibility to use part of the wealth arising from the temporary 'bonanza' for developing other 'growth poles' (Perroux, 1958, vol. II) that would stand ready to take over once the original source of export income would dry up. This is the meaning of the phrase 'sow the petroleum' that was coined in Venezuela to justify various state-financed regional and industrial development schemes. Direct fiscal linkage has often had this aim of jumping, as it were, from an ongoing activity to a wholly different one, to be created *ex nihilo*, in contrast to the seemingly plodding backward and forward linkages. Unfortunately, such jumps into uncharted territory are very risky, so that direct fiscal linkage has sometimes resulted in 'white elephants'.

But the state does not always act in this 'creative' way: more frequently its economic activities have consisted in extending the infrastructure for ongoing economic activity, through investments in transportation, communication and, later, power generation as well as health and education. These types of public investments have often been characteristic of indirect fiscal linkage, with the state's revenue accruing primarily through tariffs on imports. In these cases, the export articles which generate the dutiable imports are likely to be agricultural products whose cultivation could be further extended, and the state performs the comparatively low-risk task of facilitating such extensions. At the same time, these public investments can have the result of accentuating the country's economic structure and of relegating it more firmly to its role as a supplier of certain primary products; in the course of colonial development, indirect fiscal linkage has in fact been an important mechanism acting in this manner (Birnberg and Resnick, 1975).

LINKAGE CONSTELLATIONS AND THE STAPLE THESIS

The preceding discussion suggests that different primary commodities may have affinites for different types or 'bundles' of linkages. As already noted, the enclave conditions under which certain commodities are produced favour direct fiscal linkage, but exclude by definition any substantial backward and forward linkages. Correlatively, the non-enclave characteristics making for indirect rather than direct fiscal linkage should in due course also make for import-substituting industrialization (via the consumption linkages), and for backward linkages once agricultural technology becomes more advanced.

In this manner the linkage approach has much in common with the *staple thesis* which has been developed by a group of Canadian economic historians.

The most prominent member of the group was Harold Innis, who showed in a series of meticulous and subtle studies how Canadian development – transportation facilities, settlement patterns, new economic activities – was shaped by the characteristics and requirements of the specific primary commodities – from furs to codfish to timber, minerals, and wheat – which the country was successively supplying to world markets. The virtue of the linkage approach in comparison to the staple thesis with its detailed analysis of the impact of one commodity at a time is that it supplies a few major categories that structure the inquiry.

It is a basic tenet of the staple thesis that development of the periphery starts with the discovery of some staple that is in demand in the centre. In contrast, the 'development-of-underdevelopment' thesis (Frank, 1966) has attempted to show that it was precisely the 'successful' development of staples that has been responsible for the impoverishment of the periphery: the staple boom is said to leave nothing behind but a depressed area with depleted mines, exhausted soil, and impoverished subsistence agriculture. The historical record contains a number of situations that seem to confirm this kind of analysis: the silver mines of Potosí in Bolivia, the 'mining' of guano in Peru and the sugar plantations of the Caribbean and of Brazil's Northeast. The linkage approach can resolve the apparent contradictions between the staple and the development-of-underdevelopment theses. While originally devised to explain different patterns of *growth*, it is easily used to account for stagnation and immiserization. Some or all of the linkages can fail to materialize and an inquiry into these failures permits a preliminary sorting out of major conceivable reasons for negative developments. In the case of staples produced in enclave conditions, for example, direct fiscal linkage may of course have appeared not at all or too feebly and too late. Alternatively, the linkage may have operated, but then could have led to misinvestments of the revenue: this was precisely the case of Peru where revenues were extracted from the mid-19th-century guano boom, but were then spent on nonproductive railroad ventures (Hunt, 1985). In the case of agricultural staples, such as sugar cane, produced by slave labour on plantations, there may be a failure of both indirect fiscal linkage and of consumption linkage as much of the income accrues to absentee owners and as the income distributed to the work force is barely sufficient for subsistence and therefore provides little stimulus for additional food production on a commercial scale or for the importation of taxable consumer goods.

The various linkages, their possible failures and their changing constellations make for an increasingly complex pattern of possibilities. Moreover, in some cases a linkage can be an *obstacle* to development rather than an asset. This is the case for forward linkage when a bulky staple requires elaborate processing by technologically complex, capital-intensive methods to be transformed into a finished product. Such processing constitutes of course forward linkage, but in the case of agricultural staples like sugar cane it means that the growers themselves will often not be capable of entering the processing phase which will therefore be occupied by outside entrepreneurs; in this manner growers of the staple will be locked into their agricultural activity. The opposite situation obtains when the staple needs little processing and is compact, with a comparatively high value per unit of weight. In this case the growers themselves are able to take over the transportation and merchandizing functions. As a result the agriculturalists acquire new entrepreneurial and urban skills. Actually what goes on here is that the absence of one kind of forward linkage – elaborate, capital-intensive processing – makes for the availability of another forward link, to the merchandizing function, that can be taken advantage of directly by the staple producers. In the tropics, examples of this easy transition from agricultural production to activities in transportation, trade, and eventually to finance and industry, are supplied by the story of coffee expansion in Colombia and Brazil. In parts of Greece and of some other Mediterranean countries, the production of olive oil, nuts and raisins has made for a similarly easy transition from rural to urban pursuits (McNeill, 1978).

LINKAGES AND SOCIETY

The linkage constellations characteristic of a given staple spell out not only certain likely patterns of development (or stagnation), they also exert, through these patterns, an influence on the social order and political regime of countries where the staple occupies an important economic role. The effort to trace such influences has been called 'micro-marxism' (Hirschman, 1977), the idea being that, in searching for the effects of the 'productive forces' on the 'relations of production', it may be fruitful to go considerably beyond the macromodes of production – feudal, capitalist, etc. – specified and stressed by Marx. This is particularly so for the countries of the periphery during the period of export-led growth when each of these countries was specialized in one or a very few primary product lines, with very different linkages and characteristics. But even for countries at a different stage of development, a knowledge of the degree of affinity between key economic activities and forms of social and political organization can be useful. For example, a student of the centrally planned economies (Wiles, 1977, p. 102) has made a distinction between 'left-wing crops' and 'right-wing crops', pointing out that products requiring individual attention such as grapes and certain fruits and vegetables, are particularly unsuitable for collectivized agriculture, in contrast to the more 'left-wing' grains where operations are standardized. For the industrialized countries of the West, it has been suggested that specific sectors (textiles, steel, chemicals, automobiles) which have successively played key roles at various periods of industrial expansion, have each nurtured different political forms or tendencies (Kurth, 1979).

Such micro-marxist explorations can be insightful, but two qualifications are in order. First, there is no necessary one-to-one relationship between a specific economic activity and a 'resulting' socio-political regime. The fact that there existed for a long time a mutually supportive and reinforcing relationship between sugar cane cultivation and slavery does not mean that sugar cane does not 'fit' as well into one or several very different social and political regimes. Nevertheless, there may well be a limited number of such fits and some socio-political configurations may definitely be ill-suited to the development of a certain productive activity or technology.

Secondly, the causal connection between the productive activity, be it a staple or an industrial complex, and a socio-political regime does not flow in one direction only. The analysis has here primarily proceeded from the characteristics of a staple or an industry to their imprints on society and polity. But in many cases it is possible and inviting to reverse the direction of the inquiry: one might ask whether a certain kind of political regime is likely to exhibit a strong preference for the promotion of a certain type of industrial development, such as a petrochemical complex (Evans, 1986).

The linkage concept, in short, invites the analyst to pay close attention to the differential technological and situational features of economic activities as a means of detecting how 'one thing leads (or fails to lead) to another'. But this focus does not prejudge either the nature or the principal direction of the causal links involved in the complex interaction between technology, ideology, institutions, and development. The contention is simply that the linkage approach has a number of interesting observations to make in this area. It thus effectively challenges other approaches to propose alternative or supplementary interpretations.

BIBLIOGRAPHY

Adelman, I. 1984. Beyond export-led growth. *World Development* 12(9), September, 937–49.

Baldwin, R.E. 1956. Patterns of development in newly settled regions. *Manchester School of Economics and Social Studies* 24(2), May, 161–79.

Birnberg, T.B. and Resnick, S.A. 1975. *Colonial Development: an Econometric Study*. New Haven: Yale University Press.

Cariola, C. and Sunkel, O. 1985. The growth of the nitrate industry and socioeconomic change in Chile. In *The Latin American Economies: Growth and the Export Sector 1880–1930*, ed. R. Cortés Conde and S.J. Hunt, New York: Holmes & Meier.

Corden, W.M. 1966. The structure of a tariff system and the effective protection rate. *Journal of Political Economy* 74, June, 221–37.

Dahmén, E. 1950. *Entrepreneurial Activity and the Development of Swedish Industry, 1919–1939*. Homewood, Ill.: Irwin, 1971.

Evans, P. 1986. Generalized linkages and industrial development. In *Development, Democracy, and the Art of Trespassing: Essays in Honor of A.O. Hirschman*, ed. A. Foxley et al., Notre Dame, Ind.: University of Notre Dame Press.

Frank, A.G. 1966. The development of underdevelopment. *Monthly Review* 18(4), September, 17–31.

Furtado, C. 1967. Industrialization and inflation: an analysis of the recent course of development in Brazil. *International Economic Papers* 12, 101–19.

García, N.E. and Marfán, M. 1982. *Estructuras industriales y eslabonamientos de empleo*. Monografía sobre empleo 26, PREALC-ILO, Santiago (Chile).

Hirschman, A.O. 1958. *The Strategy of Economic Development*. New Haven: Yale University Press.

Hirschman, A.O. 1968. The political economy of import-substituting industrialization in Latin America. *Quarterly Journal of Economics* 82, February, 1–32. Reprinted in A.O. Hirschman, *A Bias for Hope*, New Haven: Yale University Press, 1971.

Hirschman, A.O. 1977. A generalized linkage approach to development, with special reference to staples. In *Essays on Economic Development and Cultural Change in Honor of Bert F. Hoselitz*, ed. M. Nash, Chicago: University of Chicago Press. Reprinted in A.O. Hirschman, *Essays in Trespassing*, Cambridge: Cambridge University Press, 1981.

Hirschman, A.O. 1979. The turn to authoritarianism in Latin America and the search for its economic determinants. In *The New Authoritarianism in Latin America*, ed. D. Collier, Princeton: Princeton University Press. Reprinted in A.O. Hirschman, *Essays in Trespassing*, Cambridge: Cambridge University Press, 1981.

Hunt, S.J. 1985. Growth and guano in nineteenth-century Peru. In *Latin American Economies: Growth and the Export Sector 1880–1930*, ed. R. Cortés Conde and S.J. Hunt, New York: Holmes & Meier.

Johnson, H.G. 1967. *Economic Policies Toward Less Developed Countries*. Washington, DC: Brookings Institution.

Jones, L.P. (ed.) 1982. *Public Enterprise in Developing Countries*. Cambridge: Cambridge University Press.

Kafka, A. 1961. The theoretical interpretation of Latin American economic development. In *Economic Development in Latin America*, ed. H.S. Ellis, New York: St. Martin's Press.

Kaufman, R.R. 1979. Industrial change and authoritarian rule in Latin America. In *The New Authoritarianism in Latin America*, ed. D. Collier, Princeton: Princeton University Press.

Kurth, J. 1979. The political consequences of the product cycle: industrial history and political outcomes. *International Organization* 33(1), Winter, 1–34.

Leff, N.H. 1978. Industrial organization and entrepreneurship in the developing countries. *Economic Development and Cultural Change* 26(4), July, 661–75.

McNeill, W.H. 1978. *The Metamorphosis of Greece since World War II*. Oxford: Blackwell.

Mellor, J.F. and Johnston, B.F. 1984. The world food equation: interrelations among development, employment and food consumption. *Journal of Economic Literature* 22(2), June, 531–74.

O'Donnell, G. 1975. Reflexiones sobre las tendencias generales de cambio en el estado burocratico-autoritario. Buenos Aires: CEDES. Also published in English as 'Reflections on patterns of change in the bureaucratic-authoritarian states' in *Latin American Research Review* 13(1), Winter 1978, 3–38.

Pearson, S.R. 1970. *Petroleum and the Nigerian Economy*. Stanford: Stanford University Press.

Perroux, F. 1958. *La coexistence pacifique*. Paris: Presses Universitaires de France.

Quarterly Journal of Economics. 1976. Various articles on measurement of linkages. 90(2), May, 308–43.

Raj, K.N. 1975. Linkages in industrialization and development strategy: some basic issues. *Journal of Development Planning* 8, 105–19.

Rostow, W.W. 1960. *The Stages of Economic Growth*. Cambridge: Cambridge University Press.

Serra, J. 1979. Three mistaken theses regarding the connection between industrialization and authoritarian regimes. In *The New Authoritarianism in Latin America*, ed. D. Collier, Princeton: Princeton University Press.

Teitel, S. and Thoumi, F. 1986. From import sustitution to exports: the recent experience of Argentina and Brazil. *Economic Development and Cultural Change* 34(3), April, 455–90.

Watkins, M.H. 1963. A staple theory of economic growth. *Canadian Journal of Economics and Political Science* 29(2), May, 141–58.

Wiles, P.J.D. 1977. *Economic Institutions Compared*. New York: Wiley.

Mahalanobis, Prasanta Chandra

SUKHAMOY CHAKRAVARTY

Mahalanobis was born in Calcutta in 1893 of a well-to-do Bengali middle-class family with a reformed outlook on Hindu religion. He was educated first at Presidency College, Calcutta, and then at Cambridge, where he graduated with a First in Natural Sciences from King's College in 1915. He became a Fellow of the Royal Society in 1946 and received many other scientific honours. While Mahalanobis served as Professor of Physics at Presidency College for nearly three decades, his scientific work consisted chiefly of developing statistical theory and techniques that had application to a wide range of subjects, beginning with meteorology and anthropology and ending in economics.

Mahalanobis established a firm international reputation on the basis of his work on the design of large-scale sample surveys (e.g. 1944) and thus laid the basis for systematic collection of a large variety of data relating to socio-economic conditions. Mahalanobis's sense of realism was combined with a deep understanding of the problems of statistical inference. This led him to place stress on 'non-sampling errors' in addition to the standard preoccupation with sampling errors. He devised his system of 'interpreting network of sub-samples' to derive among other things, an idea of 'non-sampling errors' which are inherently associated with large-scale collection of data.

Mahalanobis's work on experimental designs developed with a view to estimating crop yields (1946) was highly influential in laying down the basis for collection of agricultural statistics in India. In multivariate statistics, Mahalanobis's measure of distance between two populations (1936), usually known as Mahalanobis's D^2 statistic, is a major contribution that is much used in anthropometry and elsewhere.

Mahalanobis maintained a keen interest in problems of national planning even before India had gained Independence. He recognized very early that such planning had to have a firm statistical base, and from the beginning of the 1950s, when the Indian Five Year Plan was launched, began to devote a very large part of his time and attention to questions of estimating national income and the factors determining its rate of growth. His approach to planning issues, with its strong emphasis on quantification, was significantly different from the qualitative approach favoured by the Indian economists of his generation. However, Mahalanobis was no exclusive believer in narrowly conceived quantitative techniques. He developed an important blend between qualitative and quantitative considerations, which is reflected in his 'approach of operational research to planning' (1955).

The second Five Year Plan, whose analytical structure was largely the handiwork of Mahalanobis, stands out as a very distinguished document in the development of planning theory. Mahalanobis is generally regarded as one of the prominent advocates of the inward-looking strategy of industrialization, along with Raul Prebisch. But the analytical foundation of the Mahalanobis approach was derived from somewhat different premises. While Prebisch began his theoretical study from what he thought was a historical fact, that is, the secular decline in terms of the trade of primary producing countries, Mahalanobis developed a two-sector model of growth to deduce a strategy of industrial development which he thought was best suited to India. The classification of the economy into sectors resembled in some respects Marx's famous Departmental Schema, although they were not identical.

Mahalnobis's sector-schema (1953), distinguished between 'capital goods' and 'consumer goods', but the assumption of vertical integration made in the interest of simplicity made statistical implementation difficult. The essential point of the model is that the capacity of the capital goods sector determines the potential rate of expansion of the consumer goods sector, and not the other way round. Further, at any given instant, capacities are not directly transferable from one sector to the other. Labour is not considered to be a constraint on expanding production. The model was developed initially for a closed economy but has been subsequently extended to open economies, with an exogenously given profile of export earnings. Mahalanobis used the model to illustrate the nature of the trade-off between present and future consumption, given the objective characteristics of the two sectors.

For the dynamic closure of the model he used the ratio of the output of the capital goods sector that is ploughed back into itself ('λ_k' in his notation), to deduce a 'gradualist growth' path of consumption. For any given value λ_k maintained over time, the rate of growth of aggregate output tends, over a sufficiently long period, to a magnitude $\lambda_k \beta_k$, where β_k is the output–capital ratio of the capital goods sector. The Mahalanobis model was subsequently freed from the assumption of an exogenously stipulated λ_k. Exercises carried out by Stoleru (1965), Chakravarty (1969), Dasgupta (1969) and others introduced explicit intertemporal social utility functions along with a production technology of the Mahalanobis type. They deduced the characteristics of optimal growth paths with the help of variational calculus. $\lambda_k(t)$ was deduced as a solution of the optimizing exercise. It was shown that while the assumption of 'non-shiftability

223

critical to Mahalnobis's model could in several cases give rise to a preference for the capital goods sector in early stages of growth (a strategy preferred by Mahalanobis himself) one could not obtain a universal rule of priority for capital goods irrespective of initial conditions, or the nature of social utility functions over time.

In all these exercises, the coefficients pertaining to the 'capital goods sector', sometimes identified as the 'machine tool sector', turned out to be an important determinant of the growth process. Earlier literature on business cycle theory originating with Marx, Tugan Baranovsky and Adolph Lowe had placed emphasis on the 'machine tools sector', without linking it up with an explicit growth model. In the growth theoretic area Fel'dman alone appears to be the true predecessor of Mahalanobis as is evident from Domar's discussion (1957).

Mahalanobis extended the two-sector model to a four-sector model, to focus on issues of reduction in unemployment along with increases in income. Mahalanobis came to the 'dual development thesis', which consisted in assigning high weights to the capital goods sector in the interests of long-term growth, and emphasis on the highly labour-intensive consumer goods sector in the short run. In the literature on planning, this has on occasion been referred to as the strategy of 'walking on two legs', with authorship occasionally ascribed to Mao Tse Tung.

Towards the end of his life, Mahalanobis returned to issues of statistical methodology and concentrated on developing what he called 'fractile graphical analysis' (1960), which is based on a geometrical concept of error and can also provide a generalized measure of separation between two 'different universes' of study. He died in 1972.

Mahalanobis's work remains important for economists who are working on quantitative approaches to problems of plan formulation, especially in the context of large-sized economies. His work on sample surveys has generated a very valuable literature to which economic statisticians from India and elsewhere have made notable contributions.

SELECTED WORKS

1936. On generalized distance in statistics. National Institute of Science, India, *Proceedings* 2, 49–55.

1944. On large scale sample surveys. *Philosophical Transactions*, Series B 231, 392–451, London: The Royal Society.

1946. Sample surveys of crop yields. *Sankhya* 7, 269–80.

1953. Some observations on the process of growth of national income. *Sankhya* 12, 307–12.

1955. The approach of operational research to planning in India. *Sankhya* 16(1–2), 3–130.

1958. Science and national planning. *Sankhya* 20, 69–106.

1960. A method of fractile graphical analysis. *Econometrica* 28, April, 325–51.

1961. *Talks on Planning*. Bombay and London: Asia Publishing House.

BIBLIOGRAPHY

Bhagwati, J.N. and Chakravarty, S. 1969. Contributions to Indian economic analysis – a survey. *American Economic Review* (Supplement) 59(4), September, 1–73.

Chakravarty, S. 1969. *Capital and Development Planning*. Cambridge, Mass.: MIT Press.

Dasgupta, P.S. 1969. Optimum growth when capital is non-transferable. *Review of Economic Studies* 36(1), January, 77–88.

Domar, E.D. 1957. *Essays in the Theory of Economic Growth.* New York and Oxford: Oxford University Press.

Rao, C.R. 1973. Prasanta Chandra Mahalanobis. In *Biographical Memoirs of the Fellows of the Royal Society* 19, 445–92, London: The Royal Society.

Stoleru, L.G. 1965. An optimal policy for economic growth. *Econometrica* 33, April, 321–48.

Malthus's Theory of Population

D.R. WEIR

It is often said that Malthus was a better historian than prophet. He would be disappointed in that verdict because his intention in formulating his Theory of Population was to create a scientific basis for predicting the future state of mankind, in opposition to the speculations of utopian writers, especially Godwin. His failure to predict the Industrial Revolution is the evidence most often brought against him. But even with the benefit of hindsight, economic historians today still find it difficult to predict the Industrial Revolution from its antecedents. The crucial contribution of Malthus's theory was not its pessimism about innovation but rather its prediction of the demographic consequences of technological change and the inevitable effect of population on the standard of living. Malthus's Theory of Population continues to influence economic thought from popular discussion to policy-making, to model-building – long after many of its classical contemporaries, like the labour theory of value, have passed from the scene.

This essay will focus on the population side of Malthus's theory. We begin with a distillation of his ideas into a simple model in the modern sense of the term. Our intention is not to treat in detail all the nuanced and sometimes contradictory aspects of Malthus's writing. The *Essay on Population*, first published in 1798, was revised six times before the final seventh edition was published in 1872, some 38 years after his death. The model used here aims to portray the most essential and durable aspects of the theory. It also provides an organizational framework for discussing the evidence for and against its predictions from time periods both before and after Malthus wrote.

THE MODEL. Figure 1 portrays the essential elements of Malthusian equilibrium. There are three curves, representing three functional relationships. In the first panel is an aggregate production function showing the standard of living (or real wage, or income per capita) produced by a population of a given size. Its main feature is diminishing returns to labour – a tenet of classical economics not unique to Malthus. The second panel describes demographic behaviour. Mortality

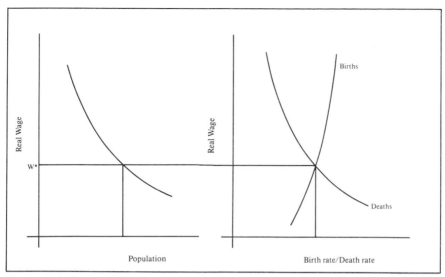

Figure 1   Malthusian equilibrium

(here, the crude death rate, which is the number of deaths per 1,000 persons) rises as the standard of living falls. This is the positive check. Fertility (here, the crude birth rate) falls as the standard of living falls. This is the preventive check. Population grows when births exceed deaths and falls when deaths exceed births. A rising population lowers the standard of living (through the production function), which in turn raises mortality and lowers fertility, eventually bringing population growth to a halt. Equilibrium in this simple version of the model is attained at zero population growth. At that point, wages do not change, and consequently the birth and death rates do not change. The equilibrium is stable, since any disturbance sets in motion compensating changes.

The stability of the equilibrium is the source of Malthusian pessimism. Imagine an expansion of land area for cultivation. The production function would shift out, raising the standard of living for the current population. Fertility would rise and mortality fall; population growth would continue to devour the gains until the wage fell to its original level. Demographic behaviour is the forge of the Iron Law of Wages. Permanent change in the standard of living can arise only from restraint of fertility (a lower birth at each wage) or a worsening of mortality (more deaths at each wage).

The smooth curves drawn above describe the long-run tendencies as envisaged by Malthus. He saw the process of adjustment, however, as anything but smooth. Population growth would tend to overshoot the equilibrium. The positive check, working through disasters like major famines or disease, would be slow to respond but would then overadjust when it did, setting off a new cycle. Malthus offered no specifics on the periodicity or amplitude of the cycle, only the prediction of oscillations around a long-run equilibrium level.

THE EVIDENCE. In discussing in detail the component parts of the model, there are three aspects of each to be considered. First is the evolution of Malthus's own ideas on the functional relationship; second, the historical evidence for or against it; and third, its relevance to the major economic and demographic transformations of the last two centuries. The importance of empirical verification was strongly emphasized by Malthus himself. Criticizing the utopians, Malthus wrote:

> A writer may tell me that he thinks man will ultimately become an ostrich. I cannot properly contradict him. But before he can expect to bring any reasonable person over to his opinion, he ought to show that the necks of mankind have been gradually elongating, that the lips have grown harder and more prominent, that the legs and feet are daily altering their shape, and that the hair is beginning to change into stubs of feathers (Malthus, 1798).

Much of the work of the later editions of the *Essay on Population* was devoted to amassing evidence on the Principle of Population at work.

A central problem with using this or any other equilibrium framework to explain co-variations in economic and demographic variables (across time or space), or with using empirical observations to 'test' the model, is the identification of exogenous shocks as distinct from endogenous responses. Malthus himself was vaguely aware of the problem as early as the first edition of his *Essay*. David Hume, noting the early age at marriage of women in China, had deduced that the population must as a consequence be very large. Malthus, taking age at marriage as endogenous rather than exogenous, concluded that the population must on the contrary be rather small and wages relatively high to induce such early marriage.

MORTALITY. Malthus gave to mortality's response to wages the name 'positive' check because it was certain and unavoidable once population had grown too large. Fertility offered a 'preventive' check in the sense that if low fertility held back the growth of population, the mortality response could be postponed.

Malthus envisaged two modes of action for the positive check. Associated with declining wages would be increasing 'misery and vice'. Misery and vice included some conditions that would raise mortality as well as lower mortality. This would yield a smooth continuous relationship like that in the diagram. The second mode of action would be sudden mortality crises to greatly reduce a population in a year or two. To put it in modern terms, the probability of a mortality crisis or any given magnitude should increase as the standard of living falls. The expected value of the death rate would show the smooth relationship to wages pictured above. Actual events would be much less regular. Adjustment to equilibrium was inevitable but not constant.

Historical studies of the positive check have approached it from two very different perspectives. One sort examines great crises to determine whether they resulted from population pressure. The other attempts to specify the extent of population pressure on resources over time and look for mortality consequences.

The Black Death of 1347 and 1348 killed between one-third and one-half of Europe's population in a single massive epidemic of bubonic plague. Hatcher (1977) concludes for England that the Black Death was 'not Malthusian', by which he means not a response to population pressure. Evidence abounds that population had been growing: rents and the relative price of basic foods had been rising for two centuries or more. There had been major famines in the 1320s. The 'anti-Malthusian' conclusion is based on the absence of a logical connection between standard of living and the scale of epidemic bubonic plague and on the fact that the mortality response was disproportionate to the population pressure. Economic responses to the Black Death were clearly Malthusian (Hatcher, 1977, pp. 101–94). It is certainly consistent with the subtler Malthus to find that an induced (endogenous) mortality response would overreact and become an exogenous disturbance driving population below its equilibrium. The study of a single episode cannot determine whether the probability of its occurrence was raised by the economic conditions preceding it. The persistence of the plague and continued population declines of the next century or more, clearly were not a consequence of the improved standard of living after the first outbreak.

Half a millenium later the Irish Potato Famine provided a tragic forum for debate over the new Malthusian ideas. Mokyr (1983) traces reliance on the potato to population pressure, through the unique funnel of Irish institutions. As was the case with the plague, the element of chance looms large in the timing and location of the potato blight itself. Unlike the Black Death, however, the means were available to alleviate the heavy mortality consequences. One wonders what might have been the fate of the Irish had not English policy-makers of the 1840s been educated in the science of Malthus's Theory of Population.

The main supporting evidence for the positive check comes from the study of subsistence crises: short-run mortality increases following harvest failures. Meuvret (1946) drew attention to the close association of grain prices and deaths in specific incidents in France. Subsequent studies have shown a regular statistical association over long periods in several countries. Improved marketing and production methods appear to have been successful in nearly eliminating the relationship in England by the end of the 16th century and in France by the middle of the 18th century.

Since Malthus wrote, life expectancy has increased from well under 40 to well over 70 in most of the now developed world. Since the standard of living has also increased, it would appear that Malthus's theory of mortality has been a better prediction that it was a description of prior history. Some scepticism on that point is voiced by Preston (1976), who finds that life expectancy across countries is not closely related to their level of per capita income at any point in time. He concludes that medical and public health technology are more important than income. Since medical technology may well be a function of per capita income in the leading country, or in the average of leading countries, his finding may indicate only that Malthus no longer applies within national boundaries.

There is, in sum, only limited evidence of the income–mortality relation postulated by Malthus. Evidence abounds that most of the variation in mortality cannot be accounted for by so simple a framework.

FERTILITY. In the first edition of the *Essay on Population* Malthus claimed that 'passion between the sexes was necessary and will remain nearly in its present state'; that is, that fertility was roughly constant and did not vary with living standards. On our diagram, the fertility curve would be vertical. He subsequently advocated delayed marriage as a check to population growth. Being a vicar of the Anglican Church, he condemned both contraception and never-marrying as 'vice'. It is one of the greatest misattributions in human history that associates the name of Malthus with the birth-control movements of the late 19th century. Nevertheless, since fertility restraint offers the only means of raising both the standard of living and length of life within his system, it is not surprising that those who believed his model but not his morals would eventually invoke his science to promote their cause.

The evidence for endogenous fertility responses is growing but is not yet convincing. Wrigley and Schofield (1981) find that long-run trends in English fertility followed long-run trends in real wages from 1541 to 1871. The lag, however, was 40 years, and the two moved in opposite directions for approximately 140 of the 330 years. Moreover, in England, as in the rest of early modern Europe, age at marriage and fertility within marriage were fairly constant, leaving changes in proportions ever-married as the main source of changes in English fertility before the Industrial Revolution (Weir, 1984).

The greatest failure of Malthus's Theory of Population is in explaining the fertility transition from high, mostly uncontrolled fertility within marriage to modern low fertility. The process began first in France at the time Malthus was writing. Parts of the United States and Hungary also began at about that time. The rest of Europe followed sometime between 1870 and 1914. In no case was the long-run downward trend in fertility caused by a downward trend in national income. In today's developing countries fertility decline has sometimes been induced by policy measures without economic development, but sustained economic growth continues to be a prescription for contraception.

Neoclassical theories of fertility, as in the work of Becker (1981), salvage Malthus's theory as an income effect in a model of the demand for children. Substitution effects from a rising price of children relative to other consumption goods may be a more important determinant of fertility trends during development, overwhelming the income effect. Such a model does help explain why the Malthusian model seems to explain cyclical fluctuations in fertility both before (Lee, 1981) and after (Easterlin, 1973) the fertility transition. Relative prices may not fluctuate as much as income. Marx, a harsh critic of Malthus, would not be surprised. He claimed that Malthus's laws of population were specific to the particular mode of production of pre-industrial Europe. Other modes of production would have other modes of reproduction. Unfortunately, he left no better guide to predicting the changes than did Malthus.

It is perhaps ironic that Malthus's Theory of Population, conceived as a prediction of long-run equilibrium, should be consistent with short-run fluctuations but not with long-run movements. Humankind has not reached the idyllic state anticipated by Malthus's utopian adversaries. Neither have we fulfilled Malthusian predictions. The separation of reproduction from 'passion between the sexes' has led the wealthiest of nations to fertility below the level needed to replace their populations while in the poorest of nations great numbers of children are born into short lives of poverty. Theories of population must acknowledge their debt to Malthus and move on.

BIBLIOGRAPHY

Becker, G.S. 1981. *A Treatise on the Family*. Cambridge, Mass.: Harvard University Press.

Easterlin, R.A. 1973. Relative economic status and the American fertility swing. In *Family Economic Behaviour: Problems and Prospects*, ed. E.B. Sheldon, Philadelphia: J.B. Lippincott.

Hatcher, J. 1977. *Plague, Population, and the English Economy, 1348–1530*. London: Cambridge University Press.

Lee, R.D. 1981. Short-term variation: vital rates, prices, and weather. In Wrigley and Schofield (1981), ch. 9.

Malthus, T.R. 1798. *An Essay on the Principle of Population, as it affects the future improvement of society. With remarks on the speculations of Mr. Godwin, M. Condorcet, and other writers*. Harmondsworth: Penguin, 1970; 7th edn, New York: Kelley, 1970.

Meuvret, J. 1946. Les crises des subsistances et la démographie de la France de l'Ancien Régime. *Population* 1(4), November, 643–50.

Mokyr, J. 1983. *Why Ireland Starved*. London: Allen & Unwin.

Preston, S.H. 1976. *Mortality Patterns in National Populations*. New York: Academic Press.

Weir, D.R. 1984. Rather never than late: celibacy and age at marriage in English cohort fertility, 1541–1871. *Journal of Family History* 9(4), Winter, 340–54.

Wrigley, E.A. and Schofield, R. 1981. *The Population History of England, 1541–1871: A Reconstruction*. Cambridge, Mass.: Harvard University Press.

Marketing Boards

PETER BAUER

With trivial exceptions, marketing boards for agricultural products fall into two distinct categories: first, boards endowed by government with monopoly power in the sale of controlled products; second, marketing boards similarly endowed with monopsony power in the purchase of controlled products. The former function mainly in advanced countries, the latter in certain poor countries.

I. To be effective, monopolistic action in a particular country requires official support and enforcement because of the multiplicity of producers of standardized commodities and the availability of imports. Without such support, agricultural markets approximate the model of perfect competition of the textbooks.

Concerted action to raise farm prices was often tried during the interwar period, and occasionally even earlier. These attempts failed because of incomplete market control. In the early 1930s, farm prices declined sharply, partly as a result of the expansion of capacity, and partly as a result of the depression. Under the influence of political pressure and because of social considerations, many governments wished to arrest the decline of farm prices and incomes. In many instances fiscal considerations were thought to preclude direct subsidies. Again, prohibition or control of competing imports was of no avail to producers of some important perishable commodities such as liquid milk and main crop potatoes. State supported or organized monopolies, termed marketing boards, were among the instruments introduced for maintaining or raising farm prices and incomes in a politically and administratively practicable and politically painless manner. The boards set up under the British Agricultural Marketing Acts of 1931 and 1933 are examples of marketing boards effectively controlled by producer representatives (Astor and Rowntree, 1938; Bauer, 1948; Warley, 1967).

The methods used by marketing boards to raise returns to producers include the following: acreage restriction (as with hops and potatoes); direct or indirect restriction of the amounts producers may market (as with potatoes); and the exercise of discriminating monopoly power, with higher prices in sheltered

232

markets and lower prices in exposed markets (in milk, the liquid market and the market for processed products respectively).

The raising prices and farm incomes are the objectives and principal effects of these marketing boards. Some other features of these boards and their operations may be of greater interest than this banal result. (a) The acreage restrictions under the potato and hops schemes conferred windfall profits on the owners of land that had quotas attached to it. (b) The boards encouraged and supported cartels of processors and distributors, and also minimum resale and retail prices for the controlled commodities. These arrangements, an example that monopoly breeds monopoly, were *prima facie* surprising since they reduced the share of the prices paid by consumers that went to the farmers. The reasons behind them may have been a wish to placate distributors and processors, or to benefit the minority of producers who were also retailers. But it appears that the Milk and Potato Boards, at any rate, were also misled by inappropriate analogy with those manufacturers of branded goods who were practising resale price maintenance. (c) The boards, established to assist farmers at the time of a sharp fall in prices and incomes, were retained, and new ones created, in radically different postwar conditions – an example of the self-perpetuating character of organizations established by governments. (d) The system involved decisions at two levels, namely the boards and the individual producers. The former were faced with sloping demand curves. In the absence of production or marketing quotas, the individual producer faced a horizontal demand curve. With such quotas, the producer faced a demand curve which was horizontal up to the assigned quota and then became vertical (or nearly so).

II. Marketing boards of the second type by statute have the sole rights to buy the designated produce for exports. During World War II, marketing boards of this type were set up in the former British West African colonies for cocoa, palm oil, palm kernels and groundnuts, and subsequently for cotton. The produce was bought for the boards by merchants as their agents. During the war and early postwar years these agents bought the controlled produce for export on the basis of official quotas calculated according to their prewar performance. Agents who exceeded their quotas paid large penalties to those who had underbought, the settlement being effected through the boards. The declared purpose of these arrangements was to prevent a collapse in the local price of cocoa (feared because of shortage of shipping and the closure of major outlets, notably Germany), and to encourage the exports of the other crops (required by the loss of Far Eastern supplies).

These arrangements were anomalous. The British Government in any case had undertaken to purchase the entire exportable output at seasonally fixed prices, so that the market available to local producers was unlimited at those prices. Monopsony of export and the imposition of buying quotas were unnecessary to maintain the local prices of cocoa, and deterred the production and exports of the other crops. The statutory monopsony *cum* quota system had been proposed in 1939 by a trade association of the major West African merchants. The quota system in effect provided statutory enforcement for their restrictive prewar marketing sharing agreements, which had limited success both because of breaches of the agreements and also because of the entry of new competitors. Buying quotas are easier to enforce where is only a single official buyer, and where over-buying is effectively penalized by that buyer. The boards also did not admit new buying agents.

In the early postwar years the quota system was abandoned in the face of its unpopularity with influential local interests and of pressure by competitors. State export monopsony was, however, retained. It was also extended to other British colonies in Africa and also to Burma. The system was continued by the governments of the new independent successor states.

The principal reason advanced officially for maintaining state export monopsony was the need for stabilization in the sense of shielding producers from the damaging effects of short-period price fluctuations. Subsidiary reasons included the usefulness of maintaining and adapting the peacetime purposes organizations established during the war; and also the impossibility of returning to the many thousands of unregistered small-scale producers the large surpluses already accumulated by the boards. The latter explanations were transparent rationalizations for self-perpetuation. Thus, if it were true that the surpluses accumulated during the war by the boards could not be returned to the producers whose output had yielded the surpluses, this would be true equally of the accumulations of the successor organizations.

According to the British Government White Paper, *Statement on the Future Marketing of West African Cocoa*, Cmnd 6950, 1946, the Cocoa Marketing Boards would prescribe seasonally fixed producer prices each year, thereby cutting the link between fluctuating world market prices and local producer prices. When world prices were high the board would make a surplus, with which it would support producer prices when market prices were low. In this way prices received by producers would be stabilized. The Cocoa White Paper stated emphatically that the board would not use its powers to underpay producers systematically and to build up increasing surpluses. The boards would act as agents and trustees for the producers, and would on no account become instruments of taxation in effect. Similar promises were made for other controlled crops.

These explicit and categoric pledges were soon broken. From their inception, the marketing boards have paid producers much less than the realized market prices. The level of taxation represented by the boards' policies has varied from time to time, and varied also between different crops. But for most products it has been extremely severe. The boards have withheld vast sums from the producers. Killick (1965) calculated that from 1939 to 1961 (when the Ghana Cocoa Marketing Boards ceased to publish annual reports) out of net export proceeds of £805 million, about £357 million, or 44 per cent was withheld from producers. For all Nigerian marketing boards the corresponding figures from 1939 to 1962 were about £1096 million and £301 million, that is, about 27 per cent (Helleiner, 1964). Reliable series are not available for more recent years, but substantial underpayment of producers has continued, especially the systematic underpayment of producers by the board in Ghana. (These calculations appropriately include the proceeds of local and export taxes, which served to siphon off directly part of the boards' surpluses.) For years on end, producers with very small annual cash incomes were taxed at rates applicable only to taxpayers in the highest income brackets in the UK. On the other hand, people with incomes far higher than those of the producers paid little or no direct taxes, and were indeed often directly subsidized by the funds of the marketing boards.

The incidence of this taxation was practically wholly on the producers. West African exports of vegetable oils and oil seeds and cotton are a very small part of world supplies, so that world prices are not affected by the boards' activities. Cocoa exports from Nigeria and Gold Coast Ghana were about 50–60 per cent of the world exports in the later 1930s, but had declined to 25–30 per cent by the early 1980s as a result of the decline of exports from Gold Coast Ghana and the expansion of supplies elsewhere. Indeed, the systematic underpayment of producers has contributed to the decline of cocoa exports from Ghana, the virtual cessation of new cocoa plantings, and the decline in exports of palm produce from Nigeria. There was some smuggling of cocoa from Ghana to the neighbouring countries where prices were higher. But the distance of some of the principal producing areas from the frontiers, the activities of armed frontier guards, and the bulky nature of the crop made smuggling difficult. The dearth of consumer goods in the cocoa areas in recent decades also suggests that smuggling was rather restricted. There was no scope for smuggling palm oil and palm kernels out of Nigeria. The decline of exports was the result of several factors, among which the underpayment of producers was almost certainly the most important.

Two sets of influences were behind the development of the marketing boards into instruments of taxation. The first was the difference in political effectiveness between the boards and the farmers. The boards were directed and administered first by British officials, and after independence by African politicians and officials. These groups have been much more powerful and articulate than the farmers; and the underpayment of producers suited their political and personal interests. The British civil servants derived prestige from the surpluses of the boards. Since independence, the reserves and revenues of the boards have served as financial power base for African politicians. Through the boards they have the power to tax producers and prescribe their living standards. They also have the power to license processors and buying agents. These powers have been a major factor in politicizing life and exacerbating political conflict in countries where export monopsonies have operated.

The policies of the marketing boards is a conspicuous instance of the disparity in political effectiveness between the urban political elites and the unorganized and inarticulate rural population. The former largely control the political and administrative machinery, the media, and usually also key elements in the military. This discrepancy in political effectiveness is a familiar feature of the scene in less developed countries, and is especially pronounced in Africa. In West Africa, notably Ghana and Southern Nigeria, the position of the urban political elites and their associates in the military, in the civil service, the media and in business, was reinforced by the removal of power and influence from the traditional tribal chiefs towards the end of colonial rule and in the early years of independence.

The second factor in the transformation of the marketing boards was the vagueness of the concept of stabilization, and the prevalence of simplistic notions about it.

Arising from the operation of the West African marketing boards, an extended academic discussion took place on issues in price or income stabilization for primary producers. This was initiated by Bauer and Paish (1952) and concluded by Helleiner (1964). In order to prevent price stabilization becoming the cloak for taxation, Bauer and Paish proposed a formula for setting producer prices by the boards which would smooth fluctuations while ensuring maintenance of contact with the trend of market prices, and thereby would clearly distinguish the smoothing of fluctuations from other objectives of policy. This article elicited several critical replies, the most significant by Friedman (1954). He argued that compulsory smoothing, even with a clearly defined formula to ensure maintenance with the trend, was unwarranted, as individual producers could always save part of their incomes in prosperity and draw on reserves in adversity. Friedman's article was an early application of his permanent income hypothesis. He also drew attention to various other disadvantages of compulsory smoothing schemes.

Bauer subsequently modified his position, partly in response to Friedman's position, and partly on the ground that in less developed countries a compulsory smoothing scheme was always liable to develop into an instrument of taxation, even in the face of specific assurances to the contrary. In fact, he and Yamey explained how a voluntary stabilization scheme could operate for small-scale agricultural producers (Bauer and Yamey, 1968).

Bauer and Paish (1952) also drew attention to major ambiguities in the concept of stabilization. Thus, stabilization can refer to money prices, money incomes, real prices or real incomes. It can mean the establishment of maximum or minimum prices or incomes. To be meaningful, the concept needs to make clear the period over which a stabilization policy is to balance surpluses and disbursements. It needs to make clear whether numerous small changes represent more or less stability than a smaller number of large discontinuous changes. The relation between open market prices and producer prices also has to be clarified.

Unless these ambiguities are resolved, stabilization becomes an empty omnibus expression, susceptible to widely different and conflicting interpretations, all of which can be invoked in support of any policy by an official monopsony. These ambiguities are exacerbated when there is a long-period tendency for prices to rise, as there has been in West African export prices since the war: the higher are the prices, the larger become the amounts necessary to maintain them at a given level, so that a particular accumulated reserve appears (or can be made to appear) to be insufficient as a reserve, and this then provides superficial justification for further accumulation of surpluses.

To have brought into the open the ambiguities of the concept of stabilization and the difficulties and dangers of price stabilization in practice may have been the most useful outcome of the protracted academic discussion about the West African Marketing Boards.

BIBLIOGRAPHY

Astor, Viscount and Rowntree, B.S. 1938. *British Agriculture.* London: Longmans & Co.

Bauer, P.T. 1948. A review of the agricultural marketing schemes. *Economica* 15, May, 132–50.

Bauer, P.T. 1954. *West African Trade.* Cambridge: Cambridge University Press. Revised edn, London: Routledge & Kegan Paul, 1963.

Bauer, P.T. and Paish, F.W. 1952. The reduction of fluctuations in the incomes of primary producers. *Economic Journal* 62, December. Reprinted in Bauer and Yamey (1968).

Bauer, P.T. and Yamey, B.S. 1968. *Markets, Market Control and Marketing Reform: Selected Papers.* London: Weidenfeld & Nicolson.

Friedman, M. 1954. The reduction of fluctuations in the incomes of primary producers: a critical comment. *Economic Journal* 64, December, 698–703.

Helleiner, G.K. 1964. The fiscal role of the marketing boards in Nigerian economic development, 1947–1961. *Economic Journal* 74, September, 582–610.

Killick, A.T. 1966. The economics of cocoa. In W. Birmingham, I. Neustadt and E.N. Omaboe, *A Study of Contemporary Ghana*: Vol. I, *The Economy of Ghana*, London: George Allen & Unwin.

Report of the Committee Appointed to Review the Working of the Agricultural Marketing Acts. 1947. Ministry of Agriculture and Fisheries, Economic Series No. 48, London: HMSO.

Statement on the Future Marketing of West African Cocoa. 1946. Colonial Office, Cmd. 6950, London: HMSO.

Warley, T.K. 1967. A synoptic view of agricultural marketing organizations in the United Kingdom. In *Agricultural Producers and their Markets*, ed. T.K. Warley, Oxford: Oxford University Press.

Market Places

POLLY HILL

It is usual to follow the *Final Report* of the British Royal Commission on Market Rights and Tolls (1891) by defining a market place as an 'authorized public concourse of buyers and sellers of commodities, meeting at a place more or less strictly limited or defined, at an appointed time', and to regard fairs, which meet far less frequently (commonly annually for a number of days in succession), as different types of assembly. While this definition broadly satisfies present purposes, some qualifications and additional emphases are required. First, the commodities (wares) must be on view so that corn exchanges and the like (and certainly stock exchanges) are disqualified; second, sellers must be quite numerous in relation to buyers, which disqualifies supermarkets as well as the small gatherings of women foodstuff vendors which are such a familiar feature of the West African scene; third, markets last for no longer than a day (or sometimes an evening), so that they constantly open and close; fourth, regular periodicity, which is most commonly based on the recognized local 'market week', is a fundamental feature; fifth, services (such as bicycle repair, food cooking or barbering) as well as commodities may be on offer; sixth, auction yards, as such, are disqualified, though sales by auction are not unknown in certain specialized market places; seventh, market places are 'public' concourses in the sense that potential buyers or onlookers may enter freely, not because they are necessarily publicly owned; eighth, taxation of sellers is usual, by means of tolls (on wares) or stall-rents; and ninth, it is the activities of the various participants (their organization) which defines the market, despite the usual emphasis on 'place'.

Traditionally, economists have displayed little interest in market places, as distinct from market principles, having condescendingly passed the subject to economic historians – see the entry on 'Market as Place of Sale' in the 1925 edition of *Palgrave's Dictionary of Political Economy*; their disdain has now become absolute in the sense that their exceedingly numerous publications on 'marketing' never include the 'place' in their indexes. This is odd since market places, especially those handling livestock or wholesaling meat, fish, vegetables

238

and other natural produce, are far from being defunct institutions in Europe; but the function of European retail markets is now so petty relative to that in the time of Samuel Pepys (when the only food shops in central London were grocers and bakers), and is so inherently uninteresting compared to that of the market place systems of the less developed world, that Europe is here ignored. (As for the United States, market places were always unimportant there.)

No disdain for history is implied by such an approach since many non-Western market place are very ancient. Cortés himself reported on the market place of Tenochtitlan, the capital city of the Aztecs, where 60,000 traders were said to assemble daily, the organization being generally familiar to Spaniards. Then, Ibn Battuta provided evidence for the existence of considerable market places over a large area of the Western Sudan in the mid-14th century; Pieter de Marees noted that every town on the Gold Coast in 1600 had its appointed market day; and in the mid-17th century Djenne, on the upper reaches of the Niger river, was accounted one of the great market places of the Muslim world. As for late Imperial China, the anthropologist G.W. Skinner (1964, p. 5) emphasizes that the regularities in central-place hierarchies there had evolved over many centuries; his analysis of hierarchical market place systems (1964, 1965, 1977) is uniquely monumental.

Fortunately, two massive bibliographies testify to the importance of non-Western markets. These are Fröhlich (1940) on African markets, which lists 406 titles including much reference material of historical interest; and the three-part series of publications on world market places and fairs, in the major European languages, which has been issued by the International Geographical Union (1977, 1979, 1985) – it has now been discontinued. Although the latter series includes a fair number of titles on marketing rather than market places; and although some items are included more than once under different geographical headings – it is significant that no fewer than 45 per cent of the 2155 entries in the two earlier issues relate to the four regions of West Africa, Middle America, South Asia and the Andean Republics. West Africa with 418 titles (19 per cent) is much the best documented region.

But the degree of documentation is not an entirely reliable indicator of the significance of market place which may happen to go unstudied in some regions. Possibly the most remarkable area of neglect is the Indian sub-continent, for it is only during the past few years that it has begun to seem likely that rural periodic market places there have long been much more important than the very unimpressive literature would suggest. It seems that in their intense preoccupation with land revenue systems the officials of the British Raj overlooked both market places and marketing generally, thus accurately reflecting the interests of contemporary economists whom they found so influential; and it is certain that independent India still remains firmly wedded to the former British approach, as in so many other socio-economic contexts affecting the countryside. In West Africa, on the other hand, where colonial administrations had been so fleeting and unimpressive compared to the Raj, and where anthropologists and travellers had long found market places fascinating, the end of colonialism was associated with an indigenous flowering of new-style historical studies, and modern research on market places has a thoroughly satisfying historical base (see Meillassoux, 1971). Nor did the deplorable 'Polanyi debate', an aberration which suddenly flourished in the 1960s, have any lasting influence there; Karl Polanyi knew little of the organization of pre-colonial West African economies and his basic notion that uncontrolled exchange in the market place was peculiar to 19th- and 20th-century industrialism seemed preposterous in a region where ordinary farmers had commonly bought chattel-slaves in public markets, for cash, in the 19th century and earlier.

Soon after geographers became the dominant students of Third World market places in the late 1960s, they began to search (as all intellectual leaders must) for a single theory of periodic marketing (R.H.T. Smith, 1978). But their search was in vain, for the functions of large rural periodic market places, which are the mainstay of all marketing systems, are very variable, both within and between regions. In some regions, most notably in late Imperial China, there is strict hierarchical ordering of market places of several levels, in accordance with the importance of their wholesaling function, grand city markets being the invariable apices. But Skinner was wrong in supposing (1964, p. 3) that the glorious structures he described were 'characteristic of the whole class of civilizations known as "peasant" or "traditional agrarian" societies', for in West Africa, for instance, the most important market in a region might be situated in the open countryside, serving as a link between ecological zones, and there is not necessarily any close association between the 'level' of a market and the size of the settlement (if any) where it is situated. Owing to its vast size and to the exceptional longevity and stability of its society, China is typical only of itself. Elsewhere there has not necessarily yet been time for the population to distribute itself so appropriately in terms of central-place theory. Only a Sinologist could assert that a close relationship between population density and crop yields is 'virtually axiomatic' in traditional agrarian societies (Skinner, 1977, p. 283).

However, the basic distinction between rural periodic market places and daily markets *is* generally useful: the latter are always situated in cities or large towns and include a fair proportion of specialist traders who occupy permanent stalls or selling positions on most days; the former always include a considerable element of cultivators, or their wives, who sell their own produce – people who are also apt to be customers themselves, but who would not have time to come to market daily.

Christaller's central-place theory, involving the drawing of hexagons, certainly had much better application to late Imperial China than to its native Germany and this may be generally true of many developing regions where the strict assumptions on which is is based, among them a flat and featureless topography, are sufficiently satisifed: but despite the best efforts of the geographers, it is too early to be sure. Of course temporal as well as spatial factors have much exercised the geographers. But the debate as to whether, for example, the four-day market week is the 'mother' of the eight-day week or *vice versa* continues to be unresolved. Skinner contended (see Hill, 1966) that market intensification in response to population growth always involves a reduction, usually a halving, in the length of the market week; Fröhlich's hypothesis was the converse, for he held that existent markets made way for new ones by lengthening their market schedules. Most writers consider that market weeks (which in any district are usually uniformly three, four, five, six, seven, eight or ten days long, though alternate-day markets occasionally occur) are economic rather than calendrical in origin, but this idea does not get us very far. Considering the widespread introduction of the European seven-day week for commercial and educational purposes, the persistence of non-seven-day market weeks in many parts of such regions as West Africa is most interesting.

Governmental attitudes to periodic market places vary greatly. In Mexico City they are said to be a well-established component of the retail structure, despite official efforts to eliminate them. In Papua New Guinea, by contrast, officialdom is endeavouring to introduce them for the first time. Indian planners emphasize the significance of urban regulated markets and despise the indigenous rural institutions, though their attitude must soon change. Kenya and Tanzania are presumably somewhat ashamed of the rarity of non-coastal markets until this century. Skinner reports (1965, p. 371) on the disastrous and unsuccessful attempt to dispense with markets in China in the late 1950s. As for city markets, everyone is apt to deplore the lack of storage facilities and the insanitary conditions in so many of them.

All attempts to formulate general theories on the relationship between market places and long-distance trading, whether or not involving caravans, are bound to fail. In some regions caravans link market places while in others they avoid them, if only because their transport-animals require adequate grazing – besides, they are themselves mobile markets following established routes. As for long-distance lorry-borne traders, they may avoid markets altogether, perhaps because they pick up their heavy loads of plantains or yams at the farms and sell them from urban sheds or lorry parks. By neglecting such considerations the geographers have strait-jacketed market studies and introduced false notions of urban-rural continua.

In earlier times when anthropologists, not geographers, ruled the roost, more emphasis was apt to be placed on the political, religious, recreational, sociological and other non-economic aspects of market places. But, again, there is much variation. In one region the market is the anonymous, safe, kinless, area where men and maidens meet; in another, Islam forbids the nubile woman from displaying her covered body there.

The geographers' emphasis on space and time neglects the actors (the customers, trader, onlookers – many of them children) who bring the market to life. Their predecessors, the anthropologists, painted colourful descriptive pictures of the people and their wares, but few of them examined the traders as economic men or women, perhaps the most notable exception being S.W. Mintz in his numerous publications on Caribbean and Latin American traders. It is generally agreed that the sellers of any commodity, who in certain important regions are mainly women, arrange themselves in clumps in the market place, and that they commonly endeavour, usually unsuccessfully, to 'fix' the prices of potentially quantifiable wares on any particular day. Although competition is usually so pronounced that price-rigging is impracticable, the frequency of 'regular customer' relationships means that it is apt to be imperfect; besides, everyone knows that the standard measures (there is seldom any weighing) are commonly suspect – as in some southern Ghanaian markets where all the kerosene tins used for measuring maize have false bottoms inserted by blacksmiths working openly in the market.

The organization of cattle markets is exceptionally interesting, especially in West Africa; the indigenous systems involving landlords and brokers, who accommodate the traders and facilitate trading with the help of credit, may best be studied there; see Hill (1985).

One 'Polanyi-supporter' has affirmed that 'for most of history' man has lived with fixed-price markets, non-price-making market places and perhaps mostly with economic systems whose essential character must be established independently of orthodox economic theory. Maybe... but such a period was the stone age of market place studies.

BIBLIOGRAPHY

Fröhlich, W. 1940. Das afrikanische Marktwesen. *Zeitschrift für Ethnologie.* (An English translation was published in 1982 by the International Geographical Union.)

Hill, P. 1966. Notes on traditional market authority and market periodicity in West Africa. *Journal of African History* 7(2), 295–311.

Hill, P. 1985. *Indigenous Trade and Market Places in Ghana 1962–4.* Jos Oral History and Literature Texts, University of Jos, Nigeria.

International Geographical Union. 1977, 1979, 1985. *Periodic Markets, Daily Markets and Fairs: a Bibliography.* 1st 2 issues ed. R.J. Bromley, University College of Swansea; last issue ed. W. McKim, Towson State University, Maryland.

Meillassoux, C. (ed.) 1971. *The Development of Indigenous Trade and Markets in West Africa.* International African Institute, London: Oxford University Press.

Skinner, G.W. 1964, 1965. Marketing and social structure in rural China. *Journal of Asian Studies,* Pt I, 24(1), November 1964, 3–43; Pt II, 24(2), February 1965, 195–228; Pt III, 24(3), May 1965, 363–99.

Skinner, G.W. (ed.) 1977. *The City in Late Imperial China.* Stanford: Stanford University Press.

Smith, R.H.T. (ed.) 1978. *Periodic Markets, Hawkers and Traders in Africa, Asia and Latin America.* Vancouver: Centre for Transportation Studies, University of British Colombia.

Moneylenders

AMIT BHADURI

The standard practice of moneylending in the unorganized credit market differs from financial intermediation by the commercial banks. Banks operating on the basis of a 'fractional reserve system' hold in cash reserve only a fraction of their total debt obligation to the public. In effect, this becomes the method of creating credit-money by the banks through the so-called 'credit multiplier'. However, there exists no ready counterpart to such credit creation by private moneylenders in the unorganized markets. In principle, a private moneylender with a good reputation for solvency can also create *private* debt obligations in the form of personal promisory notes or I-owe-you's (IOUS). And, the issue of such *private* debt obligations can even be several times the cash in reserve with him, in analogy with the credit multiplier of commercial banking. Although such *private* debt obligations are not uncommon in some less monetized rural areas or in the informal banking sector (coexisting side by side with the formal banks in urban centres) in many underdeveloped countries, the issuing of such private debt obligations must be intrinsically far more restricted in scope for at least three reasons. First, without either a legally stipulated 'cash reserve ratio' or an institutional 'lender of the last resort', private moneylenders have to rely entirely on their personal creditworthiness, in case there develops a sudden 'run' on their debt obligations. Second, *personal* reputation must normally be *spatially* restricted to relatively small areas. In turn, this tends to fragment the unorganized market for credit. Finally, many private moneylenders, especially in the poorer rural areas of underdeveloped countries do *not* act as proper financial *intermediaries*. Instead, as the name suggests, they are primarily lenders of money (usually out of their own savings), but not takers of deposits. And, not being financial intermediaries, the income or profit for this class of moneylenders cannot be explained in terms of the margin of their lending rate over the deposit rate, unlike in the case of commercial banks. This suggests a different mode of operation in terms of the profitability of private moneylending in the unorganized market. For example, the private moneylender must get a *higher* rate of return on the

243

loan he advanced from his personal savings than he could secure from deposits with banks in the organized credit market to make such activities economically worthwhile for him. It is the task of economic theory to explain how this may come about *without* financial intermediation.

Empirical studies abound (see Bhaduri, 1983, ch. 5 for references to Indian field studies; Nisbet, 1967, for Chile; and Tun Wai, 1957–8 for some earlier evidence) to suggest that in many underdeveloped countries, the rate of return on private moneylending is indeed considerably higher than say, the deposit or lending rate offered by banks. Although some economists (e.g. Bottomley, 1975) have tried to explain this in terms of the *lender's* risk margin, any such explanation can be seen to be inadequate from our preceding discussion. The lender's risk margin is supposed to cover the loss of the defaulted fraction of principal lent. According to this view a typical moneylender expects a certain proportion (q) of the total loan he advances to be defaulted and charges a sufficiently high rate of interest (i) on the loan expected to be paid back to him ($1 - q$) to cover his capital loss. In this case, his overall rate of return (r) is more or less the same as the rate of deposit (or the lending rate) with the banks in the organized credit market. This means,

$$(1 - q)(1 + i) = (1 + r) \text{ or,} \qquad i = r + q/(1 - q).$$

Clearly, given $1 > q > 0$, the private money lender's lending rate i would exceed that in the organized market (r) as it also covers the lender's risk margin due to default.

Such a theory starts with the presumption that the rate of return is 'comparatively' equalized between the organized and the unorganized credit market (e.g. at 'r' in the above calculation). It is argued therefore, that even when private moneylenders do *not* operate as financial intermediaries, they in effect earn more or less the same rate of return as the typical financial intermediaries in the organized sector. The assumption underlying is that the organized and the unorganized credit markets are thoroughly integrated. In a similar manner, explanations of higher interest rates on private lending through higher 'administrative cost' of managing such loans or higher transaction cost in general adds analytically nothing new: it is always viewed as a lender's margin over the interest rate in the organized market. Thus, explicitly or implicitly this view relies on the assumption that the organized and unorganized credit markets are integrated.

Empirically, the integration of the organized and the unorganized credit market is open to serious doubt. This is most strikingly brought out by the nearly universal fact that the poorest strata of the peasantry in many underdeveloped countries rely heavily, if not exclusively, on private moneylenders and *not* on sources of institutional finance. Indeed, financial institutions like banks and credit cooperatives typically do not consider them creditworthy. But paradoxically enough, private moneylenders do consider them creditworthy for advancing loans (Bhaduri, 1983, pp. 12–16). This would suggest *lack* of integration between the organized and the unorganized credit market, at least insofar as the criteria for creditworthiness are concerned.

Creditworthiness of a borrower generally (i.e. 'reputation' apart) depends on the collateral securities that he can offer against the loan advanced to him. The typical collateral securities that a very poor peasant can offer, for example already encumbered land, standing crops or his future labour service, do not usually have well-defined market prices. Consequently, they are not acceptable as collateral securities to usual institutional lenders like banks. On the other hand, a *local* village moneylender is willing to accept them as collateral, either because he can make personal use of them (e.g. an agriculturist moneylender may be happy to obtain the use-right of an already encumbered piece of land or the future labour service of a defaulted borrower); or, he can undervalue such collaterals substantially in a loan arrangement. In the latter case, he would indeed make some 'capital gains' in case of default of loan by the borrower, as the undervalued asset gets transferred to him in case of default. This suggests a basic difference in the mode of operation of the organized and the unorganized private credit market. In the organized market, there is risk of capital loss to the lender in case of default. However, in the unorganized market, this risk may be largely avoidable by the lender when he is in a position to sufficiently undervalue the collaterals. Indeed, default would then mean capital gain rather than capital loss to him through the transfer of such undervalued collaterals. And, because the borrower is threatened with possible capital loss in case of default, such loan arrangements can be seen to be characterized by *borrower's rather than lender's risk* (Bhaduri, 1983, ch. 5). Further, in such a loan arrangement, the lender would have a tendency to *induce* default by charging exceptionally high interest rates in order to make capital gains. This can appropriately be described as the method of *usury*, when default induced through high interest charges results in capital gains to the lender. Indeed, most 'pawn-shops' are also known to operate on a similar principle.

The helpless borrower usually goes to the pawn-shop or to the private moneylender in rural areas because he is not considered sufficiently creditworthy to obtain loans in the organized credit market. It should be evident that his helplessness as a borrower is more acute, the more desperately he needs the loan (e.g. consumption loan for survival). Analytically, the more *inelastic* is the borrower's demand function for loan, the more vulnerable he would be to this method of usury described earlier. As a matter of fact, his only defence in the extreme case of totally inelastic demand for loan may simply lie in *deliberately* defaulting, if the interest rate is raised too high by the lender. In that case, he accepts losing his collateral asset instead of trying to meet the high interest charge. However, when his loan demand function is more elastic – for example, he can decide to borrow less if the interest rate is pushed higher or the price of the collateral is pushed lower – the borrower is placed more favourably in terms of bargaining power. In such cases, the lender would *simultaneously* decide what interest rate to charge and what collateral price to offer (Basu, 1984). It is conceivable that the lender would charge a lower interest rate to entice the borrower to take a larger amount of loan; but at the same time, he would also undervalue collaterals in the hope that the borrower would not be able to pay back that larger loan so that the lender would again make capital gains through asset transfers.

BIBLIOGRAPHY

Bhaduri, A. 1983. *The Economic Structure of Backward Agriculture.* London: Academic Press.
Tun Wai, U. 1957–8. Interest rates outside the organized money markets of underdeveloped countries. *IMF Staff Papers* 6, November, 80–142.

Nationalism

SAMIR AMIN

There is a certain ambiguity in words such as nationalism, let alone economic nationalism. Indeed, a distinction must be made between the social reality which determines a nation and the degree of autonomy of States in the world system. A distinction must equally be made between theories concerning the analysis of the world economic system and normative propositions that define strategies of insertion into or confrontation with this system.

The term 'nation' presupposes certain articulations between this reality, real or alleged, and other realities such as the State, the world system of States, the economy and social classes. We currently owe these concepts and their articulation into a system to the different social theories developed in the light of the 19th-century European historical experience. Within this framework the elaboration of two sets of theories took place – as it turned out, in counterpoint to one another: on the one hand, marxism and the theory of the class struggle; on the other, nationalism and the theory of class integration into the democratic bourgeois nation-state. Both theories take account of many aspects of the immediate reality which is marked both by social struggles ending in revolutions, and by struggles between nation-states ending in war. For protagonists of these theories, they have proved to be potent guides to action.

The efficacy of political strategies was, however, dependent upon specific circumstances defined by a coincidence – apparently limited in time and space – between elements: (i) coincidence between the State and another social reality i.e. the nation; (ii) the dominant position of bourgeois nation-states in the world capitalist system and their 'central' (as opposed to marginal) character in our conceptual system; (iii) a degree of worldwide application of the capitalist sytem which led central partners to form 'autocentred' interdependent economic units enjoying a high degree of autonomy vis-à-vis each other.

These circumstances define a possible field for 'national' economic policy. The instruments of this policy – the national centralized monetary system, customs laws, the network of material infrastructures in transport and communications, the unifying effect of a 'national' language, the unified administrative system and so on – enjoy a definite autonomy in relation to the 'constraints' imposed by an economy applied world-wide. Relations between classes, however wrought with conflict, are relegated to and by the national State. In this sense, there exists an average price for the national labour force which is determined by history and by internal social relationships i.e. a national price system that reflects decisive social relationships. In this sense, the 'law of value' assumes a national dimension. True, there is no Great Wall of China to separate these national systems from the world system that they constitute. Internal social relationships are partly dependent upon positions occupied by the national States in question in the world hierarchy. All these are 'central' capitalist economies but are not equally competitive. If social relations permit, these States can improve their position by pursuing coherent national policies. This effectiveness in turn facilitates social compromise and, without 'abolishing the class struggle', puts definite limits to conflicts.

In these circumstances, what is the role of the so-called 'national' reality? *A posteriori* ideology lends an autonomous dimension to the national reality by granting it pre-existence to the State. This in fact seems questionable. For the European bourgeoisie – from the Renaissance to the Enlightenment – appears cosmopolitan rather than narrowly national. This bourgeoisie shares its loyalty between several legitimacies, religious or philosophical convictions, feudal type friendships, but also in service to the State as absolutist monarchy when it appears reasonable to do so. It still remains generally mobile, at ease in the whole of Christendom. As to the peasantry, its loyalty focuses more on the soil and the locality than on the future nation in which it does not yet share culturally nor sometimes even linguistically. But the Nation is progressively created by the absolutist monarchical State, a task which is completed by bourgeois democracy. The regional ethnolinguistic conglomerates under the same King are not 'by nature' destined to become modern European nations: it is only a potentiality.

However, at closer inspection it appears that these circumstances, pervasive but limited in time to the 19th century, are even more limited in space. Around a few 'model' nation-States, the world of the capitalist system – structured by different pasts which in turn lose their legitimacy and efficacy – remains undefined in the light of an uncertain and obscure future.

The problem changes when we quit the limited framework imposed by the central bourgeois nation-states. For this forces us to examine 'regions' more closely whether they are organized into States or not. Regions are peripheral in relation to continuously expanding capitalist reproduction. On this level there is only a central State, i.e. a State which masters external relations and submits them to the logic of autocentred accumulation. On different levels, there are only 'countries', which are administered from outside as colonies or semi-colonies; these appear to be independent but incapable not only of moulding the outside according to their needs but also of avoiding their drift and shaping from outside.

So we are confronted with the problems relating to the specific future of these regions and peripheral States. This future is implied by the worldwide application of capitalism and is based on the thesis of worldwide application of the law of value as an expressioon of value in the productive system. This thesis implies that the labour force has only one value for the whole world system. If this value has to be related to the level of development of productive forces, it follows that this level will be characteristic of the whole world productive system and not of the different national productive systems which progressively lose their reality due to the worldwide application of this system. But the price of the labour force differs from country to country. This price depends on political and social conditions which characterize each national social formation. The more the reproduction of the labour force is partially ensured by a value transfer of non-capitalist market production and non-market production, the less is the price. The formal submission of peripheral non-capitalist modes of production to a global exploitation of capital allows for a higher rate of surplus-value in real capitalist production; this contributes to the heightening of the average level of the rate of surplus-value on a world scale.

Until the end of the 19th century, this worldwide application had led to the integration of only a certain number of basic products in an international rather than worldwide market. This first stage allowed for laws of value with a national content in the framework of constraints imposed by international competition by the embryonic world capitalist law of value. At this stage, social classes were still essentially national classes, defined by social relations formed within the limits of the State. There is thus a conjunction between class struggles and the play of politics which precisely takes place within the framework of the State. From the end of the 19th century until World War II, the internationalization of monopolistic capital went parallel to the international market in basic products. But this stage was characterized by the absence of world hegemony, and monopolies which were constituted on the basis of competing central States operated preferentially in peripheral regions cut out between colonial empires and zones of influence. Due to the absence of the State or its weakness in these peripheral regions, social relations contracted within central national States continued to define the dynamics of capitalist expansion. After World War II, the stage for the worldwide application of the productive processes was elaborated by an explosion of productive systems into segments which the so-called 'transnational' form of enterprise controlled and distributed all over the planet. The hegemony of the United States constituted an adequate framework for this transnationalization.

Henceforth the world dimension of the law of value dominates over its local dimensions. This reality is clearly reflected in economic discourse; the constraint imposed by competitiveness on a world scale is hauntingly evident in speeches by those in power; it is presented as unavoidable; to ignore it is synonymous with a denial of 'progress' and so on .... But by this very fact the State – whether national or not – also loses its efficacy as a place for elaborating strategies that command or modulate capitalist expansion. Since there is no planetary State, the coincidence between conflicts and class compromise on the one hand, and politics on the other hand has disappeared.

However, in general this crises does not affect the different components of the world system to the same extent. Developed capitalist centres such as the United States, Europe and Japan are in the main not threatened by this evolution. Here we must allow for certain differences, since the historical heritage in Europe – which is still divided into separate political States despite the unfinished construction of an economic community – places Europe in a more difficult position than the United States or Japan. This leads to the questioning of American hegemony and of its eventual end, but it does not question the very existence of the Nation-states considered.

The situation is very different at the periphery of the system. Here, at the end of World War II, once political independence had been regained, the bourgeoisie of the Third World nurtured a project for 'national construction in the cadre of global interdependence' which we will characterize here as the 'Bandung Project'. This project can be defined by the following elements: (i) the will to develop productive forces, to diversify production (i.e. to industrialize); (ii) the will to ensure that it is the national State that assumes direction and control of the process; (iii) the belief that 'technical' models constitute given 'neutrals' which can only be reproduced even if they have to be mastered first; (iv) the belief that the process involves no initial popular initiative, but only popular support for State action; (v) the belief that the process is not fundamentally contradictory to participation in trade within the world capitalist system, even if this leads to short-lived conflicts.

The realization of this national bourgeois project by implication meant bringing under control through the State and by the hegemonic national bourgeois class, at least the following processes: (i) control of the reproduction of the labour force; this implies a relatively complete and balanced development so that, for example, local agriculture is capable of delivering products in reasonable quantity and at prices that ensure the valorization of capital essential to this reproduction; (ii) control over national resources; (iii) control over local markets and the capacity to penetrate the world market under competitive conditions; (iv) control over financial circuits thus enabling the centralization of surplus and the orientation of its productive use; (v) control over current technologies at a level of development reached by productive forces. The circumstances surrounding capitalist expansion in the years 1955–1970 have to a certain point favoured the crystallization of this project.

Today it is no longer possible to ignore the shortcomings of such attempts, which have not been able to resist a reversal in favourable circumstances. Agricultural and food crises, external financial debt, mounting technological dependency, fragility in the capacity to resist any future military aggressions, creeping waste in the manner of consumer capitalist models, and their influence in the areas of ideology and culture, are signs of historical limitations to these attempts. Even before the present crises opened the occasion for a 'Western offensive' which could reverse these developments, these shortcomings had already reached an impasse.

This period is now over and the focus in the new world circumstances is centred around the offensive by the capitalist West against the people and nations of the Third World. Here the objective is to subordinate their future evolution to the particularities of a redeployment of transnational capital.

Are these only temporary circumstances which will necessarily be followed by a new dawn of 'national bourgeois' advances? Or are we seeing an historical turning point which will exclude the pursuit of successive national bourgeois attempts such as those that characterized at least a century of our past history?

Our hypothesis is that the contemporary crises marks the end of an epoch; an epoch which in the case of Asia, Africa and Latin America can be called the century of the National Bourgeoisie, in the sense that it has precisely been marked by successive attempts at national bourgeois edification. Our hypothesis is that the Third World bourgeoisie now finally sees its own development in terms of the Comprador subordination imposed upon it by the expansion of transnational capitalism.

The nationalist populist political strategy known as deconnection appears at this junction as a credible future alternative. For the restoration of the Comprador system on a Third World scale is bound to be hampered by the rise of populist movements. In the initial stage, the populist form is not a surprising development since it is undefined and characterized by ambiguous ideologies. It reflects the broad character of a class alliance, in which classes are in turn uncertain of their determination and deprived of autonomy and class consciousness. But this does not exclude it as a potent world disintegrating force which under certain conditions can evolve towards positive crystallizations.

We suggest that these positive crystallizations involve a merging of three conditions. These are, first, a deconnection in the sense of a strict submission of external relations in all areas to the logic of internal choices taken without consideration of criteria relating to world capitalist rationality. Second, a political capacity to operate social reforms in an egalitarian sense. This political capacity is both a condition of deconnection – since existing hegemonic classes have no interest in it – and a possible consequence of deconnection, since this obviously implies a transfer of political hegemony. A deconnection without reform has little change of emerging. If it did emerge under certain economic conditions, it would lead to an impasse. Third, a capacity for absorption and technological invention, without which the acquired autonomy of decision making could not be realized.

Thus defined, the conditions for a positive response to the challenge of history appear severe, and any merging of such conditions seems improbable. In the immediate future, such a possibility seems remote; it may nevertheless appear to be the only reasonable solution.

North–South Economic Relations

RAVI KANBUR

North–South is the title of a book which became popularly known as 'The Brandt Report'. Published in 1980, the book had an immediate impact in terms of popular coverage and appeal. There was a conference of world leaders at Cancun to discuss the report, amidst great publicity. In 1983 there was a follow-up report which received less publicity, and in any case it can be argued that the ardour over North–South relations had cooled somewhat by then. Did the Brandt Report simply introduce a new phrase in international dialogue, or did its achievements go beyond that? In order to answer this question we have to take a step back and consider the nature of North–South economic relations.

Rather as 'the Third World' was used to signal the problems of nations that belonged neither to the developed countries of the West nor to the centrally planned economies of the East, 'North–South' is meant to signal divisions between rich nations and poor nations, in contradistinction to the 'East–West' divide. In fact, the position of the centrally planned economies in the North–South divide is ambiguous. The Brandt Report clearly wished to categorize them with the rich countries of the North, but the centrally planned economies have themselves rejected such a classification, preferring to see the poverty of the South as the result of the imperialist past of the western capitalist countries, with the attendant economic structures that are still argued to be in place today. These reservations on the part of the eastern bloc countries led to considerable discussion in the late 1970s, when a group of developing countries attempted to set an agenda for the achievement of what they termed a 'New International Economic Order'.

Even leaving aside the issues raised by the existence of the centrally planned economies, the economic relations between North and South are complex and manifold. Trade is the most obvious form of economic interaction, but associated with trade are capital flows. In the latter category are private capital flows, including investment by multinational corporations, as well as official flows of aid. The official flows category can be further subdivided into bilateral aid and aid channelled through multilateral agencies. Associated with capital flows is the question of technology transfer and the question of repatriation of profits earned in the South back to the parent company in the North.

The simplest stylized model of North–South trade is one where the South specializes in the production of primary commodities while the North specializes in the production of manufactures. This 'Argentina–England' model has become less significant as many poor countries have diversified their output and their exports to include light manufactures (such as the often referred to success stories of Korea, Taiwan, Hong Kong and Singapore) or even heavy manufactures after a period of import substitution (such as India or Brazil). However, it would nevertheless be true to say that the primary commodities/manufactures divide is the one most analysts use as a framework for thinking about North–South relations. Hence the concern in the Brandt Report with the fluctuations of primary product prices. Schemes to stabilize these prices were given great emphasis before, during and after the period in which the Report came out. UNCTAD's Integrated Program for Commodities was designed to be a major buffer stock scheme to stabilize the prices of several primary commodities. It was argued that demand fluctuations in the North impose a cost in terms of real income variability in the South, and the same was true of uncontrollable climatic factors in the South. Variability in one region was transmitted to the other through the channel of trade, and it was suggested that international cooperation was needed to overcome the costs of this particular aspect of North–South economic relations.

An even stronger claim is that the price of primary products relative to that of manufactures is on a downward secular trend. There is considerable debate regarding this 'Prebisch-Singer' hypothesis. One simple model of why there might be such a trend is that the demand for food is income inelastic while the demand for manufactures is income elastic. Thus with given supply conditions, as world income grows the shift in demand in favour of manufactures raises their prices. The problem with this argument is of course that it neglects supply conditions. Even within the framework adopted if the supply of food is relatively price elastic then the effects of a shift in demand will be mitigated. The question then turns on the elasticity of food supply, an issue which is complicated by the fact that many of the Northern countries (e.g. the USA) are major producers and exporters of food. A further complication is that food is only one component of primary commodity output. Other countries produce and export such natural products as rubber, copper and bauxite. Here it is technological innovations which are important in shifting demand away from the exports of less developed countries.

An alternative line of argument is sometimes used to theorize about the possible long-term decline in the terms of trade of the poor countries of the South. This is that while the production of primary commodities is undertaken primarily by peasant smallholders, the production of manufactures is in the hands of large oligopolistic corporations in the North who use their market power to resist downward movements in the price of manufactures relative to primary commodities.

253

Kaldor (1976) makes such an argument. Given the myriad of factors influencing the North–South terms of trade, it is perhaps not surprising that the empirical results of testing for a secular decline against the South are by no means unequivocal. Spraos (1980) summarizes the debate, which will undoubtedly continue.

Private capital flows, particularly direct investment by Northern multinational corporations in the South, have been a topic of considerable controversy. Those in favour of such investment argue that the reason why such investment is good for the South is precisely the reason why such investment is considered profitable by the multinationals. The South is labour abundant and capital scarce. Wages are low and hence investment by multinationals is profitable. But such investment should be encouraged in a capital scarce economy, since this is a way of building up capital stock and hence raising wages. Those against multinational investment argue that the technology which is transferred to developing countries in this way has been developed in the context of developed countries and hence inappropriate to the conditions prevailing in the former. In particular, it is too capital-intensive relative to the employment creation needs of developing countries. Moreover, the types of product manufactured are inappropriate to the poor in developing countries, relying rather on the demands of the rich. The technology, apart from being capital-intensive, is skill-intensive and creates a class of highly paid workers in contrast to the mass of low-paid workers elsewhere. It is therefore argued that this particular channel of North–South economic relations relies on inequality within developing countries, and perpetuates it.

Other than capital flows for investment, there is also short-term debt that the developing countries have built up, particularly in adjusting to the two oil shocks of the 1970s, and the world recession of the 1980s. If the oil price rises and commodity booms of the 1970s played their part in bringing North–South economic relations to the forefront of debate, it is the 'debt crisis' which has played that role in the 1980s. The debt levels of less developed countries as a whole have reached historic highs, and the picture has been equally dramatic for particular countries such as Brazil and Mexico. More importantly, it is clear that many of the leading banks and financial institutions in the USA and in the West generally have allowed themselves to be exposed to risk of default. Given the interlocking nature of financial institutions and of the financial system in general, events in the South have taken on a new meaning for policy-makers in the North. In days gone by, default by an entire nation could be and was taken care of by physical force. This is no longer possible, and sovereign default is a real possibility for developing countries, and a real worry for developed ones.

The solvency of a nation should be assessed by whether or not, over the long haul, it can service its debt out of growth in income. The real question then concerns not short-term liquidity but the long-term growth prospects for developing countries. But in the short term there seem to be considerable impediments to developing countries being able to export enough to service their debt. The deep recession in the West in the early 1980s meant that demand for their exports was low. Another consequence of unemployment problems in the

OECD countries has been the growing demand for protectionist measures. The deep and abiding interactions between North and South are clearly highlighted in the debt crisis. If the North adopts protectionism then the South cannot export. But if the South cannot export it cannot service its debt, which will lead to default. A default on Southern debt spells disaster for the financial system of the North, and hence for output and employment in North and South. This short-term impasse, in which the global recession is certainly playing its part, has long-term consequences as investment falls and hence future potential output is curtailed. Yet another strand in this complex weave is added when one takes into account the effect of high interest rates in the North on the Southern debt burden.

However, it is as well at this stage to note that a detailed look at specific countries reveals a more varied picture of North–South economic relations than a single and simple label might suggest. On the one hand are the fast growing newly industrializing countries such as Korea, Taiwan, Hong Kong and Singapore, which have had protectionist measures directed against their manufactured exports, and on the other hand are countries in Africa which do not have any manufactured exports. Their exports are still primarily agricultural in nature, and are suffering from a slump in demand. A stemming of the protectionist tide will not help them, and it is here that the most dire poverty in the world is to be seen.

Let us turn, then, to an answer to the question posed at the start. What was achieved by the Brandt Report, and by the push in the past decade for a New International Economic Order between North and South? One important contribution of the Report will have been to highlight the complex web of relations between North and South which make one region interdependent on the other. The global events of the past few years, in particular the debt crisis, have only served to underline this factor. But more is perhaps revealed by what the metaphor of North–South excludes than by what it includes. As noted at the start, the position of the Communist bloc in this categorization is not clear, and any attempt to place them in the Northern group has been resisted by the block itself. Some have suggested that these centrally planned economies occupy a middle position in terms of trade – they import primary products from the South and export medium technology manufactures to them. From the North they import high technology manufactures and export primary products and medium technology manufactures. They themselves have chosen to characterize North–South economic relations as emanating from a colonial past, and have excluded themselves from the categorization altogether.

But perhaps the greatest difficulty in making sense of a global concept such as North–South economic relations is the great diversity of the South. It includes labour surplus countries in Asia and land surplus countries in Africa; highly industrialized countries in Far East Asia and Latin America, and primarily agricultural ones in Africa; light manufactures exporters and heavy manufactures exporters; countries which themselves have multinationals in other Southern countries; countries in which organized labour is strong and countries in which it has been brutally suppressed; countries which have elected governments and countries

255

which have always been ruled by dictatorships. While the North–South metaphor has proved useful in crystallizing certain features of the divide between rich and poor, attention must now turn to the details of the case under consideration.

BIBLIOGRAPHY

Brandt, W. 1980. *North–South. A Program for Survival.* London: Pan.

Brandt, W. 1983. *Common Crisis. North–South: Co-operation for World Recovery.* London: Pan.

Kaldor, N. 1976. Inflation and recession in the world economy. *Economic Journal* 86, December, 703–14.

Spraos, J. 1980. The statistical debate on the net barter terms of trade between primary commodities and manufactures. *Economic Journal* 90, March, 107–28.

Nurkse, Ragnar

KAUSHIK BASU

Nurkse was born on 5 October 1907 on an estate where his father was an overseer, near the village of Viru in Estonia. His father was Estonian and his mother of Swedish origin. Ragnar Nurkse was educated in Tallinn, Tartu, Edinburgh and Vienna. From 1934 to 1945 he worked as an economist with the League of Nations and from 1945 until his death he was a professor at Columbia University. He wrote on international currency questions, trade, vicious circles of poverty and on balanced growth. In 1959 he delivered the Wicksell Lectures in Stockholm. Exhausted by the lectures, he went to Geneva and while taking a stroll on Mont Pèlerin he collapsed and died of a heart attack or stroke on 6 May 1959. The Wicksell Lectures were published posthumously (Nurkse, 1961).

One of Nurkse's two most important books was *International Currency Experience: Lessons of the Inter-War Period* (1944). It was published by the League of Nations, and though it did not carry the name of any author, this was (excepting chapter 6) the work of Nurkse. From this and several other of his writings, what comes out most clearly is Nurkse's pragmatism. Though he was one of the originators of the doctrine of balanced growth, he never minimized the role of international trade. However, he believed that the scope for trade-based expansion for Third World countries was much less in the 20th century than it was in the 19th century. Balanced growth could supplement this and even enlarge the scope for trade. Balanced growth and international trade, Nurkse argued, 'are really friends, not enemies' (Haberler and Stern, 1961, p. 257).

Nurkse had a deep concern for full employment. He viewed exchange rate adjustments and trade restrictions as legitimate measures for preventing balance of payments difficulties from translating into unemployment and domestic instability. He stressed that trade restrictions ought to be used as temporary measures. With the emergence of Keynesian macroeconomics, Nurkse came to have faith in effective-demand management as a tool for maintaining employment in the face of trade adversities. This also led him to argue for some international coordination of domestic policies.

Nurkse's other important (and, in my opinion, more important) book was *Problems of Capital Formation in Underdeveloped Countries* (1953). Here he developed the important idea that though the producer of each commodity may find an expansion unprofitable because of limitations of the market, a coordinated expansion of all productive activities could be profitable for all producers. Hence, atomistic behaviour on the part of producers could trap an economy *within* its production possibility frontier. This idea had been discussed earlier – most notably by Rosenstein-Rodan (1943) and more distantly by Young (1928) – but Nurkse took it further. While this work has been the basis of several debates in development economics (for critiques and formalizations, see Flemming, 1955; Findlay, 1959), it has the scope for further research, especially in the light of recent advances in non-Walrasian equilibrium analysis (see Basu, 1984).

The lack of formalization in Nurkse's work led to much misunderstanding – handsomely contributed to by Nurkse himself – about the policy implications of the poverty-trap doctrine. Nurkse tried to clarify these in his Ankara lectures in 1957 and his posthumously published note in *Oxford Economic Papers* (1959), both reprinted in Haberler and Stern's (1961) collection. The potential of this branch of development economics remains large.

SELECTED WORKS

1944. *International Currency Experience: Lessons of the Interwar Period*. Princeton: League of Nations.
1947. International monetary policy and the search for economic stability. *American Economic Review, Papers and Proceedings* 35, May, 569–80.
1953. *Problems of Capital Formation in Underdeveloped Countries*. Oxford: Basil Blackwell; New York: Oxford University Press.
1954. International investment today in the light of nineteenth-century experience. *Economic Journal* 64, December, 744–58.
1959. Notes on 'unbalanced growth'. *Oxford Economic Papers* 11, October, 295–7.
1961. *Patterns of Trade and Development*. The Wicksell Lectures, Oxford: Basil Blackwell; New York: Oxford University Press.

BIBLIOGRAPHY

Basu, K. 1984. *The Less Developed Economy: A Critique of Contemporary Theory*. Oxford: Basil Blackwell.
Findlay, R.V. 1959. International specialisation and the concept of balanced growth: comment. *Quarterly Journal of Economics* 73, May, 339–46.
Flemming, J.M. 1955. External economies and the doctrine of balanced growth. *Economic Journal* 65, June, 241–56.
Haberler, G. and Stern, R.M. (eds) 1961. *Equilibrium and Growth in the World Economy*: *Economic Essays by Ragnar Nurkse*. Cambridge, Mass.: Harvard University Press.
Rosenstein-Rodan, P.N. 1943. Problems of industrialization of Eastern and South-Eastern Europe. *Economic Journal* 53, June-September, 202–11.
Young, A. 1928. Increasing returns and economic progress. *Economic Journal* 38, December, 527–42.

Nutrition

C. PETER TIMMER

The economics of nutrition has both demand and supply aspects. Because nutrients for human growth, development and physical activity come almost entirely from food consumed, the demand side of nutrition economics is closely related to food consumption analysis. Because these nutrients interact with the body's health status as well as demands imposed by physical and social activities to produce 'work output', nutrition economics also relates to the burgeoning literature on the formation and productivity of human capital. And because the process of buying foods and transforming them into a family's daily diet involves primarily women's time in the household, nutrition economics also relates to analysis of the productivity of women's activities and to the 'new household economics' paradigm. In addition, biological and economic links have been established between nutrition and fertility. In combination with the influence of maternal and infant nutritional status on mortality rates, these links establish an important connection between nutrition economics and population studies and provide a vehicle for economists to contribute to that field.

At one level, the economics of nutrition touches on nearly all aspects of economic activity through its pervasive influence on demand for commodities, allocation of household time, and resulting productivity and size of a nation's workforce. At another level, nutrition is primarily a non-market issue, and many of the important analytical topics involve unobservable relationships within the household or even within the human body itself. From this viewpoint, it is not surprising that the field of nutrition economics does not contain a coherent set of empirical regularities based on common methodological frameworks and accepted data bases. The field exists as a series of niches in the broader areas of inquiry just noted – in analysis of food demand, in formation of human capital, and in household economics. The purpose of this short article is to draw together, according to an economic perspective, the aspects that specifically relate to nutrition from those diverse fields. The economic perspective is not the only one possible, of course, because nutrition has traditionally been considered primarily a topic in applied biochemistry, where health and medical professionals identify the important problems from the field that need to be solved through bench research in the laboratory.

Only in the past three decades has the bio-medical approach to nutrition – the identification, synthesis and evaluation of physiological significance of nutrients essential for human health and well-being – been broadened to include public health professionals and discipline-based social scientists, including economists. The stimulus came from two major directions.

In the first instance, the documentation of significant hunger in the United States by the Field Foundation in the early 1960s led to the rapid expansion of the Food Stamp Program, followed by the Women, Infants, and Children (WIC) Supplemental Feeding Program. As budget expenditures for the elimination of hunger rose, so too did the concern for understanding basic causes of hunger and its impact on the hungry. Of particular importance in early stages of the programmes was the identification of minimum-cost diets that met nutritional standards so that the value of Food Stamps distributed could be determined. The so-called 'Budget Plan' of diets to be followed by Food Stamp recipients became a hot political issue because its value established the financial cost of the government's most widespread welfare programme. Efforts to expand the constraints needing to be satisfied at minimum cost – eventually to include not only the palatability of the diet but also its social acceptability – led to the inclusion of a broad range of social scientists in programme design and evaluation.

Secondly, a similar but broader set of concerns arose in the 1960s in the economic development profession. Analysis of Food Stamp recipients in the United States showed that poverty was the primary reason for hunger (lack of energy) and malnutrition (imbalance of nutrients, including protein relative to energy). Consequently, nutritional problems were likely to be orders of magnitude worse in poor countries than in rich ones. At the same time, the budgetary and administrative resources available to intervene in the problem were substantially smaller. Two important lines of analysis received attention in this development context: attempts to measure the economic benefits of nutrition interventions, such as supplemental feeding programmes, in order to establish a cost-benefit basis for their expansion (Selowsky and Taylor, 1973); and attempts to understand at a highly disaggregated level the demand parameters of those individuals and families likely to be suffering from hunger or malnutrition, or both. Out of this work evolved new directions for programmes and policies for dealing more effectively with these problems (Austin and Zeitlin, 1981).

The impact of these studies on policy has often been quite significant, especially in preventing budget cuts to the WIC Program when other welfare programmes were being cut back. Important analytical approaches have been developed to address such policy issues in developed countries, but the most extensive interest in nutrition economics has come from developing countries. The reasons are easy to understand: if societies must wait until they are rich to solve their nutrition problems, then widespread hunger is likely to persist for centuries. As one component of the Basic Needs approach to development, the question was asked whether shortcuts to improved nutritional status were available, at what costs and with what benefits (Streeten et al., 1982).

The starting point for raising and analysing these issues was Alan Berg's volume for Brookings, *The Nutrition Factor: Its Role in National Development* (1973). Growing out of Berg's experiences in managing food aid shipments to India during the 1966–7 food crisis there, the book provided a holistic approach to the role of nutrition in the development process and the potential scope for government interventions. This broad vision of nutrition as a central theme linking agriculture, population, food technology, education and the income dimensions of economic growth evolved into the concept of nutrition planning, which attempted to coordinate all government activities, from macroeconomic policy to agricultural research, with the objective of improving nutritional status (Anderson and Grewal, 1976). The field spawned its own journal, *Nutritional Planning*, and several interdisciplinary doctoral programmes.

Attempts to implement nutrition plans, however, ran into serious problems. Even when political commitment to such plans was high, as in Mexico, Sri Lanka and Colombia, and ambitious policy changes were contemplated on behalf of nutritional objectives, economists were unable to specify with any precision what the nutritional outcome of changes in policy (or even programmes and projects) would be. Reutlinger and Selowsky (1976) estimated the number of under-nourished people in developing countries based on average calorie requirements, semi-log income elasticity functions for calorie intake and rough income distribution data by region. They concluded that income growth *per se* would not lead to rapid reductions in hunger, but the analysis came under fire from both economists and nutritionists for its aggregative view of the problem. Many factors other than incomes are influential in affecting nutrient intake and health outcomes, especially the prices of important foodstuffs, and the search began for the behavioural parameters that would link variables subject to governmental intervention, such as the distibution of income growth or the prices of basic grains, to decisions at the household level that had an impact on nutritional status.

The first sophisticated attempt to measure these disaggregated parameters was made by Per Pinstrup-Anderson and his colleagues (1976) at CIAT, the International Center for Tropical Agriculture in Cali, Colombia. Their goal was to determine priorities for crop research in terms of its ultimate contribution to improved diets in Colombia. Picking the simplest case to start with, they asked what would happen to nutrient intake by income class in urban areas if it were assumed that technological change would lower market prices for individual commodities. By using the Frisch methodology to estimate a full system of demand parameters and using data from two cross-section surveys to determine money flexibility by income class, Pinstrup-Anderson and his colleagues were able to trace the effects of changes in prices on nutrient intake.

When policy is used to changes prices for producers and consumers and when rural as well as urban dietary patterns are investigated, the analysis becomes much more complicated. The price changes have direct and indirect effects on rural incomes. If labour markets are connected, some of the rural dynamics are likely to be transmitted to the urban economy. Even when the question addressed is limited to the impact of food price changes on nutrition, the answer typically requires a general equilibrium approach. This broader concern for effects on production, intersectoral linkages and macroeconomic consequences of food policy, in addition to nutritional outcomes, called for an integrated analytical perspective, such as in Timmer, Falcon and Pearson (1983).

Whether the focus is projects, programmes or policies, understanding nutritional impact requires knowledge of matrices of income and price elasticities for specific foodstuffs by income class. The empirical search for these parameters has pushed consumption economics into new areas both methodologically and with respect to data sources (see Waterfield, 1985, for a review of this literature and Timmer, 1981, for the implications for consumer theory).

The project-oriented and policy-oriented literatures have evolved in somewhat different directions. The former has focussed on problems of design and implementation in targeting delivery of services, especially in rural development programmes. Johnston and Clark (1982), for example, focus on the management of integrated delivery systems for nutrition, health, and family planning services in rural areas. At the policy level, attention has generally been focused on prices because they are relatively easy for government trade and exchange rate policies to influence (see Solimano and Taylor, 1980; Timmer, 1986).

The 'supply-side' dimensions of nutrition economics have been much more difficult to specify and quantify. The long-standing 'nutritional-wage' issue has been carefully treated theoretically by Bliss and Stern (1978), but the review by Binswanger and Rosenzweig (1981) found little evidence for a nutritional floor to wages in the South Asian context, which is where the hypothesis arose. The survey of 'health and nutrition' by Behrman and Deolalikar for the *Handbook of Development Economics* concludes rather pessimistically with respect to current knowledge. It has been impossible to specify even basic energy requirements of individuals relative to measurable outcomes of interest to society, much less a direct link between nutrient intake and health status. An influential group of nutritionists and economists has emphasized the very substantial capacity of the human body to cope with low-energy intake through both metabolic and physical adaptations. The result is the hypothesis of Sukhatme (1982), Srinivasan (1981), Seckler (1982) and Payne and Cutler (1984) that people may be 'small but healthy'. Many other nutritionists and economists find this view highly controversial and wish to impose a more normative standard of achieving long-term potential rather than short-term health as the criterion for nutrient intake (Beaton, 1983; Reutlinger and Alderman, 1980). The result of this intellectual standoff is that nutrition is no longer seen as a 'tangible' marker of development where progress could be stressed (and measured) relatively independently of the broader and slower overall economic development process. Considering the significant connections between factors affecting nutrient intake and the policy environment conditioning the development process, the demise of such a shortcut mentality is perhaps healthy.

BIBLIOGRAPHY

Anderson, M.A. and Grewal, T. (eds) 1976. *Nutrition Planning in the Developing World.* New York: CARE Inc.

Austin, J.E. and Zeitlin, M.F. (eds) 1981. *Nutrition Intervention in Developing Countries.* Cambridge, Mass.: Oelgeschlager, Gunn & Hain.

Beaton, G.H. 1983. Energy in human nutrition: perspecives and problems. *Nutrition Reviews* 41(11), November, 325–40.

Behrman, J.R. and Deolalikar, A.B. 1987. Health and nutrition. In *Handbook of Development Economics,* ed. H.B. Chenery and T.N. Srinivasan, Amsterdam: North-Holland.

Berg, A. 1973. *The Nutrition Factor: its Role in National Development.* Washington, DC: Brookings Institution.

Binswanger, H.P. and Rosenzweig, M.R. 1981. *Contractual Arrangements, Employment and Wages in Rural Labour Markets: A Critical Review.* New York: Agricultural Development Council.

Bliss, C. and Stern, N. 1978. Productivity, wages and nutrition; parts I and II. *Journal of Development Economics* 5(4), 331–98.

Johnston, B.F. and Clark, W.C. 1982. *Redesigning Rural Development: A Strategic Perspective.* Baltimore: Johns Hopkins University Press.

Payne, P. and Cutler, P. 1984. Measuring malnutrition: technical problems and ideological perspectives. *Economic and Political Weekly* 19(34), New Delhi, August, 1485.

Pinstrup-Anderson, P. et al. 1976. The impact of increasing food supply on human nutrition: implications for commodity priorities in agricultural research and policy. *American Journal of Agricultural Economics* 58(2), May, 131–42.

Reutlinger, S. and Alderman, H. 1980. The prevalence of calorie-deficient diets in developing countries. *World Development* 8, 399–411.

Reutlinger, S. and Selowsky, M. 1976. *Malnutrition and Poverty: Magnitude and Policy Options.* World Bank Occasional Paper No. 23, Baltimore: Johns Hopkins University Press.

Seckler, D. 1982. Small but healthy: a basic hypothesis in the theory, measurement, and policy of malnutrition. In *Newer Concepts in Nutrition and Their Implications for Policy,* ed. P.V. Sukhatme, India: Maharashtra Association for the Cultivation of Science Research Institute.

Selowsky, M. and Taylor, L. 1973. The economics of malnourished children: an example of disinvestment in human capital. *Economic Development and Cultural Change* 22 (1), October, 17–30.

Solimano, G. and Taylor, L. 1980. *Food Price Policies and Nutrition in Latin America.* Tokyo: United Nations University.

Srinivasan, T.N. 1981. Malnutrition: some measurement and policy issues. *Journal of Development Economics* 8(1), 3–19.

Streeten, P. et al. 1982. *First Things First: Meeting Basic Human Needs.* London: Oxford University Press; New York: Oxford University Press.

Sukhatme, P.V. (ed.) 1982. *Newer Concepts in Nutrition and Their Implications for Policy.* India: Maharashtra Association for the Cultivation of Science Research Institute.

Timmer, C.P. 1981. Is there 'curvature' in the Slutsky matrix? *Review of Economics and Statistics* 62(3), August, 395–402.

Timmer, C.P. 1986. *Getting Prices Right: The Scope and Limits of Agricultural Price Policy.* Ithaca: Cornell University Press.

Timmer, C.P., Falcon, W.P. and Pearson, S.R. 1983. *Food Policy Analysis.* Baltimore: Johns Hopkins University Press for the World Bank.

Waterfield, C. 1985. Disaggregating food consumption parameters. *Food Policy* 10(4), November, 337–51.

Peasant Economy

N.H. STERN

A peasant is someone who lives in the country and works on the land (the word derives from the French *paysan*). Taking this definition, the topic 'peasant economy' concerns the analysis of the economic decisions and interactions of peasants, their relations with other agents and the rest of the economy, the determinants of the general level and distribution of their economic welfare, and how their position might move over time or be affected by policy. As such it is very broad in scope, involving the study of the economic life of around half the world's population. The term 'peasant' is sometimes used in a somewhat narrower sense in economics to mean the small farmer (tenant or smallholder) as opposed to the agricultural labourer or very large landowner. The peasant economy would then be one where farming was conducted mainly by tenants and smallholders. Even under this narrower definition it is clear that vast number of individuals are included.

There are fundamental differences amongst economists in their views of the way in which the peasant economy functions and these underlie many of the strong disagreements over policy. The main sources of the differences concern views on the 'rationality' of economic behaviour by individuals, the competitiveness and efficiency of markets, the importance and implications of the distribution of power and wealth, and the role of institutions, cultures and beliefs. Whilst we cannot provide a detailed description of these general views we shall try to give a flavour of their diversity and focus on the basis of their differences. We shall them examine some specific issues and problems including the objectives of peasants and others in terms of profit, utility and attitudes to risk; labour markets; credit; share-cropping; and relationships between size of holding and productivity. Concentration will be on the literature since World War II, although many of the issues concerned and divided some of the outstanding economists of the 19th and early 20th century.

One of the most clearly stated and definite views places the peasant economy firmly within the standard competitive analysis; see for example Schultz (1964).

Within the constraints of their knowledge, it is argued, participants in the peasant economy make the best use of the assets available to them. Each agent makes production, working and spending decisions to maximize utility or profit. This is essentially the notion of rationality in this context: individuals have preferences and act according to them. Markets for labour, land, credit, inputs and outputs, consumer purchases and so on function competitively and efficiently. The outcome for the usual reasons is therefore a Pareto efficient allocation. The role of policy is then to improve knowledge, increase assets and, if desired, to improve the distribution of income.

At another extreme we find the views of those such as Myrdal (1968), who believes that markets and prices play a minimal role. He argues that few people calculate in terms of costs and returns and that, even if they do, such calculations are not the primary determinants of their behaviour. Further, he argues that many transactions are not of the market type at all, and where markets do exist they are very far from perfect. He pleads for an insitutional analysis of behaviour and the workings of the economy. Further, he suggests direct controls to implement policy; he calls these non-discretionary controls as opposed to the manipulation of prices, where individuals are left to take their own decisions.

Away from these extremes we have varying emphases on the role of rational behaviour, incentives and market structure. For example, Lewis (1955) regards institutions, legal structures and political and regligious attitudes and practices as major determinants of the form of incentives. Thus he suggests that land reform may be a prerequisite to successful agricultural extension if, without it, farmers believe that others will reap the fruits of their improvements. In the last fifteen years or so there has been substantial concentration on the forms of peasant arrangements for cultivation, the incentives which they give and the reasons for their selection. A central example (discussed briefly below) has been the study of share-cropping following the questions and analysis of Marshall in Chapter X, Book VI, of his *Principles of Economics*. In this context individuals are seen as rational but face problems of information and supervision in designing and implementing agreements for the use of land, labour and other inputs.

Marxist writers have emphasized property and power. For example, Bhaduri (1973) suggests that landlords manipulate indebtedness over their labourers and tenants to maintain a very tight hold over their freedom. He argues from his model that landlords have an incentive to block technical change and that progress requires expropriation.

These views are generalizations about the world and no single study could provide a conclusive test between them. An empirical judgement should be based on the accumulated experience of detailed studies. Here economists have not been as active as perhaps they should in conducting economic studies of peasant societies to examine how the theories they are discussing fare in the field (compare the many studies by anthropologists; see, for example, Srinivas, 1960 and 1976, and Wiser and Wiser, 1971). Nevertheless, many studies are available (see for example, Bailey, 1957; Epstein, 1962; Haswell, 1975; Bell, 1977, Bliss and Stern, 1982, and for further references Binswanger and Rosenzweig, 1984; see also the bibliographies of village studies prepared at the Institute of Development Studies, Sussex (Lambert, 1976 and 1978)). One should not perhaps expect a clear, single picture to emerge; people and societies vary considerably. However, it seems that neither of the simple descriptions of Myrdal and Schultz are remotely adequate as generalizations. The institutional structure and conventions concerning the disposition of land and labour (for example, the form of ownership and duties of owners, structure of tenancy agreements, restrictions on the obligations of labourers and so on) will be of considerable importance in determining cultivation decisions. Individuals vary greatly in their ability to make the most of their circumstances. Nevertheless, most of the studies point to strong economic responses and these are often rapid and subtle; the Myrdal picture is clearly unacceptable.

We comment briefly on some of the particular positive issues that have been prominent in theory and applied work. The objectives of peasants have been modelled in terms of profit and utility and in varying ways relative to uncertainty (for an early discussion see Chayanov, 1925). Thus, for example, Hopper (1965) suggests that simple maximization of expected profit provided a good description of farming decisions in the village he studied in North India. This seems implausible in a poor society and for a risky activity, and a number of models of behaviour under uncertainty have been considered. These include the standard model of expected utility maximization and 'survival algorithms' where individuals attempt to minimize the probability of falling below 'disaster level'. The implications can be very different from simple profit maximization. Under expected utility maximization with risk aversion the expected value of the marginal product of an input would, in equilibrium, be above the price of the input (possibly well above) whereas with profit maximization we must have equality (see, for example, Bliss and Stern, 1982).

Two central issues in discussion of the labour market have been, first, the relationship between wages and the marginal product of labour and, second, migration. On the former some appear to have argued that the marginal product is zero. This receives little empirical or theoretical support in that an extra hour of work in agriculture usually has some contribution to production. The question of whether the withdrawals of an extra person from agriculture reduces output and by how much depends on the response to the departure by others. Whilst the marginal product of an hour or day is unlikely to be zero, it is quite possible that it may be less than the wage in the case of family labour where there are perceived costs in working for others or of hiring labour (see e.g. Sen, 1975).

Migration decisions have been examined extensively, both in theory and practice, in terms of expected differences in net incomes or utility from making a move. Of particular influence was the paper by Todaro (1969) in which he proposed a model where the probability of employment in the town was equal to the number of jobs divided by the number of seekers. If rural and urban wages and urban employment are fixed, the number of seekers adjusts to make, in equilibrium, the expected urban wage equal to the rural wage. If we associate the job seekers with the employed plus the unemployed then this is a theory of urban unemployment with the striking implication that an increase in the number of urban jobs increases unemployment. The model has been extended, elaborated and tested by many authors (see, in particular, Fields, 1975; Sabot, 1982; Todaro, 1976).

The role of credit, for example, the much easier access and cheaper rates available to the richer farmers (Griffin, 1974) and its use in manipulation and control (Bhaduri, 1973) have been major issues. It is an area where data are particularly difficult to collect and good empirical studies are rare (a notable exception in the context of fishing is Platteau et al., 1985).

Share-cropping was discussed carefully by Marshal in his *Principles*. Following the book by Cheung (1969), it has become a popular issue in recent research. Cheung contrasted his view of share-cropping as an efficient arrangement (with the tenancy contract clearly defined to stipulate inputs) with that of Marshall, who had pointed to the possibility that the tenant who receives half the output may not push the level of an input as far as someone who receives the full amount of the marginal product. Many of Cheung's arguments were, however, anticipated by Marshall in his account which contains a description of how the landlord might try to enforce higher input levels. More recently attention has been focused on share-cropping as a means of sharing risk between landlord and tenant and as providing incentives for the tenant which would not be present under simple wage labour (see Binswanger and Rosenzweig, 1984, for references).

The proposition that larger holdings may have lower output per acre has been the subject of much theoretical and empirical discussion. In Indian studies it receives more support for comparisons across districts than within villages. Possible reasons for the phenomenon, where it occurs, include more labour input per acre on smaller family plots (where labour may be applied beyond the point where the marginal product is equal to the wage) and faster population growth (and thus greater sub-division of holdings) on fertile land. For further discussion, see Sen (1975).

On the policy side some of the major issues have been land reform, the dissemination of technical change, the pricing of output and the supply and pricing of crucial inputs such as water, fertilizer and draught power. We shall be very brief since our main emphasis has been on the functioning of the peasant economy. Land reform in the sense of redistribution has been very difficult to achieve, in part because many of those who have land reform will make great efforts to resist losing it. It has sometimes been argued that the (supposed) inverse relationship between size of holding and land productivity will imply that a more egalitarian distribution of land will yield higher total output. Agricultural expansion has long been seen as part of government policy, but it has become particularly prominent with the arrival of the newer varieties of seeds (the so-called 'Green Revolution') which are particularly responsive to water and fertilizers. Of special concern has been the differential impact of the advances on different groups in the population and how the changes might be influenced to provide greater benefits to the poor.

The relative price of food and the implicit or explicit taxation of peasants have been seen as critical aspects of the availability of food (and its price) to the rest of the economy as well as influencing growth within and outside peasant agriculture. Much turns on the assumed elasticity of response. A further important feature of government policy concerns the pricing and supply of inputs. The effects on agricultural production and on the welfare of peasants and labourers can be substantial, the most obvious example being irrigation.

The study of the peasant economy is a subject for which careful economic theorizing is critical since transactions can have special structures, uncertainty will be central, and economic relations will be strongly influenced by institutional arrangements. And those theories should be tested against, and arise from, detailed empirical observation since the successful application of the theories turn on which of the structures are relevant for the particular peasant economy under examination.

BIBLIOGRAPHY

Bailey, F.G. 1957. *Caste and the Economic Frontier.* Manchester: Manchester University Press.

Bell, C.L.G. 1977. Alternative theories of share-cropping: some tests using evidence from North-East India. *Journal of Development Studies* (13)4, July, 317–46.

Bhaduri, A. 1973. Agricultural backwardness under semi-feudalism. *Economic Journal* (83)1, March, 120–37.

Binswanger, H.P. and Rosenzweig, M.R. 1984. *Contractual Arrangements, Employment, and Wages in Rural Labour Markets in Asia.* New Haven: Yale University Press.

Bliss, C.J. and Stern, N.H. 1982. *Palanpur: The Economy of an Indian Village.* Oxford: Oxford University Press.

Chayanov, A.V. 1925. *Organizatsiya krest'yanskogo khozyaistva* (Peasant farm organization). Moscow. Trans. as *The Theory of Peasant Economy*, ed. D. Thorner, B. Kerblay and R.E.F. Smith. Homewood, Ill.: Irwin (AEA Translation Series), 1966.

Cheung, S.N.S. 1969. *The Theory of Share Tenancy.* Chicago: University of Chicago Press.

Epstein, T.S. 1962. *Economic Development and Social Change in South India.* Manchester: Manchester University Press.

Fields, G.S. 1975. Rural urban migration, urban unemployment and underemployment, and job search activities in LDCs. *Journal of Development Economics* 2, 165–87.

Griffin, K.B. 1974. *The Political Economy of Agrarian Change.* London: Macmillan; Cambridge, Mass.: Harvard University Press.

Haswell, M. 1975. *The Nature of Poverty.* London: Macmillan.

Hopper, W.D. 1965. Allocation efficiency in 'traditional Indian agriculture'. *Journal of Farm Economics* 47, August, 611–24.

Marshall, A. 1920. *Principles of Economics.* 8th edn. London: Macmillan, 1959; New York: Macmillan, 1948.

Lambert, C.M. (ed.) 1976. *Village Studies I.* Institute of Development Studies, University of Sussex.

Lambert, C.M. (ed.) 1978. *Village Studies II.* Institute of Development Studies, University of Sussex.

Lewis, W.A. 1955. *The Theory of Economic Growth.* London: George Allen & Unwin; Homewood, Ill.: R.D. Irwin.

Myrdal, G. 1968. *Asian Drama: An Enquiry into the Poverty of Nations.* Harmondsworth: Allen Lane.

Platteau, J.-P., Murickan, J. and Delbar, E. 1985. *Technology, Credit and Indebtedness in Marine Fishing*. Delhi: Hindustan Publishing Corporation.

Sabot, R.H. (ed.) 1982. *Migration and the Labour Market in LDCs*. Boulder: Westview.

Schultz, T.W. 1964. *Transforming Traditional Agriculture*. New Haven: Yale University Press.

Sen, A.K. 1975. *Employment, Technology and Development*. Oxford and New York: Oxford University Press.

Srinivas, M.N. (ed.) 1960. *India's Villages*. Bombay: Asia Publishing House.

Srinivas, M.N. 1976. *The Remembered Village*. Oxford: Oxford University Press.

Todaro, M.P. 1969. A model of labour migration and urban unemployment in less developed countries. *American Economic Review* 59, 138–48.

Todaro, M.P. 1976. *Internal Migration in Developing Countries: A Review of Theory, Evidence, Methodology and Research Priorities*. Geneva: International Labour Office.

Wiser, W.H. and Wiser, C.V. 1971. *Behind Mud Walls, 1930–1960*. Berkeley: University of California Press.

Periphery

IMMANUEL WALLERSTEIN

The term 'periphery' makes sense only as part of the paired antinomy 'core(centre)–periphery'. It refers to an economic relationship that has spatial implications. This pair of terms has long been used in the social sciences, but until recently it has been used metaphorically rather than spatially, and to refer to social and political rather than to economic phenomena. Palgrave's original *Dictionary of Political Economy* (1894–9) did not know the concept.

Nor is it merely an issue of semantics. It is not the case that some other reasonably similar concept had previously been used instead. The issue is more fundamental. Mainstream 19th-century economic thought – both classical and neoclassical economics, but to a very large extent Marxism as well – had no place in its theorizing for space, except as location that might affect the cost of a factor of production. Transport costs obviously affected total costs. And location might give a natural rent advantage. Geological deposits were where they were. Water sources that could be dammed for power were located in one place but not another. Space thereupon became one more theoretically accidental, exogenous variable which had to be taken into account in concrete economic practice but was in no sense intrinsic to the functioning of the economic system.

The classic formulation of this view is to be found in the theory of comparative costs. England and Portugal each had certain natural advantages, such that it followed that it was rational, to use Ricardo's example, for Portugal to exchange her wine for English cloth even though she was able to produce cloth more cheaply than England. In this example the Methuen Treaty never entered the discussion.

It is not that no one ever raised the issue as to whether the natural advantages were not the result of political and social decisions which themselves were integral to the processes of economic behaviour. There had long been, for example, a current of theorizing which justified protectionism. Friedrich List stands out as a leading spokesman of this view in the 19th century. The protectionists did argue in effect that comparative advantage was socially structured and that therefore state policy could and should endeavour to transform inequalities. But there are two things to note about this current of protectionist thought. Firstly, it was always marginal to the leading centres of academic economics, and to the extent that its views were incorporated, state policy was once again relegated to the status of an exogenous variable. Secondly, the protectionist current did not challenge, indeed on the contrary it reinforced, a basic pillar of mainstream thought, the parallel and theoretically independent trajectories of a series of states (societies, economies), each of which was separately governed by the same economic laws.

In the interwar period, the worldwide depression in agricultural prices which dates from the early 1920s led to a revival of protectionist theorizing, particularly in those parts of the world which combined three features: a predominance of agricultural production; a small industrial sector; a reasonably large scholarly sector. The three areas which best matched this profile were eastern Europe, Latin America, and India and in all three zones such economic writings appeared. They had in fact, however, rather little impact on local policy and even less on world scholarship.

The situation changed in the post-1945 period. Although the general expansion of the world-economy was no doubt conducive to free trade ideology, the political emergence of the Third World led to some questioning of what in the 1970s would come to be known as 'the international economic order'. It is in this context that the concept of 'periphery' took shape, first of all in the work of Raúl Prebisch and his associates in the UN Economic Commission for Latin America (ECLA).

The original Prebisch thesis laid emphasis on the 'structural' factors which underlay what by the 1950s was being called 'underdevelopment'. Prebisch argued that peripheral countries were basically exporters of raw materials to industrialized core countries. He argued that there was a long-term decline of the terms of trade against raw materials exporters. Prebisch concluded that this relationship had two basic effects. It maintained the peripheral countries in a vicious cycle of lower productivity and a lower rate of savings than the core countries. And it made it impossible for them to retain the benefits of such increases in productivity as they might experience.

The explanation was 'structural', that is, that there were socio-political 'structures' that affected, even shaped the market, and thereby in (large) part determined advantage in the market. The industrialized countries had 'self-sustained' economies whereas the underdeveloped countries did not, since they functioned as peripheries to centres. The world market forces operated to maintain this undesirable 'equilibrium'. The policy implications were clear. Since the 'normal' operations of the market would only continue the same pattern, state action was required to alter it. The basic immediate recommendation was industrialization via import substitution. The long-run implication was, however, more fundamental. Unlike Ricardo's analysis, the Prebisch argument suggested that the pattern of international trade was established importantly, perhaps primarily, by political decisions and therefore could be changed by political will.

Or more generally, the determining framework for the 'world market' was more the overarching world political structure than vice versa.

This basic thesis was picked up and developed by a large number of economists and other social scientists, in Latin America to be sure, but in the Caribbean, in India and Africa as well. It also became the basic argument of a group of social scientists located in Europe and North America, although it should be noted that many of these were persons whose areas of research were in what was now being called the Third World. One of the first of this latter group was H.W. Singer, whose principal contribution was published in 1950, the same year as Prebisch's famous report. For this reason, this viewpoint is sometimes called the Prebisch-Singer thesis.

In time, the Prebisch thesis developed in the 1960s into a doctrine which was called *dependista*, because it emphasized the fact that peripheral areas were in a larger system within which they were 'dependent' as contrasted with more autonomous zones. The primary focus of criticism of the *dependistas* was a dominant mainstream model which was coming to be called 'modernization theory' or 'developmentalism'.

Developmentalism centred around the issue of how those *countries* which were 'underdeveloped' might 'develop'. Developmentalism made several assumptions Some combination of traits of a country – there was much debate about what they were – led to development. All countries could develop in similar ways, were they to ensure the proper combination of traits – in this sense, the doctrine was melioristic. Development was a patterned process. The last assumption was often expressed as a stage theory. The single most influential expression of this last argument was W.W. Rostow's *Stages of Economic Growth* (1960). Developmentalism originated as an economic doctrine, but others soon began to suggest parallel processes of political development and social development. There was much discussion of the linkages among the various 'aspects' of development and hence much encouragement of so-called interdisciplinary analysis.

By the 1960s developmentalism had become a dominant and self-conscious mode of analysis in world scholarship, particularly in any discussion of the 'Third World' or the 'underdeveloped' countries. Prebisch had argued against classical free trade ideology. The main thrust of the 'second generation' of theorizers about the periphery – that of the *dependistas* of the 1960s – was directed against these 'developmentalists' even though many of them had already accepted the legitimacy of some state intervention in the economy. This second generation was still very largely Latin American – F.H. Cardoso, T. Dos Santos, Celso Furtado, Ruy Mauro Marini, O. Sunkel, R. Stavenhagen were major figures – but there were also Lloyd Best (Trinidad), Samir Amin (Egypt) and Walter Rodney (Guyana). All of these scholars attacked in one way or another the theory of modernization and in particular the assumption that Third World countries could 'repeat' European–North American patterns of development by copying in one way or another the policies, past or present, of the presumably 'successful' states.

The contribution of André Gunder Frank to this second-generation theorizing was that he spelled out two arguments which, while present in the work of his colleagues, had not been as clearly underlined, or as widely disseminated. The first argument is to be found in the slogan he coined, 'the development of underdevelopment'. This is the argument that underdevelopment is not un-development, a primordial pre-capitalist or pre-modern state of being, but rather the consequence of the historic process of worldwide development through the linked formation of core and periphery. It followed from this perspective that the further extension and deepening of the division of labour on a world scale led not to national development (as the developmentalists argued) but to the further underdevelopment of the periphery. The policy implications of the two perspectives therefore were directly opposed one to the other.

The second argument involved a critique not of modernization theorists but of so-called orthodox Marxists. To understand this critique we have to look at the history of Marxist theory. From about 1875 on there arose a version of Marxist theory which became predominant in the two major world organizational structures, the Second and Third Internationals, and which very largely reflected the theoretical input of the German Social-Democratic Party (c1875–1920) and the Bolsheviks, later Communist Party of the Soviet Union (c1900–50). Whether this version was or was not faithful to Marx's own theorizing is not under discussion here, and is irrelevant to the issue at hand.

Since both Internationals were oriented to the issue of obtaining state power, the de facto unit of economic analysis became the state, and, in this respect, there was no real difference with neoclassical models of economic development. Furthermore, under Stalin, a very strong state model of 'modes of production' was delineated which paralleled structurally the Rostowian model, although the details were quite different.

In the period 1875–1950, the worldwide structure of capitalist development disappeared or became secondary in 'orthodox' Marxist theorizing except for a brief interval around World War I where momentarily such figures as Otto Bauer, Nikolai Bukharin, Rosa Luxemburg, and in part Lenin discussed these issues. By the 1920s all such discussion ceased, and by the 1950s Communist parties in Latin America (and elsewhere) were deriving very specific policy implications from the state-centred 'orthodox' theorizing. The reasoning went as follows. Feudalism as a stage comes before capitalism which comes before socialism. Latin America was still in the feudal stage. What was on the politico-economic agenda, and implicitly 'progressive', was national capitalist development. Ergo, Communist parties should enter into political alliances with the national bourgeoisie in order to further national development, postponing to a later date 'socialist revolution'.

The *dependistas* saw this analysis as leading to virtually the same policy results as the analysis of the modernization theory developmentalists. Since the late 1960s was also a period of increasing US-USSR political detente, they saw the theoretical 'convergence' as tied to a world-level political convergence which in turn was facilitated by the hitherto unremarked common underpinnings of analysis.

The *dependista* popularization of the concept *periphery* was abetted by two theoretical works which claimed to be Marxist in economic theory yet challenged in each case a major strand in 'orthodox' Marxist economic theorizing. The first was Paul Baran's *Political Economy of Growth*, published in 1957, and which directly inspired many *dependista* authors. Baran modified the concept of *surplus* by introducing a distinction between 'actual' and 'potential' economic surplus, suggesting that the consequence of capitalism was not merely a particular allocation of actual surplus but even more importantly the non-creation of a potential surplus. This non-created potential surplus existed throughout the system but one major component was located in the 'backwardness' of under-developed countries.

The second challenge was in Arghiri Emmanuel's *Unequal Exchange*, published in 1969. Emmanuel's book launched a direct attack on the Ricardian theory of comparative advantage, noting that its assumption, the immobility of the factors of production, had never been seriously challenged even by Marxists. Asserting that while capital is internationally mobile, labour has not been, Emmanuel argued that wages determine prices, and not vice versa. Given unequal wages (and immobile labour) internationally, international trade involves unequal exchange, since items priced identically and ensuring parity in rate of profit in fact encompass different amounts of labour. This theory thus challenges the idea that surplus is transferred only in the work process, and that space is irrelevant. The fact that frontiers are crossed is crucial to the theoretical explanation of unequal exchange.

Two other, initially separate intellectual debates entered the scene to complicate the issue further. In the late 1950s, Maurice Dobb and Paul Sweezy had a public debate (in which others then joined) about the so-called transition from feudalism to capitalism in western Europe in early modern times. They disagreed about many things: the time of the change, the motor of change, the geographical context of analysis, the very definition of feudalism and capitalism. What the debate accomplished was that it forced a reconsideration of the definition of feudalism, which was important, since many peripheral zones were being characterized as having 'feudal' characteristics. When in the late 1950s and 1960s a new debate arose on the nature of, indeed the existence of, an 'Asiatic mode of production', the debate widened. The more the debate widened, the more the distinction between what is internal and what is external (to the nation/state/society) so fundamental to 'orthodox' Marxist thought, but also to neoclassical thought, came under challenge.

There was a second debate, purely political and far outside world academic circles. It was the obscure, seemingly esoteric debate between the Soviet and Chinese state apparatuses over the process of the hypothetical transition from socialism to communism. This too occurred in the 1950s. The issue was whether states would go forward in this hypothetical transition singly or collectively. This too implied a difference concerning the unit of analysis. The Chinese position had far-reaching implications which by the late 1960s were being called 'Mao-Zedong thought'.

It was in the 1970s that these strands of thinking about the 'periphery' and related topics came together. The term '*dependista*' disappeared. Some began to speak of 'world-systems analysis'. The core-periphery relationship was now being defined as the description of the axial division of labour of the capitalist world-economy. Core and periphery were now less linked locations than linked processes which tended to be reflected in geographical concentrations. These processes had as one major consequence the formation of states within the framework of an interstate system. One could think of the interstate system as the political superstructure of the capitalist world-economy. This world-economy was an historical social system, a socially created whole which developed in specific ways over its history. The overall structure was seen as defining the parameters within which the capitalist market processes occurred. As new geographical zones had been incorporated historically into this system, they had been for the most part 'peripheralized'. This meant that various worldwide mechanisms (political, financial, and cultural) tended to make it profitable for individual entrepreneurs to segregate production processes spatially such that some zones had disproportionately high concentrations of peripheral processes – that is, processes with a high labour component and relatively low-cost labour – ensured by the involvement of wage-workers in these zones in usually reorganized household structures in which lifetime income returns from wage labour comprised a minority percentage of total real revenue.

While state policies could affect these relationships, the ability of any single state to transform the situation was constrained by its location in the interstate system and therefore depended significantly upon the changing condition of the balance of power. The interstate system varied in patterned ways between periods in which there was one hegemonic power and periods in which there was acute rivalry among several strong powers.

In addition, the ability of states to affect the processes of peripheralization was said to be a function of the cyclical rhythms of the world-economy, believed to alternate, once again in patterned ways, between periods of expansion and stagnation.

The regular cyclical rhythms and the alterations of the conditions of the interstate system led to some continuous but limited shifting in the economic roles of particular geographical zones within the system without necessarily changing the basic structuring of core–periphery relations.

Finally, it has been argued that the geographical concentration of different economic processes has been trimodal rather than bimodal, there having been at all times semiperiphal zones, defined as regions having a fairly even mix of core-like and periphery-like economic processes.

The concept 'periphery' thus has involved a basic theoretical criticism of 19th-century economic paradigms. It has not been spared counterattack from three main quarters: of course from the modernization/developmentalists under attack, most of whom have been basically Keynesians in their economic theorizing; but even more from so-called neo-liberals (the critique of P.T. Bauer has been the most trenchant), and from 'orthodox' Marxists.

The concept 'periphery' has served a polemical purpose in the last 20 years.

To advance its utility, its proponents must now come to clearer terms about the functioning interrelations of the three antinomies of the capitalist world-economy; core—periphery relations in the division of labour; A and B phase in the cyclical long waves; and periods of hegemony versus periods of rivalry in the interstate system.

BIBLIOGRAPHY

Amin, S. 1974. *Accumulation on a World Scale*. New York and London: Monthly Review Press.

Arrighi, G. 1983. *The Geometry of Imperialism*. Revised edn, London: Verso.

Baran, P. 1957. *The Political Economy of Growth*. New York: Monthly Review Press.

Bauer, P.T. 1972. *Dissent on Development*. Cambridge, Mass.: Harvard University Press.

Emmanuel, A. 1969. *Unequal Exchange*. New York and London: Monthly Review Press, 1972.

Frank, A.G. 1969. *Latin America: Underdevelopment or Revolution*. New York and London: Monthly Review Press.

Furtado, C. 1963. *The Economic Growth of Brazil*. Berkeley and Los Angeles: University of California Press.

Hilton, R. (ed.) 1976. *The Transition from Feudalism to Capitalism*. Revised edn, London: New Left Books.

Hirschman, A.O. 1958. *The Strategy of Economic Development*. New Haven and London: Yale University Press.

Hopkins, T.K. and Wallerstein, I. 1982. *World-Systems Analysis*. Beverly Hills: Sage.

Love, J.L. 1980. Raúl Prebisch and the origins of the doctrine of unequal exchange. *Latin American Research Review* 15(1), 45–72.

Prebisch, R. 1950. *The Economic Development of Latin America and its Principal Problems*. New York: United Nations.

Rostow, W.W. 1960. *The Stages of Economic Growth*. New York and London: Cambridge University Press.

Singer, H.W. 1950. The distribution of gains between investing and borrowing countries. *American Economic Review* 40(2), May, 473–85.

Wallerstein, I. 1974, 1980. *The Modern World System*. 2 vols, New York, San Francisco and London: Academic Press.

Plantations

ADRIAN GRAVES

The economic, social and political importance of plantations in many regions, the longevity and ubiquity of the institution, its association with slavery and other forms of bonded labour and with colonialism, has given rise to an extensive and rich literature which spans many scholarly disciplines including history, sociology, politics, psychology, anthropology, archaeology and geography. Economists and political economists have been preoccupied with explaining the origins of plantations and evaluating their social and economic effects, both locally and in the broader context of the world economy. A survey of the intellectual origins and thrust of the most recent economic literature, however, illustrates the immense difficulties of theorizing the plantation. The failure to derive universally applicable definitions of the plantation and of the plantation economy lies at the heart of the problem.

The meaning of 'plantation' has changed markedly over time. Originally, it referred to a plot of ground set with plants or trees. With the onset of British overseas expansion, plantation officially designated a group of settlers or their political units, hence 'Ulster Plantation' or the 'Caribbean Plantations', but this usage was eventually replaced by 'colony' and the use of 'plantation' became restricted to farms or landed estates. In this sense, the word has been applied especially in tropical or subtropical countries though units of agricultural production in temperate or non-tropical zones, such as in parts of Europe and the Middle East, have also been referred to as plantations.

The range of plantation crops is also extremely diverse, including sugar, coffee, tobacco, tea, cocoa, bananas and other tropical or sub-tropical fruits, chewing gum (chicle), rice, tree spices, such as nutmeg, cloves, cardamon, mace, vanilla, cinnamon, garden crops like ginger and pepper and industrial raw materials such as cotton, indigo, copra, oil palm, sisàl, cinchona and rubber. Although plantations are frequently typified as monocultural institutions, many plantation products were grown either as subsidiary crops or they were combined with the cultivation of cereals, temperate zone fruits such as citrus, market garden crops and even with livestock production.

Most plantations combined an agricultural with an industrial process, though they were not of necessity bifurcated institutions. The scale and sophistication of the technological forms on plantations and associated infrastructures, as well as the structures of ownership and control of plantations have varied markedly according to time and location. Plantations have also seen many modal transformations, being based on slavery, a variety of feudal forms, peonage systems, long contract migratory or indentured labour and free wage labour. There are many examples of plantations, for instance in Latin America, that operated on a mixture of labour forms, in economies which articulated around a variety of modes of production. The extraordinary diversity of geographical location, crops, sources of labour, ownership or control and technological forms over time have created major difficulties for the scientific definition of the plantation.

All definitions of the plantation attempt to differentiate it from other agricultural or agro/industrial institutions, frequently, by very general characteristics such as climate, crop type or specialization, export orientation, spatial size, number of employees, or by its system of power or authority structure. Some writers lay particular stress on labour force characteristics, its degree of bondage, skill levels, the tendency of work to be organized cooperatively around gangs, the stability or permanence of the workforce, and cultural and ethnic or racial criteria. For others, factor proportions are paramount although the emphasis on specific factor ratios varies widely in the literature. Whereas a number of writers emphasize the capital intensive nature of plantation production (such as Paige's high capital/labour approach: Paige, 1975), others (e.g. Stinchcombe, 1961) define plantations as peculiarly land intensive units of production (see Pryor, 1982, pp. 289–91).

Since most definitions are developed to service the analysis of a particular economy, region or timespan, the enormous degree of variability in plantation production has led to a plethora of definitions stressing markedly different criteria which are frequently contradictory. This is particularly evident, as we have already noted, in the literature which typifies plantations according to factor proportions, or that which lays stress on the level of work skill, which is particularly low according to some writers (e.g. Baldwin, 1956; Stinchcombe, 1961) and especially high according to others (e.g. Wolf and Mintz, 1957). Precise definitions of the plantation inevitably exclude institutions which might justifiably be considered as such: the stress on the unfree nature of the plantation labour force, for example, rules out consideration of plantations based on wage labour. The most general definitions, however, inevitably incorporate a wide range of other agricultural institutions, including production units as varied as Roman latifundia, large estates in Byzantine Egypt, feudal estates, colonial agricultural missions, cooperative estates, state farms, modern capital or labour-intensive sugar or cotton estates, ranches or pastoral stations, and large corporate farms. Needless to say, the scholarly difficulties of defining plantations are reflected in the attempts to theorize the broader concept of the plantation economy.

The theory of the plantation economy has a long and rich intellectual pedigree, drawing upon classical and marxist traditions. Its classical intellectual origins can be traced back to the debates on land/labour ratios in the early 19th century which involved Ricardo, Wakefield, Torrens, Merivale and John Stuart Mill. Merivale, in particular, stressed the dominant role of the plantation in the ex-slave economies of the West Indies. It was left to the Dutch scholar H.J. Nieboer to expand the scope of the debate by transforming the undifferentiated notion of the influence on the plantations in the tropical economies into a general theory. He characterized differing types of colonial society according to the theory of open and closed resource systems, identifying the initial absence of permanent settlement as a pre-condition of plantation production, the necessity of formal compulsion of the labour force, and the subsequent engrossment of the optimum available land as the hallmarks of plantation protection and subsequently of plantation economies and societies. In the 1930s and 1940s, Edgar T. Thompson incorporated the concepts of open and closed resource systems into a theory of social change in plantation society, through which he attempted to identify disintegrating forces inherent in the plantation which also emerged as important factors in the wider economy and society.

The influence of Nieboer and Thompson was extended by studies of wage and slave plantations undertaken in the 1950s and 1960s. The work of Mintz and Wolf stands out in this respect, especially in an important article on plantation society in Central America and the Caribbean which distinguished haciendas from plantations and developed the notion of old and new style plantations (Wolf and Mintz, 1956). Whereas the former were precapitalist with surpluses directed at conspicuous consumption, the latter were typified as capitalist enterprises driven by the process of surplus extraction to service capital accumulation. This work opened up associated discussions in marxist theory on the nature of a mode of production in which distinctions between slave plantations and capitalist institutions continue to play an important part. But it was the work in the late 1960s and early 1970s, of a group of Caribbean social scientists known as the New World Group, most prominently Lloyd Best and George Beckford, that attempted to integrate the classical literature on slave plantations with the then emerging marxist debate on underdevelopment as a means to analyse post-slave plantation production. This work has been extremely influential in the most recent literature on plantation production and warrants closer examination.

Best's contribution has been to try and develop a universally applicable model of a 'pure plantation economy'. In so doing, he drew heavily upon the intellectual heritage of Nieboer and Thompson, incorporating also Erving Goffman's notion of the 'total institution':

Where land is free to be used for subsistence production the recruitment of labour exclusively for export production imposes a need for 'total economic institutions' so as to encompass the active existence of the workforce. The plantation which admits virtually no distinction between organisation and society, and chattel slavery which deprived workers of any civil rights including the right to property, together furnish an ideal framework (Best, 1968, p. 287).

This conceptualization was subsequently elaborated by Beckford (1972) to include a vigorous critique of the dual economy and, most significantly, to demonstrate the meagre spread effects of modern plantation production.

Beckford distinguished between the mainly temperate 'colonies of settlement' (Australia, New Zealand, Canada and the United States of America) and tropical 'colonies of exploitation', observing that the pattern of agricultural production which emerged in the two types of colonies was significantly different. Generally speaking, Beckford's attempts to develop a theory of modern plantation production rests upon this basic distinction, (as does the more recent work of de Silva, 1982) with plantations being identified firmly with the tropical colonies of exploitation. Although he specified two exceptional types of plantation economy, the plantation sub-economy (USA, north-eastern Brazil, Honduras, Guatemala, Costa Rica and Panama) and the enclave plantation economy (Liberia, Kenya, Rhodesia and South Africa), Beckford based his argument about the meagre spread effects of plantations on a general model of the plantation economy, namely,

> Those countries of the world where the internal and external dimensions of the plantation system dominate the country's economic and social and political structures and its relations with the rest of the world... wherever several plantations have come to engross most of the arable farm land in a particular country which is predominantly agricultural, that country can be described as a plantation economy or society and its social and economic structure and external relations will be similar to those described for the plantation system (Beckford, 1972, p. 12).

Whilst he recognized that the potential for efficient resource use within the firm or particular plantation, Beckford argued that plantation agriculture was essentially unproductive, and that plantations exercised a pervasive economic, social and political influence over their areas which reinforced and perpetuated the underdevelopment of these economies. The fact that these local characteristics occurred within the wider context of dependent, exploitative, metropolitan/ periphery financial and trading relationships is an important component of Beckford's argument concerning the meagre spread effects of plantation production. His general conclusion was that 'regardless of the type of plantation that predominates in any given situation, the result is always the same – a persistent tendency towards underdevelopment' (Beckford, 1972, p. 213). It is important to appreciate that Beckford's typology of plantation production was meant to be appropriate for all major areas of plantation production regardless of whether or not the institution had originated in the slave based mercantilist empires of the New World.

The most recent studies of plantation economies have built upon the important work of the New World Group. Mandle in particular owes a great debt to Beckford, but he also incorporates other long-standing assumptions in the literature on plantation production. Thus he puts great stress upon the innate efficiency and inflexibility of plantation production. While this was due to a number of factors, the characteristically coerced and cheap plantation labour force was the 'key' to low productivity, because it provided planters with little incentive to innovate at the critical level of cultivation technology or to escape from their dependence upon international markets. It was partly through his stress on labour force characteristics, that Mandle underlined the importance of going beyond the analysis of the plantation merely as a productive unit (compared, for example, with the approach of the frequently quoted William O. Jones: see Jones, 1968) to embrace the distinctive kinds of social and production relations which derive from the plantation structure. On this basis, he distinguished from the growth-oriented capitalist mode of production, his notion of the 'plantation mode of production' by which he meant the 'growth inhibiting social structure' typical of plantation economies. Four attributes characterize Mandle's plantation mode of production; large-scale agriculture dominates the society; the domestic labour supply is inadequate to meet the labour demands of the agricultural sector; labour is mobilized and allocated by non-market mechanisms (coercion) which in turn define the nature of class relations in the society; and these class relations are reinforced by a distinctive culture (Mandle, 1982, pp. 37–8). The pivotal idea in Mandle's work, that the plantation mode of production inherently constrains its own technological advance and therefore the broader development of the forces of production in the plantation economy, has been supported in important studies of Louisiana agriculture by Ferleger (e.g. Ferleger 1984) and although it does not necessarily imply Mandle's model, the phrase 'plantation mode of production' is assuming a wider currency in the literature.

Although it has contributed considerably to out understanding of the institution's economic, political and social impact, the recent literature illustrates the formidable difficulties of developing a dynamic economic theory of the plantation. For one thing, it confuses model building with theorizing. Theory in history must incorporate process. Unquestionably, the recent theorists of the plantation recognize that the current state of the economies they address has historical roots. In the final analysis, however, the 'theories' of Best, Beckford and Mandle, go little beyond listing a set of distinctive, generalized characteristics of the plantation and of the plantation economy. To that extent, their typologies are static and therefore ahistorical. At another level, the primacy they place on the nature of the plantation itself and its function in the wider economy and society, effectively denies a role to human agency in the history of plantation economies.

To the extent that the literature incorporates the notion of underdevelopment, it is subject to the same sorts of criticisms which have more recently been marshalled with some force against André Gunder Frank and others (including Immanuel Wallerstein) by writers from both the marxist and neoclassical perspectives. In particular, Beckford's concern to identify the domination of the world market and the demands of capital reproduction as the arbiter of the rate of capital accumulation in plantation economies deprives his typology of the plantation of any laws of motion. Do plantation economies merely vegetate 'on the periphery of an industrializing Europe like a vast reservoir of labour-power periodically called into action by the spasmodic actions of metropolitan capital', like the underdeveloped ex-colonies of Frank and Laclau's Latin America? (Banaji, 1977, p. 14).

As to the 'plantation mode of production', other writers have noted the analytical difficulties of the more general concept of mode of production. Even within Marx, the application of the concept is confusing and even contradictory (does it mean the 'labour process' or an 'epoch of production': Banaji, 1977, pp. 4–5). But the problems of that idea are compounded substantially when it is ahistorically applied to forms of production which cover a wide chronological range, incorporating changing, even co-existing, different patterns of production relations, as McEachern (1976) has demonstrated in his criticism of Alavi's 'colonial mode of production'. The same sorts of criticisms can be addressed to Mandle's apparently timeless notion of the 'plantation mode of production'.

Beyond these broad points, a major weakness of the recent literature arises from its tendency to generalize about the impact of (exclusively sugar cane) plantations on the basis of a Caribbean/American paradigm. In respect of that region alone, other research casts doubt on the supposed inflexibility and inertia of plantation production even under slavery (Fogel and Engerman, 1974; Drescher, 1977; Ward, 1985) but also under systems of indentured labour (Saha, 1970; Beechert, 1987). Moreover, the characteristics and performance of sugar plantations in other regions, both in micro and macro terms, do not fit the Beckford/Mandle typologies. In 19th-century Queensland, Natal and Hawaii, for example, plantations did not of necessity dominate their areas and they proved to be not only highly flexible and dynamic institutions experiencing revolutionary changes in production over relatively short time periods, they stimulated rather than retarded local economic development, as have plantations more recently in Kenya (Graves and Richardson, 1982; Pryor, 1982; Beechert, 1987). Recent studies of colonial Latin America show that dynamic growth and flexible response was also a feature of plantation production in underdeveloped economies as well, not only in respect of cane sugar production but also in coffee, an important crop which is all but ignored by the theorists of the plantation economy (Duncan and Rutledge, 1977).

There is no doubt that much of the dynamism of plantations, especially in the late 19th century, was due to a revolution in the processing technology of the major plantation crops. This performance, contrary to the claims of the Mandle model, was also attributable on sugar plantations to significant innovations in the plantation cultivation process under production imperatives and structures which were unambiguously capitalist. While it is true that cane harvesting equipment was not successfully employed until the mid-20th century, the immense technical difficulties of that sort of machinery cannot be underestimated. Important innovations in cultivation technology were not confined to the more developed economies which supported plantation production. Java, for example, boasted a long history of agricultural research and development in the 19th and early 20th centuries which saw amongst other achievements, the emergence of the famous P.O.J.100 cane variety which transformed cane cultivation on an international scale. Less spectacular but no less significant innovations in the cultivation process were frequently introduced in many plantation economies by workers to raise their productivity under piece rate regimes, such as the redesigning of cane knives to suit local conditions.

Despite its weaknesses, the best recent literature on plantation production has attempted the important and urgent task of identifying the distinct economic rhythms and movements of modern colonial plantation production. Whilst the literature owes a rich debt to the classical formulations on plantations, it has also accommodated more recent theoretical approaches to colonialism and metropolitan-periphery relations. It is evident, however, that it is extremely difficult to theorize the plantation. Whilst the immense problems of defining a plantation suggest that its use as a descriptive term of agricultural organization its itself problematic, the scientific rigour of 'plantation' has very severe limitations. It appears to be unable to make analytic distinctions between agricultural production of tropical produce under the markedly different labour forms of slavery, feudal labour service, indentured labour, peonage, short-contract immigrant workers, or free labour. Nor does it distinguish between monopolistic and competitive land conditions. The revolutionary impact of changes in technology has not been sufficiently well accommodated.

Studies of plantations outside the Caribbean and the Americas indicate that the 'plantation economy' cannot be understood merely in terms of the logic and form of the plantation as a productive unit or of the plantation sector, but in the various combinations of relations of production which characterize the particular economies within which plantations operate. The explanation for the character, persistence or transformation of plantations therefore, must go beyond the discrete analysis of the institution itself and be sought more explicitly in the demands of capital accumulation under specific and changing conditions of capital markets and land ownership, labour availability and productivity, the changing technologies of cultivation and industrial processes and the consumption and distribution structures of plantation products. Only then will the laws of motion of the plantation become apparent, as will the forces tending to undermine or conserve this form of production. There is no doubt that the considerable gaps in our knowledge about plantations, despite an extraordinarily rich scholarly literature on the institution, is due to the paucity of rigorous empirical studies which address the wider conceptual issues. While that remains the case, economic theories of the plantation and of the so-called plantation economies will continue to remain unsatisfactory.

BIBLIOGRAPHY

Alavi, H. 1975. India and the colonial mode of production. In *The Socialist Register, 1975*, ed. R. Miliband and J. Saville, London: Mertin Press.

Baldwin, R.E. 1956. Patterns of development in newly settled regions. *Manchester School of Economics and Social Studies* 24, May, 161–79.

Banaji, J. 1977. Modes of production in a materialist conception of history. *Capital and Class* 3, Autumn, 1–44.

Beckford, G.L. 1972. *Persistent Poverty: Underdevelopment in Plantation Economies of the Third World.* New York: Oxford University Press.

Beckford, G.L. 1969. The economics of agricultural resource use and development in plantation economies. *Social and Economic Studies* 18(4), 321–47.

Beechert, E. 1986. Technology and the plantation. In *Proceedings of the Second World Plantation Conference*, Shreveport, 1986, ed. S. Eakin and J. Traver, Baton Rouge: Louisiana State University.

Benn, D.M. 1974. The theory of plantation economy and society: a methodological critique. *Journal of Commonwealth and Comparative Politics* 12(3), November, 249–60.

Best, L. 1968. A model of a pure plantation economy. *Social and Economic Studies* 17(3), 283–316.

Courtenay, P.P. 1965. *Plantation Agriculture.* New York: Praeger.

Drescher, S. 1977. *Econocide: British Slavery in the Era of Abolition.* Pittsburgh: University of Philadelphia Press.

Duncan, K. and Rutledge, I. 1977. *Land and Labour in Latin America: Essays on the Development of Agrarian Capitalism in the Nineteenth and Twentieth Centuries.* London and New York: Cambridge University Press.

Ferleger, L. 1984. Self-sufficiency and rural life on Southern farms. *Agricultural History* 58.

Fogel, R.W. and Engerman, S.L. 1974. *Time on the Cross.* Vol. 1, *The Economics of American Slavery;* Vol. 2, *Evidence and Methods – A Supplement.* Boston: Little, Brown.

Frank, A.G. 1967. *Capitalism and Underdevelopment in Latin America.* New York: Monthly Review Press.

Genovese, E.D. 1965. *The Political Economy of Slavery: Studies in the Economy of the Slave South.* New York: Pantheon.

Graves, A. and Richardson, P.G.L. 1980. Plantations in the political economy of colonial sugar production: Natal and Queensland, 1860–1914. *Journal of Southern African Studies* 6(2), April, 214–22.

Higman, B.W. 1969. Plantations and typological problems in geography. *Australian Geographer* 11(2), September, 192–203.

Jones, W.O. 1968. Plantations. In *International Encyclopaedia of the Social Sciences*, ed. D.L. Sills, New York: Macmillan.

Mandle, J.R. 1982. *Patterns of Caribbean Development.* New York: Gordon and Breach Science Publishers.

McBride, G.M. 1934. Plantation. In *Encyclopaedia of the Social Sciences*, New York: Macmillan.

McEachern, D. 1976. The mode of production in India. *Journal of Contemporary Asia* 6(4), 444–57.

Nieboer, H.J. 1900. *Slavery as an Industrial System. Ethnological Researches.* The Hague: Martinus Nijhoff.

Paige, J. 1975. *Agrarian Revolution: Social Movements and Export Agriculture in the Underdeveloped World.* New York: Free Press.

Pan American Union. 1959. *Plantation Systems of the New World.* Social Science Monographs No. 7, Washington, DC.

Pryor, F.L. 1982. The plantation economy as an economic system. *Journal of Comparative Economics* 6(3), 288–317.

Saha, P. 1970. *Emigration of Indian Labour (1834–1900).* Delhi: People's Publishing House.

Silva, S.B.D. de. 1982. *The Political Economy of Underdevelopment.* London: Routledge & Kegan Paul.

Stinchcombe, A.L. 1961. Agricultural enterprise and rural class relations. *American Journal of Sociology* 67, September, 165–76.

Thompson, E.T. 1975. *Plantation Society, Race Relations and the South: The Regimentation of Population.* Durham, NC: Duke University Press.

Thompson, E.T. 1983. *The Plantation: An International Bibliography.* Boston: G.K. Hall.

Wallerstein, I. 1974. *The Modern World-System: Capitalist Agriculture and the Origins of the European World-Economy in the Sixteenth Century.* New York: Academic Press.

Ward, J.R. 1985. *Poverty and Progress in the Caribbean, 1800–1960.* London: Macmillan.

Weber, M. 1927. The plantation. In M. Weber, *General and Economic History*, trans. F.H. Knight, New York: Greenburg.

Wolf, E.R. and Mintz, S.R. 1957. Haciendas and plantations in Middle America and the Antilles. *Social and Economic Studies* 6(3), September, 380–412.

Poles of Development

N. HANSEN

The term 'development pole' was first introduced by François Perroux (1955), who argued that analyses of economic development should concentrate on the processes by which various economic activities appear, grow in importance, and, in some cases, decline or disappear. Like Schumpeter, Perroux maintained that entrepreneurial innovation is primarily responsible for the development process, which involves a succession of dynamic sectors, or poles, over time. Although Perroux emphasized relations among industrial branches, the implications of the development pole notion have been elaborated mainly in terms of the geographic location of population and economic activities (Boudeville, 1972; Hirschman, 1958; Myrdal, 1957).

The concept of geographic development poles, or growth centres, gained particular prominence in the context of the balanced versus unbalanced growth controversy of the late 1940s and 1950s. A number of economists held that economic development would best be accelerated by the simultaneous balanced growth of many interdependent undertakings. The principal rationale was that investments in both directly productive activities and infrastructure that would not be profitable in isolation would become profitable for the ensemble because of mutually beneficial external economies. However, the applicability of this strategy to newly developing countries was properly questioned on the ground that the resources required for carrying it out would be so great that a country disposing of such resources would not be underdeveloped in the first place. Critics of the balanced growth approach further pointed out that economic development does not in fact appear simultaneously and uniformly throughout an economy. Hirschman (1958) in particular maintained that development strategies for developing countries should concentrate on a few sectors rather than attempt to do too much at once with very scarce resources. In his view, development is communicated from leading sectors to the followers, from one firm to another. The advantage of this phenomenon over balanced growth, where every activity expands in step with every other, is that it leaves considerable scope to induced investment decisions, and therefore economizes the principal scarce resource, namely, genuine decision-making. However, Hirschman recognized that investments may well become overconcentrated in one or a few large cities because their external economies tend to be over-rated by investment decision makers in the belief that nothing succeeds like success. Nevertheless, he believed that in the long run public investments would cease to be so concentrated in primate cities, because of national equity and unity considerations. In this regard, he was clearly overly optimistic. Finally, Hirschman suggested that while infrastructure investments may be indispensable for the development of lagging regions, this would still represent only a permissive inducement mechanism. The essential task is the provision of continuously inducing activities in industry, agriculture and services.

During the 1960s it was widely held that, as a result of Keynesian macroeconomic policies, the economies of industrialized nations could continue to experience steady growth with relatively low unemployment and inflation rates. At the same time there was increased interest in structural problems that persisted despite the favourable aggregate context. For example, the growth of large metropolitan areas and the concomitant decline of some relatively peripheral regions became a concern in many industrialized countries, as well as a continuing concern in newly developing countries. It was frequently alleged, if not proven, that large urban agglomerations were too big, in the sense that the marginal social costs of further growth outweighed the marginal social benefits. Yet such places continued to grow because new entrants benefited from economies of agglomeration but did not bear the full costs associated with their entry. Critics argued that under these conditions, congested large cities and the nation as a whole would benefit if the growth of population and economic activity could be diverted to medium-size development poles, whose accelerated growth could be induced by government policies with respect to infrastructure, taxation, capital subsidies and similar incentives. Proponents of this development pole strategy emphasized the advantages of economies of agglomeration in a relatively few urban centres and argued against policies that would spread development outlays too thinly over the national territory. The induced development poles would thus be economically efficient counter-magnets to the spontaneous development poles deemed to be too large. It was further argued that the induced development poles would generate beneficial 'spread effects' to their surrounding hinterland areas, so that in the long run the entire national territory would be characterized by 'balanced growth'. An example of this strategy was the French spatial development policy of the 1960s, which designated eight metropolitan areas whose favoured growth would, it was hoped, counteract the growth of the Paris region.

The development pole strategies that were adopted in the 1960s fit in well with the hierarchical diffusion of innovations paradigm popular at the time. This approach to spatial-temporal development processes maintains that there are two principal features that characterize the spatial organization of economic activities: (1) a hierarchical system of cities, arranged according to the number and quality of functions performed by each city; and (2) a corresponding set of urban spheres of influence (urban fields) surrounding each of the cities in the system. Within this framework, development-inducing innovations are transmitted simultaneously in three ways: (1) outward from one or a few dominant national metropolitan areas to major regional urban centres; (2) downward from higher-order to lower-order cities in the urban hierarchy, in a pattern of hierarchical diffusion; and (3) outward from urban centres into their surrounding hinterland areas, that is, through radiating spread effects. The hierarchical diffusion of innovation paradigm is essentially a top–down model of development because it places considerable emphasis on continuing innovation adoption in the largest cities as the critical element for the subsquent extension of development over the entire urban-economic system.

Given this general setting, the role that induced development poles play in regional development can be regarded as a particular case of the general process of innovation diffusion. More specifically, development pole policies can be introduced if diffusion mechanisms are perceived to be operating too slowly, if 'cumulative causation' leads to increasing regional income disparities rather than to their reduction, or if institutional or historical barriers impede diffusion processes. The purpose of spatially selective public investments in development poles would be to hasten the focused extension of development to lower echelons of the urban hierarchy in peripheral regions, and to link the development poles more closely to the national urban system via higher-echelon cities in the urban hierarchy. It should be remarked that the innovation diffusion justification for a development pole policy does not deal with the issue of the actual or potential social costs of very large cities. Such places are viewed in an exclusively positive light, as the seedbeds of innovation, or at least the initial adopters of innovations conceptually generated elsewhere.

In retrospect, what have development pole policies accomplished? This is difficult to evaluate because it is hard to find any example of a development pole policy that has been vigorously implemented in practice. In many countries, development pole strategies have not really passed the stage of paper plans, and in many others the resources committed to implementing the plans have been too few to represent a genuine test of the strategy. Yet another pervasive problem has been the political difficulty of being selective in the choice of geographical development poles. Policies that have begun by attempting to concentrate investments in a relatively few urban centres have been diluted over time by pressures to include ever more centres, thus precluding the inducement of extensive economies of agglomeration in any one place.

In addition to the foregoing problems, the context for regional development policies has altered considerably over time, and especially since the mid-1970s. Here it is instructive to distinguish between the advanced industrial countries and the newly developing countries.

In the industrialized nation context, mounting evidence indicates that the hierarchical diffusion paradigm cannot be supported empirically. Development-inducing linkages run not only from larger to smaller cities, but also in the reverse order as well as between cities of similar size. Moreover, the notion that induced development poles will in turn induce development in their respective hinterlands has been undermined by evidence that interfirm and intersectoral linkages for the most part involve relatively distant locations. From the viewpoint of regional development policy, the problem of how to create local linkages has yet to be resolved. Although large city size is associated with technological progress in the hierarchical diffusion paradigm, there is no evidence that this is necessarily the case. Even in broadly regional terms, new industrial sources of innovation increasingly are widely dispersed. Finally, in many countries the aims of development pole strategies have tended to be realized since 1970, though few would attribute this phenomenon to such policies. Very large metropolitan areas have been declining in population or else have experienced much slower rates of growth than in the past; and many once stagnant or declining peripheral areas have experienced at least a modest degree of population increase and economic revival. In general, then, while spontaneous development poles continue to emerge outside of older industrial regions, the impetus to formulate deliberate policies to promote induced development poles has receded.

Development pole policies in newly developing countries have taken a number of forms. Some have concentrated on infrastructure in order to provide a critical minimum level of power, water, transportation and other public overhead facilities. Others have been based on the intermediate or heavy manufacturing activities of public enterprises; these projects have typically involved industrial complexes organized around such sectors as iron and steel, aluminium, petro-chemicals and heavy engineering. What all these efforts have had in common is emphasis on the direct use of large-scale investment resources to generate structural changes through accelerated economic growth. However, the selection of development pole locations has typically been based on urban population growth projections and/or on national sectoral projections, but not on the development potential or demand of the surrounding hinterland areas. Consequently, polarized development undertakings have had only a very limited impact on their surrounding areas because the linkages involved in the development process have been largely with distant suppliers and markets, and because the derived demand for labour and for agricultural outputs has often stimulated migration and supplies from outside the regions where development poles have been located. In addition, the highly capital-intensive nature of development pole activities has generated relatively low levels of employment in view of the considerable total resources invested.

In general terms, the principal criticism of polarized development strategies as applied in developing countries has been their failure to improve the social and economic well being of the large numbers of poor persons who live in rural peripheral regions. In recent years there has been a broadly based reaction against 'top–down' development efforts in favour of 'bottom–up' approaches that emphasize highly divisible, labour-intensive technologies applied to agriculture and to small and medium-size enterprises with direct linkages to agriculture and to rural and small town markets.

Despite criticisms of development pole policies, they are still being formulated in some countries, including Mexico and South Korea, where in each case decentralization away from the large, congested national capital is a major national objective. The evidence suggests that if such policies are to be successful they need to be broadened to include political, social and institutional changes as well as sectoral measures. Induced development poles need to be placed within a larger human settlement system framework, and human resource development policies need to be integrated with spatial-sectoral policies. The dissipation of scarce resources should be avoided by greater selectivity in location choices, and measures need to be taken to reduce the enclave nature of development poles. And political will needs to be sustained in the context of sufficiently long planning horizons.

In brief, then, prevalent attitudes toward development pole strategies have passed from an initial phase of optimism, to one of pessimism, to an emerging broader perspective that would include induced development poles as but one aspect of more comprehensive development planning (Hansen, 1981).

BIBLIOGRAPHY

Boudeville, J. 1972. *Aménagement du territoire et polarisation*. Paris: Génin.

Hansen, N. 1981. Development from above: the centre–down development paradigm. In *Development from Above or Below?*, ed. W.B. Stöhr and D.R. Fraser Taylor, New York: John Wiley and Sons.

Hirschman, A.O. 1958. *The Strategy of Economic Development*. New Haven: Yale University Press.

Myrdal, G. 1957. *Rich Lands and Poor*. New York: Harper and Brothers.

Perroux, F. 1955. Note sur la notion de pôle de croissance. *Economie Appliquée* 8, Series D, January-June.

Prebisch, Raúl

J.G. PALMA

Prebisch was born on 17 April 1901 in Tucumán, Argentina, and died in 1986 at the age of 84 in Santiago de Chile. He graduated in Economics at the University of Buenos Aires in 1923 having already written nine articles (six of which had been published in different journals); the first of them – written at the age of 17 – being (not surprisingly) on industrialization.

He was Professor of Political Economy at the School of Economics of the University of Buenos Aires from 1925 to 1948. In addition he held various other positions in Argentina; the two most important being Under-Secretary of Finance (1930–32) and the first Director-General of the Argentine Central Bank (1935–43). Then he moved to the UN, being appointed Executive Secretary of ECLA (Economic Commission for Latin America) in 1950. In January 1963 he moved to UNCTAD (United Nations Conference on Trade and Development) as Secretary-General. When his term of office with UNCTAD was over (1969), he went back to Santiago de Chile as Director-General of the UN Latin American Institute for Economic and Social Planning.

Although his main intellectual concern was always the process of industrialization in peripheral countries, he acknowledged in a magazine interview that he viewed it mainly from a conventional point of view until he witnessed the Great Depression and read the *General Theory*. After writing several articles and an influential book on Keynes, he began to develop his well-known ideas on the problems of economic development in the periphery at the end of the 1940s. His work became well known all over the world in the 1950s when he led the ECLA team into the formulations of the structuralist approach to the analysis of these problems.

In this approach, Prebisch was basically concerned with what he saw as the four stylized facts of underdevelopment: (i) the growing gap in the level of income between centre and periphery; (ii) the persistent unemployment in the periphery; (iii) the persistent balance of payments disequilibrium in the periphery which imposed an important external constraint on the process of economic growth; and (iv) the tendency to deterioration of the terms of trade of the periphery.

His main analytical concern was to build a theoretical framework to be able to explain these four phenomena, tracing their causes both to the level of circulation (pattern of international trade) and of production (economic structure) of the periphery.

At the core of Prebisch's analysis lies his differentiation of the economic structure of the centre and periphery. In the first, the economic structure is seen as homogeneous and diversified, in the latter, as heterogeneous and specialized (see STRUCTURALISM). The problem of unemployment of the periphery is associated with the structural heterogeneity; that of the balance of payments and terms of trade with the excessive degree of specialization. Both together are responsible for increasing income differentials between centre and periphery.

His best-known thesis is the tendency to deterioration of the terms of trade of the periphery, the development of which coincided in time with Hans Singer's theory on the subject (1950). (It is not clear that he saw this as the most important part of his work but by its own nature it was a seductive challenge to that part of the North American academic world which is ever anxious to extract from the structuralist approach unidimensional hypotheses referring to clearly established variables for its own consumption.) Prebisch was concerned with the effect of economic growth on the terms of trade of the periphery. His hypothesis is that from both the demand for imports and supply of exports points of view there are reinforcing elements that – if left to an unregulated international market – would tend to work against the terms of trade of the periphery.

In a very simple and summarized way, the tendency towards deterioration of the terms of trade of the periphery could be expressed as shown in Figure 1.

From the point of view of the consumption path, the Prebisch hypothesis is that the income elasticity of imports of the periphery is greater than one and (much) greater than that of the centre. Therefore the consumption path of the periphery would be biased for trade (say, ODE'), i.e. as incomes grow the proportion of importables (from the centre) in local consumption of the periphery increases.

From the point of view of the production path there would be the same phenomenon, i.e. it would also be biased for trade in the periphery (say, ODF') for reasons of supply and demand. From the supply side, Prebisch put great emphasis on the peculiarities of productivity change. For him there was one similarity and two differences in terms of the creation and diffusion of technological change between the centre and the periphery. The similarity is that technological change and increases in productivity are relatively high in both export sectors. The differences are, on the one hand, that those of the manufacturing sector tend to spread more to the rest of the economy (externalities are higher) than those of primary production (export-led growth based on primary commodities could in fact reinforce structural heterogeneity). On the other hand, the increases in productivity in the manufacturing sector of the centre do not tend to be transferred into lower prices as happens to those of primary production in the periphery (mainly due to market imperfections in the centre both in product and labour markets).

In the case of the demands for exports, the hypothesis is that the price elasticity

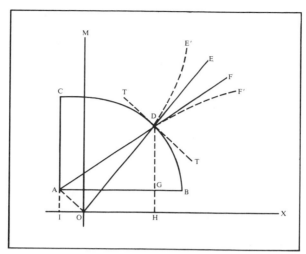

Figure 1 X = exportable of the periphery (primary commodity); M = importable of the periphery (manufacturing good); ABC = transformation curve of the periphery; ODE = neutral consumption path; ADF = neutral production path; OA = TT = terms of trade of the periphery; DH = consumption of M; DG = local production of M; GH (AI) = imports of M; IH = production of X; OH = local consumption of X; IO = exports of X.

is lower for primary commodities than for manufactured ones. The combination of both factors (supply and demand for exports) and the need to produce in the periphery the necessary foreign exchanges to pay for the consumption path being biased for trade would tend to make the production path of the periphery also biased for trade, and more so than that of the centre.

The end result would be that for the same rate of growth in both poles, the periphery would tend to have a path more biased for trade in consumption and production and, therefore, an excess demand for imports of manufactured goods (from the centre) and supply of exports of primary commodities (to the centre), resulting in the tendency towards the deterioration of the terms of trade of the periphery. Within this context, the recipe for avoiding it is to produce locally more of the highly income elastic importables and to diversify exports towards more price elastic, productivity spreading commodities, i.e. a process of industrialization that should eventually lead towards exports of manufactured goods from the periphery. (In one of his last articles Prebisch summarizes his and ECLA's task as having been that of 'showing that industrialization was an unavoidable prerequisite for development'; 1980, p. viii.)

This theory contradicts not only Ricardo's comparative advantage theory – for Prebisch, the higher the rate of growth of productivity in the export sector of the periphery (primary commodities), the higher the need for import substituting industrialization (1983, p. 1082) – but also the classical approach to the terms of trade that argued that in the long term they should move in favour

293

of primary production (see for example J.S. Mill, 1848 and J.M. Keynes, 1920). On the other hand, Prebisch would certainly be in agreement with Joan Robinson (1979) when she argues that in Ricardo's classical example Portugal would end up with a low rate of accumulation and having destroyed its promising textile industry, while England ended up with an industrial revolution.

From this point of view it is important to stress that for Prebisch the argument for industrialization is not only due to differences in income elasticities of demand for imports and/or for price elasticities of demand for exports (arguments at the level of circulation of commodities) but is also due *to the very nature of manufacturing production*, especially its externalities (an argument at the level of production).

For the traditional criticism of Prebisch ideas, see the article on Structuralism. Some additional problems to which the literature on Prebisch has not given due consideration are: (i) although this was not at all Prebisch's intention, his ideas have undoubtedly led to a clear bias against the production of primary commodities in the periphery *per se*; (ii) Prebisch's work does not sufficiently take into account that the centre is a major (and increasing) producer of primary commodities, and the periphery one of manufactured goods, and that there are important conflicts of interest within the periphery (for example, for a peripheral country there could be significant gains in the short or medium term if it expands rapidly its exports of a given primary commodity when its competitors in the periphery are controlling their own output); (iii) Prebisch did not sufficiently stress that in order to have the real benefits of industrialization the periphery should not only produce at home the highly income elastic importables but should also diversify its exports towards manufacturing goods as soon as possible.

SELECTED WORKS

1949. The economic development of Latin America and its principal problems. *Economic Bulletin for Latin America* 7, 1962, 1–22. (First published by ECLA in 1949.)

1951a. The spread of technical progress and the terms of trade. In United Nations, *Economic Survey of Latin America, 1949*, New York: UN Department of Economic Affairs, 46–61.

1951b. *Problemas teóricos y prácticos del crecimiento económico*. Santiago: UN, ECLA.

1959. Commercial policy in the underdeveloped countries. *American Economic Review, Papers and Proceedings* 49, May, 251–73.

1962a. Economic aspects of the Alliance for Progress. In *The Alliance for Progress*, ed. J.C. Dreier, Baltimore: Johns Hopkins Press.

1962b. El falso dilema entre desarollo económico y estabilidad monetaria. *Boletin Económico de América Latina* 6(1).

1963. *Towards a Dynamic Development Policy for Latin America*. New York: United Nations.

1964. *Towards a New Trade Policy for Development. Report of the Secretary-General of the United Nations Conference on Trade and Development*. New York: United Nations.

1968. A new strategy for development. *Journal of Economic Studies* 3(1), March, 3–14.

1971a. *Latin America: a problem in development*. Austin: Austin Institute of Latin American Studies, University of Texas at Austin.

1971b. *Change and Development – Latin America's Great Task: Report submitted to the*

Inter-American Development Bank. New York and London: Praeger; Mexico: Fondo de Cultura Económico (1970).

1976. A critique of peripheral capitalism. *CEPAL Review* (UN ECLA), 1, 9–76.

1980. Prologo. In Rodriguez (1980).

1981. *Capitalismo periférico: crisis y transformación.* México: Fondo de Cultura Económico.

1983. Tres etapas de mi pensamiento económico. *El Trimestre Económico* 50(2), 1077–96.

BIBLIOGRAPHY

Di Marco, L.E. 1972. The evolution of Prebisch's economic thought. In *International Economics and Development: Essays in Honour of Raul Prebisch*, ed. L.E. Di Marco, New York and London: Academic Press, 3–13.

Keynes, J.M. 1920. *Economic Consequences of the Peace.* London: Macmillan; New York: Harper & Row, 1971.

Mill, J.S. 1848. *Principles of Political Economy.* London: Longmans, 1948; New York: A.M. Kelley.

Robinson, J.V. 1979. *Aspects of Development and Underdevelopment.* Cambridge and New York: Cambridge University Press.

Rodriguez, O. 1980. *La teoria del subdesarrollo de la CEPAL.* Mexico: Siglo XXI Editores.

Singer, H. 1950. The distribution of gains between investing and borrowing countries. *American Economic Review* 40, 473–85.

Rosenstein-Rodan, Paul Narcyz

RICHARD S. ECKAUS

Rodan was one of the founders and first leaders of the field of development economics. Born in 1902, his formative intellectual years were in the Austrian School of economics at the University of Vienna. He moved to the Department of Political Economy at University College, London, in 1931.

Rodan's early essays in economics show a preoccupation with themes which reappeared throughout his professional career: the interaction and complementarity of economic processes (1933) and their temporal patterns (1934). Rodan's seminal article on developing countries (1943) argued that complementarities and externalities in demand and production created a need for the programming of investment. The arguments were subsequently extended to justify the need for an across-the-board 'big push' for a successful start to the development process (1963). He was among the first to apply the concept of 'disguised unemployment', described by Joan Robinson (1936), to developing countries as a persisting rather than cyclical problem.

Rodan first became actively engaged in development policy during his tenure at the World Bank from 1947 to 1954. In 1954 he moved to the Department of Economics at the Massachusetts Institute of Technology, where he produced an influential article (1961) which demonstrated that feasible levels of assistance to developing countries would substantially improve their growth performance. After retirement from MIT in 1968 he moved to the University of Texas and then to Boston University in 1972, where he established and worked in the Center for Latin American Development Studies until his death in 1985. Rodan was an active policy adviser to international agencies and governments of many countries and served on the Panel of Experts, the 'Nine Wise Men' of the Alliance for Progress, from 1961 to 1966.

SELECTED WORKS

1933. La complementarita, prime delle tre fase del progresso della teoria economica pura. *Riforma Sociale* 44, 257–308.

1934. The role of time in economic theory. *Economica*, NS 1, 77–97.

1943. Problems of industrialization of Eastern and South-Eastern Europe. *Economic Journal* 53, 202–11.

1956. Disguised unemployment and underemployment in agriculture. *Monthly Bulletin of Agricultural Economics and Statistics* 6, 1957, 1–6.

1961. International aid for underdeveloped countries. *Review of Economics and Statistics* 43, 107–38.

1963. Notes on the theory of the 'Big Push' in economic development. In *Proceedings of a Conference of the International Economics Association*, ed. H.S. Ellis, London: Macmillan.

BIBLIOGRAPHY

Robinson, J. 1936. Disguised unemployment. *Economic Journal* 46, 225–37.

Schultz, Theodore Wilhain

MARY JEAN BOWMAN

A scholar, research entrepreneur, and intellectual catalyst, Schultz has been motivated through a long and active life by a drive to deepen economic understanding and to foster enlightened policies in the furtherance of human welfare. Although he has served as adviser to agencies of the United States, the United Nations, other governments and many non-profit organizations, Schultz has always maintained independence. He has received many honours, including the Walker award (the highest given by the American Economic Association) and a Nobel prize for contributions to development economics.

Schultz was born in 1902. Growing up on a farm in South Dakota, he never attended secondary school, but as a young man he tested for entrance to South Dakota State College where he obtained an MS degree (1928), going on to an economics PhD from the University of Wisconsin (1930). For most of his professional life Schultz has been at the University of Chicago, to which he came from Iowa State College in 1943.

Initially Schultz focused on problems faced by agriculture in the United States during the 1930s and the war years. A vital young department head, he brought together a lively group of colleagues, stimulating them and students to explore strategies for dealing with the impact of economic fluctuations and of the vagaries of weather on farmers and farming. As important as his 1945 book on *Agriculture in an Unstable Economy* was his active involvement in dissemination to both lay and professional audiences, reflected in the bibliography attached to my essay on Schultz in the *Scandinavian Journal of Economics* (1980). Two themes that recur both in this and in later work are distortions of incentives and dealing with change and uncertainty.

With his increasing interest in economic development around the world, and in less developed countries in particular, Schultz came increasingly to consider the importance of agricultural development for general economic growth. His understanding of what rural poverty can mean, his respect for the shrewdness of unschooled practical men, and his appreciation of the value of education were joined in *Transforming Traditional Agriculture* (1964). This book challenged the 'zero marginal product' hypothesis in agriculture and proposed that ultimately farmers' education could be a low-cost investment in acquiring a 'permanent income stream'.

Though his roots are in agricultural economics, in the late 1950s Schultz began his pursuit of human capital theory on a broad front, gleaning fresh insights (as he often does) from the wisdom of great predecessors (Marshall, Knight, Irving Fisher). His contributions to the economics of education have been distinctive in their dynamic emphasis, in contrast to most of the technical econometric studies that proliferated following early contributions of Gary Becker and Jacob Mincer. Thus Schultz has stressed the importance of enhanced 'ability to deal with disequilibria' as an essential component in economic progress, and more recently he has given particular attention to innovative behaviour in his continuing pursuit of a dynamic approach to the present and the future. Schultz has never stood still, but a continuity of emphasis on incentives, on change and uncertainty, and on human potentials is ever present in his work.

SELECTED WORKS

1932. Diminishing returns in view of progress in agricultural production. *Journal of Farm Economics* 14(4), October, 640–49.

1934. Trade and tariff problems related to agriculture. In *Report of the Committee of Inquiry into National Policy in International Economic Relations*, Minneapolis: University of Minnesota Press.

1940. Capital rationing, uncertainty, and farm tenancy reform. *Journal of Political Economy* 48, June, 309–24.

1941. Economic effects of agricultural programs. *American Economic Review* 30, February, 127–54.

1944. Two conditions necessary for economic progress in agriculture. *Canadian Journal of Economics and Political Science* 10, August, 298–311.

1945a. *Agriculture in an Unstable Economy*. New York: McGraw-Hill.

1945b. Food and agriculture in a developing economy. In *Food for the World*, ed. T.W. Schultz, Chicago: University of Chicago Press. Reprinted, New York: Arno Press, 1976, in the 'World Food Supply' Series.

1950. Reflections on poverty within agriculture. *Journal of Political Economy* 43, February, 1–15.

1951. Declining economic importance of agricultural land. *Economic Journal* 61, December, 725–40.

1953. *The Economic Organization of Agriculture*. New York: McGraw-Hill. (Translated into Spansih, Portuguese, French, Japanese, Italian).

1956. The role of the government in promoting economic growth. In *The State of the Social Sciences*, ed. L.D. White, Chicago: University of Chicago Press. 372–83.

1960. Capital formation by education. *Journal of Political Economy* 68, December, 571–83. (Translated into Spanish.)

1961. Investment in human capital. *American Economic Review* 51, March, 1–17. (Presidential address: Reprinted at least 20 times, and translated into Slovak, Spanish, Portuguese, Hungarian, Italian, French and Japanese.)

1963. *The Economic Value of Education.* New York: Colombia University Press. (Translated into Spanish, Portuguese, Japanese, Greek.)

1964. *Transforming Traditional Agriculture.* New Haven: Yale University Press. (Translated into Japanese, Korean, Portuguese, Spanish.) Reprinted, 1976, New York: Arno Press.

1965. Investing in poor people: an economist's view. *American Economic Review* 45, May, 510–20.

1968. Institutions and the rising economic value of man. *American Journal of Agricultural Economics* 50, December, 1113–22.

1971. *Investment in Human Capital: The Role of Education and Research.* New York: Free Press and Macmillan. (Translated into 9 other languages.)

1975. The value of the ability to deal with disequilibria. *Journal of Economic Literature* 13(3), 827–46.

1980. *Investing in People; The Economics of Population Quality.* San Francisco: University of California Press. (Translated into 9 other languages.)

Schumacher, E.F. (Fritz)

G.D.N. WORSWICK

Economist, journalist, industrial adviser and eventually 'guru' with a world wide following, Schumacher was born a German citizen in 1911 and died a British citizen in 1977. One of the first German Rhodes scholars at Oxford University after World War I, he spent much of the 1930s studying and working in Britain and United States. When World War II came he cast his lot with Britain. Interned as an 'enemy alien', he was released to work as a farm labourer and then allowed to return to Oxford. His credentials as an economist were quickly established in a memorandum (1943a) on a multilateral clearing union for postwar international payments, similar to the famous 'Keynes Plan' put forward by the British at Bretton Woods. Another paper, written jointly with Michael Kalecki (1943b), proposed an International Investment Board as a means to inject liquidity into the international economy, an idea revived twenty years later as the 'Link'. He was also one of a group of economists working out policies for full employment.

Schumacher had early shown a desire to grapple with big questions, and to participate in great events. He became economic adviser to the British Control Commission in Germany, and then became adviser to the British coal industry, which had been nationalized after the war. Notwithstanding the glut of Middle East oil in the 1950s and 1960s, he stood for maintaining the output of British coal, albeit with an emphasis on conservation. Nuclear energy he rejected on the grounds that it would create an environmental and ecological problem of waste disposal of 'monstrous magnitude'. A visit to Burma in 1955 aroused his interest in developing countries, and for economics the most striking outcome was his idea of 'intermediate technology'. In developing countries the indigenous technology required little equipment for each worker, but the outcome was low productivity and low standards of living. With only limited amounts of capital, poor countries adopting advanced technology might achieve much higher output but would gain little in employment. What was needed was an intermediate technology adapted to the special needs of a developing country. This idea unquestionably changed the direction of thought about economic development, although its practical implementation has proved far from easy, since it runs against the grain of large-scale multinational capitalist enterprise.

While in Burma, Schumacher became a Buddhist (he was later to become a Roman Catholic) and this coloured his subsequent attitude to conventional Western economics. Capitalism, he argued, might bring higher living standards through competition and efficiency, but only at the cost of debasing human culture. Bigness, whether of industrial firms or cities, was anathema. The planet's resources were finite and should be conserved. These ideas were brought together in a set of essays with the brilliantly evocative title *Small is Beautiful,* whose publication in 1973 marked the transformation of an economic programme into something like a religious movement.

SELECTED WORKS

1943a. Multilateral clearing. *Economica* 10, May, 150–65.
1943b. (With M. Kalecki.) International clearing and long-term lending. *Oxford University Institute of Statistics Bulletin* 5, Supplement 6, August, 29–33.
1971. Industrialisation through 'intermediate technology'. In *Developing the Third World: The Experience of the Nineteen-Sixties,* ed. R. Robinson, Cambridge Commonwealth Series, New York and London: Cambridge University Press.
1972. The work of the intermediate technology development group in Africa. *International Labour Review* 106(1), July, 75–92.
1973. *Small is Beautiful. A study of economics as if people mattered.* London: Blond & Briggs.

Seers, Dudley

ROSEMARY THORP

Born in 1920, Seers was educated at Rugby and Pembroke College, Cambridge, and served in the Royal Navy during World War II. Once the war was over he joined the Prime Minister's Office in New Zealand, but by 1946 had moved to Oxford. He became a leading economist in the field of development studies, moving from his early work in statistics and national income to a wide range of topics in development and an extraordinary diversity of country studies. In his later work he turned back to the problems of developed countries, in two major edited volumes on the European Economic Community. His claim was one that increasingly finds echo: the study of the underdeveloped world provides much insight into the structural problems of the developed countries.

Perhaps his outstanding characteristic as an economist, apart from exceptional professional competence, was his passionate concern that the subject should deal with people and real issues, fearlessly crossing discipline boundaries if necessary. His instinctive ability to see the subject in the terms of people is apparent in his first book, written while at the Institute of Statistics, Oxford, in the 1940s. Discussing the difficulty of assessing shifts in income distribution, he wrote:

> One may find a wage-earner with a large family in a council house who was unemployed before the war and has enjoyed a great rise in living standard. His brother may be an engine driver and vegetarian, who has been forced to rent furnished rooms and can afford much less pipe tobacco than he could in 1939 (Seers, 1949, p. 3).

These interests led him naturally to the 'structuralist' school when he worked at the UN and in 1957–61 for the UN Economic Commission for Latin America. In 1962 he published what was to become a seminal article in the structuralist view of inflation: an eloquent and precise presentation of the view that inflation results not from monetary expansion but from rigidities inherent in the economic, social and political system (Seers, 1962). As the structuralists became more radical, and the 'dependency' school emerged, Seers was a sympathetic critic, insisting

303

in his edited volume in 1981 that its insights were real and important: it 'raises the right questions – much more relevant ones than those derived from neo-classical economics' (Seers, 1981).

This preoccupation with 'the right questions' runs through his writing, and led to his best-known articles: those on methodology and the development of the discipline. Although not a writer for whom it is easy to identify 'seminal contributions', his role as *agent provocateur* was truly original and of great value. In this way the same personality trait that led him to list his recreation in *Who's Who* as 'teasing bureaucrats', led him to provoke and stimulate also at a professional level. In 'The Limitations of the Special Case' in 1963, he argued that the corpus of economic theory is in fact based on the special case; the few highly industrialized economies comprising a small minority of the world population. His analysis of 'the typical case', the unindustrialized economy, although dated by now, remains a prophetic statement of the need for a different 'text book economics' more helpful to teachers, students and practitioners in LDCs. The challenge is unmet more than twenty years later.

In addition to his stimulating role as a persistent questioner, he was also a careful empirical economist, as witnessed in the thoroughness of his many country studies, including his book on Cuba, edited in 1964 with Richard Jolly and for some years the only serious and accessible study in English of the Cuban economy, and the ILO report on employment in Colombia, of which he was the chief author.

His desire to link academic thinking and the real world led him to become also an institution builder – first at the new Ministry of Overseas Development established in 1964 where with Barbara Castle as Minister and Andrew Cohen as Permanent Secretary he shaped the new Ministry's work, and subsequently as the first Director of the Sussex Institute of Development Studies. He was Director 1967–72 and a Fellow till his death. He played a minor role in establishing the international reputation of the IDS and in leading the effort to link academics and policy advice.

The willingness to step into 'real life' was reflected also in his work as Chairman of the World University Service Awards for Chile (1974–8), following the collapse of Allende's government and the ensuing wave of refugeese to the UK.

Dudley Seers died in 1983 at the age of 62, in the midst of continued productive work: he had just arrived in Washington to edit for the World Bank a series of papers by 'pioneers' in development thinking.

SELECTED WORKS

1949. *The Levelling of Incomes since 1938*. Oxford: Basil Blackwell.
1962. Inflation and growth: a summary of experience in Latin America. UNECLA, *Economic Bulletin for Latin America* 7, February, 23–51.
1963. The limitations of the special case. *Bulletin of the Oxford University Institute of Economics and Statistics* 25(2), May, 77–98.
1981. *Dependency Theory: a Critical Reassessment*. London: Frances Pinter.

Shadow Pricing

RAVI KANBUR

When a businessman evaluates a project, he does it with a view to calculating the prospective profit from it. These calculations can be seen as taking place in two steps. At the first step, all the physical consequences of relevance to the businessman – the inputs to and outputs from the project – are assessed. At the second stage, these inputs and outputs are converted into costs and revenues, using *market prices*. It is natural that a private businessman should use the ruling market prices for costing inputs and for valuing sales, since these are the prices at which transactions take place and hence profit is generated.

Consider now the evaluation of a project by a government. Such evaluation will differ at each of the two steps referred to above. At the first step, the government will be interested in *all* of the repercussions of the project, however indirect. This is because it is the government rather than a private businessman concerned with his own narrowly defined activities. At the second step, the government will wish to use not the ruling market prices but prices which reflect social costs and social benefits, in order to calculate what might be termed social profit. These prices are referred to as *shadow prices*, or accounting prices (see Little and Mirrlees, 1974), and the name suggests that they are to be used in lieu of the actual market prices.

Market prices are what they are. But how are shadow prices to be calculated? Clearly they depend on the government's objective function and on the constraints it faces. The shadow prices should be such that the social profit from the project is positive if and only if the project increases the value of the government's objective function. In a general competitive equilibrium, if the government's objective is economic efficiency, then it can be argued that for a small project the shadow prices do in fact coincide with market prices. If the government's objective includes the pursuance of equity, but it has lump sum instruments to carry this out, then shadow prices still coincide with market prices. Basically the government should use redistributive lump sum taxation to pursue equity and use the project to pursue increases in aggregate economic welfare.

But if the government does not have a sufficient range of instruments to pursue effective redistribution without distortion it may be the case that, even with a full competitive equilibrium, shadow prices may differ from market prices. In addition to this, if the economy is not in a full competitive equilibrium, then the case for using shadow prices different from market prices can be argued strongly.

In programming terms, shadow prices are simply dual to the changes in the government's objective function. One justification for their use is the benefits of decentralization: local project evaluators are better equipped to analyse the physical consequences of a project, and this localized knowledge should be used in conjunction with centrally determined shadow prices to evaluate the social profitability of projects. But the real difficulties arise in specifying the objectives of the government and in specifying its constraints, and this is in turn related to who is thought of as doing the project evaluation.

The standard assumption is one of a unitary government with a given social welfare function – a benevolent dictator. But the reality is one where the project evaluator is either part of a government which is a coalition of interests, or the project evaluation is being done by an international agency which faces a government made up of conflicting and competing objectives. The logical procedure for an international agency should be clear – in evaluating a project it should incorporate a model of the political process to clarify the responses of various government instruments to the project. Sen (1972) gives an illuminating discussion of a project which requires importing an input on which there is already a quota – so that the border price of the input is very different from its domestic scarcity value. The Little and Mirrlees (1974) method of using border prices is predicated on the assumption that it is these prices which represent the transformation possibilities for the economy as a whole. But if the assessment of the political realities is such that this quota will not be removed by the government – because of the overriding influence of interest groups that benefit from the rents generated by the quota – then the domestic scarcity value should be used in costing the input.

Similarly, any project which alters significantly the distribution of income will have repercussions on the political process – and there will be attempts by groups who are adversely affected to restore their standard of living. Project evaluation in general, and shadow pricing in particular, should take these into account. Consider, for example, the shadow cost of labour. If the labour used on the project comes from the agricultural sector, and if this labour is a constraint on output, then agricultural output will fall. If government revenue depends on taxation of this output, this will fall too. If, in turn, government expenditure is a major source of non-agricultural (urban) incomes, then at constant fiscal deficit urban incomes will fall. This change in the distribution of income will be an important element in the shadow cost of labour. But suppose now that the political processes are such as not to allow a decline in urban living standards. Rather, government expenditure remains constant and the fiscal deficit increases. Now it is the increased burden on future generations which has to be taken into account. Either way, it should be clear that a model of the political process is crucial in specifying shadow prices even if the project evaluator (be it an international agency or a project evaluation unit within the government) is clear about what the objectives are. Braverman and Kanbur (1985) have provided a prototype analysis of how such constraints might be taken into account, in the specific context of projects in West Africa.

BIBLIOGRAPHY

Braverman, A. and Kanbur, S.M.R. 1985. Urban bias, present bias, and the shadow cost of labour for agricultural projects: the West African context. The World Bank, Mimeo.

Little, I.M.D. and Mirrlees, J.A. 1974. *Project Appraisal and Planning for Developing Countries*. London: Heinemann.

Sen, A.K. 1972. Control areas and accounting prices: an approach to economic evaluation. *Economic Journal* 82, Supplement, 486–501.

Sharecropping

JOSEPH E. STIGLITZ

Sharecropping is a form of land tenancy, in which the landlord allows the tenant to use his land, in return for a stipulated fraction of the output (the 'share'). It is an institutional arrangement which has prevailed in many parts of the world. Though today sharecropping is most commonly found in l.d.c.'s, sharecropping arrangements exist even in more advanced countries (such as the United States).

The sharecropping relationship may take on a variety of forms. The landlord may share in the costs (other than labour), or may bear none of the costs or all of the costs. If he shares in the cost, the fraction of the costs he bears may or may not be equal to the fraction of output which he receives. A variety of restrictions may be imposed on the tenant (e.g. concerning what crops to be grown, how much non-labour inputs have to be supplied, etc.).

Since the early 1970s there has been a resurgence of interest in sharecropping, for two reasons. First, sharecropping *appears* to be an inefficient institutional arrangement, since workers receive less than their marginal product. The question naturally arises, how could such an inefficient system seem to flourish in so many places and over such a long duration? The New Institutional Economics begins with the presumption that one should not simply take the institutional structure of the economy as given, but should attempt to explain it, to identify the economic rationale for the observed features of the economy. (This is not to say that inefficient economic institutions might not persist, but one must explain why that is the case.) Thus, researchers in the theory of rural organization have attempted to explain not only the persistence of sharecropping, but also the particular features which it exhibits.

Secondly, it has increasingly become clear that the sharecropping relationship is, in fact, quite similar to a number of other economic relationships, found in both developed and less developed countries. For instance, capitalists often let others use their capital, in return for a fixed share in the profits; thus understanding sharecropping may provide insights into understanding modern capital markets (stock markets). Thus, the sharecropping model has served as the basic paradigm for a wider class of relationships known as principal-agent relationships. This basic similarity was noted in Stiglitz (1974); this entry draws heavily upon that paper.

Views on the reasons for, and efficiency of, sharecropping relationships have gone through several stages. The earlier view that depicted sharecropping as simply an inefficient institutional arrangement was followed by a view that it represented an efficient institutional arrangement for risk-sharing, in an environment where other forms of insurance were not available; the landlord and the tenant shared in the risks associated with the fluctuations in output caused by weather, disease, etc., as well as those associated with the vicissitudes in the prices of marketed commodities. Sharecropping contracts had the distinct advantage over rental contracts in that the landlord, who because of his higher wealth was in a better position to bear risks, bore a larger fraction of those risk than he did under the rental agreement (where the worker bore all the risks). Cheung (1969) went so far as to suggest that there were not, in fact, any efficiency losses, provided that the sharecropping contract specified the labour required of the worker.

Three objections were raised to these conclusions. First, if sharecropping were just a risk-sharing institution, why did not the landlord bear still more of the risk? Secondly, it was shown that *the same risk-sharing opportunities could be provided without sharecropping, simply by having workers mix wage contracts and rental contracts*. Thirdly, if sharecropping was primarily a risk sharing contract, then the terms (shares) should vary accordingly to the riskiness of the crops grown and the differences in wealth between the landlord and the tenant. Though terms did vary from place to place, the variations did not appear to be of the magnitude that the risk-sharing theory would have suggested.

Moreover, it seemed implausible that the landlord could perfectly monitor the worker, so that a contract which specified precisely the labour to be applied would not be enforceable.

Thus Stiglitz (1974) argued that sharecropping was an institutional arrangement designed both to share risks and to provide incentives, in a situation where monitoring effort (labour supply) was costly. Sharecropping represented a *compromise*: while rental contracts provided (in the absence of bankruptcy) perfect incentives (since the individual kept all of the value of his marginal product), it provided no risk sharing; on the other hand, wage contracts shifted all of the risk on to landlords, who were in the best position to bear it, but provided no incentives. To ensure that workers did not shirk, the landlord would have to spend resources monitoring the workers.

In this approach, it appears as if the sharecropping contract has certain optimality properties: indeed, the contract is usually represented as maximizing the welfare of the worker, subject to the landlord obtaining a particular value of expected rents from his land. (Even the inefficiency associated with the worker receiving less than the value of his marginal product may be mitigated with long-term contracts; workers who fail to produce a sufficiently high level of output over a long enough period may find their tenancy contract terminated.)

This general approach could be used to explain not only the persistence of sharecropping, but also some of its important features:

(a) The landlord had an incentive to encourage the tenant to use inputs (such as fertilizer) which raised the workers' marginal product, and which therefore resulted in the workers working harder. This explains why the landlord might bear a fraction of the costs of inputs that exceeded the fraction of the output that he received.

(b) Important externalities might arise between land markets and credit markets; these externalities can explain the interlinking between credit and land markets that is frequently observed in l.d.c.'s (i.e. the landlord is also the lender). An increase in the amount of outstanding debt affects both workers' efforts and their choice of technique (risk). These, in turn, affect the return to the landlord. Conversely, a change in the terms of sharecropping contract will in general affect the probability of default, and hence the return to the lender. See Braverman and Stiglitz (1982).

This analysis leaves three questions outstanding:

(1) To implement a cost sharing contract, costs have to be observable. If costs are observable, then the contract could, in principle, specify the level of inputs; no 'moral hazard' problem need arise. Why then are cost sharing contracts so widespread? Again, the answer lies in an information asymmetry: the worker often is more informed than the landlord about what the appropriate level of inputs are. Thus, the contract should provide the worker with an incentive to use his superior information; and this the cost sharing contract does.

(2) The theory predicts a wider variation in the terms of the contract than is in fact observed. Shares of between $\frac{1}{2}$ and $\frac{2}{3}$ are observed in widely varying circumstances. Allen (1985) provides an interesting explanation of this phenomenon. He argues that unless the worker is provided adequate incentives (a large enough share) he will have an incentive to abscond with the entire output. Assume, for instance, that if a worker were to do so, he would remain unemployed for one period, and then obtain land (at similar terms) in another village. If his output is Q, the present discounted value of his absconding is

$$Q + \alpha Q / (1 + r)r$$

where α is the share the worker receives, and r is the rate of interest; if he does not abscond, the present discounted value of his income is

$$(1 + r)\alpha Q / r.$$

Hence, if he is not to abscond,

$$\alpha > (1 + r)/(2 + r)$$

If r is not too great, this is approximately 0.5. Thus, if this constraint is binding, changes in economic circumstances will have little affect on the terms of the contract.

(3) Economic theory predicts that, in general, the share received by the worker should be a function of the level of output and not a constant. One explanation

310

for why the share would be a constant is that, if it were not, the effective price received by different farmers would differ. Then there would be opportunities for arbitrage.

There may be a simpler explanation: the gains to the use of non-linear contracts are not worth the additional costs of implementing them. In particular, the exact form of the 'optimal non-linear contract' (to be described below) may be sensitive to details concerning the probability distribution of the random variables affecting output, the nature of the technology, and the utility function of workers. Much more limited information is required to implement the optimal linear sharecropping contract. Indeed, in the standard specifications of the optimal contract, the share contracts should be random, under quite general conditions. The fact that they are not suggests that something important is left out of the analysis.

Current views on sharecropping suggests that while it may not have the deleterious consequences suggested by the earlier views, it may not have the optimality properties associated with the 'principal-agent' view. First, though the contracts are 'locally efficient' (that is, they maximize the expected utility of the worker, given the expected rents to be received by the landlord), they are not 'general equilibrium efficient', that is, there exist, in general, taxes and subsidies which could lead to Pareto improvements.

Secondly, for a variety of reasons, one may be concerned with the level of production in the economy; and sharecropping may have a deleterious effect on this. A sharecropping contract with a 50 per cent share has the same effects that a tax on output of 50 per cent would have; there is a presumption that such a tax might significantly decrease output, unless the labour supply schedule was backward bending. If this is the case, then a land reform, in which workers receive the land which they formally worked as sharecroppers, may increase agricultural productivity significantly.

There has also been some concern that the contractual form may affect the adoption of innovations. It undoubtedly does: innovations which increase output (at any level of input of labour), but which decrease the marginal product of labour (and hence reduce workers' incentives to work) will be resisted by landlords (they may impose restrictions on the use of such technologies). But these innovations would, at the same time, have reduced agricultural productivity.

DETERMINATION OF THE EQUILIBRIUM CONTRACT. The analysis of sharecropping contracts depends critically on the set of admissible contracts. Three sets of contracts have been investigated: (a) fixed shares; (b) linear contracts; and (c) non-linear contracts.

In the case where the share is fixed (by convention, say), then the problem of the landlord is a simple one. The 'competitive' landlord takes the opportunity cost of a worker as given, represented by his reservation utility level U^*; he must offer a contract which generates at least that level of utility. For simplicity, we assume all workers and all land are identical.

Output per acre is assumed to be a function of a random variable (S) and labour input per unit land, which in turn is a function of the effort level of workers

(e) and the number of workers per acre (a):

$$q = f(S, ea)$$

We simplify by using the multiplicative form,

$$q = Sf(ea).$$

The worker chooses his effort level to maximize his expected utility, given his outside wage opportunities and the terms of the contract. For simplicity, for the moment we ignore the outside opportunities. His utility is a function of his effort and his income, y; y in turn depends simply on the share and the amount of land he has, i.e.

$$y = \alpha q/a,$$

where α is the share (q is the output per acre, and $1/a$ is the number of acres the representative tenant worker has). He then maximizes

$$EU(\alpha q/a, e).$$

The solution yields effort, and his output, as a function of the contract terms a and α:

$$y = y(a, \alpha).$$

We denote the maximized value of expected utility by $V(\alpha, a)$. The landlord thus

$$\underset{\{\alpha, a\}}{\text{maximizes}} \, E(1 - \alpha)q$$

subject to the constraint that

$$V(\alpha, a) \geqslant U^*.$$

In the case, where α is dictated by custom, there are two possible patterns of equilibrium.

(a) Increasing the density (reducing the amount of land per worker) has two effects; it reduces his welfare, and this income effect induces him to work harder; and it reduces the marginal return to his effort, and this induces him to work less hard. If the individual has outside opportunities, he may spend more of his energies on these outside activities. It is thus possible that reducing acreage per worker below a certain level actually reduces output per acre. There may thus exist an interior solution to the unconstrained problem,

$$\underset{\{a\}}{\max} \, Eq.$$

Denote the solution by a^*. Denote the available worker/land ratio by a'. If

$$a^* < a',$$

then some individuals will get land, with plot sizes $1/a^*$; there will be unemployed individuals (or individuals who work in non-agricultural occupations, at a lower expected utility); but they cannot persuade any landlords to give them land.

On the other hand, if

$$a^* > a',$$

then in equilibrium everyone will get land, with plot size $1/a'$.

(b) By the same token, if there is no interior solution, then the equilibrium plot size will be simply determined by the available land/labourer ratio.

The analysis when the share can be determined endogenously follows along parallel lines. We now need to solve again the unconstrained problem. (The optimal share in the unconstrained problem will be between zero and one; at $\alpha = 0$, the worker has no incentive to work; and at $\alpha = 1$, the landlord receives nothing.) Thus, at the optimal value of $\{\alpha, a\}$, if $a^* < a'$, then some individuals will not be successful in obtaining the use of land.

Linear contracts. The next most complicated set of sharecropping contracts involves a fixed payment (either to or from the landlord) plus a share. Many contractual relations may have an implicit or explicit provision calling for such fixed payments; payments from the landlord to the worker to finance stipulated inputs, like fertilizer, can be interpreted this way. Now, the income of the worker can be written

$$y = \alpha q / a + \beta.$$

The mathematical formulation follows exactly along the lines of the previous case. This formulation has the advantage that it can generate, as limiting cases, a pure rental contract (where $\alpha = 1$, $\beta < 0$) and a pure wage contract ($\alpha = 0$, $\beta > 0$). Not surprisingly, the exact form of the contract depends both on the properties of U and f, as well as the magnitude of the uncertainty. If, for instance, workers were risk neutral, a pure rental contract will be used; the greater the risk aversion and the greater the risk, the closer the optimal contract approximates a pure wage contract. Moreover, the greater the (compensated) labour supply elasticity, i.e. the more sensitive the worker is to incentive, the greater α, i.e. the closer to a rental contract. (If the worker supplied labour inelastically, again a wage contract would be efficient.) (For detailed formulae, see Stiglitz, 1974.)

Non-linear contracts. In the formulations presented thus far, it makes little difference whether workers supply their effort before or after S is known (though the contract must be signed before S is known). (Most of the sharecropping literature focuses on the case where the effort decision is made before S is known.) This is no longer true when non-linear contracts are employed.

The simplest case is that where effort must be applied before S is known, and there are unbounded penalties (no restrictions on the set of admissible contracts). In the case where there is a finite range to S, the landlord calculates what the first-best optimal level of effort would be, i.e.

313

$$\max_{e} U(\bar{y} + \beta, e)$$

(where $-\beta$ is his rent and $\bar{y} = Ey$). Denote this by e^{**}. He then calculates the minimum output associated with this

$$\min_{\{S\}} \{f(S, e^{**}a')\}.$$

The worker gets a fixed wage, regardless of output, provided output per acre exceeds this level; and he gets an infinite punishment if it falls short (being thrown off the land may suffice, if alternative opportunities are unavailable).

Thus, in this case, optimal contracting will never entail sharecropping, but will always involve a wage contract, with a severe penalty for deficient performance. Though the landlord may be able to detect deficient performances only in extreme cases, the severe punishment in those situations is enough to provide the worker with the requisite incentives. (This result does not, however, appear to be robust to changes in information structure.)

The other situation is that where effort is applied after S is known. Consider the simplest case where there are only two states of nature, S_1 and S_2. The landlord will, ex post, be able to distinguish which of the two states has occurred by observing the output (one can show that this will always be the case with optimally chosen incentive structures).

An incentive structure provides a relationship between output and what the worker gets, i.e. assuming for simplicity that everyone has one unit of land, it specifies

$$y = \tilde{y}(q).$$

For each incentive function, we could calculate the levels of effort and output in the two states and hence the landlord's expected income; if the two states are equally likely, his expected income is

$$R = 1/2\{q_1 - y_1 + q_2 - y_2\}.$$

We then look for that function $\tilde{y}$ which maximizes this, subject to the workers' reservation utility constraint. It is easier, however, if we simply ask, what are the values of $\{q_i, y_i\}$ which maximize rents, subject to the reservation utility constraint, and subject to the 'self-selection constraints' which enable us to differentiate among the two states (that is, the self-selection constraint ensure that, when the state is state 1, the individual undertakes the action which we intended in state 1, and similarly for state 2). Formally, then, the optimal sharecropping contract is that set of $\{y_i, q_i\}$ which

$$\max R$$

subject to

$$V(y_i, q_i, S_i) > V(y_j, q_j, S_i) \qquad i \neq j \text{ (the self-selection constraint)}$$

and subject to

$$\Sigma V(y_i, q_i, S_i) p_i > U^*,$$

where u^* is the reservation utility constraint, p_i is the probability of state i, and where

$$V(y, q, S) = U[y, l(q, S)],$$

the utility in state S when output is q and income is y; where $l(q, S)$ is the labour (effort) required to produce output q in state S.

BIBLIOGRAPHY

Allen, F. 1985. On the fixed nature of sharecropping contracts. *Economic Journal*, March, 30–48.

Braverman, A. and Stiglitz, J.E. 1982. Sharecropping and the interlinking of agrarian markets. *American Economic Review* 72(4), September, 695–715.

Cheung, S. 1969. *The Theory of Share Tenancy*. Chicago: University of Chicago Press.

Stiglitz, J.E. 1974. Incentives and risk sharing in sharecropping. *Review of Economic Studies*, April, 219–55.

Structuralism

J.G. PALMA

Structuralism is basically a method of enquiry which challenges the assumptions of empiricism and positivism. This method is found in literary criticism, linguisitics, aesthetics and social sciences both Marxist and non-Marxist.

The principal characteristic of structuralism is that it takes as its object of investigation a 'system', that is, the reciprocal relations among parts of a whole, rather than the study of the different parts in isolation. In a more specific sense this concept is used by those theories that hold that there are a set of social and economic structures that are unobservable but which generate observable social and economic phenomena.

In anthropology, structuralism is particularly associated with Lévi-Strauss and Godelier. The main structuralist current in Marxist thought has its origins in Althusser and stands in opposition to the version of Marxist theory developed by Lukacs, Gramsci and the Frankfurt School. While structuralism seeks to explain social phenomena by reference to the underlying structure of the mode of production (hence, trying not to be 'humanistic' or 'historicist' in a technological sense), the second group of Marxist theories stress the role of human consciousness and action in social life, with a concept of history in which (arguably) some idea of 'progress' is either implicit or explicit.

In economics structuralism is primarily associated with the school of thought originated in ECLA (United Nations' Economic Commission for Latin America), and in particular with the work of its first Director, Raul Prebisch.

The key to the internal unity of ECLA thought lies in its early postulation of the original ideas and hypotheses around which its subsequent contributions would be organized. The starting point was the idea that the world economy was composed of two poles, the 'centre' and the 'periphery', and that the *structure of production* in each differed substantially. That of the centre was seen as homogeneous and diversified, that of the periphery, in contrast, as heterogeneous and specialized; heterogeneous because economic activities with significant differences as to productivity existed side by side, with the two extremes provided by an export sector with relatively high productivity of labour, and a subsistence agriculture in which it was particularly low; specialized because the export sector would tend to be concentrated upon a few primary products, with production characteristically confined to an 'enclave' within the peripheral economic structure, or, in other words, having very limited backward and forward linkage effects with the rest of the economy. It was this structural difference between the two types of economy which lay behind the different function of each pole in the international division of labour, and this in turn had the effect of reinforcing the structural difference between the two.

Thus the two poles were closely bound together, and were mutually and reciprocally conditioning. Therefore, the structural difference between centre and periphery could not be defined or understood in static terms, as the transformation of either pole would be conditioned by the interaction between them. Centre and periphery formed a single system, dynamic by its very nature.

The nucleus of ECLA analysis was the critique of the conventional theory of international trade (as expressed in the Heckschler–Ohlin–Samuelson version of Ricardo's theory of comparative advantages); it aimed to show that the international division of labour which conventional theory claimed was 'naturally' produced by world trade was of much greater benefit to the centre (where manufacturing production is concentrated) than to the periphery (which was destined mainly to produce primary products, be they agricultural or mineral). The analysis of ECLA has a unity and an internal coherence which is not always perceptible at first sight, as its component parts are scattered through numerous documents published over a period of years (mainly in the 1950s and 1960s). Several contributions had their origins in the examination of specific problems, around which a series of theoretical arguments were articulated, in an attempt to isolate their causes and to justify the economic policy measures recommended to resolve them.

The ECLA analysis turns on three tendencies which are considered inherent to the development of the periphery: unemployment of the labour force, external disequilibrium, and the tendency to deterioration of the terms of trade (see Rodriguez, 1980).

(i) *Structural heterogeneity and unemployment.* The problem of employment in the periphery has two facets: the absorption of additions to the active population, and the re-absorption of the labour force of the most backward areas into economic activities in which productivity is higher. As the ECLA analysis assumes that demand for labour is proportionate to the level of investment (its rate of growth is directly related to the rate of capital accumulation), and this takes place almost exclusively in the modern sector, full employment of the labour force at adequate levels of productivity can only be achieved if the rate of capital accumulation in the export sector and in import-substituting manufacturing activities is sufficient not only to absorb the growth in the whole of the active population, but also to reabsorb labour from the traditional sector. Thus the level of employment depends on the balance between the growth of the active population and the rhythm of the expulsion of labour from the traditional sector, and on the level of capital accumulation in the modern sector. It is from the heavy burden on the modern sector to provide full employment in the economy at an adequate level of productivity that the structural tendency towards unemployment in the peripheral economies is deduced.

(ii) *Specialization in production and external disequilibrium.* The structure of production in the periphery is specialized in a double sense: mainly primary products are exported, and the economies are in general poorly integrated. From this it follows that a significant proportion of the demand for manufactured products is oriented towards imports, and given that their income elasticity is greater than unity, imports tend to grow faster than the level of real income. The opposite is the case in the centre, as imports from the periphery consist essentially of primary products, for which income elasticity is usually less than unity; hence they grow less rapidly than real income.

Thus for a given rate of growth real income in the centre, the disparity between the income elasticities of imports at each pole will impose a limit upon the rate of growth of real income in the periphery (unless the latter is able to diversify its productive structure). This will not only tend to be less than that of the centre, but to be less in proportion to the degree of the disparity between the respective income elasticities of demand for imports. If the periphery attempts to surpass this limit, it will expose itself to successive deficits in its balance of trade; the only long term alternative will be an increased effort to satisfy the highly income-elastic demand for manufactured products with internal production, and to diversify its export trade towards income-elastic products. Only a process of industrialization, given these assumptions, can allow that and enable the periphery to enjoy a rate of growth of real income higher than that determined by the rate of growth in the centre and the disparity between income elasticities of demand for imports.

As this process of industrialization also generates a need for imports which can exceed the availability of foreign currency deriving from the slow expansion of primary exports, ECLA argues in its documents that there is a role for foreign capital in the first stages of the process, both to remedy the shortage of foreign currency, and to complement internal savings.

(iii) *Specialization, heterogeneity, and the tendency to deterioration of the terms of trade.* The explanation for the phenomena of the tendency to deteriorating terms of trade and the disparity in incomes which it brings with it are, in the thought of ECLA, a logical analytical deduction from the phenomena of specialization and heterogeneity. (It is not, as it is usually assumed, the starting point of ECLA thought, but – given its assumptions and hypotheses – a natural analytical deduction.)

There are, basically, a demand and a supply element behind this tendency to deterioration of the terms of trade of the periphery (see the article on Prebisch for a more detailed analysis of this point). The basic problem is the effect of economic growth on the terms of trade. From a demand point of view – given the problem of specialization and the differences in income elasticities for imports between the centre and periphery – the 'consumption path' of the periphery is biased towards trade (i.e. as incomes grow the proportion of importables in total consumption increases). From the point of view of supply – given the effect of heterogeneity on technological change and the differences in price elasticity of supply of exports between the centre and the periphery – the 'production path' of the periphery is also biased towards trade (i.e. as output grows the proportion of exportables in domestic production increases). The combined effect would be a tendency towards an increased demand for imports of manufacturing goods and an increased supply of primary products from the periphery. If left to the 'invisible hand' of international markets, this would tend to push up prices of imports and push down prices of exports of these countries as a whole; thus the tendency towards deterioration of the terms of trade of the periphery.

According to ECLA, it is possible to escape from this vicious circle through a process of transformation of the economic structure of the periphery capable, ideally, of providing those economies with a rapid and sustained rate of growth, and avoiding unemployment, external disequilibrium, and the deterioration of the terms of trade. The central element in this structural transformation is the process of industrialization, which could provide those highly income-elastic importables and eventually also produce more price-elastic exportables; thus Prebisch, in a recently published article, summarizes ECLA's task as having been that of 'showing that industrialization was an unavoidable prerequisite for development' (1980, p. viii). Furthermore, the article in question appears at times to use the concepts 'industrialization' and 'development' as synonyms.

In other words, to achieve accelerated and sustained economic growth in the periphery a necessary condition (and, some ECLA writings seemed to suggest, a sufficient one) was the development of a process of industrialization. But this process could not be expected to take place spontaneously, for it would be inhibited by the international division of labour which the centre would attempt to impose, and by a series of structural obstacles internal to the peripheral economies. Consequently, a series of measures was proposed, intended to promote a process of deliberate or 'forced' industrialization; these included state intervention in the economy both in the formulation of economic policies oriented towards these ends and as a direct productive agent. Among the economic policies suggested were those of 'healthy' protectionism, exchange controls, the attraction of foreign capital into manufacturing industry, and the stimulation and orientation of domestic investment. The intervention of the state in directly productive activities was recommended in those areas where large amounts of slow-maturing investment were needed, and particularly where this need coincided with the production of essential goods or services.

The dimensions of the thought of ECLA are based then not only upon its breadth and internal unity, but also upon its structuralist nature. The three most important characteristics of the development of the economy in the periphery – unemployment, external disequilibrium, and the tendency to deterioration of the terms of trade – are derived directly from the characteristics of the structure of production in the periphery, thus the possibility of tackling them is seen in terms of an ideal pattern of transformation, which indicates the conditions of proportionality which must hold if those features are to be avoided. This leads to the formulation, tacitly or explicitly, of the law of proportionality in the transformation, which will avoid heterogeneity and will thus allow full employment at adequate levels of productivity, avoid specialization and thus permit the escape from external disequilibria, and thus counteract the tendency towards deterioration of the terms of trade.

Nevertheless, it is also in this very structuralist nature that the limitations of ECLA thought lie; at this level of analysis no consideration is given to the social relations of production which are at the base of the process of import-substituting industrialization, and of the transformation in other structures of society that this brings in its wake.

ECLA proposes an ideal model of sectoral growth – and hence of global growth – designed in such a way that the three tendencies peculiar to economic development of the periphery are not produced; from this are derived the necessary conditions of accumulation which will allow the proportionality required in the transformation of the different sectors of material production. Nevertheless, even when pushed to the limits of its potential internal coherence, the structural approach is inadequate for the analysis of the evolution in the long term of the economic system as a whole, as it clearly involves more than the transformation of the structure of production alone. The theories of ECLA describe and examine certain aspects of the development of the forces of production (to the extent that they deal with the productivity of labour and the degree of diversification and homogeneity of the structures of production), but do not touch on relations of production, nor, as a result, on the manner in which the two interact.

Furthermore, the analysis of the inequalities of development cannot be carried out solely in terms of the patterns of accumulation necessary to avoid the creation of certain disproportions between the different sectors of material production, as inequalities of development are clearly linked to the possibility of saving and accumulation in each pole. That is to say, the requirements as far as accumulation is concerned are derived from those disproportions, but their feasibility depends more upon the general conditions in which accumulation occurs at world level than upon those disproportions. In other words, if the intention is to analyse the bipolarity of the centre–periphery system, it is not enough to postulate the inequality of development of the forces of production; it is necessary also to bear in mind that those forces of production develop in the framework of a process of generation, appropriation and utilization of the economic surplus, and that process, and the relations of exploitation upon which it is based, are not produced purely within each pole, but also between the two poles of the world economy.

It is not particularly surprising that ECLA should have attracted its share of criticism, particularly as it went beyond theoretical pronouncements to offer packages of policy recommendations. It was critized from sectors of the left for failing to denounce sufficiently the mechanisms of exploitation within the capitalist system, and for critizing the conventional theory of international trade only from 'within' (see for example Frank, 1967 and Caputo and Pizarro, 1974). On the other hand, from the right the reaction was immediate and at times ferocious: ECLA's policy recommendations were totally heretical from the point of view of conventional theory, and threatened the political interests of significant sectors. A leading critic in academic circles was Haberler (1961), who accused ECLA of failing to take due account of economic cycles, and argued that single factorial terms of trade would be a better indicator than the simple relationship between the prices of exports and imports (see also Baldwin, 1955).

On the political front, the right accused ECLA of being the 'Trojan horse of Marxism', on the strength of the degree of coincidence between both analyses. In both cases the principal obstacle was located overseas (international division of labour imposed by the centre), and both share the conviction that without a strenuous effort to remove the internal obstacles to development (the traditional sectors) the process of industrialization would be greatly impeded.

Furthermore, the coincidence between crucial elements in the analysis of the two respective lines of thought is made more evident by the fact that the processes of reformulation in each occurred simultaneously. Thus when it became evident that capitalist development in Latin America was taking a path different from that expected, a number of ECLA members began a process of reformulation of the traditional thought of that institution, just at the time that an important sector of the Latin American left was breaking with the traditional Marxist view that capitalist development was both necessary and possible in Latin America, but hindered by the 'feudal–imperialist' alliance. Moreover, both reformulations had one extremely important element in common: *pessimism* regarding the possibility of capitalist development in the periphery (see DEPENDENCY).

Some of the ECLA analysis reemerged in the 1980s in some North American academic circles (see especially Taylor, 1983), but in a way more as conventional economic analysis attempting to integrate some of the assumptions and hypotheses of the traditional ECLA analysis, or as an attempt to formalize classical ECLA thought – which has, nevertheless, proved to be an important contribution (and a much needed one) to mainstream economics – rather than an attempt to use structuralism as a new method of enquiry into economic analysis.

BIBLIOGRAPHY

Bacha, E.L. 1978. An interpretation of unequal exchange from Prebisch to Emmanuel. *Journal of Development Economics* 5, 319–30.

Baer, W. 1962. The economics of Prebisch and ECLA. *Economic Development and Cultural Change* 10, 169–82.

Baldwin, R.E. 1955. Secular movements in the terms of trade. *American Economic Review, Papers and Proceedings* 45, 259–69.

Bhagwati, Y. 1960. A skeptical note on the adverse secular trend in the terms of trade of underdeveloped countries. *Pakistan Economic Journal* 8, 235–48.

Cardoso, F.H. 1977. The originality of the copy: CEPAL and the idea of development. *CEPAL Review* 4, 7–40.

Caputo, O. and Pizarro, A. 1974. *Dependencia y relaciones internationales.* Costa Rica: EDUCA.

Di Marco, L.E. (ed.) 1972. *International Economics and Development: Essays in Honour of Raul Prebisch.* New York and London: Academic Press.

ECLA. 1963. *El desarrollo social de América Latina en la post-guerra.* Buenos Aires: E. Solar-Hachette.

ECLA. 1964. *El desarrollo económico de América Latina en la post-guerra.* Santiago: UN (CEPAL).

ECLA. 1965. *El financiamiento externo de América Latina.* Santiago: UN (CEPAL).

ECLA. 1966. *El proceso de industrialización de América Latina.* Santiago: UN (CEPAL).

ECLA. 1969. *El pensamiento de la CEPAL.* Santiago: Editorial Universitaria.

ECLA. 1973. *Bibliografía de la CEPAL. 1948–1972.* Santiago: UN (CEPAL).

Ellsworth, P.T. 1956. The terms of trade between primary producing and industrial countries. *Interamerican Economic Affairs,* Summer.

Flanders, F.J. 1964. Prebisch on protectionism: an evaluation. *Economic Journal* 74, 305–26.

Frank, A.G. 1967. *Capitalism and Underdevelopment in Latin America: Historical Studies of Chile and Brazil.* New York: Monthly Review Press.

Johnson, H.G. 1972. *Economic Policies Towards Less Developed Countries.* New York: Brookings.

Haberler, G. 1961. Terms of trade and economic development. In *Economic Development of Latin America,* ed. H.S. Ellis, New York: St. Martin's Press, 275–97.

Hirschman, A. 1961. Ideologies of economic development. Reprinted in A. Hirschman, *A Bias for Hope,* New Haven: Yale University Press, 1971.

Kindleberger, C.P. 1956. *The Terms of Trade: a European Case Study.* New York: The Technology Press of MIT and J. Wiley & Son.

Mynt, M. 1954. The gains from international trade and the backward countries. *Review of Economic Studies* 22(2), 234–51.

Palma, J.G. 1981. Dependency and development: a critical overview. In *Dependency Theory: a Critical Reassessment,* ed. D. Seers, London: Francis Pinter.

Pinto, A. 1965. La concentración del progreso técnico y de sus frutos en el desarrollo. *El Trimestre Económico* 25, 3–69.

Pinto, A. 1973. *Inflación: raices estructurales.* Mexico: Fondo de Cultura Económico.

Pinto, A. 1974. Heterogeneidad estructural y el modelo de desarrollo reciente. In *Desarrollo Latinoamericano, ensayos criticos,* ed. J. Serra, Mexico: Fondo de Cultura Económico.

Pinto, A. and Knakel, J. 1973. The centre–periphery system twenty years later. *Social and Economic Studies,* March, 34–89.

Prebisch, R. 1980. Prologo. In Rodriguez (1980).

Rodriguez, O. 1980. *La teoria del subdesarrollo de la CEPAL.* Mexico: Siglo XXI Editores.

Taylor, L. 1983. *Structuralist Macroeconomics.* New York: Basic Books.

UNESCO. 1949. *Postwar Price Relations Between Under-developed and Industrialized Countries.* New York: UN.

Viner, J. 1953. *International Trade and Economic Development.* Oxford: Clarendon Press; Glencoe, Ill.: Free Press, 1952.

Terms of Trade and Economic Development

H.W. SINGER

One of the most widely discussed theories concerning the terms of trade of developing countries is the Prebisch–Singer hypothesis independently published in 1950 (Prebisch, 1950; Singer, 1950). This hypothesis proclaimed a structural tendency for the terms of trade of developing countries to deteriorate in their dealings with industrial countries. In the original form this related mainly to the terms of trade between primary commodities and manufactured goods from the industrial countries. The historical statistical basis was an analysis of British terms of trade during the period 1873–1938 which corresponded to this image of exports of manufactured goods in exchange for primary commodities.

During the first half of the 19th century the historical statistical experience regarding British terms of trade was in the opposite direction. British import prices of primary commodities such as cotton, wool, etc. increased in relation to the prices of British manufactured products (with textile manufactures prominent among exports at that time). This was in line with classical thinking according to which there would be diminishing returns in the production of primary products, due to the scarcity of land and mineral resources (Malthus, Ricardo and extended by Jevons to the cases of coal and minerals more generally). In classical thinking, up to and including John Stuart Mill, it was taken for granted that there was a tendency for the prices of primary commodities to rise in relation to manufactures, especially since the pressure of surplus population and the process of urbanization would keep wages and cost of production in manufacturing low; this was indeed in line with actual experience in the first half of the 19th century and formed the basis of Marx's theory of surplus value and was later applied by Arthur Lewis to conditions in developing countries in his emphasis on the role of unlimited supplies of labour in economic development (Lewis, 1954).

Thus when Singer in 1947/48 prepared for the United Nations his analysis of British terms of trade after 1873 (*Relative Prices of Exports and Imports of*

Under-developed Countries, New York: United Nations, 1949) which subsequently formed the basis of the Prebisch–Singer hypothesis, this ran contrary to traditional thinking. Hence, there was a great reluctance even to accept the empirical evidence for this period. In particular the question of transport costs and also the question of improving quality of manufactured goods were used by critical economists to contest the empirical basis of the UN study and the Prebisch–Singer hypothesis (Viner, 1952; Haberler, 1961; Ellsworth, 1956 and Morgan, 1959). However, subsequent analysis has shown that correction for shipping costs and changing quality would not destroy the empirical basis for the hypothesis (Spraos, 1980 and 1983).

The extension of the Prebisch–Singer hypothesis to the post-war period has also been questioned empirically. At the time the hypothesis was formulated in 1949/50 primary commodity prices were high as a result of wartime disruption and restocking needs after the war, and rose even further subsequently in 1950/51 as a result of the Korean war. Hence while the hypothesis is empirically supported if both the 1873–1938 period and the period since 1949–50 are considered separately, some doubts have been expressed about the postwar period and about the period since 1873 considered as a whole. However the doubts about the post-war period expressed by Spraos (1983) are only partial doubts; they only applied to the net barter terms of trade (NBTT) (and even there of doubtful validity) but vanished when looked at the 'Employment Corrected Double Factorial Terms of Trade' (ECDFTT). The double factorial terms of trade take the relative productivities into account as well as relative prices. The employment correction allows for the fact that the manufactured products from the North are produced under conditions of full employment, while the South was subject to chronic unemployment. (The first part of this correction would hardly be made for current measurement.) This shift to ECDFTT seems perfectly compatible with the Prebisch–Singer hypothesis since its main concern was with the welfare impact of terms of trade upon industrial and developing countries respectively which is a matter of productivity and employment as well as prices. Moreover, more detailed analysis of the post-war period or of the whole period since 1873 seems to confirm the hypothesis empirically even as far simple NBTT are concerned. For example, Sapsford (1985) extended Spraos's analysis into the early eighties and applied statistical analysis to the whole series since 1900 to account for the wartime break and found that the Prebisch–Singer hypothesis was strongly borne out not only for the pre-war period since 1900 and the post-war period separately, but also for the whole period in spite of the wartime upward displacement. He determined the downward trend in the NBTT over the period 1900 to 1982 as 1.2% per annum. A.P. Thirlwall (1983, pp. 52–354) and Prabirjit Sarkar in a forthcoming paper on 'The terms of trade experience of Britain since the nineteenth century' also have no doubt about the genuineness and validity of the long-term declining trend in NBTT for primary commodity exports.

The empirical basis for a continuing post-war declining trend of terms of trade of developing countries or of primary exporters, in confirmation of the Prebisch–Singer hypothesis, can of course be taken as established only if oil prices are excluded. However, this exclusion of oil prices seems fully justified. The Prebisch–Singer hypothesis clearly refers to normal international market processes, while the rise in oil prices was due to the application of producer power by a producer cartel in 1973 and again in 1979 to set aside market forces. In fact the need for such producer action and the need for international commodity agreements to raise and stabilize primary commodity prices is one of the possible policy conclusions arising from the Prebisch–Singer hypothesis. It could, of course, be taken as a weakness of Prebisch–Singer that it does not allow for such reaction to market pressures; but then the OPEC case has remained fairly isolated and it is by no means certain that market pressures will not in the end have the last word.

The underlying economic argument in explaining the trend towards deteriorating terms of trade observed and projected by Prebisch–Singer can be put under four headings:

(1) Differing elasticities of demand for primary commodities and manufactured goods. Primary commodities being inputs have a lower elasticity of demand because a 10 per cent drop (rise) in the price of the primary input will only mean a fractional drop in the price of the finished product – say 2 per cent instead of 10 per cent – and hence no great effort on demand can be expected. This means that in the case of a drop in prices there is no compensation in balance-of-payments terms (or 'income terms of trade') as a result of increasing volume. In the case of food the low price elasticity of demand is due to the fact that food is a basic need – and hence much of the income set free by a fall in the price of food will be devoted to other consumption goods rather than an increase in food consumption. Today the developing countries are net importers rather than exporters of food although this was not the case when the Prebisch–Singer hypothesis was developed in 1949/50. This low elasticity of demand, especially when combined with low elasticity of supply as emphasized by the classical analysis, also means that there is great instability of primary commodity prices and hence terms of trade – both upward and downward. The Prebisch–Singer analysis did not always quite clearly distinguish the disadvantages of the present system of world trade for primary exporters due to price instability from those due to a deteriorating trend. In terms of instability, the Prebisch–Singer hypothesis was much more widely accepted and for example strongly anticipated by Keynes (1938), and also in the various memoranda and proposals by Keynes at the Bretton Woods conference aiming at an International Commodity Clearing House or even a world currency based on commodities.

(2) Demand for primary commodities is bound to expand less than demand for manufactured products. This is due partly to the lower income elasticity of demand for primary products, especially agricultural products (Engel's Law), and partly to the technological superiority of the industrial countries exporting manufactures. Part of that technological superiority is devoted to economies in the use of primary commodities and also to the development of synthetic substitutes for primary commodities. The latter has been a striking feature of economic development which has markedly accelerated since it was first

emphasized by Prebisch–Singer (Singer, 1950). The tendency towards balance of trade deficits for developing countries arising from such divergent demand trends will enforce currency depreciations which will introduce a further circle of terms of trade deterioration (although hopefully not of income terms of trade).

(3) The technological superiority of the industrial countries means that their exports embody a more sophisticated technology the control of which is concentrated in the exporting countries and especially in the large multinational firms located in those countries. This means that the prices of manufactured exports embody a Schumpeterian rent element for innovation and also a monopolistic profit element because of the size and power of multinational firms.

(4) The structure of both commodity markets and labour markets is different in industrial and developing countries. In the industrial 'centre' countries, labour is organized in trade unions and producers in strong monopolistic firms and producers' organizations, all very powerful at various times. This means that the results of technical progress and increased productivity are largely absorbed in higher factor incomes rather than lower prices for the consumers. In the developing 'peripheral' countries, to the contrary, where labour is unorganized, the rural surplus population (Lewis, 1954) and its partial transfer into urban unemployment, open or disguised as explained in the Harris–Todaro model (Todaro, 1969), make for a situation in which results of increased productivity are likely to show in lower prices, benefiting the overseas consumer rather than the domestic producer. As long as we deal only with domestic production, such shifts in internal terms of trade between consumers and producers may not matter too much, partly because the two bodies are largely the same people, and partly because internal terms of trade can be influenced by domestic fiscal and other policies. But in international trade, the producers and consumers are in different countries; hence a tendency for productivity improvements mainly benefiting producers in the industrial countries but not in the developing countries will clearly affect terms of trade and international income distribution. Moreover, in many developing countries some of the major 'domestic' producers benefiting from higher productivity would be foreign investors and the higher profits flowing abroad would be equivalent in results to worsening terms of trade.

It will be noted that some of the four explanations for a deteriorating trend in terms of trade of developing countries relate as much or more to the characteristics of different types of *countries* – their different level of technological capacity, different organization of labour markets, presence or absence of surplus labour, etc. – as to the characteristics of different *commodities*. This indicates a general shift in the terms of trade discussion away from primary commodities *versus* manufactures and more towards exports of developing countries – whether primary commodities or simpler manufactures – *versus* the exports products of industrial countries – largely sophisticated manufactures and capital goods as well as skill-intensive services including technological know-how itself. As already mentioned, the initial hypothesis was formulated at a time when there was relatively little export of manufactures from developing countries. Since then there has been a considerable shift towards manufactures, including intensifying the export of primary commodities embodied in more highly processed manufactures. Although the early exponents of the Prebisch–Singer approach were often criticized for recommending import substituting industrialization (ISI) as a main policy conclusion, another equally logical policy conclusion would be export substituting industrialization (ESI) to get exports away from the deteriorating primary commodities. In fact this policy advice was given by some early followers of Prebisch–Singer to countries like India, where the possibilities of ESI seemed to exist at the time. However, the fact that some of the explanation for deteriorating terms of trade now relates to the characteristics of countries rather than commodities means that even ESI, a shift away from primary commodities to manufactures in the exports of developing countries, has not disposed of the problem. The type of manufactures exported by developing countries in relation to the different types of manufactures exported by the industrial countries shared some of the disadvantages pointed out by Prebisch–Singer for primary commodities in relation to manufactures.

This can be demonstrated from some recent data. Taking trend equations for the period 1954–72 we find that in constant export unit values the prices of the primary commodities of developed countries fell by an annual average of 0.73%, but those of primary commodities of developing countries fell by 1.82% p.a. (both co-efficients significant at 1% level). This difference shows the existence of both commodity and country influences reinforcing each other. Similarly it can be shown that while the terms of trade for manufactures improved, they did so less for the manufactures of developing countries than those of industrial countries. Hence the deterioration in terms of trade of developing countries during this period can be attributed to three distinct factors:

(1) the rate of deterioration in prices of their primary commodities compared with those of primary commodities exported by industrial countries;

(2) a fall in prices of the manufactures exported by developing countries relative to the manufactures exported by industrial countries; and

(3) the higher proportion of primary commodities in the exports of developing countries which means that the deterioration of primary commodities in relation to manufactures affected them more than the industrial countries.

A quantitative weighting of these three factors is difficult, but a broad estimate seems to show that they are of more or less equal importance. The original Prebisch–Singer hypothesis based on characteristics of commodities emphasized only the third factor, while the more recent formulations in terms of characteristics of countries include also the first two factors. It also shows that ESI mitigates the problem but does not entirely dispose of it. The shift in emphasis from commodity factors to country factors is particularly associated with the various theories of dependency (Prebisch and the work of the UN Economic Commission for Latin America (ECLA); Furtado, 1964), of centre–periphery analysis (Seers, 1983); and particularly of unequal exchange (Emmanuel, 1972).

BIBLIOGRAPHY

Ellsworth, P.T. 1956. The terms of trade between primary producing and industrial countries. *Inter-American Economic Affairs* 10, Summer, 47–65.

Emmanuel, A. 1972. *Unequal Exchange*. New York and London: Monthly Review Press.

Furtado, C. 1964. *Development and Underdevelopment*. Berkeley: University of California Press.

Haberler, G. 1961. Terms of trade and economic development. In *Economic Development for Latin America*, ed. H.S. Ellis, London: Macmillan.

Keynes, J.M. 1938. The policy of government storage of foodstuffs and raw materials. *Economic Journal* 48, September, 449–60.

Lewis, W.A. 1954. Economic development with unlimited supplies of labour. *Manchester School of Economics and Social Studies* 22, May, 139–91.

Morgan, T. 1959. The long-run terms of trade between agriculture and manufacturing. *Economic Development and Cultural Change* 8, October, 1–23.

Prebisch, R. 1950. *The Economic Development of Latin America and its Principal Problems*. New York: UN Economic Commission for Latin America.

Sapsford, D. 1985. The statistical debate on the net barter terms of trade between primary commodities and manufactures: a comment and some additional evidence. *Economic Journal* 95(379), September, 781–8.

Seers, D. 1983. *The Political Economy of Nationalism*. Oxford: Oxford University Press.

Singer, H.W. 1950. The distribution of gains between investing and borrowing countries. *American Economic Review* 40, May, 473–85.

Spraos, J. 1980. The statistical debate on the net barter terms of trade between primary commodities and manufactures. *Economic Journal* 90(357), March, 107–28.

Spraos, J. 1983. *Inequalising Trade?* Oxford: Clarendon Press.

Spraos, J. 1985. A reply. *Economic Journal* 95(379), September, 789.

Thirlwall, A.P. 1983. *Growth and Development, with special reference to developing economies*. 3rd edn, London: Macmillan.

Todaro, M.P. 1969. A model of labour migration and urban unemployment in less developed countries. *American Economic Review* 59(1), March, 138–48.

Viner, J. 1952. *International Trade and Economic Development*. Glencoe, Ill.: Free Press; Oxford: Clarendon Press, 1953.

Unequal Exchange

EDNALDO ARAQUEM DA SILVA

Marxists have long attempted to explain the uneven development of 'productive forces' (labour productivity) and the resulting income differences in the world capitalist economy primarily by means of the 'surplus drain' hypothesis (see Emmanuel, 1972; Andersson, 1976). Adopting Prebisch's division of the world capitalist economy into the 'centre' and 'periphery', Marxists have argued that surplus transfer has restrained the economic development of the periphery and exacerbated its income gap vis-à-vis the centre.

Before Emmanuel's work, the surplus transfer argument consisted of a loose intertwining of Prebisch's thesis over the secular deterioration of the terms of trade in the periphery, Marx's writings on 'the colonial question', and Lenin's theory of imperialism. Although presented inelegantly in terms of Marx's tableaux, Emmanuel introduced a coherent surplus drain theory utilizing Marx's transformation of values into production prices.

Emmanuel (1972) formulated his theory of surplus transfer through unequal exchange by comparing values with Marxian prices of production (see Okishio, 1963, pp. 296–8). Subsequently, Braun (1973) introduced unequal exchange utilizing Sraffa's framework (see Evan's, 1984, critical survey), Bacha (1978) introduced a neoclassical counterpart, and Shaikh (1979) suggested an alternative preserving Marx's theory of value.

Departing from recent reformulations, it is helpful to explain Emmanuel's unequal exchange theory within its original Marxist framework. The value (t) of a product is the sum of constant capital (c), variable capital (v), and surplus value (s), whereas its corresponding Marxian production price (p) includes the average profit rate (r):

$$t = c + v + s \tag{1}$$

$$p = (1 + r)(c + v) \tag{2}$$

In a world capitalist system consisting of the centre (A) and periphery (B) as

329

trading partners, unequal exchange is defined as the difference (g) between Marxian production prices and values (see Marelli, 1980, p. 517). In fact, unequal exchange compares two terms of trade under different assumptions about the wage rate in each country:

$$g_i = p_i - t_i \qquad i = A, B \tag{3}$$

A positive g denotes a *surplus gain* for exporters, while a negative g denotes a *surplus loss*.

Emmanuel's theory rests on the assumptions of a single world-wide profit rate resulting from international capital mobility, and the existence of a wage gap resulting from the immobility of labour from the periphery to the centre. The wage rate is an independent variable. Based on these assumptions, Emmanuel showed that unequal exchange depends on a country's rate of surplus value and on its organic composition of capital in relation to world average. Subtracting (1) from (2), we obtain:

$$g_i = r(c_i + v_i) - s_i. \tag{4}$$

Now consider these definitions:

(a) $s_i = e_i v_i$ rate of surplus value,
(b) $r = e/(1 + k)$ average profit rate,
(c) $c_i = k_i v_i$ organic composition of capital.

After substituting the definitions for the rate of surplus value, the average profit rate, and the organic composition of capital into equation (4), we obtain a formula to measure unequal exchange:

$$g_i = v_i \left\{ e \frac{1 + k_i}{1 + k} - e_i \right\}. \tag{5}$$

Unequal exchange will disappear when the profit rate of the centre or the periphery approaches the world average profit rate, i.e. $r_i = r$. This is satisfied when these conditions hold:

(i) $e_i = e$ and   (ii) $k_i = k$.

Emmanuel's distinction between the *broad* and *strict* definitions of unequal exchange can be easily understood by referring to equation (5). Even when the wage rates and thus the rate of surplus are equalized between the centre and the periphery, unequal exchange in the 'broad sense' occurs resulting from differences in the organic composition of capital. This type of unequal exchange can also exist *within* a country because of the differences in the organic composition of capital among sectors.

If condition (i) is satisfied and the rates of surplus value in the centre and periphery are equalized, the unequal exchange equation (5) becomes:

$$g_i = v_i e \left\{ \frac{1 + k_i}{1 + k} - 1 \right\}. \tag{5'}$$

As a result, there will be a surplus gain through trade when the individual organic composition of capital exceeds the world average. Likewise, if condition (ii) is satisfied and the organic compositions of capital are equal in both the centre and the periphery, the unequal exchange equation (5) becomes:

$$g_i = v_i(e - e_i). \tag{5''}$$

In this case, corresponding to Emmanuel's unequal exchange in the 'strict sense', there will be a surplus gain through trade when the world average rate of surplus value exceeds the individual rate.

The periphery tends to transfer surplus through trade because its rate of surplus value is higher than the world average, resulting from an international wage gap favouring workers in the centre. Therefore, even if the organic compositions of capital are equalized, unequal exchange results from the existence of a wage gap between the centre and the periphery, expressed as the rate of surplus value being lower in the centre than in the periphery (the rate of surplus value can be expressed as one over the value of labour power or 'wage share' minus one, $e = ((1/w) - 1)$. According to Emmanuel, unequal exchange in the 'strict sense' characterizes the trade relations between the centre and periphery.

Emmanuel's (1972, p. 61) basic conclusion is that 'the inequality of wages as such, all other things being equal, is alone the cause of the inequality of exchange'. As a corollary, Emmanuel (1972, p. 131) argued that 'by transferring, through non-equivalent [exchange], a large part of its surplus to the rich countries, [the periphery] deprives itself of the means of accumulation and growth'. Thus, an important implication of Emmanuel's theory is that a widening wage gap leads to a deterioration of the periphery's terms of trade, and a subsequent reduction in its rate of economic growth.

Emmanuel's work generated an interesting international debate. One contentious issue is the relationship of Emmanuel's theory to Marx's theory of value, leading to reformulations of Emmanuel's theory within the context of the Marx–Sraffa debate (Gibson, 1980; Mainwaring, 1980; Dandekar, 1980; Evans, 1984; Sau, 1984). Another view holds that Emmanuel's theory does not sufficiently explain uneven development because it omits the 'blocking of the productive forces' by entrenched and reactionary social classes in the periphery (Bettelheim, in the Appendix to Emmanuel, 1972). Bettelheim also argues that the rate of surplus value is higher in the centre resulting from its higher labour productivity, thus giving rise to unequal exchange reversal.

At the same time, Amin (1977) has emphasized non-specialized trade between the centre and the periphery, claiming the 'end of a debate', while the debate survived a virulent 'exchange of errors' among Marxists in India (see Dandekar, 1980; Sau, 1984). De Janvry and Kramer (1979) criticize unequal exchange as a theory of underdevelopment because capital mobility tends to eliminate wage differences by exhausting the 'reserve army' in the periphery, an argument which is challenged by Gibson (1980). Andersson (1976) surveys some pre-Emmanuel views, adding a formalization similar to Braun (1973), while Liossatos (1979) and Marelli (1980) have recast Emmanuel's theory in a modern, Morishima-like Marxian framework.

Although Emmanuel's primary objective involes 'model building', it is important to recognize that his references to standard trade theory are dated, largely confined to the literature of the 1950s, perhaps indicating that his work suffered from a long gestation period. Therefore, one should be cautious about treating Emmanuel's work as a critique of standard trade theory. Outside of Ricardian and Marxian circles, the reception of Emmanuel's work has been tepid if not neglectful.

Looking ahead, Harris (1975) suggests that a convincing theory of economic development should include a theory of value and distribution and a theory of accumulation on a world scale. Emmanuel's theory of unequal exchange, especially in subsequently more rigorous formulations (Andersson, 1976; Liossatos, 1979; Marelli, 1980; Gibson, 1980; Evans, 1984; Sau, 1984) has an assured place in this curriculum. In this way, Emmanuel's theory of unequal exchange is definitely linked to the original theory of Prebisch, Singer, Lewis and Baran, on trade and development.

BIBLIOGRAPHY

Amin, S. 1977. *Imperialism and Unequal Development*. New York: Monthly Review Press.

Andersson, J. 1976. *Studies in the Theory of Unequal Exchange Between Nations*. Abo: Abo Akademi.

Bacha, E. 1978. An interpretation of unequal exchange from Prebisch-Singer to Emmanuel. *Journal of Development Economics* 5(4), December, 319–30.

Braun, O. 1973. *International Trade and Imperialism*. Atlantic Highlands, NJ: Humanities Press, 1984.

Dandekar, V. 1980. Unequal exchange of errors. *Economic and Political Weekly* 15(13), March, 645–48. Continued in 16(6), February 1981, 205–12.

De Janvry, A. and Kramer, F. 1979. The limits of unequal exchange. *Review of Radical Political Economics* 11(4), Winter, 3–15.

Emmanuel, A. 1972. *Unequal Exchange: A Study of the Imperialism of Trade* (with additional comments by Charles Bettelheim). New York: Monthly Review Press.

Evans, D. 1984. A critical assessment of some neo-Marxian trade theories. *Journal of Development Studies* 20(2), January, 202–26.

Gibson, B. 1980. Unequal exchange: theoretical issues and empirical findings. *Review of Radical Political Economics* 12(3), Fall, 15–35.

Harris, D. 1975. The theory of economic growth: a critique and reformulation. *American Economic Review* 65(2), May, 329–37.

Liossatos, P. 1979. Unequal exchange and regional disparities. *Papers of the Regional Science Association* 45, November, 87–103.

Mainwaring, L. 1980. International trade and the transfer of labour values. *Journal of Development Studies* 17(1), October, 22–31.

Marelli, E. 1980. An intersectoral analysis of regional disparities in terms of transfers of surplus value. *Revista internazionale di scienze economiche e commerciali* 27(6), June, 507–26.

Okishio, N. 1963. A mathematical note on Marxian theorems. *Weltwirtschaftliches Archiv* 91(2), 287–98.

Sau, R. 1984. *Underdeveloped Capitalism and the General Law of Value.* Atlantic Highlands, NJ: Humanities Press.

Shaikh, A. 1979. Foreign trade and the law of value: Part I. *Science and Society* 43(3), Fall, 281–302. Part II was published in 44(1), Spring.

Uneven Development

DONALD J. HARRIS

In considering the general character of the process of capitalist development as it has appeared historically across many different countries over a long period of time, one of its most striking characteristics is the phenomenon of uneven development. By this is meant specifically that the process is marked by persistent differences in levels and rates of economic development between different sectors of the economy.

This differentiation appears at many levels and in terms of a multiplicity of quantitative and qualitative indices. Relevant measures which sharply identify the pattern of differentiation would include, for instance, the level of labour productivity in different sectors, the level of wages, occupational and skill composition of the labour force, the degree of mechanization of production techniques, the level of profitability as measured by sectoral rates of profit, the size structure of firms, and rates of growth at the sectoral level. This phenomenon appears regardless of the level of aggregation or disaggregation of the economy, except for the extreme case of complete aggregation – in which case, of course, one cannot say anything about the structural properties of the economy. For example, it appears at the level of comparing the broad aggregates of manufacturing industry and agriculture. It appears also at the level of individual industries within the manufacturing sector. It appears on a regional level as well as on a global scale within the international economy. In this latter context, one form that it takes is the continued differentiation between underdeveloped and advanced economies, usually identified as the problem of underdevelopment.

These disparities appear from observing the economy as a whole at any given moment and over long periods of time. And while the relative position of particular sectors may change from one period to another, nevertheless, there is always a definite pattern of such differentiation. We might say, therefore, and certainly it is an implication of these observations, that these disparities are continually reproduced by the process of development. Uneven development, in this sense, is an intrinsic or inherent property of the economic process. Far from being merely transitory, it seems to be a pervasive and permanent condition.

Now, it is an equally striking fact that, when we examine the theoretical literature on economic growth, we find the completely opposite picture. In particular, the dominant conception of the growth process that has motivated the post-World-War II literature is one that is constructed in terms of uniform rates of expansion in output, productivity and employment in all sectors of the economy. It is largely a literature of steady-state growth. Furthermore, much of existing economic theory predicts that, given enough time, many of the features of differentiation which we observe empirically would tend to wash out as a result of the operation of competitive market forces. Such differentiation should therefore be viewed only as a transitory feature of the economic process. But, in fact, we observe the opposite.

Thus, on the one side, we find a historical picture of uneven development as a persistent phenomenon. On the other side, we find a theory which essentially negates and denies this fact. It is as if the theory existed on one side and the historical reality on the other, and never the twain shall meet. However, it is possible to go some of the way towards bridging this gap. Accordingly, I consider here a strategy for analysis of uneven development that breaks through the narrow limits of the existing steady-state theory and advances towards a historically and empirically relevant theory. A detailed review and critique of the analytic foundations of steady-state theory is presented in Harris (1978; 1985).

THE ANALYSIS OF UNEVEN DEVELOPMENT. In order to go beyond the analysis of steady-state growth, it is necessary to start by recognizing the intrinsic character of the individual firm as an expansionary unit of capital. Various efforts have been made to develop a theory of the firm on this basis. (See, for instance, Penrose, 1959; Baumol, 1959; and Marris, 1967.) In this conception, growth is the strategic objective on the part of the firm. This urge to expand is not a matter of choice. Rather, it is a necessity enforced upon the firm by its market position and by its existence within a world of firms where each must grow in order to survive. It is reinforced also by sociological factors, such as the social status and power associated with being the owner, director, or manager of an expanding enterprise. It is this character of the firm which constitutes the driving force behind the process of expansion of the economy.

This is a crucial starting point because it establishes the idea of growth as the outcome of a process which is driven by active agents and not by exogenous factors. In particular, in the context of the capitalist economy, growth is the outcome of the self-directed and self-organizing activity of firms, each seeking to expand and to improve its competitive position in relation to the rest. Once this principle is recognized it becomes possible to move towards an understanding of the problem of uneven development.

The imperative of growth impels the firm constantly to seek out new investment opportunities wherever they are to be found. Such investment may occur in existing product lines, in new products and processes, or in the takeover of existing firms. The emergency of growth centres or leading sectors is a reflection of this underlying process. It is a consequence of the effort on the part of many firms to create or to rush into those spheres in which a margin of profitability exists that allows them to capture new growth opportunities. Such new spheres are always being opened up as a consequence of the ongoing innovative activity of firms and the competitive interactions among them. It is this constant flux, consisting of the emergence of new growth centres, their rapid expansion relative to existing sectors, and the relative decline of other sectors, which shows up in the economy as a whole as uneven development.

The form that this process takes, as it appears at the level of particular industries and product lines, has been well documented through empirical research. These studies show that the growth of many new industries and products follows a life-cycle pattern which may be represented by an S-shaped curve as in Figure 1. There are correspondingly three phases of expansion. In the initial phase, total output of the new industry is a minute share of the overall aggregate output in the economy and the rate of growth of output is low. This is followed by a phase of rapid growth in which this sector's output expands rapidly relative to overall output and its share of aggregate output grows. Then there is a third phase in which the sector reaches a threshold beyond which the growth rate tends to level off and perhaps to decline.

Of course, the process does not come to an end at that point. We must understand this sequence, schematically described here, as but a small segment of the time sequence characterizing the historical evolution of the economy. Given that firms are growing, making profits, and seeking to continue to grow, it would

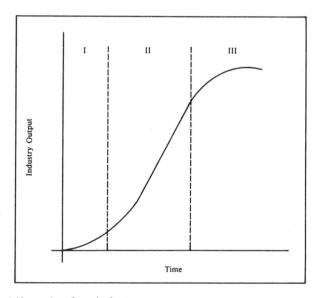

Figure 1   Life-cycle of an industry

be necessary for them, having entered into phase III, to launch out into new sectors. They will therefore actively seek to find new products that will initiate a corresponding new sequence.

It follows that we can map out the dynamic evolution of the economy in terms of a *sequential process*, where the overall growth is accountable for on the basis of (1) the individual growth of particular new sectors, (2) the growth of pre-existing sectors, each of which is growing at a different rate depending on the particular phase reached in its life-cycle, and (3) the constant accretion of new sectors into the economy owing to the introduction of new products. In this context also, the relative position of any region or country on a relevant index of development could be seen as a matter of the particular products or industries it has managed to capture as a result of the previous pattern of accumulation and the ongoing activity of firms operating within it and the particular timing of their entry into the life-cycle of new products.

We can go further in understanding the anatomy of this process if we take account of the technological innovation process tied up with it. In this connection it is helpful to drawn upon Kuznets's suggestive characterization of general features of the innovation process of 'major' innovations. Specifically, Kuznets (1979) identifies a sequence of four distinct phases as constituting the life-cycle of an innovation. It begins with a *pre-conception* phase in which necessary scientific and technological preconditions are laid. This is followed by a phase of *initial application* involving the first successful commercial application of the innovation. Then comes the *diffusion* phase marked by spread in adoption and use of the innovation throughout the economy along with continued improvements in quality and cost. Finally, there is a phase of *slowdown* and *obsolescence* in which further potential of the innovation is more or less exhausted and even some contraction may occur. This taxonomy is useful and suggestive in pointing to a certain internal logic of the innovation process related to 'the purely technological problems in breaking through to an effective invention and resolving the difficulties in development, prototype production, etc,... [and] ... the complementary and other organizational and social adjustments that would assure adequate diffusion and economic success' (pp. 64–5). It suggests, furthermore, that different firms, regions, and countries may be differently situated in terms of their capacity to undertake or enter the innovation process and hence to realize the growth advantages/disadvantages associated with different phases of that process. The case for such differentiation has been cogently argued, for instance, by Hirsch (1967).

The anatomy of this process can be further understood by taking account of its connection with the changing firm-structure of the industry. In particular, it has been observed that, for many industries, there is a proliferation of small firms in phase I of the industry's life cycle. But as the diffusion of the product occurs and growth speeds up, there is a 'shaking out' process by which many of the smaller firms disappear and the available market is concentrated in the remaining firms. When the industry reaches 'maturity', in phase III, there is a high degree of concentration.

This association between industry life cycle and firm-structure of the industry suggests that the dynamic of expansion through innovation is simultaneously a process of the concentration of capital. Further investigation of this link may provide a key to understanding the internal mechanisms and forces which feed the expansion process and account for its character as a process of uneven development. Without going into these in depth, it may be suggested here that there are a number of factors at work.

One is the phenomenon of economies of scale in production and marketing. Such economies give to the larger firms a decisive advantage in exploiting an innovation. Small firms may well have special advantages in the research and development phase of innovation and, in many cases, are observed to lead the process in that phase. But they often lose out to the larger firms at the stage of standardization, mass production and mass marketing of the product. The larger firms, on their part, may gain from foregoing the risks associated with the first phase and choosing to enter at a later stage through adoption of a proven innovation or takeover of a successful firm.

Another factor is the power of finance. The capacity to command finance is a powerful lever in the expansion process, deriving its significance from the substantial financial outlays involved in product development, production, and marketing, that have to be made well in advance of sales. This capacity depends both on the generation of internal funds and on access to external funds. Large firms have an advantage here because of their larger profits, to begin with, and because of their superior ability to borrow.

Because of these complementary relationships one might say that it is the large firms which drive the process, at least within certain phases of it. It is still a process which is driven by the expansion of firms, but it turns out that some firms are more equal than others in this process.

What role is to be assigned to demand as a factor in this process? At the level of individual consumer products or industries, a common conception is demand acts as an autonomous factor with a definite influence on the life-cycle pattern of evolution of the product. That influence is exerted in the early phase of introduction of a new product because of an element of resistance due to 'habit' formed in a customary pattern of consumption. It is exerted also in the maturity phase because of the operation of 'saturation effects' in consumption. But there are reasons to doubt the strength and effectiveness of such factors, as well as their supposed autonomy.

First of all, in an economy undergoing regular and rapid change, it is not evidence what role there is for habit except for the habit of change itself. The experience of and adaptation to change may create a high degree of receptivity to change. What then becomes decisive in the evolution of demand for consumer goods is the growth of income, and the changing relative prices and quality of products.

Second, insofar as these latter factors are crucial to the formation of demand, it may be argued that there is a certain self-fulfilling aspect of the expansionary process at the level of industry demand. In particular, investment generates the demand that provides the market for the new products which the investment itself creates. This occurs in two ways. First, investment generates income both directly in the sector undergoing rapid expansion and indirectly, via backward and forward linkages, through the stimulation of demand and investment in other sectors. In this respect, structural interdependence in the economy at the level of both production and expenditure patterns, allows for the possibility of a certain mutual provisioning of markets when expansion takes place on a broad front. Second, as a new product unfolds through the stages of the innovation process, it undergoes both improvements in quality and a decline in price relative to other products. This development provides a substantive basis for making inroads into the market for existing closely related products and hence promotes demand through a shift from 'old' to 'new' products. It is perhaps this *shift effect* which is mistakenly identified as a *saturation effect* by adopting a one-sided and static view of a dynamic and interdependent process.

Of course, though investment generates demand in these various ways, there is no guarantee that in the aggregate there is always sufficient demand for all products. It is here that the argument comes full circle, so to speak, back to the problem of overall effective demand that motivated the early post-war growth theory initiated by Harrod (1948) and Domar (1957). This problem was a central focus of the analysis of steady-state growth. It appears now that it cannot be escaped in making the transition to the analysis of uneven development.

In general, it must be recognized here that all of the preceding argument concerns the pattern of sectoral growth viewed at the level of individual industries, products, and firms. There is nothing in that argument to indicate how the patterns of sectoral growth translate into aggregate expansion at the level of the economy as a whole, or how the various sectoral patterns fit together to form a complete whole. This is a substantive problem requiring further analytical treatment on its own terms. Its significance derives from the recognition that the economy as a whole is not just the sum of its parts. Hence, the motion of the economy cannot simply be deduced from the movement of its parts.

Another aspect of the problem is associated with the manifold and complex ways in which growth in one sector mutually conditions and is conditioned by growth in all other sectors. Such mutual interaction is a necessary consequence of economic interdependence. The existence of such interaction implies that there is a certain cumulative effect intrinsic in the growth process. Understanding the exact mechanisms through which this effect operates is one of the central analytical problems for the analysis of uneven development.

BIBLIOGRAPHY

Baumol, W.J. 1959. *Business Behavior, Value and Growth*. New York: Harcourt, Brace and World.

Domar, E.D. 1957. *Essays in the Theory of Economic Growth*. New York: Oxford University Press.

Harris, D.J. 1978. *Capital Accumulation and Income Distribution*. Stanford: Stanford University Press.

Harris, D.J. 1985. The theory of economic growth: from steady states to uneven development. In *Contemporary Issues in Macroeconomics and Distribution*, ed. G. Feiwel, London: Macmillan.

Harrod, R.F. 1948. *Towards a Dynamic Economics*. London: Macmillan; New York: St. Martin's Press, 1954.

Hirsch, S. 1967. *Location of Industry and International Competitiveness*. Oxford: Clarendon Press.

Kuznets, S. 1979. Technological innovations and economic growth. In S. Kuznets, *Growth, Population, and Income Distribution, Selected Essays*, New York: Norton.

Marris, R. 1967. *The Economic Theory of 'Managerial' Capitalism*. London: Macmillan; New York: Free Press of Glencoe, 1964.

Penrose, E.T. 1959. *The Theory of the Growth of the Firm*. Oxford: Blackwell; New York: Wiley.

Contributors

Mahmoud Abdel-Fadil Professor of Economics, Cairo University; Associate Editor *Cambridge Journal of Economics*. Consultant, International Institute of Educational Planning. *La planification des prix en économie socialiste* (1975); *Development, Income Distribution and Social Change in Rural Egypt: 1952–70* (1975); *Papers on the Economy of Oil* (ed., 1979); *The Political Economy of Nasserism* (1980); *Informal Employment in Egypt* (1983).

Samir Amin Professor of Economics, University of Paris VIII. *Unequal Development* (1976); *Imperialism and Unequal Development* (1977); *The Law of Value and Historical Materialism* (1978); *The Arab Nation* (1978); *Class and Nation, Historically and in the current crisis* (1980).

Alice H. Amsden Visiting Professor, Department of Civil Engineering and Urban Studies and Planning, Massachusetts Institute of Technology; Faculty Member, Harvard Business School. *International Firms and Labour in Kenya* (1971); 'The division of labour is limited by the type of market: the Taiwanese machine tool industry', *World Development* (1977); *The Economics of Women and Work* (1980); 'The state and economic development in Taiwan', *States and Social Structure* (ed. P. Evans et al., 1985); 'The direction of trade – past and present – and the "learning effects" of exports to different directions', *Journal of Development Economics* 23 (1986); *Asia's Next Giant: Late Industrialization in South Korea* (1989).

Amiya Kumar Bagchi Professor of Economics and Director, Centre for Studies in Social Sciences, Calcutta. Dr. V.K.R.V. Rao Award for Economics, 1980. *Private Investment in India 1900–1939* (1972); *Change and Choice in Indian Industry* (ed., with N. Banerjee, 1981); *The Political Economy of Underdevelopment* (1982); *The Evolution of the State Bank of India: the roots, 1806–1876* (1987); *Public Intervention and Industrial Restructuring in China, India and the Republic* *of Korea* (1987); *Economy, Society and Polity: Essays in the Political Economy of Indian Planning* (ed., 1988).

Kaushik Basu Professor of Economics, Delhi School of Economics, University of India. Member, Institute for Advanced Study, Princeton, 1985–86; Associate Editor, *Journal of Development Economics*; Associate Editor, *Journal of Public Economics*; CORE Fellow, 1981–82. 'Cardinal utility, utilitarianism and a class of invariance axioms in welfare analysis', *Journal of Mathematical Economics* 12 (1983); 'Implicit interest rates, usury and isolation in backward agriculture', *Cambridge Journal of Economics* 18 (1984); *The Less Developed Economy: A Critique of Contemporary Theory* (1984); 'Poverty measurement: a decomposition of the normalisation axiom', *Econometrica* 53 (1985); 'One kind of power', *Oxford Economic Papers* 38 (1986); 'Technological stagnation, tenurial laws and adverse selection', *American Economic Review* (1989).

Peter Bauer Fellow of Gonville and Caius College, Cambridge, 1946–1960; Emeritus Professor of Economics, London School of Economics. Baron Bauer of Market Ward, City of Cambridge; Fellow, British Academy. *The Rubber Industry* (1948); *West African Trade* (1954); *Dissent on Development* (1972); *Reality and Rhetoric: Studies in the Economics of Development* (1984).

Jere K. Behrman William R. Kenan, Jr. Professor of Economics, University of Pennsylvania. Fulbright 40th Anniversary Distinguished Fellow; Fellow, Econometric Society; Compton Fellow, 1980–81; Guggenheim Fellow, 1979–80; Ford Fellow, 1971–2. 'Supply response in underdeveloped agriculture: a case study of four major annual crops in Thailand 1937–1963', *Contributions to Economic Analysis* 55 (1968); *Commodity Exports and Economic Development: The Commodity Problem and Policy in Developing Countries* (with F.G. Adams, 1982); 'Parental preferences and provision for progeny', (with R.A. Pollock and P. Taubman) *Journal of Political Economy* 90(1), (1982); 'The quality of schooling: the quantity alone is misleading', (with Nancy Birdsall) *American Economic Review* 73(5), (1983); 'Will developing country nutrition improve with income? A case study for rural south India', (with Anil B. Deolalikar) *Journal of Political Economy* 95(3), (1987); 'Health and nutrition', (with Anil B. Deolalikar) in *Handbook of Development Economics* 1 (ed. Hollis B. Chenery and T.N. Srinivasan, 1988).

Clive Bell Professor of Economics, Vanderbilt University. 'A bargaining theoretic approach to cropsharing contracts', (with P. Zusman) *American Economic Review* 66 (1976); 'Alternative theories of sharecropping: some tests using evidence from North-East India', *Journal of Development Studies* 13 (1977); *Project Evaluation in Regional Perspective* (with P. Hazell and R. Slade, 1982); 'Shadow prices for project evaluation under alternative macroeconomic specifications', (with S. Devarajan) *Quarterly Journal of Economics* 97 (1983); 'Intertemporally consistent shadow prices in an open economy: estimates for Cyprus', (with

S. Devarajan) *Journal of Public Economics* 32 (1987); 'Credit markets and interlinked transactions', in *Handbook of Development Economics* (ed. Hollis B. Chenery and T.N. Srinivasan, 1988).

Amit Bhaduri 'Agricultural backwardness under semi-feudalism', *Economic Journal* 83(1), (1973); *The Economic Structure of Backward Agriculture* (1983); 'Accumulation and exploitation: an analysis in the spirit of Marx, Sraffa and Kalecki', (with J. Robinson) *Cambridge Journal of Economics* 4 (1980); 'The Complex dynamics of the simple Ricardian system', (with D.J. Harris) *Quarterly Journal of Economics* 102(4), (1987).

Ester Boserup Author and consultant. Honorary degrees in Economics, University of Copenhagen; Agricultural Science, University of Wageningen; Human Letters, Brown University. *The Conditions of Agricultural Growth* (1965); *Women's Role in Economic Development* (1970); *Population and Technological Change* (1981).

Mary Jean Bowman Professor of Economics and of Education, University of Chicago; World Bank Consultant. Guggenheim Fellow, 1974. 'Schultz, Denison, and the contribution of EDS to national income growth', *Journal of Political Economy* 72(5), (1964); 'From guilds to infant training industries', in *Education and Economic Development* (ed., with C.A. Anderson, 1965); 'Schooling, experience, and gains and losses in human capital through migration', (with Robert G. Meyers) *Journal of American Statistical Association* 62(3), (1967); *Educational Choice and Labor Markets in Japan* (with H. Ikeda and Y. Tomada, 1981); 'An integrated framework for analysis of the spread of schooling in less developed countries', *Comparative Education Review* (1984); 'Education, population trends and technological change', *Economics of Education Review* 4(1), (1985).

Sukhamoy Chakravarty Professor of Economics, Delhi School of Economics, Delhi University; Chairman, Indian Council of Social Science Research, Government of India, New Delhi. Fellow of the Econometric Society; President, Indian Econometric Society 1983–87; President, Indian Economic Association 1986; Honorary President, International Economic Association. 'The logic of investment planning', *Contributions of Economic Analysis* 27 (1959); *Capital and Development Planning* (1969); *Contributions to Indian Economic Analysis – A Survey* (with J. Bhagwati, 1969); *Alternative Approaches to a Theory of Economic Growth: Marx, Marshall, Schumpter*, R.C. Dutt Memorial Lectures (1982); *Development Planning: The Indian Experience* (1987); 'The state of development economics', *Journal of the Manchester School of Economics* (June 1987).

Hollis B. Chenery Thomas D. Cabot Professor of Economics, Harvard University. Fellow, Econometric Society; Member, American Academy of Arts and Sciences; Honorary Doctorate, Erasmus University. *Interindustry Economics* (with P. Clark and J. Wiley, 1959); *Studies in Development Planning* (ed., 1971); *Redistribution with Growth: An Approach to Policy* (with N. Ahluwalia, C. Bell, J. Duloy and R. Jolly, 1974); *Patterns of Development, 1950–70* (with M. Syrquin, 1978);

Structural Change and Development Policy (1979); *Industrialization and Growth: A Comparative Study* (with S. Robinson and M. Syrquin, 1986).

Ednaldo Araquém da Silva Assistant Professor, New School for Social Research; Fulbright Visiting Professor, CEDEPLAR, Federal University of Minas Gerais, Brazil, 1985. 'Wage-profit trade-offs in Brazil: an input/output analysis', *Science and Society* 51 (1987); 'Measuring the incidence of rural capitalism: a discriminant analysis of survey data from Northeast Brazil', *Journal of Peasant Studies* 12 (1984); 'Preços e distribuiçao de renda no Brasil: uma análise de insumo/produto, 1975', *Pesquisa and Planejamento Econômica* 18 (1988).

Richard S. Eckaus Ford International Professor of Economics, Massachusetts Institute of Technology. *Planning for Growth* (with K. Parikh, 1968); 'The factor proportions problem in economic development', *American Economic Review*; *Appropriate Technologies for Developing Countries* (1977); 'Energy-economy interactions in Mexico', (with C. Blitzer) *Development Economics* 21(2), (1986); 'How the IMF decides on its conditionality', *Policy Sciences* 19(3), (1986); 'Prospects for development finance in India', (with R. Dernberger) in *Financing Asian Development* (1988).

Éprime Eshag Fellow of Economics, Wadham College, Oxford; Senior Research Officer, Institute of Economics and Statistics, Oxford University. *From Marshall to Keynes* (1963); 'Economic and social consequences of orthodox economic policies in Argentine in the post-war years', *Bulletin of the Oxford University Institute of Economics and Statistics* (1965); 'A comparison of economic developments in Ghana and the Ivory Coast since 1960', *Bulletin of the Oxford University Institute of Economics and Statistics* (1967); 'Agrarian reform in the United Arab Republic (Egypt)', *Bulletin of the Oxford University Institute of Economics and Statistics* (1968); 'The relative efficiency of monetary policy in selected industrial and less-developed countries', *Economic Journal* (1971); *Fiscal and Monetary Policies and Problems in Developing Countries* (1983).

Ronald Findlay Professor of Economics, Columbia University. *Trade and Specialization* (1970); 'Relative prices, growth and trade in a simple Ricardian system', *Economica* 92(1), (1974); 'Relative backwardness, direct foreign investment, and the transfer of technology: a simple dynamic model', *Quarterly Journal of Economics* 92(1), (1976); 'An "Austrian" model of international trade and interest equalization', *Journal of Political Economy* 86(6), (1978); 'The terms of trade and equilibrium growth in the world economy', *American Economic Review* 70 (1980); 'International distributive justice', *Journal of International Economics* 13 (1982).

Albert Fishlow Professor of Economics, University of California at Berkeley. David Wells Prize, 1963; Joseph Schumpeter Prize, 1971; Guggenheim Fellow, 1972–73. *American Railroads and the Transformation of the Ante Bellum Economy*

(1965); 'Brazilian size distribution of income', *American Economic Review* (1982); 'Origins and consequences of import substitution in Brazil', in *International Economic and Development* (ed. L. Di Marco, 1972); 'Lessons from the past: capital markets during the 19th century and the interwar period', *International Organization* 39(3), (1985); 'Latin American adjustment to the oil shocks of 1973 and 1979', in *Latin American Political Economy* (ed. J. Hartlyn and S. Morley, 1986); 'Financial requirements for the developing countries in the next decade', *Journal of Development Planning* 17 (1987).

E.V.K. FitzGerald Professor of Economics, Institute of Social Science, The Hague. 'The problem of balance in the peripheral socialist economy', *World Development* 13(1), (1985).

A.K. Ghose Senior Research Economist, International Labour Office, Geneva; formerly Economist, Queen Elizabeth House, Oxford University; Member, Indian Statistical Institute, Calcutta. 'Farm size and land productivity in Indian agriculture: a reappraisal', *Journal of Development Studies* (1979); 'Food supply and starvation: a study of famine with reference to the Indian sub-continent', *Oxford Economic Papers* 34(2), (1982); *Agrarian Reform in Contemporary Developing Countries* (ed., 1983); 'The new development strategy and rural reforms in post-Mao China', in *Institutional Reform and Economic Development in the Chinese Countryside* (ed. K. Griffin, 1984); 'Rural poverty and relative prices in India', *Cambridge Journal of Economics* (1988).

Adrian Graves Lecturer, Department of Economic and Social History, University of Edinburgh. 'Plantations in the political economy of colonial sugar production: Queensland and Natal', (with P. Richardson) *Journal of Southern African Studies* 6(2), (1980); *Crisis and Change in the International Sugar Economy, 1860–1914* (1984); *The World Sugar Economy in War and Depression, 1914–40* (ed., with B. Albert, 1988); *Cane and Labour: The Political Economy of the Queensland Sugar Industry 1862–1906* (1989).

Christopher A. Gregory Lecturer, Department of Prehistory and Anthropology, Australian National University. *Gifts and Commodities* (1982); *Observing the Economy* (with J. Altman, 1989).

Niles Hansen Leroy G. Denmar, Jr. Regents Professor in Economics, University of Texas, Austin. Fulbright Program 40th Anniversary Distinguished Fellow, 1987. *French Regional Planning* (1968); *France in the Modern World* (1969); *Rural Poverty and the Urban Crisis* (1970); *Location Preference, Migration, and Regional Growth* (1973); *Improving Access to Economic Opportunity* (1976); *The Border Economy: Regional Development in the Southwest* (1981).

Donald J. Harris Professor of Economics, Stanford University. National Research Council, Ford Foundation Fellow, 1984–85. 'Inflation, income distribution, and

345

capital accumulation in a two-sector model of growth', *Economic Journal* 77 (1967); 'Income, prices, and the balance of payments in underdeveloped economies: a short run model' *Oxford Economic Papers* 22 (1970); 'On Marx's scheme of reproduction and accumulation', *Journal of Political Theory* 80 (1972); *Capital Accumulation and Income Distribution* (1978); 'Profits, productivity, and thrift: the neoclassical theory of capital and distribution revisited', *Journal of Post-Keynesian Economics* 3 (1981); 'Accumulation of capital and the rate of profit in Marxian theory', *Cambridge Journal of Economics* 7 (1983).

Polly Hill Emeritus Reader in Commonwealth Studies, University of Cambridge; Emeritus Fellow, Clare Hall, Cambridge. *The Migrant Cocoa Farmers of Southern Ghana* (1963); *Studies in Rural Capitalism in West Africa* (1970); *Rural Hausa: A Village and a Setting* (1972); *Population, Prosperity and Poverty: Rural Kano 1900 and 1970* (1977); *Dry Grain Farming Families: Hausaland (Nigeria) and Karnataka (India) compared* (1982); *Development Economics on Trial: The Anthropological Case for a Prosecution* (1986).

Albert O. Hirschman Emeritus Professor of Social Science, Institute for Advanced Study, Princeton. Distinguished Fellow, American Economic Association; Member, National Academy of Sciences; Talcott Parsons Prize for Social Science; Frank E. Seidman Distinguished Award in Political Economy; numerous honorary degrees. *National Power and the Structure of Foreign Trade* (1945); *The Strategy of Economic Development* (1958); *Journeys towards Progress: Studies of Economic Policy-Making in Latin America* (1963); *Exit, Voice, and Loyalty* (1970); *The Passions and the Interests* (1976); *Rival Views of Market Society and Other Recent Essays* (1986).

Helga Hoffman Staff Member, United Nations Office of the Director-General for Development and International Economic Cooperation. *Desemprego e subemprego no Brasil* (1977); 'The export orientated development strategy in Brazil', *Intereconomics* 3/4 (1978); *Social Indicators and their Role in Development Policy in Latin America* (1978); 'Towards Africa? Brazil and the South–South trade', in *South–South Relations in a Changing Word Order* (ed. Jerker Carlsson, 1982); 'Poverty and property in Brazil: what is changing?', in *Incomplete Transition: Brazil since 1945* (ed. E. Bacha and H.S. Klein, forthcoming).

Ravi Kanbur Director of Development Economics, Research Centre, Warwick University. 'How to analyse commodity price stabilization?', *Oxford Economic Papers* (1984); 'North–South interaction and commodity control', (with D.A. Vines) *Journal of Development Economics* (1985); 'Food subsidies and poverty alleviation', (with T. Besley) *Economic Journal* (1988).

M. Ali Khan Abraham G. Hutzler Professor of Political Economy, Johns Hopkins University. Gonner Prize 1969. 'Some remarks on the core of a large economy', *Econometrica* 44 (1974); 'Some equivalence theorems', *Review of Economic Studies* 41 (1974); 'The Harris–Todaro hypothesis and the Heckscher–Ohlin–Samuelson trade model', *Journal of International Economics* 10 (1980); 'Development policies in less developed countries with several ethnic groups: a theoretic analysis', (with T. Chauduri) *Zeitschrift für Nationalökonomie* 45 (1985); 'Equilibrium points of non-atomic games over a Banach space', *Transactions of the American Mathematical Society* 293 (1986); 'An extension of the second welfare theorem to economics with non-convexities and public goods', (with R. Vahra) *Quarterly Journal of Economics* (1987).

James McIntosh Associate Professor of Economics, Concordia University, Montreal. 'Growth and dualism in less-developed countries', *Review of Economic Studies* 42 (1975); 'The econometrics of growth and underdevelopment: a test of the dual hypothesis', *Review of Economic Studies* 45 (1978); 'Dynamic interrelated factor demand systems: the United Kingdom 1950–78', *Economic Journal* 92 (1982); 'Reproductive behaviour in peasant societies: a theoretical and empirical analysis', *Review of Economic Studies* 50 (1983); 'An oligopsonist model of wage determination in agrarian societies', *Economic Journal* 94 (1984); 'North–South trade-export led growth with abundant labour', *Journal of Development Economics* 24 (1986).

Michael S. McPherson Chair, Economics Department, Williams College, Massachusetts. Member, Institute for Advanced Study, Princeton 1981–82; Senior Fellow, Brookings Institution, 1984–86. 'Efficiency and liberty in the productive enterprise: recent work in the economics of work organization', *Philosophy and Public Affairs* (1983); 'Moral theory in modern economics: Hirschmann, Schelling and Sen', *Partisan Review* (1984); 'Limits on self-seeking: the role of morality in economic life', in *Neoclassical Political Economy* (ed. D. Colander, 1984); 'The social scientist as constructive skeptic: on Hirschman's role', in *Democracy, Development and the Art of Trespassing: Essays in Honor of Albert O. Hirschman* (ed. A. Foxley, M. McPherson and G. O'Donnell, 1986); 'On Rawlsian justice in political economy: capitalism, "property-owning democracy", and the welfare state', (with R. Krouse) in *Democracy in the Welfare State* (ed. A. Gutmann, 1987); 'The logic of liberal equality: John Stuart Mill and the origins of the political theory of welfare-state liberalism', (with R. Krouse) in *Poverty, Welfare and Charity: The Theory and Practice of the Welfare State* (ed. D. Moon, 1988).

J. Gabriel Palma University Lecturer and Fellow, Faculty of Economics and Politics, Sidney Sussex College, Cambridge. 'Dependency: a formal theory of underdevelopment, or a methodology for the analysis of concrete situations of underdevelopment?', *World Development* (July 1978); 'From an export-led to an import-substituting economy, Chile 1918–1935', in *Latin America in the 1930's* (ed.

R. Thorp, 1984); 'On Kaldor's "Economic Problems of Chile": the long-term economic costs of the 'discreet charm' of the Chilean bourgeoisie', *Cambridge Journal of Economics* (April 1989); *Growth and Structure of Chilean Manufacturing Industry from 1830 to 1935: Origins and Development of a Process of Industrialization in an Export Economy* (1989); *Dependency and Development: a critical evaluation of the structuralist and dependency schools' contribution to the analysis of development* (1989).

S.K. Rao Economic Advisor to the Ministry of Commerce, Government of India.

Gustav Ranis Frank Altschul Professor of International Economics, Yale University. Chair, M.S. Bicentennial Symposium on the Role of Technology and Science in Development, 1976; Honorary Doctorate, Brandeis University, 1982. *Development of the Labor Surplus Economy: Theory and Policy* (with J. Fei, 1964); *Sharing in Development: A Programme of Employment, Equity and Growth for the Phillippines* (Chief of Mission and main author, 1974); *Growth with Equity: the Taiwan Case* (with J. Fei and S. Kuo, 1979); 'Science, technology and development: a retrospective view', in *Science, Technology and Economic Development: A Historical and Comparative Study* (ed., with W. Beranek, 1979); 'Latin American debt and adjustment', *Journal of Development Economics* (special issue, ed. P. Harden, A. Fishlow and J. Behrman, 1988); 'Analytics of development: dualism', in *Handbook of Development Economics* (ed. H. Chenery and T. Srinivasan, 1988).

Tibor Scitovsky Emeritus Professor of Economics, Stanford University. *Welfare and Competition* (1951); *Economic Theory and Western European Integration* (1958); *Papers on Welfare and Growth* (1964); *Money and the Balance of Payments* (1970); *The Joyless Economy* (1976); *Human Desire and Economic Satisfaction* (1986).

H.W. Singer Emeritus Professor, University of Sussex; Professorial Fellow, Institute of Development Studies, Sussex. Frances Wood Memorial Prize, Royal Statistical Society; Honorary Fellow, Institute of Social Studies, The Hague. *Unemployment and the Unemployed* (1940); *International Development, Growth and Change*; *Technologies for Basic Needs* (1977); 'The terms of trade controversy and the evolution of soft financing: early years in the U.N.', in *Pioneers in Development* (ed. G. Meier and D. Seers, 1984); *Food Aid, The Challenge and the Opportunity* (with J. Wood and T. Jennings, 1987); *Rich and Poor Countries* (with J. Ansari, 1988).

Nicholas Stern Professor of Economics, London School of Economics and Political Science; Chair, Suntory Toyota International Centre for Economics and Related Disciplines. Fellow, Econometric Society. *An Appraisal of Tea Production on Smallholdings in Kenya* (1972); *Theories of Economic Growth* (ed., with J. Mirrlees, 1973); *Crime, The Police and Criminal Statistics* (with R. Carr-Hill,

1979); *Palanpur: The Economy of an Indian Village* (with C. Bliss, 1982); *The Theory of Taxation for Developing Countries* (ed., with D. Newbery, 1987).

Joseph E. Stiglitz Professor of Economics, Stanford University. Fellow, American Academy of Arts and Sciences; Fellow, National Academy of Sciences; John Bates Clark Medal, American Economic Association. *Collected Scientific Papers of P.A. Samuelson* (ed., 1965); *Readings in Modern Theory of Economic Growth* (ed., with H. Uzawa, 1969); *Lectures in Public Finance* (with A.B. Atkinson, 1980); *The Economic Impact of Price Stabilization* (with D. Newbery, 1980).

Rosemary Thorp Fellow, St Anthony's, Oxford; University Lecturer in Latin American Economics. *Peru 1890–1977: Growth and Policy in an Open Economy* (with T. Betram, 1978); *Latin America in the 1930s: the role of the periphery in world crisis* (ed., 1984); 'Latin America and the international economy 1913–39', in *Cambridge History of Latin America* (ed. Bethell, 1986); *Latin American Debt and the Adjustment Crisis* (ed., with L. Whitehead, 1987); 'The APRA alternative in Peru: a preliminary evaluation on Garcia's economic policy', *Bulletin of Latin American Research* (1987); 'Trends and cycles in the Peruvian economy', in *International Trade, Investment, Macropolicies and History* (ed. Bardhan, Behrman and Fischler, 1988).

C. Peter Timmer Thomas D. Cabot Professor of Development Studies, At Large, Harvard University. 'On measuring technical efficiency', *Food Research Institute Studies* 9(2), (1970); *Small Scale Rural Industry in China* (with D. Perkins et al., 1977); *Food Policy Analysis* (with W. Falcon and S. Pearson, 1983); *Getting Prices Right: The Scope and Limits of Agricultural Price Policy* (1986); *The Corn Economy of Indonesia* (contributing editor, 1987); 'The agricultural transformation', in *The Handbook of Development Economics* Vol. I (ed. H. Chenery and T. Srinivasan, 1988).

Michael P. Todaro Professor of Economics, New York University; Senior Associate, Centre for Policy Studies, The Population Council, New York. 'A model of labor migration and unemployment in less developed countries', *American Economic Review* 59(1), (1969); 'Migration, unemployment and development: a two-score analysis', (with J. Harris) *American Economic Review* 60(1), (1970); *Internal Migration In Developing Countries* (1976); *Economics for a Developing World* (1983); *Economic Development in the Third World* (1989).

Immanuel Wallerstein Distinguished Professor of Sociology and Director, Fernand Braudel Center, State University of New York at Binghampton. Doctor Honoris Causa, University of Paris, 1976. *The Modern World-System* (3 vols: 1974, 1980, 1988); *The Capitalist World-Economy* (1979); *The Politics of the World-Economy* (1984); *Historical Capitalism* (1985).

Alan Walters Professor of Economics, Johns Hopkins University. *Money in Boom and Slump* (1968); *An Introduction to Econometrics* (1968); *The Economics of Road User Charges* (1968); *Noises and Prices* (1975); *Microeconomic Theory* (with R. Layard, 1978); *Britain's Economic Renaissance* (1986).

David R. Weir Associate Professor of Economics, Yale University. 'Life under pressure: France–England, 1670–1870', *Journal of Economic History* (1984); 'Rather never than late: celibacy and age at marriage in English cohort-fertility 1541–1871', *Journal of Family History* 9(4), (1984); 'Market and mortality in France 1600–1789', in *Death in the Social Order* (ed. Roger Schofield and John Walther, forthcoming).

Donald Winch Professor of Historical Economics, University of Sussex. Fellow of the British Academy. *Classical Political Economy and the Colonies* (1965); *Economics and Policy* (1969); *Adam Smith's Politics* (1978); *S. Collini and J. Burron: that noble science of politics* (1983); *Malthus* (1987).

G.D.N. Worswick Fellow and Tutor in Economics, Magdalen College, Oxford, 1945–65; Director, National Institute of Economic and Social Research, London, 1965–1982. Fellow of the British Academy; President, Royal Economic Society, 1982–84. *The Economics of Full Employment* (contributor, 1944); *The British Economy 1945–50* (joint editor, 1952); *The British Economy in the 1950's* (joint editor, 1962); *The Uses of Economics* (ed., 1972).